Environmental Sociology

Environmental Sociology

From Analysis to Action

3rd Edition

Edited by Leslie King
and Deborah McCarthy Auriffeille

ROWMAN & LITTLEFIELD PUBLISHERS, INC.
Lanham • Boulder • New York • Toronto • Plymouth, UK

Published by Rowman & Littlefield Publishers, Inc.
A wholly owned subsidiary of The Rowman & Littlefield Publishing Group, Inc.
4501 Forbes Boulevard, Suite 200, Lanham, Maryland 20706
www.rowman.com

10 Thornbury Road, Plymouth PL6 7PP, United Kingdom

British Library Cataloguing in Publication Information Available

Library of Congress Cataloging-in-Publication Data

Environmental sociology : from analysis to action / [edited by] Leslie King and
Deborah McCarthy Auriffeille. — 3rd edition.
    pages cm
  Includes bibliographical references and index.
  ISBN 978-1-4422-2075-1 (cloth : alk. paper) — ISBN 978-1-4422-2076-8 (pbk. :
alk. paper) — ISBN 978-1-4422-2077-5 (electronic) 1. Environmental sociology.
2. Environmental justice. 3. Environmentalism—North America. I. King, Leslie,
1959– II. Auriffeille, Deborah McCarthy. 1966–
  GE195.E588 2014
  333.72—dc23

                                                          2013019797

Printed in the United States of America

Contents

PART I
Imagining Nature

PART II
Political Economy

PART III
Environmental Inequalities

PART IV
Social Construction of the Environment— Identity, Emotions and Community

PART V
Perspectives on Disaster

PART VI
Globalization

Acknowledgments

Thanks are still in order for those who helped with our first edition: Brian Romer, our first-edition editor, and our fantastic student assistant, Elisabeth Gish. Alan McClare, our second edition editor, provided much patience and encouragement and he is missed. For their excellent work on the second edition, we also thank Ella Hartenian, Olivia Ryan, Kia Jenkins, and Meredith Trevino. Thanks also to Krista Harper, Daniel Faber, Angela Halfacer, Tracy Burkett, and several anonymous reviewers for comments and suggestions on various parts of the text and thanks to Terri Boddorff for assistance on obtaining permissions to use our excerpts. For this third edition, we thank our editor at Rowman & Littlefield, Sarah Stanton, and her assistant editor, Kathryn Knigge. This edition, like previous editions, also benefitted from useful ideas from anonymous reviewers. Finally, we thank Claire Johnson, Rebecca Turner, Vivian Mintz King and Jane Austin for all sorts of help, including many excellent comments and suggestions.

Preface

We both strongly believe that humans have come to a turning point in terms of our destruction of ecological resources and the endangerment of human health. A daily look at the major newspapers points, without fail, to worsening environmental problems and sometimes (but not often enough) a hopeful solution. Humans created these problems, and we have the power to resolve them. Naturally, the longer we wait, the more devastating the problems will become; the more we ignore the sociological dimensions of environmental decline, the more our proposed solutions will fail.

Out of our concern for and dedication to bringing about a more sustainable future, we have both worked hard to develop environmental sociology courses that not only educate students about environmental issues but also show them their potential role as facilitators of well-informed change. This reader results in large part from our commitment to the idea that sociology can be a starting point for social change, and we have sought to include in it work that reflects our vision. Sociology, however, can be good at critiquing social arrangements and not as good at highlighting positive change and explaining how that change has come about. We tried to include a few selections that show how groups of people have been able to effect positive changes, but be warned that some of the selections in this reader, reflecting the discipline of sociology, reveal problems in which solutions may seem elusive.

Anthologies seek to accomplish different things. One of our goals has been to provide students and their instructors with shortened versions of fairly recent academic research. Mostly, the articles and chapters included here were intended for an academic audience; to make them more accessible to students new to the discipline, we have shortened most of the selections and tried to provide a bit of context for each one.

We actively looked for readings that interest, motivate, and make sense to an undergraduate audience. Choosing which selections to include has been exciting and thought provoking, but it was not without a few dilemmas. Our selection process has evolved over the three editions, and this edition is most pointedly focused on pieces that would provoke productive discussion, whether for students in small seminars or for students in larger classes. We do not include the "classical" or foundational works; instead, we provide an overview of more recent work in the field to give students a sense of what types of research environmental sociologists are currently engaging in. That choice sprang from our observation that undergraduate students tend to be more interested in current work.

In addition, several other good edited volumes and readers include the "classics," so we did not see a need to reinvent the wheel. One of our most difficult decisions was to leave out many "big name" researchers who have profoundly influenced the field. Some of this work represents a dialogue with a long and intertwined body of thought and research. Understanding such a dialogue would require reading the lineage of research leading up to it. In addition, much of the theoretical work in environmental sociology (as in most of our subdisciplines) engages important, but very specialized, issues.

As a way of providing students with a beginning understanding of this lineage, our introductory chapter presents a brief overview of the field for students wishing to explore specific theoretical perspectives in greater depth. The works in the book itself balance this introductory chapter—recent articles and book chapters illustrate a wide variety of ways that sociologists might address environmental questions. The introductory chapter of the third edition reflects changes that have occurred in the focus of the discipline over the last several years.

We also wanted this reader to be accessible to a maximum number of instructors, whether or not they are specialists in environmental sociology. Most sociologists and social scientists we know speak the language of inequalities, political economy, and social constructionism; we tend not to be as fluent in the biological and mechanical details of energy production, watershed management, or climate change. Thus, we organized our reader not by environmental issue but by sociological perspective. The reader frames the issues in terms of sociological concepts and seeks to show students how sociologists might go about examining environment-related issues. We do want to emphasize, though, that in developing the reader's conceptual blocks, we were careful to cover a broad range of topics—from coal mining to food justice to climate change.

Ultimately, we think the most important feature of the reader is not the topics we chose or how we decided to organize the different pieces into categories; rather, it is that woven throughout the collection in the choice of material is the connection between power and environmental decision making. All of the pieces address either systems of power relations (e.g., the relations between the globalization of Western culture and the impact of the automobile infrastructure on lower-income countries) or individual levels of power (e.g., what motivates people to become environmental activists). We believe that good environmental decision making must incorporate sociological perspectives, and we hope that increasing numbers of activists, policymakers, and academics will benefit from these frameworks.

Introduction:
Environmental Problems
Require Social Solutions

Deborah McCarthy Auriffeille
and Leslie King

What Is Environmental Sociology?

What is environmental sociology? The answer, of course, involves exploring two ideas: sociology and environment. Sociology is, above all else, a way of viewing and understanding the social world. It allows us to better understand social organization, inequalities, and all sorts of human interaction. Sociology is a multifaceted discipline that researchers use in diverse ways and, along with many others (e.g., Feagin and Vera 2001), we think it has the potential to help us create a more just world. *Environment*, like *sociology*, can be an elusive term. Is the environment somewhere outside, "in nature," untouched by humans? Or are humans part of the environment? Does it include places where you live and work and what you eat and breathe? Or is it more remote: the rolling valleys of the Blue Ridge Mountains, the pristine waters of Lake Tahoe, the lush rain forests of Brazil?

For environmental sociologists the answer is that the "environment" encompasses the most remote regions of the earth as well as all the bits and pieces of our daily lives—from the cleaners we use to wash our carpets to the air we breathe on our way to work each day. We sociologists assume, first and foremost, that humans are part of the environment and that the environment and society can only be fully understood in relation to each other. We build on this understanding to point to fissures that are developing in the relationship between humans and nature. These are problems that humans both have contributed to and are feverishly attempting to solve. Our lack of understanding about the human/nature relationship has led to some of our worst environmental problems—climate change, ozone depletion, and so on—and has limited our ability to solve those problems.

In fact, some of our attempts to solve environmental problems have actually made them worse. The Green Revolution is an example. The goal of the Green Revolution was to increase world food yields through the transfer of Western agricultural techniques, fertilizers, pesticides, knowledge, and equipment to lower-income countries. This shift in agricultural methods massively reorganized agricultural production on a global scale. Although the global rates of food production increased, the revolution, with its focus on export crop production, for-profit rather than sustainable agriculture, mechanization, and heavy pesticide and fertilizer use, contributed to the destabilization of social, political, and ecological systems in many regions of the world (Dowie 2001: 106–40). For example, farmers must now engage in a money economy in order to pay for pesticides and herbicides and, as a result, many small-scale, less affluent farmers have lost their land (Bell 1998). What is more, as Peter Rosset and colleagues (2000) point out, an increase in food production does not necessarily lead to a decrease in hunger. In their words, "Narrowly focusing on increasing production—as the Green Revolution does—cannot alleviate hunger because it fails to alter the tightly concentrated distribution of economic power, especially access to land and purchasing power. . . . In a nutshell—if the poor don't have the money to buy food, increased production is not going to help them." With a better understanding of how humans and nature interact and a willingness to learn from past mistakes and misunderstandings, we can prevent such problems from occurring again and build a more socially and environmentally sustainable future. This collection of readings represents a broad sample of work by many writers and researchers who are attempting to do just that.

Environmental Problems Are Social Problems

Sociologists, by focusing their research on questions of inequality, culture, power and politics, the relationship between government and economy, and other societal issues, bring a perspective to environmental problem solving that is quite different from that of most natural and physical scientists. Take the following examples: the catastrophe in Bhopal, India, in 1984; the 1989 *Exxon Valdez* oil spill in Alaska; the devastating impact of the 2005 Hurricane Katrina on communities in Louisiana and Mississippi; the 2010 Deepwater Horizon oil spill in the Gulf of Mexico; the 2011 Fukushima Daiichi nuclear disaster in Japan; the ongoing air pollution problems in the United States; and global climate change. Why are those not uniquely "natural science" or engineering issues? The answer is that these "disasters" are not out of our control; they are not merely "accidents," as we sometimes hear them referred to in the news media. In each of these cases (briefly summarized below), and many other cases too numerous to mention, it was social organization—a series of identifiable managerial steps, a collection of beliefs, a set of regulations, or other social structures—that led to the environmental problems.

- BHOPAL, INDIA: In 1984, the Union Carbide pesticide plant in Bhopal leaked forty tons of lethal methyl isocyanate (MIC) into the low-income communities of Bhopal. Varying estimates indicate that between three thousand and sixteen thousand people died immediately, and at least five hundred thousand more were permanently injured. This was far from a mere "technological accident." As many social science and journalistic studies attest, the mismanagement of the Bhopal plant almost guaranteed a disaster. In short, Union Carbide, in an attempt to cut costs, took advantage of a repressed and desperate workforce to construct and manage the plant in an unsafe manner. Nearly thirty years later the site, which was turned over to the state government in 1998, still has not been cleaned up. Though over twenty thousand people continue to live in slums in close proximity to the site, and though community members experience a host of illnesses (including gastrointestinal, gynecological, neurological, immunological, and respiratory ailments; cancers; and birth defects), the degree of contamination to soil and water has never been adequately tested.[1]
- *EXXON VALDEZ*: The story of the *Exxon Valdez* disaster along Alaska's shoreline is also, sadly, the story of a preventable "accident." Exxon, as well as other members of the oil industry, had waged a successful public relations campaign to convince Congress that requiring tankers to use double hulls would be too expensive and therefore dangerous to the industry's profits. Exxon also had spent the 1960s and 1970s working to delay and avoid Alaska's attempts to raise taxes on tankers that didn't comply with the state's regulations. The groundwork for the largest-ever crude oil disaster in U.S. history had been successfully laid; in 1989 the *Exxon Valdez* tanker got stuck on Bligh Reef and spewed over thirty-eight thousand tons of oil into Prince William Sound (BBC News World Edition 2002), contaminating approximately 1,200 miles of coastline and a national forest, four national wildlife refuges, three national parks, five state parks, four state critical habitat areas, and a state game sanctuary. In just one example of the impact of

the spill on wildlife, it killed an estimated 3,500 to 5,500 sea otters and 300,000 to 675,000 birds (Vicini 2008; Greenpeace 1999). The spill also nearly devastated the local fishing and seafood-packaging industries (not to mention the serious impact on the national insurance industry).[2] Despite the widespread ecological and economic damage caused by the spill, Exxon Mobil used the legal system to successfully fight payment of punitive damages. A federal jury originally ordered Exxon Mobil to pay $5 billion in damages. Later a federal judge reduced this to $4.5 billion, and an appeals court then further reduced it to $2.5 billion. Finally in 2008, the U.S. Supreme Court reduced the $2.5 billion in damages to $507.5 million (Vicini 2008).

- HURRICANE KATRINA: Hurricane Katrina hit the Gulf Coast of Louisiana and Mississippi on August 29, 2005. With a storm surge of twenty to thirty-two feet, Katrina did enormous damage; over 1,800 people were killed and between seven hundred thousand and 1.2 million people were displaced (Gabe, Falk, McCarty, and Mason 2005; Picou and Marshall 2007). New Orleans was devastated, as its levees were breeched and much of the city flooded. While hurricanes are typically considered "natural disasters," Katrina's extreme consequences must be considered as the result of social and political failures. Prior to Katrina, it was known that New Orleans was at risk for flooding in the event of a powerful storm. According to author Jenni Bergal (2007: 4), "Numerous studies before Katrina cautioned that storm protection plans weren't moving fast enough, that the levees might not hold in a strong hurricane, that the U.S. Army Corps of Engineers had used outdated data in its engineering plans to build the levees and floodwalls and that the wetlands buffering the area from storms were disappearing." Coastal land that protected New Orleans had been lost due to human activities including settlement, the building of canals to promote shipping, and the digging of channels for oil and gas pipelines (Hiles 2007). The levee system that provided additional protection was vulnerable due, among other things, to design errors, and the emergency response that should have assisted residents in the aftermath of the storm proved grossly inadequate (McQuaid 2007).

- DEEPWATER HORIZON OIL SPILL: While the *Exxon Valdez* disaster occurred in the process of transporting oil, the more recent BP disaster of 2010 happened while drilling for oil five thousand feet under the sea floor in the Gulf of Mexico (Krauss 2012). An explosion on the Deepwater Horizon rig caused the death of eleven people and resulted in a breeched wellhead; oil spilled for three months and, by the time the well was capped, an estimated 4.9 million barrels (or about two hundred million gallons) of oil had flowed into the Gulf (Freudenburg and Gramling

2011). In addition, 1.8 million gallons of dispersants to dissolve the oil were applied, and there are serious safety concerns about these dispersants (Foster 2011).

The U.S. Department of Interior (2012) reported that the impacts of the spill were extensive and affected "important species and their habitats across a wide swath of the coastal areas of Alabama, Florida, Louisiana, Mississippi, and Texas, and a huge area of open water in the Gulf of Mexico. When injuries to migratory species such as birds, whales, tuna and turtles are considered, the impacts of the Spill could be felt across the United States and around the globe."

The stage was set for this disaster by a series of human decisions guided by BP's desire to cut costs and the failure of the U.S. government to strictly regulate and monitor the actions of the companies drilling in the Gulf (Freudenburg and Gramling 2011). According to a report by PBS's *Frontline* and ProPublica (PBS 2010) BP, in order to cut costs and increase profits, had a history of failing to prioritize for the safety of workers and the environment. Prior to the Deepwater Horizon disaster, there had been an explosion in one of BP's Texas City, Texas, refineries in 2005 that killed twenty-six people, and there had been a major oil spill in Alaska in 2006 that resulted from a ruptured pipeline.

A reporter for the New Orleans *Times Picayune* (Hammer 2010) wrote, "The rig's malfunctioning blowout preventer ultimately failed, but it was needed only because of human errors. . . . [T]he engineers repeatedly chose to take quicker, cheaper and ultimately more dangerous actions, compared with available options. Even when they acknowledged limited risks, they seemed to consider each danger in a vacuum, never thinking the combination of bad choices would add up to a total well blowout."

- FUKUSHIMA NUCLEAR DISASTER: In March 2011, a powerful earthquake struck off the coast of Japan in the Pacific Ocean, generating an enormous tsunami and ultimately causing catastrophic meltdowns at the Fukushima Daiichi Nuclear Plant. The tsunami disabled the backup generators that would have been used to cool reactors that were shut down as a result of the earthquake. The resulting disaster was the worst nuclear accident since the meltdown at the Chernobyl plant in Ukraine in 1986. Radiation releases at the Fukushima plant necessitated the evacuation of ninety thousand people (Fackler 2012) and caused extensive damage to Japan's food and water supplies.

The Japanese government and the power company that ran the plant, Tokyo Electric Power (TEPCO), have subsequently been criticized for failing to institute adequate safety measures, given that the plant was built in an earthquake- and tsunami-prone area (Fackler

2012; Nöggerath et al. 2011). The plant was designed in the 1960s, when knowledge and understanding of earthquakes and tsunamis was somewhat limited; however, since that time, scientists have compiled a substantial amount of data on these phenomena. A group of scientists writing in the *Bulletin of Atomic Sciences* wrote, "The knowledge, generally available by about 1980, that magnitude 9 mega-quakes existed as a class should probably have triggered a re-examination of the earthquake and tsunami counter-measures at the Fukushima power station, but it did not" (Nöggerath et al. 2011: 40).

New York Times journalist Martin Fackler (2012) explained that a cozy relationship between government officials and industry leaders led to a lax regulatory climate. For example, a number of years before the disaster, a seismologist serving on a high-level committee on offshore earthquakes in northeastern Japan "warned that Fukushima's coast was vulnerable to tsunamis more than twice as tall as the forecasts of up to 17 feet put forth by regulators and TEPCO." He was completely ignored, and to the *New York Times*, he stated, "They completely ignored me in order to save TEPCO money."

Similar to the examples above, the accident at the Fukushima plant was not attributable to "natural" causes (i.e., the earthquake and subsequent tsunami) alone. And while one could argue that design flaws led to the accident, it is also clear that money and power—social relations—played an important role in the decisions that were made by the Japanese government and TEPCO.

The Bhopal, *Exxon Valdez*, Hurricane Katrina, Deepwater Horizon, and Fukushima events represent crises that occurred in a flash and left immediately visible human and ecological tragedies in their wakes. Environmental disasters also occur in slow motion and inflict damages that are harder to detect but are no less severe. This is the kind of disaster that we all are watching as air pollution and climate warming, among other problems, continue to worsen. Like *the fast-moving environmental crises discussed above*, these "slow motion" environmental problems also have their roots in human decision making and social structure.

- AIR POLLUTION IN THE UNITED STATES: Outdoor air pollution is a major environmental problem, with serious health implications for millions of people around the world. According to the World Health Organization (2011), outdoor urban air pollution accounts for 1.3 million deaths worldwide each year. In the United States, as in other parts of the world, the ongoing danger presented by a host of air pollution problems has roots in many social processes, one being the inability of governmental policies and laws to regulate industry amid the rise of neoliberal style economics, with its emphasis on deregulation and corporate rights, and the increasing monetary and political power of corporations. The 1970 Clean Air Act (and its 1977 and 1990 amendments), sets standards for air pollution levels, regulates emissions from stationary sources, calls for state implementation plans for achieving federal standards, and sets emissions standards for motor vehicles (Rosenbaum 2011). While air quality has improved since 1970 (EPA 2012), the nation's air remains unhealthy in several important respects. For example, as of 2010, some 124 million people in the United States still live in areas where outdoor levels of air pollution exceed federal health-based standards and, thereby, breathe air that is dirty enough to cause health problems (EPA 2012). This is especially true of two kinds of air pollution—ground-level ozone (which forms when sunlight reacts with dirty air) and fine particulates (particles smaller than the diameter of a human hair); both of these are created by fuel combustion, among other sources, and they continue to persist at dangerous levels in the United States (American Lung Association 2012). Both ground-level ozone and fine particulate matter can cause pulmonary inflammation, decreased lung function, exacerbation of asthma, and other pulmonary diseases. Fine particulate matter is also associated with cardiovascular morbidity and mortality (Laumbach 2010). One study found that, despite improvements in air quality in recent decades, in the year 2005, ozone pollution was related to 4,700 deaths, and fine particulate pollution was related to 130,000 deaths in the United States (Fann et al. 2012). In addition, as will be discussed below, the release of greenhouse gases in the United States, particularly carbon dioxide, continues to increase at an alarming rate.

- GLOBAL CLIMATE CHANGE: The Intergovernmental Panel on Climate Change (IPCC) and most scientists believe that the warming of our global climate is unequivocal and is evident from documented increases in average air and ocean temperatures, widespread melting of snow and ice, and a rising average sea level (IPCC 2007a). Global warming is caused primarily by the increasing amounts of greenhouse gases released into the atmosphere, produced in large part by the burning of fossil fuels. It is causing significant changes in climate patterns worldwide. The most recent IPCC report (2007—a new one is expected in 2014) confirms that most of the observed climate change has been and is projected to be due to human-caused and not natural emissions of greenhouse gases (IPCC 2007b). Greenhouse gases trap heat, and they are predicted to warm the earth by .2 degrees Celsius (.36 degrees Fahrenheit) per decade over the next two decades. Even if greenhouse gases were held constant at year 2000 levels, a further warming of .1

degree Celsius (.18 degrees Fahrenheit) per decade is expected. Significant warming has already occurred; environmentalist Bill McKibben (2012) noted that May of 2012 was the warmest May on record for the Northern Hemisphere and "the 327th consecutive month in which the temperature of the entire globe exceeded the 20th-century average." McKibben also notes that the average temperature has been raised .8 degrees Celsius and that this increase has already caused "far more damage than most scientists expected," including the loss of a third of summer sea ice in the Arctic, more acidity in the oceans, and wetter atmosphere above the oceans, increasing the likelihood of floods. Some of the expected ramifications of climate change include increased mortality, malnutrition and other health problems, and economic loss due to increased flooding, increased drought, extremely dangerous temperature increases in some regions of the world, and increased severe weather (IPCC 2001; 2007a; EPA 2004). As with other environmental problems, those with the fewest resources will tend to suffer most from the negative consequences of these changes.

Climate warming continues to worsen, in part, because of national and international political practices and regulatory structures that place the interests of corporations over the interests of citizens. The United States has failed to ratify the Kyoto Protocol, which sets binding obligations on nations to reduce greenhouse gas emissions, and those countries that have signed on have found it difficult to agree on specific action plans (see Parks and Roberts 2010). In addition, national governmental policies and many international treaties, such as NAFTA, exacerbate the release of fossil fuels into the atmosphere by subsidizing road construction rather than public transportation, and by encouraging long-distance trade in which businesses produce goods in one place only to transport them across the globe for consumption in another. Under this "business as usual" scenario, average global temperatures may be expected to increase anywhere from 2°F to 11.5°F by 2100 (National Research Council 2010).

Some sociologists follow the crumb trail of social facts left behind by climate change and other ecological stories in order to envision a more just and sustainable future. Why should we assume that human ingenuity begins and ends with the invention of a deadly, yet extraordinarily powerful, pesticide, such as Bhopal's methyl isocyanate? We have put our minds together to invent automobiles (which contribute to sprawl, asthma, and greenhouse gas production), polyvinyl chlorides (which are carcinogenic), and nuclear energy (which has led to the nuclear waste problem). Can we not put the same creative optimism and energy into preventing the worst impacts of global climate change, regulating polyvinyl chlorides and other carcinogens, and developing safe forms of renewable energy?

The answer is, "Yes, but . . ." On the one hand, the twentieth century brought the passage of several environment-related laws in the United States, as well as the explosion of environmental activism and legislation that marked the 1970s as the "environmental decade." This one decade alone, for example, is witness to the successful passage of the 1970 National Environmental Policy Act (NEPA), the 1970 Clean Air Act, the 1972 Water Pollution Control Act (Clean Water Act), the 1976 Toxic Substances Control Act, and the 1977 Surface Mining Control and Reclamation Act, to name a few.[3] There is little doubt that ecological problems in the United States would be much worse absent these environmental laws and the current system of regulation. On the other hand, it is increasingly apparent, as noted earlier, that many of our environmental problems have worsened, and several new environmental problems have appeared since the "environmental decade." For example, industries across the United States continue to pump billions of pounds of toxic chemicals into our air, land, and water each year. In terms of releases to the air and water, in just one year, U.S. facilities released seventy million pounds of carcinogens, ninety-six million pounds of chemicals linked to developmental problems (i.e., birth defects and learning disabilities), thirty-eight million pounds of chemicals linked to reproductive disorders, 1.5 million pounds of respiratory toxicants, and 826 million pounds of suspected neurological toxicants (U.S. PIRG 2007). People are routinely put in danger in their own homes by ingesting household dust laced with toxic chemicals (Wu et al. 2007). Globally, the air quality picture is increasingly similar to, or much worse than, that of the United States as countries around the world increasingly engage in environmentally destructive economic development patterns (World Health Organization 2011).

A good deal of our failure to successfully address these problems can be linked to a lack of understanding of what seemingly separate issues—like the Bhopal industrial leak and global climate change—have in common. The linkages among environmental abuse, poverty, inequality, racism, lack of democracy, and the increasing concentration of power within corporations form a complex social nexus that allows environmental degradation to continue and that prevents meaningful policy from being enacted. In almost all parts of the world, environmental laws have been poorly enforced and, when they are enforced, it is usually after the damage has already been done. In other words, they focus on controlling pollutants/toxins after they have been released rather than preventing them from posing a threat.

Environmental sociologists contend that environmental problems are inextricably linked to societal issues (such as inequality, governance, and economic practices). Endocrine-disrupting hormones, bioengineered foods, ocean dumping, deforestation, asthma, and so on are each interwoven with economics, politics, culture, television, religious worldviews, advertising, philosophy, and a whole complex tapestry of societal institutions, beliefs, and practices. Environmental sociologists tend not to ask whether something—such as the methyl isocyanate used to produce pesticide in Bhopal—is inherently good or bad. Rather, the social organization of the pesticide industry is problematic. Blaming methyl isocyanate for the death toll in Bhopal's factory leak is like cursing the chair after you stub your toe on it. Humans invent pesticides, and humans decide how to manage those chemicals once they have been produced—or they can decide to halt production. Who decides whether to ban or regulate a toxin? How do we decide this? Do some citizens have more say than others? How do the press, corporate advertising, and other forms of media shape our understanding of a dangerous chemical or pollutant? These are just a whisper of the chorus of questions sociologists are asking about environmental problems and their solutions.

While science and technology can help us to invent "safer" pesticides, they cannot tell us what is safe. Is it safe enough that a new pesticide causes one in one hundred thousand of those exposed to develop a form of cancer? What about one in one million? What do you do when the scientific studies contradict each other? Who decides which studies represent the "facts," and how do they decide? Or, finally, as a colleague commented, "We scientists might be able to tell you how much of a toxic chemical you can dump in the ocean without killing all the fish; but the important question—and one that the natural sciences can't answer—is 'Why are we dumping that chemical in the first place?'"

Sociology can also help us see that environmental concerns are not merely about individuals. Some people disregard environment-related problems, explaining that "life itself is a risky business and the issue is ultimately about choice and free will." Along this line, the argument is that just as we choose to engage in any number of risky activities (like downhill skiing without a helmet or eating deep-fried Twinkies), we also choose to risk the increased cancer rates that are associated with dry-cleaning solvents in order to have crisp, well-pressed suits and dress shirts. A sociologist, however, would begin by pointing out that not everyone is involved in that choice and not every community experiences the same level of exposure to that toxin. The person who lives downstream from a solvent factory may not be the same person who chooses the convenience (and the risk) of dry-cleaned clothing (Steingraber 2000).

A Brief History of Environmental Sociology

In this section, we provide a broad and, by necessity, partial, overview of the emerging subdiscipline of environmental sociology. Let's start at the beginning: Auguste Comte first coined the term *sociology* in 1838. However, it wasn't until the late 1960s and the 1970s that a significant number of sociologists began studying the impacts of natural processes on humans and its reverse—the social practices that organize our development and use of the products and technologies that impact ecological *and* human communities. Certainly many people in the early part of the twentieth century were interested in a wide range of environmental issues—from the conservation of vast expanses of wilderness to the improvement of urban spaces (see Taylor 1997). So why the long wait for an environment-focused sociology?

Part of the answer lies in the efforts of sociologists to establish the discipline of sociology as separate from other areas of study, especially the natural sciences (Hannigan 1995). Sociology provides an important counterpoint to the natural sciences by showing how social interaction, institutions, and beliefs shape human behavior—not just genetics, physiology, and the natural environment. In addition, the sociological perspective has been a crucial tool for dismantling attempts to use the natural sciences to justify ethnocentrism, racism, sexism, and homophobism. Sociologists have traditionally been reluctant, therefore, to venture outside the study of how various social processes (e.g., politics, culture, and economy) interact to look at human/nature interactions.[4] Writing about this trend in the discipline, Riley Dunlap and William Catton argued in the 1970s that sociologists should claim the study of the environment and not leave the "natural" world to natural and physical scientists (Catton and Dunlap 1978; Dunlap 1997). Catton and Dunlap thought environmental sociology ought to examine how humans alter their environments and also how environments affect humans. They developed a "new ecological paradigm," which represented an initial attempt to explore society-environment relations.

During the first decades of environmental sociology (the 1960s and 1970s), researchers focused primarily on the same issues that the emerging environmental movement highlighted, including air and water pollution, solid and hazardous waste dumping, litter, urban decay, the preservation of wild areas and wildlife, and fossil fuel dependence. These problems were easy to measure and see: think of polluted rivers catching on fire, visible and smelly urban smog, ocean dumping of solid and hazardous wastes, and the appearance of refuse along the side of the road. Most early sociological studies focused on people's attitudes toward problems and the impacts of those problems on demographic trends (for instance, trends in health and mortality).[5]

As public and academic awareness of environmental issues has intensified, so has our understanding of the complexity of environmental problems. Potential and currently existing hazards that are socially, politically, and technologically complex, difficult to detect, potentially catastrophic, sometimes long-range in impact, and attributable to multiple causes (e.g., environmental racism, acid rain, rain forest destruction, ozone depletion, loss of biodiversity, technological accidents, and climate change)[6] began to attract the attention of the nascent environmental sociology community in the 1980s. Environmental sociologists of the late twentieth and early twenty-first centuries are studying a broad range of issues—from environmental racism to the international trade in electronic waste to lead poisoning.[7]

Social scientists have developed a number of specialist lenses to explore the increasingly complex relationships between environments and societies. Environmental sociologists frequently focus on power and inequalities. They tend to ask who (which groups or individual actors) have the power not only to make policy decisions but also to create knowledge and set the terms of debate. In addition, most sociologists see all things—from material items to institutions to "nature"—as imbued with meaning by humans.

Environmental sociologists interested in power dynamics often explore intersections between political and economic practices and structures; we often use the term *political economy* to characterize this work. Rudel, Roberts, and Carmin (2011: 222) state that for sociologists, "the political economy of the environment refers to how people control and, periodically, struggle for control over the institutions and organizations that produce and regulate the flows of materials that sustain people (corporations and the state)." Often, researchers using political economy frameworks see environmental devastation and resource exhaustion as inevitable consequences of capitalist accumulation.[8]

While there are numerous ways to approach a political economy of the environment (see Rudel et al. 2011 for a review), many environmental sociologists engage with one of two central and somewhat competing theories: the "treadmill of production," which sees capitalism as inherently problematic, and "ecological modernization," which is a bit more hopeful about the potential of capitalism to become environmentally sustainable.

The concept of the "treadmill of production," developed by Allan Schnaiberg (1980), emphasizes the tendency of capitalist production to constantly seek to expand. According to Schnaiberg and his colleagues, this emphasis on growth leads to increased resource consumption as well as the increased generation of wastes and pollutants (both from the by-products of production and from consumption). Thus, according to this perspective, capitalist production, by its very nature, is at odds with efforts to clean up or improve the environment.

Scholars working within the ecological modernization paradigm are typically somewhat less critical of existing social and economic structures (e.g., Mol 1997; Spaargarten and Mol 1992). Ecological modernization calls our attention to the ways in which environmental degradation may be reduced or even reversed within our current system of institutions. Theorists working within this framework believe that our institutions may be capable of transforming themselves through the use of increasingly sophisticated technologies, and that production processes in the future will have fewer negative environmental consequences. Maurie Cohen (2006) has recently argued that the inability of the U.S. environmental movement to embrace the principles of ecological modernization to produce change has deprived the United States of some of the sustainability successes witnessed in northern European countries, especially in regard to energy efficiency and the development of clean production technologies.

Other theoretical lenses to emerge in the realm of environmental sociology address the intersections of science and risk analysis. Ulrich Beck (1999), for example, has written that people in modern times feel increasingly at risk, due in large part to environmental degradation. Beck developed the concept of the *risk society*, which Michael Bell (1999: 193) describes as "a society in which the central political conflicts are not class struggles over the distribution of money and resources but instead non-class-based struggles over the distribution of technological risk." According to Beck (1999: 72), we are now at "a phase of development in modern society in which the social, political, ecological and individual risks created by the momentum of innovation increasingly elude the control and protective institutions of industrial society." Beck examines how risks, and especially the social stresses associated with our perceptions of risks, are fostering deterioration in our quality of life. In Beck's words, the risk society concept "describes a stage of modernity in which the hazards produced in the growth of industrial society become predominant" (1999: 74).

The study of risks and the study of health are necessarily interconnected, and many environmental sociologists focus their research on the health consequences of environmental risks and other types of degradation. For example, in one recent study, Kari Marie Norgaard (2007) documents how, in a rural region of Northern California, controversy arose over the U.S. Forest Service's proposed use of herbicides on spotted knapweed. The Karuk tribe and other community members, who perceived that they would suffer disproportionate health risks, successfully fought the Forest Service's plans for herbicide application. Norgaard shows that the question of who faces risks from modern technology, as well as perceptions about the existence of risks, is influenced by sociological factors such as gender, race, and power. In the case study by Norgaard, conflict arose partly because citizens had been left out of policy deliberations over how to deal with the weed problem. Phil Brown and his colleagues (see, for example, Brown and Mikkelsen 1990; Brown 2007), meanwhile, have documented and promoted the idea of "popular epidemiology"—a process whereby nonscientist citizens become active producers and users of scientific data.[9]

Finally, some authors (e.g., Greider and Garkovich 1994; Hannigan 1995; Burningham and Cooper 1999; Scarce 2000; Yearley 1992) specifically use a social constructionist framework to examine environment-related questions. Social constructionism emphasizes the process through which concepts and beliefs about the world are formed (and reformed) and through which meanings are attached to things and events. Early on, some environmental sociologists drew a distinction between the "realists," who preferred not to question "the material truth of environmental problems" (Bell 1999: 3), and the "constructionists," who emphasized the creation of meaning—including the meaning of "environment" and "environmental problems"—as a social process (see Bell 1999; Lidskog 2001). However, it is important to note that all sociology is, to some extent, constructionist (see Burningham and Cooper 1999). The debate between "realists" and "constructionists" has largely disappeared from the work of environmental sociologists. All along, the difference was more in the extent to which the authors *emphasized* the process through which meanings are created.

Theoretical perspectives such as the treadmill of production, ecological modernization, the risk society, and popular epidemiology have been developed specifically to help us better understand the human/environment nexus. Many researchers, including those summarized above, also draw on more traditional sociological perspectives, such as social constructionism, to study environment-related issues. Working within the tradition of sociological research that is interested in the creation and perpetuation of inequalities, some sociologists apply theories of gender, race, and class to environmental injustices. The study of environmental justice is a major development that derives from a combination of social scientists' long-standing interest in inequalities and social movement activism that has sought to remedy environmental inequities. Finally, sociologists have long been interested in the cause and consequences of social movement activism, and researchers working in this area of sociology have increasingly examined environmental social movement organizations—such as Greenpeace or the Sierra Club—and environmental movement objectives—such as reducing toxins (see Pellow and Nyseth 2013 for a review of research in environmental sociology as well as several disciplines that speak to—or have influenced—it).

A Look at What's Included in the Reader

The roots of environmental sociology run deep and wide for such a relatively new field of study. The terrain of environmental sociology could perhaps best be described as a collage rather than a cohesive structure of theory and research. This collage reflects the increasingly complex and global nature of our environmental challenges. Our intent in creating this reader is to provide a buffet of issues and perspectives on environmental sociology so that you can sample a wide variety of pieces. Later, when you know what you like, go to the library for seconds!

As mentioned above, often the theories used by sociologists and other social researchers to study environment-related topics build upon the same theories sociologists use to study most anything else. The pieces presented in our reader reflect that theoretical lineage. The first selection, by Hillary Angelo and Colin Jerolmack, argues that social forces affect how we see and understand "nature." Next, we include four works that use a political economy perspective, examining, for example, how economic growth often leads to environmental destruction. Some sociologists adapt ideas about capitalism developed by Karl Marx to analyze the relationship between environment and society. In one provocative essay, John Bellamy Foster argues that we have on our hands an ecological crisis so dire as to warrant an "ecological revolution" that would also be a social revolution because, he contends (as do many environmental sociologists), without addressing fundamental inequalities we cannot tackle climate change and other environmental issues (chapter 2).[10] Longo and Clausen use a Marxist framework to examine overfishing of tuna in the Mediterranean (chapter 3). In a piece very different from the previous two, Benjamin Vail (chapter 4) describes Sweden's broad-reaching environmental policy and asks to what extent it has been guided by the precepts of ecological modernization. Next, Richard York and his colleagues (chapter 5) use a political economy lens to examine the ecological footprint of China, India, Japan, and the United States from 1962 to 2003. The authors show that increased efficiency does not lead to smaller ecological footprints. Many of the authors in this section of the reader argue that there is a fundamental conflict between capitalism's need for constant expansion and the protection of the environment, and they are wary of technological solutions that, they argue, often fail to produce safer, healthier environmental conditions.

In the following section, the authors examine the relationship between social inequality and environmental degradation—an issue central to many recent sociological studies of the environment. These studies ask how, for example, class, race, and gender inequalities foster environmental injustices or inequities. Using case studies of the Kayuk tribe of California and a food collaborative in West Oakland, Alison Alkon and Kari Norgaard develop the concept of food justice, explaining how historically oppressed or disenfranchised populations may be denied access to healthy and culturally appropriate food as a result of institutional racism (chapter 6). The piece by Lois Bryson, Kathleen McPhillips, and Kathryn Robinson (chapter 7) examines the gender and class dimensions of Australian lead pollution policies and public health projects. Finally, Robert Bullard (chapter 8) describes how transportation is an environmental justice issue. Transportation is closely related to employment and access to services and is also closely connected to health issues, such as asthma.

The next section of the reader includes pieces that examine how people's understandings of nature and environment are produced and maintained. J. Sanford Rikoon (chapter 9) analyzes how different groups may have more or less power to impose their own understandings of nature. The chapter (chapter

10) by Kari Norgaard is a case study on perceptions about global warming in Norway; she examines what prevents some people from engaging in environmental change activities. And Shannon Bell and Richard York (chapter 11) describe the power of industry—in this case the coal mining industry—to shape communities' cultural identity.

In the section called "Perspectives on Disaster," the excerpt by Thomas Beamish (chapter 12) uses organizational theories to illuminate an ongoing, slow-motion "accident" (an oil spill that continued for many years) and how workers and managers in the corporation responsible failed to respond. The piece by Ritchie, Gill, and Picou (chapter 13) reflects on the social psychological impacts of the *Exxon Valdez* and BP oil spills for people living along affected coastlines.

The process of globalization has profound implications for local and global environments as well as for social movement activists working to improve environmental quality. Daniel Faber (chapter 14) explains how environmental inequalities have deepened as a result of globalization. Peter Freund and George Martin examine the spread of automobile culture and infrastructure across the globe and its impacts on lower-income nations (chapter 15).

A large number of studies in environmental sociology focus on knowledge, science, health, and/or risk. Sherry Cable, Thomas Shriver, and Tamara Mix (chapter 16) examine how employers and other powerful actors contest workers' claims of environment-related illnesses. In chapter 17, Eric Bonds describes how powerful government agencies and corporations may shape what the public knows about potentially toxic substances. In a study of scientific testing in post-Katrina New Orleans, Scott Frickel and M. Bess Vincent (chapter 18) point to the limits of scientific practices in providing adequate public health and environmental safety information. Because much of the scientific information that reaches the public does so through the news media, we include a chapter (chapter 19) by Norah MacKendrick that analyzes how the Canadian news media has covered "body burdens" (internal contaminant load that most of us—especially those of us in industrialized nations—carry in our bodies).

As students become aware of environmental and social inequalities and injustices, many naturally want to use their sociological knowledge to change things. Some find it frustrating that while sociology reveals many grave societal problems, it does not tell them what to do about those problems. Indeed, there is no one grand sociological recipe for change. To some extent, just learning more about specific issues is the beginning of change. We have to know about and understand issues such as body burdens in order to even think about doing something about that problem. We believe that in almost every sociological study, one can find implied ideas—or "mini-recipes"—for how to work toward solving some of the dilemmas illuminated by environmental sociologists. However, sometimes it is valuable to have specific and explicit examples of how change might occur. Our final section contains pieces with ideas for environmental change and studies of social movements that have advocated for environment-related improvements. The chapter by Michael Maniates (chapter 20) emphasizes the limits of individualism and argues that we need to come together as citizens, rather than act as individual consumers, to seek important structural changes. The piece by Juliet Schor (chapter 21), however, focuses on the types of changes we *can* make as individual consumers (with a focus on the garment industry). David Pellow (chapter 22) describes how a small group of activists in Mozambique succeeded, with the help of transnational social movement actors, in halting an effort (funded by a Danish development organization) to burn obsolete fertilizer and pesticide stocks. Finally, in chapter 23, Myran and Penina Glazer delineate the factors that allow people to commence and remain engaged in social change work.

A Final Word

There are two main reasons we wanted to edit this book. First, we know that people are increasingly interested in ecological change. Environmental interest and support is especially evident in academic institutions, and new courses and programs relevant to environmental studies appear each year (see Galbraith 2009; Johnston 2012; Jones et al. 2010; Schmit 2009). Universities and colleges not only offer environmental courses but also are becoming more active as positive models of environmental change. Around the United States, institutions of higher education are increasingly engaging in environmentally sustainable practices (see Barlett 2011; Barlett and Chase 2004). Some colleges and universities are working to "green" their dining services by including, for example, more organic and locally produced foods or offering the possibility to compost food waste (see Barlett 2011). College campuses are also increasingly stressing energy and water conservation, green building, recycling, and other environment-oriented actions (see Barlett 2011; Elefante 2011). As part of our work as professors we, as well as many of our students, are a part of this ongoing dialogue and activity on our own campuses. We see this book as another way we can contribute to the work we find so important.

Our second reason for compiling this book is to make it easier for nonspecialist sociologists to teach environmental sociology courses. We have spent many hours on our own and, later, in collaboration with each other, to design environmental sociology courses that reflect our values and teaching philosophies. We believe that this is a tremendously important field of research and one that students should have the option to explore as part of their college experience. As sociologists continue to learn about the interconnectedness of our ecological problems with other social problems (e.g., toxic waste and racism), it becomes ever more clear that our ecological health is dependent on our understanding of broader social issues (e.g., democracy, inequality, economics, mass media, etc.) and vice versa. The degree to which we progress in one area (or regress) will echo into every other area of social thought and change. Environmental problems involve power relations; they derive from cultural and institutional practices, and they are unequally distributed among populations. Environmental problems require social solutions.

Notes

1. For more detailed accounts of the Bhopal disaster, see Faber (2008: 188–89); Sengupta (2008); Dinham and Sarangi (2002); Jasanoff (1995); Dembo, Morehouse, and Wykle (1990); Weir (1987); and Everest (1986).

2. For a brief summary of the *Exxon Valdez* disaster and the social conditions leading up to it, see Karliner (1997: 180–82).

3. For a current list of environmental laws and executive orders, see the Environmental Protection Agency website (www.epa.gov/lawsregs/laws). Also, for a comprehensive history of environmental legislation in the United States, see Rosenbaum (2011).

4. It is important to note that sociological thought has always, to some degree, included the consideration of ecological factors. For example, some scholars at the Institute for Social Research in Frankfurt worked on environment-related issues, such as the question of domination of nature, in the mid-twentieth century (see Merchant 1999 for a review). Brief summaries of the history of sociological thought on nature and environment can be found in Hannigan (1995) and Buttel and Humphrey (2002). In addition, more recently, environmental sociologists have begun to draw on previously overlooked ideas in classical sociological theory and have revealed that the classical theorists were more ecologically oriented than many subsequent sociologists realized (see Pellow and Nyseth 2013).

5. Sample titles of articles from sociological journals during this time include: "Support for Resource Conservation: A Prediction Model" (Honnold and Nelson 1979); "The Costs of Air Quality Deterioration and Benefits of Air Pollution Control: Estimates of Mortality Costs for Two Pollutants in 40 U.S. Metropolitan Areas" (Liu 1979); "The Public Value for Air Pollution Control: A Needed Change of Emphasis in Opinion Studies" (Dillman and Christenson 1975); and "The Impact of Political Orientation on Environmental Attitudes and Actions" (Dunlap 1975).

6. Sample titles of articles from sociological journals during the 1980s include: "The Social Ecology of Soil Erosion in a Colombian Farming System" (Ashby 1985); "Manufacturing Danger: Fear and Pollution in Industrial Society" (Kaprow 1985); "Cultural Aspects of Environmental Problems: Individualism and Chemical Contamination of Groundwater" (Fitchen 1987); "Blacks and the Environment" (Bullard and Wright 1987); and "Exxon Minerals in Wisconsin: New Patterns of Rural Environmental Conflict" (Gedicks 1988).

7. For a summary of the history of environmental sociology and the change in focus of environmental studies over time, see Dunlap, Michelson, and Stalker (2002).

8. For an early overview of this body of theory, see O'Connor (1988: 11–38). For a collection of O'Connor's work, see the 1998 book *Natural Causes: Essays in Ecological Marxism*. More recent work in this area is being conducted by scholars such as John Bellamy Foster and others (see, for example, the excerpts in this reader).

9. For example, Brown and Mikkelson's (1990) book, *No Safe Place*, describes how residents of Woburn, Massachusetts, identified and sought remediation for a cancer cluster caused by toxic chemicals in the water supply in certain parts of the town.

10. With a few notable exceptions (e.g., Spaargarten and Mol 1992), sociologists have strong reservations about the long-term sustainability of capitalism.

References

Abramovitz, Janet N. (Worldwatch Institute). 2003. *Vital Signs 2003: The Trends That Are Shaping Our Future*. New York: W.W. Norton.

American Lung Association. 2012. *State of the Air 2012*. Washington, DC: American Lung Association. http://www.stateoftheair.org/2012/assets/state-of-the-air2012.pdf.

Ashby, Jacqueline A. 1985. "The Social Ecology of Soil Erosion in a Columbian Farming System." *Rural Sociology* 50 (3) (Fall): 377–96.

Barlett, Peggy. 2011. "Campus Sustainable Food Projects: Critique and Engagement." *American Anthropologist* 113 (1): 101–15.

Barlett, Peggy F., and Geoffrey W. Chase (eds.). 2004. *Sustainability on Campus: Stories and Strategies for Change*. Cambridge, MA: The MIT Press.

BBC News World Edition. 2002. "Comparing the Worst Oil Spills." November 19, 2002. http://news.bbc.co.uk/2/hi/europe/2491317.stm (retrieved December 30, 2003).

Beck, Ulrich. 1999. *World Risk Society*. Malden, MA: Polity Press.

Bell, Michael M. 1998. *An Invitation to Environmental Sociology*. Thousand Oaks, CA: Pine Forge Press.

Bergal, Jenni. 2007. "The Storm." Pp. 1–6 in Jenni Bergal, Sara Shipley Hiles, Frank Koughan, John McQuaid, Jim Morris, Katy Reckdahl, and Curtis Wilkie, *City Adrift: New Orleans before and after Katrina*. Baton Rouge: Louisiana State University Press.

Brown, Phil. 2007. *Toxic Exposures: Contested Illnesses and the Environmental Health Movement*. New York: Columbia University Press.

Brown, Phil, and Edwin J. Mikkelsen. 1990. *No Safe Place: Toxic Waste, Leukemia, and Community Action*. Berkeley: University of California Press.

Bullard, Robert D., and Beverly Hendrix Wright. 1987. "Blacks and the Environment." *Humboldt Journal of Social Relations* 14 (1–2) (Fall–Summer): 165–84.

Burningham, Kate, and Geoff Cooper. 1999. "Being Constructive: Social Construction-ism and the Environment." *Sociology* 33 (2): 297–316.

Buttel, Frederick H., and Craig R. Humphrey. 2002. "Sociological Theory and the Natural Environment." Pp. 32–69 in Riley E. Dunlap and William Michelson (eds.), *Handbook of Environmental Sociology*. Westport, CT: Greenwood Press.

Catton, William R., and Riley E. Dunlap. 1978. "Environmental Sociology: A New Paradigm." *American Sociologist* 13: 41–49.

Cohen, Maurie J. 2006. "Ecological Modernization and Its Discontents: The American Environmental Movement's Resistance to an Innovation-Driven Future." *Futures* 38: 528–47.

Dembo, David, Ward Morehouse, and Lucinda Wykle. 1990. *Abuse of Power: Social Performance of Multinational Corporations: The Case of Union Carbide.* New York: New Horizons Press.

Dillman, Don A., and James A. Christenson. 1975. "The Public Value for Air Pollution Control: A Needed Change of Emphasis in Opinion Studies." *Cornell Journal of Social Relations* 10 (1) (Spring): 73–95.

Dinham, Barbara, and Satinath Sarangi. 2002. "The Bhopal Gas Tragedy 1984 to ? The Evasion of Corporate Responsibility." *Environment and Urbanization* 14 (1): 89–99.

Dowie, Mark. 2001. "Chapter 6: Food." Pp. 106–40 in *American Foundations: An Investigative History.* Cambridge, MA: MIT Press.

Dunlap, Riley E. 1997. "The Evolution of Environmental Sociology: A Brief History of the American Experience." Pp. 21–39 in Michael Redclift and Graham Woodgate (eds.), *The International Handbook of Environmental Sociology.* Northampton, MA: Edward Elgar.

———. 1975. "The Impact of Political Orientation on Environmental Attitudes and Actions." *Environment and Behavior* 7 (4): 428–54.

Dunlap, Riley E., William Michelson, and Glenn Stalker. 2002. "Environmental Sociology: An Introduction." Pp. 1–32 in Riley E. Dunlap and William Michelson (eds.), *Handbook of Environmental Sociology.* Westport, CT: Greenwood Press.

Elefante, Carl. 2011. "The Full and True Value of Campus Heritage." *Planning for Higher Education* 39(3).

EPA (U.S. Environmental Protection Agency). 2012. *Our Nation's Air—Status and Trends through 2010.* www.epa.gov/airtrends/2011.

———. 2004. "Climate." Environmental Protection Agency website. yosemite.epa.gov. oar/globalwarming.nsf/content/climate/html (retrieved January 1, 2004).

Everest, Larry. 1986. *Behind the Poison Cloud: Union Carbide's Bhopal Massacre.* Chicago: Banner Press.

Faber, Daniel. 2008. *Capitalizing on Environmental Injustice: The Polluter Industrial Complex in the Age of Globalization.* New York: Rowman & Littlefield.

———. 1993. *Environment under Fire: Imperialism and the Ecological Crisis in Central America.* New York: Monthly Review Press.

Fackler, Martin. 2012. "Nuclear Disaster in Japan Was Avoidable, Critics Contend." *New York Times*, March 9.

Fann, Neal, Amy D. Lamson, Susan Anenberg, Karen Wesson, David Risley, and Bryan J. Hubbell. 2012. "Estimating the National Public Health Burden Associated with Exposure to Ambient PM2.5 and Ozone." *Environmental Sciences and Pollution Management* 32 (1): 81–95.

Feagin, Joe, and Hernán Vera. 2001. *Liberation Sociology.* Boulder, CO: Westview Press.

Fitchen, Janet M. 1987. "Cultural Aspects of Environmental Problems: Individualism and Chemical Contamination of Groundwater." *Science, Technology, and Human Values* 12 (2): 1–12.

Foster, Joanna. 2011. "Impact of Gulf Spill's Underwater Dispersants Is Examined." *New York Times*, August 26.

Freudenburg, William R., and Robert Gramling. 2011. *Blowout in the Gulf: The BP Oil Spill Disaster and the Future of Energy in America.* Cambridge, MA: The MIT Press.

Gabe, Thomas, Gene Falk, Maggie McCarty, and Virginia Mason. 2005. *Hurricane Katrina: Social-Demographic Characteristics of Impacted Areas.* Washington, DC: Congressional Research Service, Library of Congress.

Galbraith, Kate. 2009. "Sustainability Field Booms on Campus." *New York Times,* August 19.

Gardner, Gary T., Chris Bright, and Linda Starke (Worldwatch Institute). 2003. *State of the World 2003.* New York: W.W. Norton.

Gedicks, Al. 1988. "Exxon Minerals in Wisconsin: New Patterns of Rural Environmental Conflict." *Wisconsin Sociologist* 25 (2–3): 88–103.

Greenpeace. 1999. "Remembering the *Exxon Valdez.*" www.greenpeaceusa.org/features/exxontext.htm (retrieved December 30, 2003).

Greider, Thomas, and Lorraine Garkovich. 1994. "Landscapes: The Social Construction of Nature and the Environment." *Rural Sociology* 59 (1): 1–24.

Hammer, David. 2010. "5 Key Human Errors, Colossal Mechanical Failure Led to Fatal Gulf Oil Rig Blowout." *Times Picayune,* September 5.

Hannigan, John. 1995. *Environmental Sociology: A Social Constructionist Perspective.* New York: Routledge.

Hiles, Sara Shipley. 2007. "The Environment." Pp. 7–19 in Jenni Bergal, Sara Shipley Hiles, Frank Koughan, John McQuaid, Jim Morris, Katy Reckdahl, and Curtis Wilkie, *City Adrift: New Orleans before and after Katrina.* Baton Rouge: Louisiana State University Press.

Honnold, Julie A., and Lynn D. Nelson. 1979. "Support for Resource Conservation: A Prediction Model." *Social Problems* 27 (2): 220–34.

IPCC (Intergovernmental Panel on Climate Change). 2007a. *Climate Change 2007: Synthesis Report, Summary for Policy Makers.* www.ipcc.ch/ (retrieved July 16, 2008).

———. 2007b. *Climate Change 2007: The Physical Science Basis, Summary for Policy Makers.* www.ipcc.ch/ (retrieved July 16, 2008).

———. 2001. *Climate Change 2001: Synthesis Report.* http://www.ipcc.ch/ipccreports/tar/vol4/english/ (retrieved December 31, 2003).

Jasanoff, Sheila (ed.). 1995. *Learning from Disaster: Risk Management after Bhopal.* Philadelphia: University of Pennsylvania Press.

Johnston, Lucas F. (ed.). 2012. *Higher Education for Sustainability: Cases, Challenges, and Opportunities from across the Curriculum.* New York: Routledge.

Jones, Paula, David Selby, and Stephen Sterling (eds.). 2010. *Sustainability Education: Perspectives and Practice across Higher Education.* New York: Routledge.

Kaprow, Miriam Lee. 1985. "Manufacturing Danger: Fear and Pollution in Industrial Society." *American Anthropologist* 87 (2): 342–56.

Karliner, Joshua. 1997. *The Corporate Planet: Ecology and the Politics in the Age of Globalization.* San Francisco: Sierra Club Books.

Krauss, Clifford. 2012. "In BP Indictments, U.S. Shifts to Hold Individuals Accountable." *New York Times,* November 15.

Laumbach, Robert J. 2010. "Outdoor Air Pollutants and Patient Health." *American Family Physician* 81 (2): 175–80.

Lidskog, Rolf. 2001. "The Re-Naturalization of Society? Environmental Challenges for Sociology." *Current Sociology* 49 (1): 113–36.

Liu, Ben-Chieh. 1979. "The Costs of Air Quality Deterioration and Benefits of Air Pollution Control: Estimates of Mortality Costs for Two Pollutants in 40 U.S. Metropolitan Areas." *American Journal of Economics and Sociology* 38 (2): 187–95.

McKibben, Bill. 2012. "Global Warming's Terrifying New Math." *Rolling Stone*, July 19.

McQuaid, John. 2007. "The Levees." Pp. 20–41 in Jenni Bergal, Sara Shipley Hiles, Frank Koughan, John McQuaid, Jim Morris, Katy Reckdahl, and Curtis Wilkie, *City Adrift: New Orleans before and after Katrina*. Baton Rouge: Louisiana State University Press.

Merchant, Carolyn (ed.). 1999. *Key Concepts in Critical Theory: Ecology*. Amherst, NY: Humanity Books.

Mol, Arthur P. 1997. "Ecological Modernization: Industrial Transformations and Environmental Reform." Pp. 138–49 in Michael Redclift and Graham Woodgate (eds.), *The International Handbook of Environmental Sociology*. Northampton, MA: Edward Elgar.

National Research Council. 2010. *Advancing the Science of Climate Change*. National Research Council. The National Academies Press, Washington, DC, USA. http://nas-sites.org/americasclimatechoices/sample-page/panel-reports/87-2/.

Nöggerath, Johannis, Robert J. Geller, and Viacheslav K. Gusiakov. 2011. "Fukushima: The Myth of Safety, the Reality of Geoscience." *Bulletin of the Atomic Scientists* 67 (5): 37–46.

Norgaard, Kari Marie. 2007. "The Politics of Invasive Weed Management: Gender, Race, and Risk Perception in Rural California." *Rural Sociology* 72 (3): 450–77.

O'Connor, James. 1998. *Natural Causes: Essays in Ecological Marxism*. New York: Guilford Press.

——. 1988. "Capitalism, Nature, Socialism: A Theoretical Introduction." *Capitalism, Nature, Socialism* 1 (Fall): 11–38.

Parks, Bradley C., and J. Timmons Roberts. 2010. "Climate Change, Social Theory and Justice." *Theory, Culture and Society* 27 (2–3): 134–66.

PBS (Public Broadcasting Service). 2010. "The Spill." (PBS *Frontline* and ProPublica). http://www.pbs.org/wgbh/pages/frontline/the-spill/ (retrieved December 2012).

Pellow, David, and Hollie Nyseth. 2013 (forthcoming). "An Environmental Sociology for the 21st Century." *Annual Review of Sociology*, V39.

Picou, J. Steven, and Brent Marshall. 2007. "Katrina as Paradigm Shift: Reflections on Disaster Research in the Twenty-First Century." Pp. 1–20 in David Brunsma, David Overfelt, and J. Steven Picou (eds.), *The Sociology of Katrina: Perspectives on a Modern Catastrophe*. New York: Rowman & Littlefield.

Rosenbaum, Walter A. 2011. *Environmental Politics and Policy*. Washington, DC: CQ Press.

Rosset, Peter, Joseph Collins, and Frances Moore Lappe. 2000. "Lessons from the Green Revolution." *Tikkun Magazine*, March 1.

Rudel, Thomas K., J. Timmons Roberts, and JoAnne Carmin. 2011. "Political Economy of the Environment." *Annual Review of Sociology* 37: 221–38.

Scarce, Rik. 2000. *Fishy Business: Salmon, Biology, and the Social Construction of Nature*. Philadelphia: Temple University Press.

Schmit, Julie. 2009. "As Colleges Add Green Majors and Minors, Classes Fill Up." *USA Today*, December 28.

Schnaiberg, Allan. 1980. *The Environment: From Surplus to Scarcity*. New York: Oxford University Press.

Sengupta, Somini. 2008. "Decades Later, Toxic Sludge Torments Bhopal." *New York Times*, July 7. www.nytimes.com/2008/07/07/world/asia/07bhopal.

Spaargarten, Gert, and Arthur P. Mol. 1992. "Sociology, Environment, and Modernity: Ecological Modernization as a Theory of Social Change." *Society and Natural Resources* 54 (4): 323–444.

Steingraber, Sandra. 2000. "The Social Production of Cancer: A Walk Upstream." In Richard Hofrichter (ed.), *Reclaiming the Environmental Debate: The Politics of Health in a Toxic Culture*. Cambridge, MA: MIT Press.

Taylor, Dorceta E. 1997. "American Environmentalism: The Role of Race, Class and Gender in Shaping Activism 1820–1995." *Race, Gender & Class* 5 (1): 16–62.

U.S. Department of Interior. 2012. *Deepwater Horizon Oil Spill Phase I Early Restoration Plan and Environmental Assessment*. http://www.doi.gov/deepwaterhorizon/upload/Final-ERP-EA-ES-041812.pdf (retrieved December 2012).

U.S. PIRG. 2007. *Toxic Pollution and Health Analysis of Toxic Chemicals Released in Communities across the United States: Executive Summary US PIRG Report*. www.uspirg.org/home/reports/report-archives/healthy-communities/.

Vicini, James. 2008. "*Exxon Valdez* $2.5 Billion Oil Spill Ruling Overturned." http://www.reuters.com/article/idUSWBT00926720080625 (retrieved April 16, 2013).

Weir, David. 1987. *The Bhopal Syndrome*. San Francisco: Sierra Club Books.

World Health Organization. 2011. *Fact Sheet No. 313, "Air Quality and Health."* http://www.who.int/mediacentre/factsheets/fs313/en/index.html (retrieved February 1, 2013).

Worldwatch Institute. 2004. *State of the World 2004: Progress Towards a Sustainable Society*. London: Earthscan.

Wu, Nerissa, Thomas Herrmann, Olaf Paepke, Joel Tickner, Robert Hale, Ellen Harvey, Mark La Guardia, Michael McClean, and Thomas Webster. 2007. "Human Exposure to PBDEs: Associations of PBDE Body Burdens with Food Consumption and House Dust Concentrations." *Environment, Science, and Technology* 41 (5): 1584–89.

Yearley, Steven. 1992. *The Green Case*. London: Routledge.

PART

Imagining Nature

Nature's Looking Glass
Hillary Angelo and Colin Jerolmack

The authors of this first piece use a case study of New York City hawks, Violet and Bobby, and their human web cam followers to illustrate how people hold very different views on the meaning of nature. Some mystify nature and view "pure" nature as separate from people. In this "asocial nature" view, just the presence of humans might despoil nature. Others see a "social nature" in which animals are adaptable rather than mystic. According to this viewpoint "social nature" is neither pure nor impure, the mix of human society with other animal societies and ecosystems is taken as a given. These differing perspectives can lead to conflicts over how, and whether, humans should intervene in phenomena such as a hawk pair nesting on a New York city ledge. The authors suggest that both views of nature are important. Belief in a "pure nature" may motivate us to protect nature. On the other hand, the understanding that nature is always, at least on some level, social, encourages us to appreciate the potential and real biodiversity surrounding us.

After a month of courtship and nest-building, two red-tailed hawks began patiently tending to three speckled eggs in April 2011. Given that red-tailed hawks are a common American species, the event would seem no more than a footnote in the rites of spring; but this nest happened to be on a 12th floor window ledge of NYU's Bobst Library, overlooking Washington Square Park in Manhattan.

Within days, the birds, christened "Bobby" and "Violet," had their own Facebook page and Twitter account, and were stars of a streaming reality television show (thanks to a web camera installed by the *New York Times*). Building on New Yorkers' recent infatuation with the famous 5th Avenue hawks known as Pale Male and Lola, Violet and Bobby soon gathered a devoted following who watched anxiously as the pair raised their hatchling ("Pip") on squirrels and rats captured from the park. The public participated with "tweets," chatroom conversations, blog posts, and face-to-face meet-ups. As articulated by the *Times* and reflected in statements by NYU's president, witnessing the hawks' efforts to start a family—up-close—enabled a rare moment of human encounter with "transcendent" nature in the city.

The environmental historian William Cronon writes that people turn to nature because it is seen as untainted by the "social ills" of civilization. He calls this the "wilderness fantasy." Yet paradoxically, rather than facilitating a socially unspoiled nature experience in the comfort of urban homes, the "hawk cam" instead revealed its impossibility: the band around Violet's swollen foot marked her as a raptor that had already encountered human hands; the Department of Environmental Protection opened up a case file on the hawks, declaring the state's authority over them; hawk devotees debated online whether humans should intervene to remove Violet's band, fortify the nest, or even help break open the eggs; and the hawks' choices of inorganic nesting materials—a thick sheet of white plastic, a soiled hand towel, and artificial Easter grass—frustrated viewers, who criticized the hawks' use of these "unnatural" items.

Although some viewers embraced the hawks as "city birds" whose resourcefulness reflected an admirable adaptation to the urban environment they inhabited, fans seeking an asocial nature experience protested when signs of the social world interrupted their image of the hawks as a kind of miniature wilderness. Much as Frederick Olmsted's design for Central Park had aimed to create an experience of nature that hid the city surrounding it, many hawkwatchers had a strong desire to maintain the myth of wild, unsullied nature.

The hawk cam, just one of hundreds of popular web cameras streaming the trials and tribulations of wild animals to a global audience, exemplifies a central paradox of our urbanized society's relationship to the environment: on the one hand, we believe that encounters with nature allow us to transcend social life, and yet, on the other, our experience of nature is profoundly shaped by social forces. To emphasize the fact that our relationships with the environment are always socially mediated, sociologists often place quotes around "nature" or refer to *socio-nature*. While the idea of nature as a realm free of social interests may indeed be a fantasy, as a cultural ideal it nonetheless organizes the ways people experience the environment. The conception of asocial nature, in interaction with the reality of "social nature," impacts how humans interpret and respond to the nonhuman world. Perhaps the incursion of the social world spoils the imagery of Bobby and Violet's nest as a microcosm of "pure" wilderness, but the collective human response to this alleged interruption is itself a microcosm of our social struggles over how to live with nature.

Asocial Nature

Classical sociological concerns regarding modernization have centered on topics like people's migration from rural villages to large cities, the rise of capitalism, and the reorganization of community life. More recently, though, social scientists have begun looking at how society's relationship to the physical environment has been transformed. After all, the Industrial Revolution, Karl Marx and Friedrich Engels observed, was founded on the "subjection of nature's forces to man."

Much as the rationalization of work and social life was said to produce a sort of collective malaise (what social theorist Max Weber called "disenchantment"), sociologist James Gibson tells a parallel story of contemporary society's increasing estrangement from nature. Gibson reports that many pre-modern societies revered nature and believed it was animated by spirits, but that the rise of science promoted a mechanistic view of nature "as inert matter." In turn, capitalism reduced nature to a commodity. Gibson and other environmental scholars argue that the physical defilement of the natural world and people's increasing geographic separation from nature through urbanization have led to nature's spiritual profanation. The art and literary critic John Berger looks to our relationships with animals as clear evidence of this estrangement: the transformation of the wolf to working farm dog and then to handbag Chihuahua simultaneously marks the retreat of wild, asocial nature and the disappearance of our respect and awe for it. Scholars like Gibson and Berger see our desecration and humanization of nature as harmful to both the environment (which we are socialized to exploit as a means rather than an end) and society (which is spiritually impoverished because the plants and animals around us are no longer endowed with otherworldly significance).

If the entrance of social interests into our relationship with nature despoils it conceptually and physically, then solving the ecological crisis requires that we supersede instrumentalist orientations and reinvest nature with sacred meaning. Gibson believes it's already happening. He finds a growing number of people "who long to rediscover and embrace nature's mystery and grandeur" and "who look to nature for psychic regeneration and renewal." Gibson interprets New Yorkers' fascination with the red-tailed hawks Pale Male and Lola—and, presumably, Bobby and Violet—as an expression of their desire to seek momentary sanctuary from the concrete jungle in the experience of "kinship" with nature. In his view, the hawks are ambassadors of the wild and our celebration of them is a consecration of nature, a transcendence of the social. Strands of this "culture of enchantment" are evident in the narratives of the environmental movement, which often focuses its attention on the majesty of rugged mountain peaks or charismatic fauna (rather than, say, a suburban park or snails). The implied ideal is preserving, or even reconstructing, "pristine" nature.

The enchanted nature thesis guides many preservationists' efforts and compellingly captures the asocial wilderness ideal that many use to frame their interpretations of the nonhuman world. Yet, as Cronon has said, by reproducing "the dualism that sets humanity and nature at opposite poles," this quixotic standard does not offer a blueprint of "what an ethical, sustainable, *honorable* human place in nature might look like." As Gibson concedes, "unrealistic expectations of purity" can impede appreciation and respect for the hybrid landscapes we actually inhabit. Stories such as *Grizzly Man* and *Into the Wild* show how efforts to realize the wilderness fantasy can in fact be harmful or tragic. By threatening to pigeonhole socially mediated relations with nature— which, in reality, includes *all* relations with nature—as somehow less "pure" or "meaningful" than nature encounters that appear to be asocial, this perspective misses an opportunity to examine how the explicit comingling of the natural and the social can be beneficial for both the environment and society.

Social Nature

A second sociological tradition, dating back to classical sociologist Emile Durkheim, highlights how the social and the natural are inextricably intertwined. In studying pre-modern aboriginal clans that practiced totemism, a belief system in which a clan adopts a particular plant or animal as its symbol and considers it sacred, Durkheim rejected the assumption that aborigines actually worshipped nature. The totem species was sacred, rather, because it stood for the clan; worshipping it was a way of expressing social solidarity. Though perhaps in different ways, our relations to the nonhuman world remain inherently social. Every landscape, sociologists Thomas Greider and Lorraine Garkovich write, is a "symbolic environment created by the human act of conferring meaning." The meanings we ascribe to the environment reflect our self-definitions and are grounded in particular social contexts. For example, in studying an English exurban village, sociologist Michael Bell found that residents identified as "country people" who, by living close to nature, believed that they led more authentic and wholesome lives than city dwellers. Still, Bell found important differences in villagers' relationships with nature that were patterned by their class position. Wealthier residents, for instance, prized open vistas of the countryside and sculpted their backyards to create clear sight lines, but working-class residents had a more hands-on relationship with the land and paid less attention to "the view," even planting shrubs that impeded it. Though all of the villagers believed nature offered them an escape from the ills of society, in reality their experience of the environment still mapped onto familiar social categories.

"Social nature" analyses undermine the wilderness fantasy by exposing how the social and natural worlds are conjointly constituted. They also help us understand the social motivations behind idealizing nature. Bell found that salient class tensions threatened to undermine group solidarity in the village he studied, and that grounding their sense of selves in nature was a way for villagers to overcome social divisions and rally around a shared identity—a sort of secular totemism. Historically, Cronon argues that urban elites in the U.S.—who themselves never lived close to the land—cultivated the wilderness fantasy as a national project because untamed nature was a monument to America's heroic frontier myth and "the last bastion of rugged individualism." Culture and context always frame our understandings of nature. The idea of asocial nature is itself a social frame.

The principle that nature is just as social as race or gender challenged assumptions about environment-society relations and helped open up a domain of inquiry long considered the realm of the natural sciences. It forces us to see the encroachment of the social world into Bobby and Violet's nest as an inherent part of our experience of nature, not contamination. The chatroom discussions, "expert" opinions rendered in the news, and the face-to-face meetups under the nest aren't ancillary to the "first hand" experience of the hawks—they are the means by which the hawks become meaningful and knowable to people.

While the pristine, asocial nature ideal spurred important environmental legislation like the creation of treasured national parks, scholars like Cronon point to the troubling social and material consequences of the wilderness fantasy: it has too often meant evicting those who inhabited the land (like Native Americans and farmers) and erasing any trace of their existence; and it can foster apathy toward the "impure" environments that most humans actually inhabit. Further, the "not in my backyard" environmental activism of the middle and upper classes may lead to the siting of toxic facilities in poor and minority communities. "Social nature" analyses can help us see environmental justice and social justice as inherently linked ideals.

Scholarship on the social experience of nature falls short of its potential if it simply debunks the wilderness fantasy or subjects it to an ideological critique. For, while the notion that nature is always social may now be sociological commonsense, the experience of nature that people strive to create and maintain is an asocial one. Bell acknowledges that we must continue to account for the imaginative pull of this paradigmatic frame in the urbanized Western world. For most people, there is something fundamentally distinct about encountering the "wild." We can warn hawk-cam viewers that their quest for asocial nature is foolhardy, yet they will still fix their eyes on the screen hoping to capture the moment when Violet feeds her baby beak-to-beak. Interactions with superficially asocial nature in the city—a hike on Central Park's wooded trails or a glimpse of soaring red-tailed hawks—give us an experiential analog that we reflexively connect to a grander image of the kind of nature we wish to preserve and immerse ourselves in, the rugged mountain peak or lion on the savannah we may never know. Few consider the animal-filled circus or weeds in a vacant lot "nature experiences," and most of Violet and Bobby's fans remain unmoved by the pigeons picking at the remains of a bagel below the hawks' nest.

Frame Breaks

If asocial nature is an interpretive frame, then what sociologist Erving Goffman called "frame breaks"—moments when the taken-for-granted way we see the world is disrupted—are telling. Because these interruptions contain *both* the enchanted ideal and the social reality, they provide analytically rich data and moments for education and reflection.

Environmental educators are fluent in putting these contrasts to work. A visit to a natural history museum is unlike wilderness immersion in a wooded park in part because, in order to educate people about "nature," the exhibits quite deliberately play with the tension between social and asocial nature frames. Like going to a movie, habitat dioramas (or, more recently, IMAX films) are self-consciously short-term immersive experiences explicitly designed to mimic an at-risk "natural" environment in order to show us what we would be missing if it disappeared. They are effective in part because the frame is *visible*: stepping back, you see the edges of the glass, hear the echoing cries of the children around you, and feel the wilderness recede. There is no question that this window is an illustration, that the dioramas use a clearly fabricated image of asocial nature to provoke critical reflection about humanity's alteration of the environment. Although proponents of animal welfare decry the collision of caged animals and entertainment, zoos increasingly rely on similar visual techniques to try to educate about conservation through what might be called "living dioramas."

When it comes to the camera that frames Bobby and Violet, however, sublime nature seekers treat it not as a manmade window that illustrates some aspect of the natural world, but as a window into "real," asocial nature. That is why viewers are apt to complain when human hands intervene in Violet's nest, yet watch in fascination as a zookeeper feeds peanuts to an elephant or a museum employee exposes a diorama's artificiality by entering to repair a perfectly rendered plant or animal form.

Yet the frame breaks that hawk-cam viewers continually confront need not be a tragedy. Like a diorama, these moments can foster awareness and even appreciation for the ways that the natural and the social are co-constituted. The presence of a plastic bag in Violet's nest can be a platform for discussing the adaptability of animals (and humans) to built environments and for thinking about how we can alter the cityscape to create a more sustainable habitat for "wild" species. And, rather than deploring the Department of Environmental Protection's intervention in Bobby and Violet's affairs as unnatural or simply holding it up as evidence that nature is always social, we can use the moment to illuminate the constellation of institutions that influence our relationship with other species in the city. Understanding this organizational ecology is more than an academic exercise; it can help environmental advocates find their bureaucratic allies and apply pressure to their opponents. It can also reveal the social structures that govern how access to "natural goods" like clean air, safe drinking water, green spaces, and farmer's markets is distributed in the city.

Spared the toil of the farm or the awesome but terrifying experience of taming the wilderness frontier, contemporary urbanites idealize nature as an environment uncorrupted by people. And though that asocial nature is a chimera, our *belief* in it often serves as a prime motivator for helping the environment. It infuses our encounters with the "wild" with a sense of mystery. By the same token, seeing the social in nature need not threaten our desire to associate with and protect it. The hawk chatroom and in-person meet-ups continued long after Pip fled the nest. The community that sprang up around the hawks abetted people's sense of connection to Bobby, Violet, their baby, and, in some cases, the urban ecology around them. And catching a glimpse of Pip eating her first pigeon becomes meaningful not only because hawk devotees bear witness to the cycle of life, but also because they can blog about it or talk about it in person with each other.

Our own research highlights how the social experience of nature can enhance our appreciation of it and how asocial and social experiences of nature are interconnected. In studying a group of Turkish male immigrants in Berlin who kept domestic pigeons, for instance, Jerolmack was able to show how the birds enabled the men to experience a connection to nature in the midst of the city. Yet the men also said they appreciated keeping pigeons in Berlin because it enabled them to experience a connection to their homeland and express their ethnicity. This social tie to *nation* augmented, rather than mitigated, the immigrants' enjoyment of *nature*. And, in a study of two very different types of bird enthusiasts, Angelo demonstrated the interdependence of asocial and social nature experiences. While ornithologists draw the ire of birdwatchers by shooting and skinning birds to create specimens, their social practices produce the knowledge—in the form of field guides—that birdwatchers rely upon to identify avian species while imaginatively immersing themselves in "wildernesses" big and small. Socially mediated "nature," in the form of bird specimens in a scientific collection, enables the asocial nature experience that birdwatchers enjoy through binoculars. Both practices—though very different—can be understood as driven by, and resulting in, admiration for the nonhuman world.

The journalist Robert Sullivan writes that nature is prospering in cities like New York (Queens contains more species of birds than Yellowstone and

Yosemite Parks combined), but that many residents haven't noticed because this isn't the nature they are looking for—it is less precious, less "pure." Yet these species, many of which have learned to adapt their behaviors to the habits of people, powerfully demonstrate the extent to which the social and the natural are intertwined. Pigeons and squirrels "beg" humans for food in Washington Square, and crows crack open nuts by dropping them into car traffic. Given the likelihood of continued ecological disruption, ecologists predict a future in which more and more species will fashion their survival strategies around human societies. Learning to appreciate and promote the biodiversity hiding in our cities expands the terrain of environmental conservation and may in fact offer clues for how to model sustainable human and nonhuman cohabitation.

William Cronon writes that, while humans must be conscious of our place in the natural world in order to live mindfully within it, we must also "recognize and honor nonhuman nature as a world we did not create." The magical experience of asocial nature is not something to blindly embrace, nor is it something that we should—or could—rid ourselves of. Rather than conceptualizing "asocial nature" and "social nature" as moral or experiential opposites, we would do better to think of them as overlapping modes of experience that can both foster greater appreciation of, and concern for, the environment *and* society.

Note

Hillary Angelo and Colin Jerolmack. 2012. "Nature's Looking Glass." *Contexts* 11(1): 24–29.

References

Bell, Michael. 1994. *Childerley: Nature and Morality in a Country Village*. Chicago: University of Chicago Press. Describes how a rural community uses the idea of asocial nature to construct an image of themselves as moral people.

Cronon, William. 1996. "The Trouble with Wilderness." *Environmental History* 1(1): 7–28. Examines the origins, and negative environmental consequences, of the wilderness ideal.

Freudenburg, William R., Scott Frickel, Robert Gramling. 1995. "Beyond the Society/ Nature Divide: Learning to Think about a Mountain." *Sociological Forum* 10(3): 361–392. Surveys the ways in which the social and the natural are conjointly constituted.

Gibson, James. 2009. *A Reenchanted World: The Quest for a New Kinship with Nature*. New York: Holt. Frames recent environmentalist efforts to protect animals and open spaces as reflecting a "culture of enchantment" that attempts to make nature sacred once again.

PART II

Political Economy

Why Ecological Revolution?

John Bellamy Foster

In the next four selections, the authors examine the intersections between politics, economics, and the environment. The sociological study of politics and economics challenges our tendency to take current systems, like capitalism, for granted by critically examining how power and wealth intersect with ecology and environment. Many environmental sociologists draw on the ideas of classical political/ economic theorists, like Karl Marx and Friedrich Engels, to argue that capitalism's need for constant expansion contributes to resource depletion and environmental degradation. The articles in this section encourage us to question a modern global, capitalist economic system that must constantly expand and grow in order to thrive. Although the messages of these articles are often cautionary, they can also be read as positive. For while the current levels and future predictions of environmental degradation are frightening, they are human made. And if we can make a system of production and consumption that harms the environment then we can unmake it.

John Bellamy Foster's essay sounds the alarm bells. He argues not just that the earth is experiencing an urgent ecological crisis, but potentially the final crisis. Drawing on research indicating that environmental problems, like global climate change, are accelerating and in danger of reaching irreversible "tipping points", Foster contends that technological fixes are not enough and only an ecological revolution—a major change in our social relations and our relationship to the environment—will save our planet, and ourselves, from collapse.

It is now universally recognized within science that humanity is confronting the prospect—if we do not soon change course—of a planetary ecological collapse. Not only is the global ecological crisis becoming more and more severe, with the time in which to address it fast running out, but the dominant environmental strategies are also forms of denial, demonstrably doomed to fail, judging by their own limited objectives. This tragic failure, I will argue, can be attributed to the refusal of the powers that be to address the roots of the ecological problem in capitalist production and the resulting necessity of ecological and social revolution.

The term "crisis," attached to the global ecological problem, although unavoidable, is somewhat misleading, given its dominant economic associations. Since 2008, we have been living through a world economic crisis—the worst economic downturn since the 1930s. This has been a source of untold suffering for hundreds of millions, indeed billions, of people. But insofar as it is related to the business cycle and not to long-term factors, expectations are that it is temporary and will end, to be followed by a period of economic recovery and growth—until the advent of the next crisis. Capitalism is, in this sense, a crisis-ridden, cyclical economic system. Even if we were to go further, to conclude that the present crisis of accumulation is part of a long-term economic stagnation of the system—that is, a slowdown of the trend-rate of growth beyond the mere business cycle—we would still see this as a partial, historically limited calamity, raising, at most, the question of the future of the present system of production.[1]

When we speak today of the world ecological crisis, however, we are referring to something that could turn out to be *final*, i.e., there is a high probability, if we do not quickly change course, of a *terminal crisis*—a death of the whole anthropocene, the period of human dominance of the planet. Human actions are generating environmental changes that threaten the extermination of most species on the planet, along with civilization, and conceivably our own species as well.

What makes the current ecological situation so serious is that climate change, arising from human-generated increases in greenhouse gas emissions, is not occurring gradually and in a linear process, but is undergoing a dangerous acceleration, pointing to sudden shifts in the state of the earth system. We can therefore speak, to quote James Hansen, director of NASA's Goddard Institute of Space Studies, and the world's most famous climate scientist, of "tipping points . . . fed by amplifying feedbacks."[2] Four amplifying feedbacks are significant at present: (1) rapid melting of arctic sea ice, with the resulting reduction of the earth's albedo (reflection of solar radiation) due to the replacement of bright, reflective ice with darker blue sea water, leading to greater absorption of solar energy and increasing global average temperatures; (2) melting of the frozen tundra in northern regions, releasing methane (a much more potent greenhouse gas than carbon dioxide) trapped beneath the surface, causing accelerated warming; (3) recent indications that there has been a drop in the efficiency of the carbon absorption of the world's oceans since the 1980s, and particularly since 2000, due to growing ocean acidification (from past carbon absorption), resulting in faster carbon build-up in the atmosphere and enhanced warming; (4) extinction of species due to changing climate zones, leading to the collapse of ecosystems dependent on these species, and the death of still more species.[3]

Due to this acceleration of climate change, the time line in which to act before calamities hit, and before climate change increasingly escapes our control, is extremely short. . . .

Many of the planetary dangers associated with current global warming trends are by now well-known: rising sea levels engulfing islands and low-lying coastal regions throughout the globe; loss of tropical forests; destruction of coral reefs; a "sixth extinction" rivaling the great die-downs in the history of the planet; massive crop losses; extreme weather events; spreading hunger and disease. But these dangers are heightened by the fact that climate change is not the entirety of the world ecological crisis. For example, independently of climate change, tropical forests are being cleared as a direct result of the search for profits. Soil destruction is occurring, due to current agribusiness practices. Toxic wastes are being diffused throughout the environment. Nitrogen run-off from the overuse of fertilizer is affecting lakes, rivers, and ocean regions, contributing to oxygen-poor "dead zones."

Since the whole earth is affected by the vast scale of human impact on the environment in complex and unpredictable ways, even more serious catastrophes could conceivably be set in motion. One growing area of concern is ocean acidification due to rising carbon dioxide emissions. As carbon dioxide dissolves, it turns into carbonic acid, making the oceans more acidic. Because carbon dioxide dissolves more readily in cold than in warm water, the cold waters of the arctic are becoming acidic at an unprecedented rate. Within a decade, the waters near the North Pole could become so corrosive as to dissolve the living shells of shellfish, affecting the entire ocean food chain. At the same time, ocean acidification appears to be reducing the carbon uptake of the oceans, speeding up global warming.[4]

There are endless predictive uncertainties in all of this. Nevertheless, evidence is mounting that the continuation of current trends is unsustainable, even in the short-term. The only rational answer, then, is a radical change of course. Moreover, given certain imminent tipping points, there is no time to be lost. Catastrophic changes in the earth system could be set irreversibly in motion within a few decades, at most.

The IPCC [United Nations Intergovernmental Panel on Climate Change], in its 2007 report, indicated that an atmospheric carbon dioxide level of 450 parts per million (ppm) should not be exceeded, and implied that this was the fail-safe point for carbon stabilization. But these findings are already out of date. "What science has revealed in the past few years," Hansen states, "is that the safe level of carbon dioxide in the long run is no more than 350 ppm," as compared with 387 ppm today. That means that carbon emissions have to be reduced faster and more drastically than originally thought, to bring the overall carbon concentration in the atmosphere down. The reality is that, "if we burn all the fossil fuels, or even half of remaining reserves, we will send the planet toward the ice-free state with sea level about 250 feet higher than today. It would take time for complete ice sheet disintegration to occur, but a chaotic situation would be created with changes occurring out of control of future generations." More than eighty of the world's poorest and most climate-vulnerable countries have now declared that carbon dioxide atmospheric concentration levels must be reduced below 350 ppm, and that the rise in global average temperature by century's end must not exceed 1.5°C.[5]

Strategies of Denial

The central issue that we have to confront, therefore, is devising social strategies to address the world ecological crisis. Not only do the solutions have to be large enough to deal with the problem, but also all of this must take place on a world scale in a generation or so. The speed and scale of change necessary means that what is required is an ecological revolution that would also need to be a social revolution. However, rather than addressing the real roots of the crisis and drawing the appropriate conclusions, the dominant response is to avoid all questions about the nature of our society, and to turn to technological fixes or market mechanisms of one sort or another. In this respect, there is a certain continuity of thought between those who deny the climate change problem altogether, and those who, while acknowledging the severity of the problem at one level, nevertheless deny that it requires a revolution in our social system.

We are increasingly led to believe that the answers to climate change are primarily to be found in new energy technology, specifically increased energy and carbon efficiencies in both production and consumption. Technology in this sense, however, is often viewed abstractly as a *deus ex machina*, separated from both the laws of physics (i.e., entropy or the second law of thermodynamics) and from the way technology is embedded in historically specific conditions. With respect to the latter, it is worth noting that, under the present economic system, increases in energy efficiency normally lead to increases in the scale of economic output, effectively negating any gains from the standpoint of resource use or carbon efficiency—a problem known as the "Jevons Paradox." . . . .

Technological fetishism with regard to environmental issues is usually coupled with a form of market fetishism. So widespread has this become that even a militant ecologist like Bill McKibben, author of *The End of Nature*, recently stated: "There is only one lever even possibly big enough to make our system move as fast as it needs to, and that's the force of markets."[6]

Green-market fetishism is most evident in what is called "cap and trade"— a catch phrase for the creation, via governments, of artificial markets in carbon trading and so-called "offsets." The important thing to know about cap and trade is that it is a proven failure. Although enacted in Europe as part of the implementation of the Kyoto Protocol, it has failed where it was supposed to count: in reducing emissions. Carbon-trading schemes have been shown to be full of holes. Offsets allow all sorts of dubious forms of trading that have no effect on emissions. Indeed, the only area in which carbon trading schemes have actually been effective is in promoting profits for speculators and corporations, which are therefore frequently supportive of them. Recently, Friends of the Earth released a report entitled *Subprime Carbon?* which pointed to the emergence, under cap and trade agreements, of what could turn out to be the world's largest financial derivatives market in the form of carbon trading. All of this has caused Hansen to refer to cap and trade as "the temple of doom," locking in "disasters for our children and grandchildren."[7]

. . .

Recognizing that world powers are playing the role of Nero as Rome burns, James Lovelock, the earth system scientist famous for his Gaia hypothesis, argues that massive climate change and the destruction of human civilization as we know it may now be irreversible. Nevertheless, he proposes as "solutions" either a massive building of nuclear power plants all over the world (closing his eyes to the enormous dangers accompanying such a course)—or geoengineering our way out of the problem, by using the world's fleet of aircraft to inject huge quantities of sulfur dioxide into the stratosphere to block a portion of the incoming sunlight, reducing the solar energy reaching the earth. Another common geoengineering proposal includes dumping iron filings throughout the ocean to increase its carbon-absorbing properties.

Rational scientists recognize that interventions in the earth system on the scale envisioned by geoengineering schemes (for example, blocking sunlight) have their own massive, unforeseen consequences. Nor could such schemes solve the crisis. The dumping of massive quantities of sulfur dioxide into the stratosphere would, even if effective, have to be done again and again, on an increasing scale, if the underlying problem of cutting greenhouse gas emissions were not dealt with. Moreover, it could not possibly solve other problems associated with massive carbon dioxide emissions, such as the acidification of the oceans. [8]

The dominant approach to the world ecological crisis, focusing on technological fixes and market mechanisms, is thus a kind of denial; one that serves the vested interests of those who have the most to lose from a change in economic arrangements. Al Gore exemplifies the dominant form of denial in his new book, *Our Choice: A Plan to Solve the Climate Crisis*. For Gore, the answer is the creation of a "sustainable capitalism." He is not, however, altogether blind to the faults of the present system. He describes climate change as the "greatest market failure in history" and decries the "short-term" perspective of present-day capitalism, its "market triumphalism," and the "fundamental flaws" in its relation to the environment. Yet, in defiance of all this, he assures his readers that the "strengths of capitalism" can be harnessed to a new system of "sustainable development."[9]

The System of Unsustainable Development

In reality, capitalism can be defined as *a system of unsustainable development*. In order to understand why this is so, it is useful to turn to Karl Marx, the core of whose entire intellectual corpus might be interpreted as a critique of the political economy of unsustainable development and its human and natural consequences.

Capitalism, Marx explains, is a system of generalized commodity production. There were other societies prior to capitalism in which commodity markets played important roles, but it is only in capitalism that a system emerges that is centered entirely on the production of commodities. A "commodity" is a good produced to be sold and exchanged for profit in the market. We call it a "good" because it is has a use value, i.e., it normally satisfies some use, otherwise there would be no need for it. But it is the exchange value, i.e., the money income and the profit that it generates, that is the exclusive concern of the capitalist.

What Marx called "simple commodity production" is an idealized economic formation—often assumed to describe the society wherein we live—in which the structure of exchange is such that a commodity embodying a certain use value is exchanged for money (acting as a mere means of exchange), which is, in turn, exchanged for another commodity (use value) at the end. Here, the whole exchange process from beginning to end can be designated by the shorthand C-M-C. In such a process, exchange is simply a modified form of barter, with money merely facilitating exchange. The goal of exchange is concrete use values, embodying qualitative properties. Such use values are normally consumed—thereby bringing a given exchange process to an end.

Marx, however, insisted that a capitalist economy, in reality, works altogether differently, with exchange taking the form of M-C-M'. Here money capital (M) is used to purchase commodities (labor power and means of production) to produce a commodity that can be sold for more money, M' (i.e., M + Δm or surplus value) at the end. This process, once set in motion, never stops of its own accord, since it has no natural end. Rather, the surplus value (profit) is reinvested in the next round, with the object of generating M''; and, in the following round, the returns are again reinvested with the goal of obtaining M''', and so on, *ad infinitum*.[10]

For Marx, therefore, capital is self-expanding value, driven incessantly to ever larger levels of accumulation, knowing no bounds. "Capital," he wrote, "is the endless and limitless drive to go beyond its limiting barrier. Every boundary is and has to be a [mere] barrier for it [and thus capable of being surmounted]. Else it would cease to be capital—money as self-reproductive." It thus converts all of nature and nature's laws as well as all that is distinctly human into a mere means of its own self-expansion. The result is a system, fixated on the exponential growth of profits and accumulation. "Accumulate, accumulate! That is Moses and the prophets!"[11]

Any attempt to explain where surplus value (or profits) comes from must penetrate beneath the exchange process and enter the realm of labor and production. Here, Marx argues that value added in the working day can be divided into two parts: (1) the part that reproduces the value of labor power (i.e., the wages of the workers) and thus constitutes necessary labor; and (2) the labor expended in the remaining part of the working day, which can be regarded as surplus labor, and which generates surplus value (or gross profits) for the capitalist. Profits are thus to be regarded as residual, consisting of what is left over after wages are paid out—something that every businessperson instinctively understands. The ratio of surplus (i.e., unpaid) labor to necessary (paid) labor in the working day is, for Marx, the rate of exploitation.

The logic of this process is that the increase in surplus value appropriated depends on the effective exploitation of human labor power. This can be achieved in two ways: (1) either workers are compelled to work longer hours for the same pay, thereby increasing the surplus portion of the working day simply by adding to the total working time (Marx calls this "absolute surplus value"); or (2) the value of labor power, i.e., the value equivalent of workers' wages, is generated in less time (as a result of increased productivity, etc.), thereby augmenting the surplus portion of the working day to that extent (Marx calls this "relative surplus value").

In its unrelenting search for greater (relative) surplus value, capitalism is thus dependent on the revolutionization of the means of production with the aim of increasing productivity and reducing the paid portion of the working day. This leads inexorably to additional revolutions in production, additional increases in productivity, in what constitutes an endless treadmill of production/accumulation. The logic of accumulation concentrates more and more of the wealth and power of society in fewer and fewer hands, and generates an enormous industrial reserve army of the unemployed.

This is all accompanied by the further alienation of labor, robbing human beings of their creative potential, and often of the environmental conditions essential for their physical reproduction. "The factory system," Marx wrote, "is turned into systematic robbery of what is necessary for the life of the worker while he is at work, i.e., space, light, air and protection against the dangerous or the unhealthy contaminants of the production process."[12]

For classical political economists, beginning with the physiocrats and Adam Smith, nature was explicitly designated as a "free gift" to capital. It thus did not directly enter into the determination of exchange value (value), which constituted the basis of the accumulation of private capital. Nevertheless, classical political economists did see nature as constituting public wealth, since this was identified with use values, and included not only what was scarce, as in the case of exchange values, but also what was naturally abundant, e.g., air, water, etc.

Out of these distinctions arose what came to be known as the Lauderdale Paradox, associated with the ideas of James Maitland, the eighth Earl of Lauderdale, who observed in 1804 that private riches (exchange values) could be expanded by destroying public wealth (use values)—that is, by generating scarcity in what was formerly abundant. This meant that individual riches could be augmented by landowners monopolizing the water of wells and charging a price for what had previously been free—or by burning crops (the produce of the earth) to generate scarcity and thus exchange value. Even the air itself, if it became scarce enough, could expand private riches, once it was possible to put a price on it. Lauderdale saw such artificial creation of scarcity as a way in which those with private monopolies of land and resources robbed society of its real wealth.[13]

Marx (following Ricardo) strongly embraced the Lauderdale Paradox, and its criticism of the inverse relation between private riches and public wealth. Nature, under the system of generalized commodity production, was, Marx insisted, reduced to being merely a *free gift to capital* and was thus robbed. Indeed, the fact that part of the working day was unpaid and went to the surplus of the capitalist meant that an analogous situation pertained to human labor power, itself a "natural force." The worker was allowed to "work for his own life, i.e. *to live*, only in so far as he works for a certain time gratis for the capitalist . . . [so that] the whole capitalist system of production turns on the prolongation of this gratis labour by extending the working day or by developing the productivity, i.e., the greater intensity of labour power, etc." Both nature and the unpaid labor of the worker were then to be conceived in analogous ways as free gifts to capital.[14]

Given the nature of this classical critique, developed to its furthest extent by Marx, it is hardly surprising that later neoclassical economists, exercising their primary role as apologists for the system, were to reject both the classical theory of value and the Lauderdale Paradox. The new marginalist economic orthodoxy that emerged in the late nineteenth century erased all formal distinctions within economics between use value and exchange value, between wealth and value. Nature's contribution to wealth was simply defined out of existence within the prevailing economic view. However, a minority of heterodox economists, including such figures as Henry George, Thorstein Veblen, and Frederick Soddy, were to insist that this rejection of nature's contribution to wealth only served to encourage the squandering of common resources characteristic of the system. "In a sort of parody of an accountant's nightmare," John Maynard Keynes was to write of the financially driven capitalist system, "we are capable of shutting off the sun and the stars because they do not pay a dividend."[15]

For Marx, capitalism's robbing of nature could be seen concretely in its creation of a rift in the human-earth metabolism, whereby the reproduction of natural conditions was undermined. He defined the labor process in ecological terms as the "metabolic interaction" between human beings and nature. With the development of industrial agriculture under capitalism, a rift was generated in the nature-given metabolism between human beings and the earth. The shipment of food and fiber hundreds, and sometimes thousands, of miles to the cities meant the removal of soil nutrients, such as nitrogen, phosphorus, and potassium, which ended up contributing to the pollution of the cities, while the soil itself was robbed of its "constituent elements." This created a rupture in "the eternal natural condition for the lasting fertility of the soil," requiring the "systematic restoration" of this metabolism. Yet, even though this had been demonstrated with the full force of natural science (for example, in Justus von Liebig's chemistry), the rational application of scientific principles in this area was impossible for capitalism. Consequently, capitalist production simultaneously undermined "the original sources of all wealth—the soil and the worker."[16]

Marx's critique of capitalism as an unstainable system of production was ultimately rooted in its "preconditions," i.e., the historical bases under which capitalism as a mode of production became possible. These were to be found in "primitive accumulation," or the expropriation of the commons (of all customary rights to the land), and hence the expropriation of the workers themselves—of their means of subsistence. It was this expropriation that was to help lay the grounds for industrial capitalism in particular. The turning of the land into private property, a mere means of accumulation, was at the same time the basis for the destruction of the metabolism between human beings and the earth.[17]

. . .

Marx's whole critique thus pointed to the reality of capitalism as a system of unsustainable development, rooted in the unceasing exploitation and pillage of human and natural agents. As he put it: "*Après moi le déluge!* is the watchword of every capitalist and of every capitalist nation. Capital therefore takes no account of the health and the length of life of the worker [or the human-nature metabolism], unless society forces it to do so . . ."[18]

Toward Ecological Revolution

If the foregoing argument is correct, humanity is facing an unprecedented challenge. On the one hand, we are confronting the question of a terminal crisis, threatening most life on the planet, civilization, and the very existence of future generations. On the other hand, attempts to solve this through technological fixes, market magic, and the idea of a "sustainable capitalism" are mere forms of ecological denial: since they ignore the inherent destructiveness of the current system of unsustainable development—capitalism. This suggests that the only rational answer lies in an ecological revolution, which would also have to be a social revolution, aimed at the creation of a just and sustainable society.

In addressing the question of an ecological revolution in the present dire situation, both short-term and long-term strategies are necessary, and should complement each other. One short-term strategy, directed mainly at the industrialized world, has been presented by Hansen. He starts with what he calls a "geophysical fact": most of the remaining fossil fuel, particularly coal, must stay in the ground, and carbon emissions have to be reduced as quickly as possible to near zero. He proposes three measures: (1) coal burning (except where carbon is sequestered—right now not technologically feasible) must cease; (2) the price of fossil fuel consumption should be steadily increased by imposing a progressively rising tax at the point of production: well head, mine shaft, or point of entry—redistributing 100 percent of the revenue, on a monthly basis, directly to the population as dividends; (3) a massive, global campaign to end deforestation and initiate large-scale reforestation needs to be introduced. A carbon tax, he argues, if it were to benefit the people directly—the majority of whom have below average per-capita carbon footprints, and would experience net gains from the carbon dividends once their added energy costs were subtracted—would create massive support for change. It would help to mobilize the population, particularly those at the bottom of society, in favor of a climate revolution. Hansen's "fee and dividend" proposal is explicitly designed not to feed the profits of vested interests. Any revenue from the carbon tax, in this plan, has to be democratically structured so as to redistribute income and wealth to those with smaller carbon footprints (the poor), and away from those with the larger carbon footprints (the rich).[19]

Hansen has emerged as a leading figure in the climate struggle, not only as a result of his scientific contributions, but also due to his recognition that at the root of the problem is a system of economic power, and his increasingly radical defiance of the powers that be. Thus, he declares: "the trains carrying coal to power plants are death trains. Coal-fired plants are factories of death." He criticizes those such as Gore, who have given in to cap and trade, locking in failure. Arguing that the unwillingness and inability of the authorities to act means that desperate measures are necessary, he is calling for mass "civil resistance." In June 2009, he was arrested, along with thirty-one others, in the exercise of civil resistance against mountain top removal coal mining.[20]

In strategizing an immediate response to the climate problem, it is crucial to recognize that the state, through government regulation and spending programs, could intervene directly in the climate crisis. Carbon dioxide could be considered an air pollutant to be regulated by law. Electrical utilities could be mandated to obtain their energy increasingly from renewable sources. Solar panels could be included as a mandatory part of the building code. The state could put its resources behind major investments in public environmental infrastructure and planning, including reducing dependence on the automobile through massive funding of public transportation, e.g., intercity trains and light rail, and the necessary accompanying changes in urban development and infrastructure.

Globally, the struggle, of course, has to take into account the reality of economic and ecological imperialism. The allowable carbon-concentration limits of the atmosphere have already been taken up as a result of the accumulation of the rich states at the center of the world system. The economic and social development of poor countries is, therefore, now being further limited by the pressing need to impose restrictions on carbon emissions for the sake of the planet as a whole—despite the fact that underdeveloped economies had no role in the creation of the problem. The global South is likely to experience the effects of climate change much earlier and more severely than the North, and has fewer economic resources with which to adapt. All of this means that a non-imperialistic, and more sustainable, world solution depends initially on what is called "contraction and convergence"—a drastic *contraction* in greenhouse gas emissions overall (especially in the rich countries), coupled with the *convergence* of per-capita emissions in all countries at levels that are sustainable for the planet.[21] Since, however, science suggests that even low greenhouse gas emissions may be unsustainable over the long run, strategies have to be developed to make it economically feasible for countries in the periphery to introduce solar and renewable technologies—

reinforcing those necessary radical changes in social relations that will allow them to stabilize and reduce their emissions.

For the anti-imperialist movement, a major task should be creating stepped-up opposition to military spending (amounting to a trillion dollars in the United States in 2007) and ending government subsidies to global agribusiness—with the goal of shifting those monies into environmental defense and the meeting of the social needs of the poorest countries, as suggested by the *Bamako Appeal*.[22] It must be firmly established as a principle of world justice that the wealthy countries owe an enormous ecological debt to poorer countries, due to the robbing by the imperial powers of the global commons and the pillage of the periphery at every stage of world capitalist development.

Already, the main force for ecological revolution stems from movements in the global South, marked by the growth of the Vía Campesina movement, socialist organizations like Brazil's MST, and ongoing revolutions in Latin America (the ALBA countries) and Asia (Nepal). Cuba has been applying permaculture design techniques that mimic energy-maximizing natural systems to its agriculture since the 1990s, generating a revolution in food production. Venezuela, although, for historic reasons, an oil power economically dependent on the sale of petroleum, has made extraordinary achievements in recent years by moving toward a society directed at collective needs, including dramatic achievements in food sovereignty.[23]

Reaching back into history, it is worth recalling that the proletariat in Marxian theory was the revolutionary agent because it had nothing to lose, and thus came to represent the universal interest in abolishing, not only its own oppression, but oppression itself. As Marx put it, "the living conditions of the proletariat represent the focal point of all inhuman conditions in contemporary society. . . . However, it [the proletariat] cannot emancipate itself without abolishing the conditions which give it life, and it cannot abolish these conditions without abolishing all those inhuman conditions of social life which are summed up in its own situation."[24]

Later Marxist theorists were to argue that, with the growth of monopoly capitalism and imperialism, the "focal point of inhuman conditions" had shifted from the center to the periphery of the world system. Paul Sweezy contended that, although the objective conditions that Marx associated with the proletariat did not match those of better-off workers in the United States and Europe in the 1960s, they did correspond to the harsh, inhuman conditions imposed on "the masses of the much more numerous and populous underdeveloped dependencies of the global capitalist system." This helped explain the pattern of socialist revolutions following the Second World War, as exemplified by Vietnam, China, and Cuba.[25]

Looking at this today, I think it is conceivable that the main historic agent and initiator of a new epoch of ecological revolution is to be found in the third world masses most directly in line to be hit first by the impending disasters. Today the ecological frontline is arguably to be found in the inhabitants of the Ganges-Brahmaputra Delta and of the low-lying fertile coast area of the Indian Ocean and China Seas—the state of Kerala in India, Thailand, Vietnam, Indonesia. They, too, as in the case of Marx's proletariat, have nothing to lose from the radical changes necessary to avert (or adapt to) disaster. In fact, with the universal spread of capitalist social relations and the commodity form, the world proletariat and the masses most exposed to sea level rise—for example, the low-lying delta of the Pearl River and the Guangdong industrial region from Shenzhen to Guangzhou—sometimes overlap. This, then, potentially constitutes the global epicenter of a new environmental proletariat.[26]

The truly planetary crisis we are now caught up in, however, requires a world uprising transcending all geographical boundaries. This means that ecological and social revolutions in the third world have to be accompanied by, or inspire, universal revolts against imperialism, the destruction of the planet, and the treadmill of accumulation. The recognition that the weight of environmental disaster is such that it would cross all class lines and all nations and positions, abolishing time itself by breaking what Marx called "the chain of successive generations," could lead to a radical rejection of the engine of destruction in which we live, and put into motion a new conception of global humanity and earth metabolism. As always, however, real change will have to come from those most alienated from the existing systems of power and wealth. The most hopeful development within the advanced capitalist world at present is the meteoric rise of the youth-based climate justice movement, which is emerging as a considerable force in direct action mobilization and in challenging the current climate negotiations.[27]

What is clear is that the long-term strategy for ecological revolution throughout the globe involves the building of a society of substantive equality, i.e., the struggle for socialism. Not only are the two inseparable, but they also provide essential content for each other. There can be no true ecological revolution that is not socialist; no true socialist revolution that is not ecological. This means recapturing Marx's own vision of socialism/communism, which he defined as a society where "the associated producers govern the human metabolism with nature in a rational way, bringing it under their collective control . . . accomplishing it with the least expenditure of energy and in conditions most worthy and appropriate for their human nature."[28]

One way to understand this interdependent relation between ecology and socialism is in terms of what Hugo Chávez has called "the elementary triangle of socialism" (derived from Marx) consisting of: (1) social ownership; (2) social production organized by workers; and (3) satisfaction of communal needs. All three components of the elementary triangle of socialism are necessary if socialism is to be sustained. Complementing and deepening this is what could be called "the elementary triangle of ecology" (derived even more directly from Marx): (1) social use, not ownership, of nature; (2) rational regulation by the associated producers of the metabolic relation between humanity and nature; and (3) satisfaction of communal needs—not only of present but also future generations (and life itself).[29]

As Lewis Mumford explained in 1944, in his *Condition of Man*, the needed ecological transformation required the promotion of "basic communism," applying "to the whole community the standards of the household," distributing benefits "according to need, not ability or productive contribution." This meant focusing first and foremost on "education, recreation, hospital services, public hygiene, art," food production, the rural and urban environments, and, in general, "collective needs." The idea of "basic communism" drew on Marx's principle of substantive equality in the *Critique of the Gotha Programme*: "from each according to his ability, to each according to his needs!" But Mumford also associated this idea with John Stuart Mill's vision, in his most socialist phase, of a "stationary state"—viewed, in this case, as a system of economic production no longer geared to the accumulation of capital, in which the emphasis of society would be on collective development and the quality of life.[30] For Mumford, this demanded a new "organic person"—to emerge from the struggle itself.

An essential element of such an ecological and socialist revolution for the twenty-first century is a truly radical conception of sustainability, as articulated by Marx:

> From the standpoint of a higher socio-economic formation, the private property of particular individuals in the earth will appear just as absurd as the private property of one man in other men [i.e., slavery]. Even an entire society, a nation, or all simultaneously existing societies taken together, are not the owners of the earth. They are simply its possessors, its beneficiaries, and have to bequeath it in an improved state to succeeding generations as *boni patres familias* [good heads of the household].[31]

Such a vision of a sustainable, egalitarian society must define the present social struggle; not only because it is ecologically necessary for human survival, but also because it is historically necessary for the development of human freedom. Today we face the challenge of forging a new organic revolution in which the struggles for human equality and for the earth are becoming one. There is only one future: that of sustainable human development.[32]

Notes

Foster, John Bellamy. "Why Ecological Revolution?" Monthly Review: An Independent Socialist Magazine; Jan 2010, Vol. 61 Issue 8, p1.

1. On the long-term aspects of the current financial-economic crisis, see John Bellamy Foster and Fred Magdoff, *The Great Financial Crisis* (New York: Monthly Review Press, 2009).

2. James E. Hansen, "Strategies to Address Global Warming" (July 13, 2009), http//www. columbia.edu.

3. Ibid.; "Seas Grow Less Effective at Absorbing Emissions," *New York Times*, November 19, 2009; S. Khatiwala. F. Primeau and T. Hall, "Reconstruction of the History of Anthropogenic CO2 Concentrations in the Ocean," *Nature* 462, no. 9 (November 2009), 346–50.

4. "Arctic Seas Turn to Acid, Putting Vital Food Chain at Risk," October 4, 2009, http://www. guardian.com.uk.

5. Hansen, "Strategies to Address Global Warming"; AFP, "Top UN Climate Scientist Backs Ambitious CO2 Cuts," August 25, 2009.

6. Bill McKibben, "Response," in Tim Flannery, *Now or Never* (New York: Atlantic Monthly Press, 2009), 116; Al Gore, *Our Choice: A Plan to Solve the Climate Crisis* (Emmaus, PA: Rodale, 2009), 327.

7. Friends of the Earth, "Subprime Carbon?" (March 2009), http://www.foe. org/ subprimecarbon, and *A Dangerous Obsession* (November 2009), www.foe.co.uk/ resources/ reports/dangerous_obsession.pdf; James E. Hansen, "Worshipping the Temple of Doom" (May 5, 2009), http//www.columbia.edu.

8. James Lovelock, *The Revenge of Gaia* (New York: Basic Books, 2006), and *The Vanishing Face of Gaia* (New York: Basic Books, 2009), 139–58; Gore, *Our Choice*, 314–15. Hansen, it should be noted, also places hope in the development of fourth generation nuclear power as part of the solution. See James Hansen, *Storms of My Grandchildren* (New York: Bloomsbury USA, 2009), 194–204.

9. Gore, *Our Choice*, 303, 320, 327, 330–32, 346.

10. Karl Marx, *Capital*, vol. 1 (London: Penguin 1976), 247–80. On how Marx's M-C-M′ formula serves to define the "regime of capital," see Robert Heilbroner, *The Nature and Logic of Capitalism* (New York: W.W. Norton, 1985), 33–77.

11. Karl Marx, *Grundrisse* (London: Penguin, 1973), 334–35, 409–10, and *Capital*, vol. 1, 742; John Bellamy Foster, "Marx's Grundrisse and the Ecological Contradictions of Capitalism," in Marcelo Musto, *Karl Marx's Grundrisse* (New York: Routledge, 2008), 100–02.

12. Marx, *Capital*, vol. 1, 552–53.

13. The discussion of the Lauderdale Paradox is based on John Bellamy Foster and Brett Clark, "The Paradox of Wealth," *Monthly Review* 61, no. 6 (November 2009): 1–18.

14. Karl Marx, *Capital*, vol. 3, (London: Penguin, 1981), 949, *Critique of the Gotha Programme* (New York: International Publishers, 1938), 3, 15.

15. John Maynard Keynes, "National Self-Sufficiency," in *Collected Writings* (London: Macmillan/Cambridge University Press, 1982), vol. 21, 241–42.

16. Karl Marx, *Capital*, vol. 1, 636–39, *Capital*, vol. 3, 948–50, and *Capital*, vol. 2 (London: Penguin 1978), 322; Foster, *The Ecological Revolution*, 161–200.

17. See Foster, "Marx's Grundrisse and the Ecological Contradictions of Capitalism," 98–100.

18. Marx, *Capital*, vol. 1, 381.

19. James Hansen, et al., "Target Atmospheric CO2: Where Should Humanity Aim?" *Open Atmospheric Science Journal* 2 (2008): 217–31; James E. Hansen, "Response to Dr. Martin Parkinson, Secretary of the Australian Department of Climate Change" (May 4, 2009), http://www.columbia.edu; Hansen, "Strategies to Address Global Warming" and "Worshipping the Temple of Doom"; Frank Ackerman, et al. "The Economics of 350," October 2009, www. e3network.org, 3–4.

20. James E. Hansen, "The Sword of Damocles" (February 15, 2009), "Coal River Mountain Action" (June 25, 2009), and "I Just Had a Baby, at Age 68" (November 6, 2009), http://www. columbia.edu; Ken Ward, "The Night I Slept with Jim Hansen" (November 11, 2009), www. grist.org.

21. Tom Athanasiou and Paul Baer, *Dead Heat* (New York: Seven Stories Press, 2002).

22. John Bellamy Foster, Hannah Holleman, and Robert W. McChesney, "The U.S. Imperial Triangle and Military Spending," *Monthly Review* 60, no. 5 (October 2008), 9–13. The Bamako Appeal can be found in Samir Amin, *The World We Wish to See* (New York: Monthly Review Press, 2008), 107–34.

23. An important source in understanding Cuban developments is the film "The Power of Community: How Cuba Survived Peak Oil," http:// www.powerofcommunity. org/cm/index.php. On Venezuela see Christina Schiavoni and William Camacaro, "The Venezuelan Effort to Build a New Food and Agriculture System," *Monthly Review* 61, no. 3 (July-August 2009): 129–41.

24. Karl Marx and Frederick Engels, *The Holy Family* (Moscow: Foreign Languages Publishing House, 1956), 52. Translation follows Paul M. Sweezy, *Modern Capitalism and Other Essays* (New York: Monthly Review Press, 1972), 149.

25. Sweezy, *Modern Capitalism*, 164.

26. John Bellamy Foster, "*The Vulnerable Planet* Fifteen Years Later," *Monthly Review* 54, no. 7 (December 2009): 17–19.

27. On the climate justice movement see Tokar, "Toward Climate Justice."

28. Marx, *Capital*, vol. 3, 1959.

29. On the elementary triangles of socialism and ecology see Foster, *The Ecological Revolution*, 32–35. The failure of Soviet-type societies to conform to these elementary triangles goes a long way toward explaining their decline and fall, despite their socialist pretensions. See John Bellamy Foster, *The Vulnerable Planet* (New York: Monthly Review Press, 1999), 96–101.

30. Lewis Mumford, *The Condition of Man* (New York: Harcourt Brace Jovanovich, 1973), 411; Marx, *Critique of the Gotha Programme*, 10: John Stuart Mill, *Principles of Political Economy* (New York: Longmans, Green and Co., 1904), 453–55.

31. Marx, *Capital*, vol. 3, 911, 959.

32. Paul Burkett, "Marx's Vision of Sustainable Human Development," *Monthly Review* 57, no. 5 (October 2005): 34–62.

The Tragedy of the Commodity

The Overexploitation of the Mediterranean Bluefin Tuna Fishery

Stefano B. Longo and Rebecca Clausen

In a famous essay published in 1968, ecologist Garrett Hardin argued that a "tragedy of the commons" occurs when land—or any resource—is held in common. Hardin argued that when herders, for example, all used the same land to graze sheep, that land would ultimately be over-used and depleted. This notion has since been widely deployed to justify the privatization of land, water, and other resources. Utilizing the overfishing of the Mediterranean bluefin tuna as a case study, Stefano Longo and Rebecca Clausen provide an alternative explanation; they argue that capitalism, which must constantly expand in order to survive, and the privatization associated with capitalism cause environmental degradation and resource depletion. They call this the "tragedy of the commodity."

Hegel remarks somewhere that all great, world-historic facts and person-
ages occur, as it were, twice. He has forgotten to add: the first time as
tragedy, the second as farce.

—Karl Marx, *The Eighteenth Brumaire of
Louis Bonaparte*, 1852 (Tucker 1978, p. 594)

In the late 20th century, the tragedy of the commons emerged as a leading
thesis to explain the social origins of environmental resource depletion
(Hardin, 1968). This framework has become one of the most cited theories
in environmental social sciences, used consistently to explain a variety of ecological "tragedies" (e.g., Corral-Verdugo, Frías-Armenta, Pérez-Urias, Orduña-
Cabrera, & Espinoza-Gallego, 2002; McHugh, 1977; Nickler, 1999). Using a
political economic framework, this article will develop a critique of this well-
known theory. In doing so, we offer an alternative framework, the tragedy of
the commodity, for examining the social drivers of environmental degradation.
We argue that Marx's explanation of capitalist private property, commodity
production, and the general formula for capital provide powerful theoretical
guides for clarifying the social relations of production that have driven the
overexploitation of fisheries in the recent past. We develop a case study of
Atlantic bluefin tuna (ABFT) production, with an emphasis on the traditional
Sicilian trap fishery, to illustrate the tragedy of the commodity.

The decline of ABFT provides important perspective on the sociological
processes that affect marine ecosystems. By examining a historic fishery in the
Mediterranean that is undergoing massive depletion as well as rapid technological change, we provide alternative explanations to oft-misunderstood problems in fisheries management. Relying on historical and qualitative data, the
case study demonstrates the ways in which the socioeconomic imperative of
capitalist private property toward accumulating surplus-value directs production, reorganizes social relations, and transforms nature into an instrumental
input that can more easily serve the needs of capital.

. . . Latest research reveals that every square mile of the world's oceans
has been affected by anthropogenic forces, of which overfishing is a primary
concern (Halpern et al., 2008). More than 90% of the ocean's top predators
have been overexploited and are ecologically threatened, including the bluefin
tuna (Myers & Worm, 2003). Throughout the world, fisheries are in fast decline
and aquaculture has become a major source of marine protein for human consumption (Food and Agriculture Organization of the United Nations, 2007).
Indeed, the depletion of fisheries and growth of aquaculture are interrelated
phenomena that can be illuminated by sociological analysis.

Our analysis of social and ecological transformations of global marine
fisheries centers on three main themes: (a) refuting the dominant discourse

of "inevitable" ocean decline due to the tragedy of the commons, (b) exposing the underlying structural factors of capitalist development that drive ocean depletion and disruptions in ocean ecosystems, and (c) exploring how the political economy of fisheries enables a tragedy of the commodity in modern bluefin tuna production . . .

The Tragedy of the Commons

Overexploitation in modern fisheries is often referred to as a manifestation of the "tragedy of the commons." The concept was developed by Garret Hardin (1968) to describe the conditions that shape the degradation of resources held in "common." Hardin's model is based on the notion that land, or other natural resources that are common property, will be degraded due to the competing individual interests of the users. In the absence of control or coercion by private entities or the state, Hardin maintained that the self-serving motivations of individual users inevitably lead to the destruction of commonly held nature.

. . . The classic illustration of the tragedy of the commons involved herders adding additional livestock to common grazing land to increase individual benefits. Hardin (1968) contended that individual "herdsmen" would attempt to acquire the benefits offered by the commons, while socializing costs to all the herders. By adding an extra animal to the pasture the herder reaps all the benefit but pays only a fraction of the environmental costs. As each actor is motivated by individual maximization of benefit, it is assumed that the herdsmen will increasingly introduce grazing animals into a finite ecological system, which leads to the tragic despoliation of the land. Therefore, Hardin (1968) concluded "freedom in commons brings ruin to all" (p. 1244).

The tragedy of the commons theory assumes that individuals are not constrained by conscience or by custom. This approach is essentially built on the notion that humans, in their inherent nature, are self-serving, will make rational cost–benefit decisions, and that resource users, typically, will not be motivated or constrained by altruism or the common good. This leads to a critical examination of the liberal ideology of personal freedom, in that, in order to avert tragedy, individuals must be constrained by either state and/or private actors (including firms). . . .

Hardin was a staunch defender of the liberal notion of private property, which served as a linchpin to his theory. The approach contends that private property, as exclusionary property relations, can prevent society from undermining resources and the destruction of natural systems. Although acknowledging that this property arrangement is not necessarily a just or fair distribution, Hardin claimed that private property allows for control over resource depletion by barring some users access as well as investment in and/or protection of crucial resources to support long-term production.

For Hardin, and many others who have adopted this perspective, private property arrangements are offered as a leading policy solution for avoiding ecological tragedies.

Tragedy of the commons theorists also acknowledge the potential for state action and management as alternative arrangements for promoting resource conservation (Dietz, Dolsak, Ostrom, & Stern, 2002). The type of state control promoted by Hardin's thesis can be best characterized as an approach to resource protection that excludes or coerces users through creating the legal structure to sustain resource extraction within a competitive market economy and capitalist private property arrangements. For example, legal codes enforce limited access through licensing or individual quotas, sometimes referred to as "catch shares" (Costello, Gaines, & Linham, 2008). In essence, the tragedy of the commons theory promoted the notion that the role of the state is to enclose the commons, sometimes resulting in individual entry permits and/or transferable quotas, usually bypassing local users, and creating broad management schemes over vast natural resources (Ostrom, 1999). Generally speaking, the tragedy of the commons was built on the premise that only private control or state (top-down) management can prevent ecological devastation and the tragedy of the commons (Hardin, 1998).

. . . [T]he theory has not been without its critics. McCay, Acheson, and others have made key contributions to the literature on the commons (Acheson, 1975, 1988; Feeny, Berkes, McCay, & Acheson, 1990; McCay, 1998; McCay & Acheson, 1987; McEvoy, 1986). These scholars have examined differing examples and definitions of "the commons" and the ways in which local cultural factors, historical conditions, and community settings can play a role in maintaining viable "common property" fisheries. In addition, Dietz, Ostrom, and others (Dietz et al., 2002; Dietz, Ostrom, & Stern, 2003; Ostrom, 1999; Ostrom, Burger, Field, Norgaard, & Policansky, 1999) have developed major works in this area. Their focus has been on examining the role of common ownership as a viable property regime and contextualizing some economic assumptions of the tragedy of the commons. This research has revealed that private control and state regulation can be conflated or that the "drama of the commons" (Dietz et al., 2002) depends on the composition of state policies and governance, together with political economic and historical conditions. Furthermore, governments can, potentially, promote environmental sustainability or advance environmental tragedies (Ostrom et al., 1999).

. . . We extend the critique of the tragedy of the commons by drawing on Marxist political economy to highlight the fundamental contradictions of capitalist agri-food production that are driving the oceanic crisis. By making use of the theoretical frame provided by the tragedy of the commodity, we aim to clarify the root dynamics that shape the historical context for agri-food production and environmental degradation in the modern era. We illustrate this using Atlantic bluefin tuna as a case study.

Capitalist Production and the Tragedy of the Commodity

Much has been made of the tragedy of the commons theory as an explanatory model. Surely, it provides descriptive power in that it can explain the behaviors of individual actors in given social circumstances. Nevertheless, the crude formulation neglects historically specific conditions, taking them as transhistorical constants. The tragedy of the commodity approach, emerging from a historical materialist perspective, contends that an analysis of human agency must include a thorough understanding of the historical social organization of production and consumption.

Marx's (1977) systematic critique of the categories of political economy in *Capital* is at the same time a systematic elaboration of the "capitalist mode of production, and the relations of production and forms of intercourse [*Verkehrsverhältnisse*] that correspond to it" (p. 90) . . .

[Marx's] political economy described social conditions as the outcome of historical processes and its specific social forms, not a reflection of invariant natural laws (Sweezy, 1942). That is to say,

> Nature does not produce on the one hand owners of money or commodities, and on the other hand men possessing nothing but their own labour-power. This relation has no basis in natural history, nor does it have a social basis common to all periods in human history. It is clearly the result of past historical developments, the product of many economic revolutions, of the extinction of a whole series of older formations of social production. . . . *Definite historical conditions are involved in the existence of the product as a commodity.* (Marx, 1977, p. 273, italics added)

This examination of the commodity unveils the fundamental makeup of the capitalist system of production. Here, the commodity forms a microcosm of the social organization and its consequent relations of production; "a system that appears as an 'immense collection of commodities'" (Marx, 1977, p. 125).

Marx explained the underlying characteristics of commodities as usevalue and exchange-value. That is, "Every useful thing . . . may be looked at from the two points of view of quality and quantity" (Marx, 1977, p. 125). Extending this simple formulation by the force of a historical materialist analysis, the dual character of the commodity reveals a central contradiction of capitalist production. That is, the quantitative form of value is divorced from its qualitative dimension, and social production is accordingly organized along this historical form. To elucidate this analytical insight, we provide a brief overview of Marx's analysis of capitalist commodities and valorization.

Value, Growth, and the Exploitation of Nature

In the general formula for capital, Marx (1977) distinguished between simple circulation of commodities and the circulation of money as capital. In the former, depicted as C-M-C, commodities are the beginning and end of the process. Although mediated by money, it reaches conclusion with the use of a commodity, "in short use-value, is therefore its final goal" (Marx, 1977, p. 250). The outcome results in a qualitatively different form that serves a particular need, and circulation is complete. Conversely, in capitalist commodity production, money or exchange-value are the beginning and end result. Depicted as M-C-M, money is put into circulation to return money, a quantity for a quantity, "its driving and motivating force is therefore exchange-value" (p. 250). Accordingly, the process is fundamentally transformed from one organized around the exchange of qualities to the exchange of quantities.

In a capitalist exchange of two quantities, beginning with M and ending with M, it would be nonsensical unless the quantity at the end of the exchange was different (larger) than that existing at the outset. Marx explained that the complete depiction of the general formula for capital consists of M-C-M', where M' is equal to M +ΔM. Thus, capitalist circulation requires the realization of surplus-value within ΔM, or what forms the basis of profit and capital accumulation. Providing the impetus for reinvestment, it becomes the central aim of production.[1] Marx unambiguously described how capitalist production prioritizes surplus-value when he stated, "The absolute value of a commodity is, in itself, of no interest to the capitalist who produces it. All that interests him is the surplus-value present in it, which can be realized by sale" (Marx, 1977, p. 437).

Under capitalist social relations of production, labor itself becomes a commodity for sale. The capitalist buys labor power, and "the worker receives a means of subsistence for his labour power" (Tucker, 1978, p. 209). Although labor is often misinterpreted or misunderstood as the single domain of value production, commodified labor-power *and* nature come together to produce values. In the "Critique of the Gotha Program," Marx made clear that both human labor and nature are fundamental to the production process (Tucker, 1978). "Marx does *not* see abstract labour time as an adequate representative or measure of wealth—including the wealth of nature" (Burkett, 2006, p. 28). Human nature acts along with and on extra-human nature, generating a useful form.

As the capitalist valorization process requires a quantitative difference in value when capital is circulated, and labor and nature are providing the material means for producing value, the disparity in value must be found in the materiality of the commodity production process. Profit does not appear through "a mystical source of self-valorization" that results from circulation "independent of its production process," as presented by many modern economists (Marx, 1992, p. 204). The capitalist valorization process requires the exploitation of labor and nature, which forms the locus of surplus-value. Therefore, capital does not pay the entire costs of production. Referring to the "free gifts" of nature, Marx clarified that capitalist commodity production appropriates nature and its use-value, which permits the production and realization of surplus-value. Although nature is not a product of wage labor, it is expropriated *gratis* by capital through commodity production (Burkett, 2006).

Because exchange-value, and its embodied surplus-value, is the ultimate goal of capitalist commodity production, profit realization becomes an endless process. The process begins and ends with money (quantities), and the result of one cycle is the beginning of the next. "The movement of capital is therefore limitless" (Marx, 1977, p. 253). At each stage of circulation there is a new starting point, relatively larger than the last, resulting in an ever-increasing scale of profit accumulation as the quantitative nature of commodity production knows no restriction or limits (Foster, Clark, & York, 2010). To be sure, in order to realize surplus-value, the commodity must be sold, thus fueling the sales effort toward increasing effective demand (Baran & Sweezy, 1966).

. . . [U]nbounded accumulation of capital becomes the motor force of capitalist production (Sweezy, 1942). Under the compulsion of competition, capitalist producers expropriate value to expand and accumulate capital, staying ahead of their competitors. As such,

> The development of capitalist production makes it necessary constantly to increase the amount of capital laid out in a given industrial undertaking, and competition subordinates every individual capitalist to the immanent laws of capitalist production, as external and coercive laws. It compels him to keep extending his capital, so as to preserve it, and he can only extend it by means of progressive accumulation. (Marx, 1977, p. 739)

The capitalist production process is geared toward producing surplus-value, and generally this is accomplished by extending the working day (absolute surplus-value) or by increasing productivity (relative surplus-value). Intensifying technological investments so as to expand the productivity of capital allows it to stay ahead of real or potential competitors. As there are defined limits on absolute surplus-value, increasing relative surplus-value becomes an essential method of capital accumulation and growth. Consequently, capitalist production must be continually transformed or revolutionized (Braverman, 1998).

In what Schumpeter (1962) called "creative destruction," capital relentlessly seeks new ways to develop the productive forces of labor and nature and expropriate value. This "creative destruction" is often implemented through the means of technological change, which expands capital efficiency and must, first and foremost, meet the needs of capital. As Braverman (1998) made clear, "Technology instead of simply *producing* social relations is *produced* by the social relations," and furthermore, "The social form of capital, driven to incessant accumulation as the condition for its own existence, *completely transforms technology*" in its own image (p. 14).

The historical tendency of capitalist accumulation was described by Marx (1977) as a process of expropriation, whereby individual private property is "supplanted by capitalist private property, which rests on the exploitation of alien, but formally free labor" (p. 928). This formulation is an important conceptual distinction that aids our understanding of "the great transformation" (Polanyi, 1957) and is particularly relevant to this case study. The need to transform land into capitalist private property is the driving force of the enclosure of the commons. That is, capitalist private property is the social form that promotes enclosures, and the process of primitive accumulation, so as to conform to the needs of commodity production described above. This occurred during the prehistory of capitalist production, but also continues into the present via the power of capital to sweep away traditional production systems, including the individual private property of small-scale industry, that do not easily conform to the essential characteristics of capitalist development, particularly the expropriation of surplus-value. Thus, "It has to be annihilated; it is annihilated" (Marx, 1977, p. 928).

Our case study of the Atlantic bluefin tuna in the Mediterranean illustrates how the tragedy of the commodity leads to both the catastrophe of ABFT depletion as well as the chimera of technological solutions to address the bluefin tuna's recent demise. We suggest that the first consequence of the historically specific form of commodity production is the *tragedy* of resource degradation (i.e., overfishing). As Marx's addendum to Hegel's remark alludes, the consequences of commodification do not end there. They manifest in a second occurrence as the *farce* of technological "solutions" to the original problem (i.e., tuna ranching and aquaculture).

Commodification and Overexploitation

The Mediterranean bluefin tuna fishery is one of the oldest and, at one time, likely one of the most productive fisheries in the world. Human societies have been capturing bluefin tuna in this region for about 10,000 years. Circa 1000 CE, a trapping system developed that fixed this fishery as a Mediterranean icon

(Sarà, 1998). Traditional trap fishing allowed for an ecologically sustainable harvest of bluefin tuna that was viable for centuries.

The history of the Sicilian trap fishery, *la tonnara*,[2] can help illuminate the present circumstances in the Mediterranean and the emergence of the tragedy of the commodity. Historical research on the *tonnara* displays a pattern of attention by the managers, owners, and workers regarding the impacts that particular technologies might have on the bluefin populations. Many actors associated with the fishery maintained that practices promoting intensified capture methods would have damaging consequences for the long run of the fishery.

La Mantia (1901) described contestations between active *tonnare* over the amount, location, and technology used in fishing for bluefin tuna as well as other species during the bluefin spawning season. He noted that disputes occurred as early as the 16th century. For example, in the Sicilian city of Palermo, there were concerns among managers and fishers that the location of the *tonnara* in Arinella was too close to that in Mondello, which began proceedings to enact minimum distances between active bluefin fishing. Also, bans were put in place regarding the types of fishing nets that could be used in the vicinity of the *tonnara,* and the capture of smaller tuna species was prohibited by a number of decrees in 1784, 1785, and 1794 in Sicily as a result of concerns among those representing established trap fishing (La Mantia, 1901). Furthermore, D'Amico (1816) discussed the potential damage to the bluefin fishery by practices that resulted in overfishing and the capture of juvenile fish, arguing that these practices "sterilized" the fishery.[3]

Interviews with *tonnaroti* (tuna fishers) revealed a deep understanding of the bluefin reproductive processes and an awareness of issues related to overfishing. On more than one occasion, fishermen clearly expressed that it was necessary to "leave fish for next year" and that this was a traditional fishing ethic. Unlike the herders in Hardin's theory, who disregard the future implication of overgrazing, many participants who took part in this study were unquestionably mindful of the future of the fishery and future generations. For example, this was explained in terms of the *tonnara's* selectivity. Because of its design, methods, and stationary nature, the trap did not deplete the fishery.

Although the traditional Sicilian fishery may be considered a "commons," there were many social arrangements surrounding access, methods of capture, and distribution of resources (Consolo, 1986; Sarà, 1998). Historical research, substantiated by in-depth interviews, suggests that the traditional trap fishery was undoubtedly integrated into community life, and the sustainability of the fishery was associated with the welfare of the community. Thus, legal decrees, fishing practices, and traditions in the trap fishery indicate a relatively sophisticated understanding of resource sustainability. Unfortunately, this was not carried over into the recent phase of bluefin fishing.

Within the last half-century, the Mediterranean ABFT fishery has been dramatically over-fished, first by industrial long-lines and most recently by purse-seines (International Commission for the Conservation of Atlantic Tunas [ICCAT], 2010b). As the fishery entered the modern era, new methods of production were sought to ensure increases in production and value. Fishing vessels grew in size, power, and on-board equipment, and the development of capital- and technology-intensive methods significantly reduced the demand for labor (Safina, 2001). Making use of modern technology with lethal efficiency, powerful fishing gear, including radar, sonar, and spotter planes, increased captures in earnest during the 1980s and continued for more than 20 years (ICCAT, 2010a). At the same time, the labor-intensive traditional trap technology was on the decline or had collapsed.

Furthermore, governments and industry groups pushed for expansion of fishing capacity and technology in the name of food security and jobs.[4] This resulted in massive subsidies entering into the fishery offered by regional governments and the European Union. The subsidies have been used to "modernize" the fleet, develop tuna ranching facilities, and research bluefin tuna aquaculture (Bregazzi, 2005; Doumenge, 1999; Tudela, 2002). By the mid-1990s, bluefin tuna "ranching" emerged as the newest technology for providing this high-value commodity for the global market. Soon after, ranches were the leading sources of bluefin tuna originating from the Mediterranean.

The expansion of production is readily observed in the era following the Second World War. The growth of investment in more technologically intensive fishing efforts with the intention of increasing production developed at an unprecedented rate (Bregazzi, 2005). As a result, bluefin tuna captures in this region increased from about 5,000 tons in 1950 to about 40,000 tons in 1994 and close to 60,000 tons in 2007 (ICCAT, 2010b).

During this era, the ABFT became a global commodity that was associated with possibly the highest value of all fish species. With prices that could run as high as $1,000 per kilogram, the potential for large returns drew in transnational capital (Normile, 2009). Fishing technology in the Mediterranean ABFT fishery was shaped by a globalized industry led by transnational firms such as the Mitsubishi Corporation, the largest in the fishery, and fishing industry interests in the region. A thriving global market for sashimi-grade tuna thrust the bluefin tuna into stardom. With skyrocketing prices that reflected its global fame, it became a culinary status symbol, particularly in Japan (Bestor, 2001; Issenberg, 2007).

In the modern era, the global bluefin tuna market grew as a luxury food product or a "boutique species" (Safina, 2001). Thus, its value as a commodity stemmed not from its nutritive capacity but from market exchange. That is, in its commodified form, it has a high exchange-value, but low use-value. While other food products, such as beef, have been historically tied to high status, the sociocultural phenomenon surrounding bluefin tuna is unique. Little physical sustenance is garnered from 10 to 20 grams of sashimi-grade tuna, the largest global market for bluefin tuna. This became a symbol for the global elite, and later the middle class. Socially constructed notions of prestige that display one's position in the social hierarchy and fashionable perceptions of sushi/sashimi shaped global market demand in wealthy nations, which were pushed by marketing and other powerful media sources (Issenberg, 2007).

The political-economic power of the industry is evidenced in the many unsuccessful attempts by nongovernmental organizations to reign in captures through policy and management by ICCAT or the Convention on International Trade in Endangered Species during the first decade of the 21st century (Bregazzi, 2006; Vasquez, 2010). Incidentally, it is indicative that the management practices developed by ICCAT, essentially a private quota system, were very likely influenced by the logic of the tragedy of the commons theory, which maintains that private property arrangements are a practical solution to overfishing.[5]

The traditional bluefin tuna trap fishery was dually affected by the transformations in the Mediterranean. First, the *tonnara* has a limited capacity for expansion and investors slowly abandoned it for more powerful technologies. The industrial fleets increased the size of the total catch and lowered the total costs of labor.[6] Second, over time, fishing by industrial fleets diminished the trap fishery's captures due to the heavy impact on Mediterranean bluefin populations. The capture levels in the traditional fishery showed significant declines in the latter decades of the 20th century (ICCAT, 2010b). Within a short time the Sicilian tonnare disappeared, and the traditional trap fishery throughout the Mediterranean has been decimated. Many practices and relationships that developed in the traditional fishery, such as the *tonnara*, focused on qualitative concerns including community welfare and future generations, which came to stand in contradiction with the concerns of capital.

Ranching Bluefin Tuna

The practice of bluefin tuna ranching involves capturing live ABFT from the open ocean and transferring them to holding pens to increase the fat content of the tuna. As ABFT sushi/sashimi is highly prized for its fatty or oily texture, something that only a short time ago was looked on disapprovingly by consumers, bluefin ranching develops as a method to add value to the commodity (Longo, 2011). Bluefin ranching in the Mediterranean originated in Cueta, Spain, to fatten postspawning tuna (Miyake et al., 2003). Because of the fact that bluefin tuna exert high energy and feed less frequently during spawning, their fat content and weight declines during this phase of the life cycle. Fattening postspawning ABFT could add value when its condition was considered suboptimal for market. However, recent ranching practices began capturing ABFT during the spawning period to further increase fat and weight before they are shed through the reproductive process.

Ranching is a method that can be economically efficient but is ecologically harmful. For example, bluefin tuna food conversion ratio estimates are as high as 30:1, meaning that it can take up to 30 pounds of feed to increase the weight of a bluefin tuna by 1 pound (Relini, 2003; Tudela, 2002). Capturing live ABFT for fattening has no material benefits for human subsistence. That is, there is no increase in the total protein available or calories produced for human development. More energy and protein are consumed in ranching than are gained. Furthermore, tuna ranching operations increase pressure on wild bluefin tuna stocks because they capture live fish for fattening. Capturing ABFT during their spawning migration disrupts their life cycle, a prime example of what has been referred to elsewhere as the metabolic rift (Foster 1999; Longo, in press). Thus, bluefin tuna ranching has been ecologically damaging to Mediterranean bluefin stocks and ocean ecosystems.

Ranching has played an important role in the impending development of ABFT aquaculture. Aquaculture entails closed captivity of the species during its entire life cycle. These facilities have provided a testing ground for confined production and have been used as resources for research and development. Recent European Union–funded efforts have conducted multimillion dollar research programs to "domesticate" ABFT for commercial production (SELF-DOTT, 2010). This has been regarded as the sustainable alternative, as it seeks to avoid the overexploitation of bluefin and maintain industry growth. However, tuna aquaculture is still susceptible to many of the ecological and social contradictions associated with ranching, most notably the challenges associated with bluefin tuna's food conversion ratio.

The Tragedy of the Commodity, Capitalist Valorization, and Bluefin Tuna

The inherent dynamics and logic of the social conditions of "capitalist private property" (Marx, 1977) create the historical context for environmental tragedies to unfold. In the marine environment, the drive to accumulate has spurred the capitalist commodification processes, leading to an oceanic crisis (Clausen & Clark, 2005). This crisis exemplifies both resource overexploitation as well as the unintended ecological and social consequences resulting from technological developments . . .

The traditional trap fishery was not subject to this tragedy until very recently. This fishery operated for close to a millennium and has been devastated within a few decades. Its demise occurred at precisely the time that the species underwent an unprecedented market metamorphosis. The collapse of this traditional fishery has been due, in no small part, to the processes of capitalist valorization, illustrating a tragedy of the commodity. As capital reaches ecological and social boundaries to realizing surplus-value, it seeks to overcome them in various ways (Foster et al., 2010).

To overcome these boundaries, capital searches for new geographic areas for exploitation along with the creation of new commodities and markets for investment and consumption. Bluefin tuna consumption expanded worldwide, particularly in Japan, with the increasing popularity of sashimi-grade bluefin tuna, which became a highlight on the menus of elite eating establishments (Bestor, 2001; Issenberg, 2007). As the Mediterranean became one of the last areas of abundant bluefin tuna stocks, global capital rushed in. In the process, the *tonnara* was "creatively" destroyed, or as Marx stated, it was "annihilated."

Capital slowly took a dominant role in the Mediterranean bluefin fishery, and there was a period of coexistence between traditional trap fishing and modern fishing. Yet even as individual private property, the *tonnara* was limited as a result of social and technical boundaries, and therefore inadequate to the dictates of capitalist private property. By examining this closely, it becomes clear that the "tragedy" of the *tonnara* emerged within the transformations in the social relations of production.

As noted, the capacity for expansion is constrained in the traditional trap fishery. First, it is a passive (stationary) trap and subject to variations in natural systems and contingency. Second, it is a labor- and knowledge-intensive system, which relies little on capital or high-technology intensive methods. The method of production is fundamentally linked to the natural metabolism of the bluefin and its reproductive cycles (Longo, in press). Thus, in 18th or 19th century Sicily, for example, any potential for growth was constrained to increasing absolute surplus-value by reducing the number of laborers and expanding the working day, or simply good fortune (Calleri, 2006). Because of the social and technical character of the capture system, expansion had clear limits.

The *tonnara* required a work force that had comprehensive knowledge of the local oceanic conditions. This is most clearly evidenced by the senior tuna fisherman or *tonnaroti* (Longo, in press). Many members of the crew were not easily replaceable. The social, technological, and knowledge barriers to expanding surplus-value could only be superseded by revolutionary changes in the methods of bluefin production, increasing relative surplus-value, and social abandonment of the *tonnara*. The expansion of capitalist private property and social power of capitalist commodity production created a dynamic that undermined sustainable harvesting methods, such as the *tonnara*.

Today, the Mediterranean fishery is at the brink of economic and ecological collapse (ICCAT, 2007; MacKenzie, Mosegaard, & Rosenberg, 2009). ABFT population levels have been depleted to historically low levels. Indeed, captures in the broader Mediterranean have peaked, even with increasing effort[7] (ICCAT, 2010a). In addition, the onset of tuna ranching has only exacerbated the problem by adding other environmental concerns to the mix, including overfishing of feed-fish species. Very recent developments in bluefin tuna domestication and aquaculture are regarded as the technical fix toward achieving sustainability. However, this will be plagued with its own set ecological problems, many of which have been displayed in other modern aquaculture systems based on capitalist private property (Naylor et al., 1998).

These phenomena can be regarded as the latest wave of technologies driven by capitalist valorization. The logic that prevails is bound by capitalist private property, which seeks to revolutionize the means of production in the process of finding new avenues for realizing surplus-value. Capturing and ranching a high-trophic-level species such as ABFT is ecologically inefficient and socially detrimental (Longo, in press). Nevertheless, it converts low-value "feed" species (e.g., sardines) into high-value fatty bluefin sushi/sashimi (*maguro toro*).

Tuna ranching serves as a clear example of a technological development that expropriates value from nature to maximize revenues, a fact that is unlikely to be disputed by almost anyone in the industry. Yet this erodes ocean resources and externalizes the costs of production. This process will be further complicated by a complete transition to bluefin tuna domestication. ABFT aquaculture in the Mediterranean is not yet commercially viable, but there are ongoing efforts to advance it as a lucrative enterprise. A species such as ABFT, with its high metabolic rate and physical size, is an ecologically irrational choice for domestication and aquaculture. The (ir)rationality of these decisions lies purely in the market realm, where exchange-value determines production outcomes.

It is erroneous to deem the recent technological transformations as driven by the individual fishing boats and self-interested bureaucrats, or a self-driven process of "pure" scientific advancement. The increase in captures was fundamentally tied to the expansion of productive capacity and the effectiveness of technological adaptations that brought high returns for the fishing industry and transnational capital. The tragedy of the commodity approach highlights that this is characteristic of the commodification process, constantly pushing the bounds of productivity seeking relative surplus-value (Braverman, 1998). Thus, commodification drives the ecological tragedy.

. . . Transformations in the ABFT fishery were based on expanding the global bluefin market, led by the social construction of a luxury food item. Nevertheless, for capitalist commodity production, "the nature of the needs, whether they arise, for example, from the stomach, or the imagination, makes no difference" (Marx, 1977, p. 125). Such are the consequences of the capitalist valorization process. The high market value of this global food commodity and the needs of capitalist private property propelled increased fishing effort and caused dramatic alterations in the production process and the ecology of the fishery.[8]

Conclusion

The logic of economic growth at all costs, ignoring ecological boundaries, is essential to capitalist production in part due to a real, or perceived, competitive structure and the drive for capital accumulation. When analyzing complex resource concerns such as those occurring in the Mediterranean bluefin tuna fishery, the seemingly logical tragedy of the commons explanatory model of individual selfishness and negligence is oversimplified. This perspective ignores the broader sociostructural and historical realities that are centrally important when analyzing these issues.

According to the tragedy of the commons theory, problems are formulated largely as relations between humans and nature, neglecting how this relationship is mediated through social relations of production (Foster, 2002). Historically, specific circumstances and social relations affect the ways in which communities access common property resources such as the oceans (Berkes, Feeny, McCay, & Acheson, 1989). The dominant discourse on ABFT, focusing on individual culpability, universal human characteristics, and population, overlooks the systemic structure of capitalist private property and commodity production and its inherent expansionary and exploitative character.

Contrary to Hardin's (1968) theory, the forces of overexploitation in the Mediterranean are not individual selfishness or resource users that are rational utility maximizers. Rather, the drivers of bluefin tuna depletion are fundamentally based in the historically specific relations of capitalist private property and commodity production. The tragedy of the commodity emerged as the quantitative form of value, and the inherent surplus-value embodied in it became divorced from its qualitative dimension. Capitalist private property seeks every avenue to expand into all aspects of social life and extinguish methods of production that can encumber the endless accumulation of surplus-value (Braverman, 1998).

In the case of ABFT, we do *not* find that the tragedy of the commons is causing the demise of the species. Rather, Atlantic bluefin tuna suffers from the tragedy of the commodity as capital creates opportunities for investors to increase the rate of returns, driving production decisions and technological developments. As Burkett (2006) makes clear, "The real tragedy of the commons has been the depletion and despoliation of communal resources by private, market-driven economic activity, that is, the inadequate recognition and enforcement of communal property in the form of strict user rights and responsibilities" (p. 82).

Historically, the traditional trap fishery in Sicily, the *tonnara,* was a system of production that allowed resource users access, yet social restrictions were imposed and material circumstances were limiting. This common resource was organized around social conditions that were not yet fully penetrated by capitalist private property. Modern ABFT production, born of capitalist private property and the unending quest to maximize surplus-value, became the form-determinant of fishing methods, technology, and the labor process in the modern era, resulting in a host of social and ecological contradictions. Thus, ecologically inefficient and environmentally destructive practices are implemented in the name of economic growth.

Applying Hegel's and Marx's aphorism, if overfishing in the Mediterranean is a tragedy, then ABFT ranching and aquaculture are a farce. Overexploitation is one of the manifestations of the tragedy of the commodity and is devastating in and of itself. However, the historical phenomenon of commodification deals a second blow by introducing tuna ranching and aquaculture. The destruction of bluefin tuna populations, as well as other ocean species, can only be addressed by confronting the tragedy of the commodity. In doing so, we begin to challenge the dominant assumptions that have governed modern natural resource management strategies.

Notes

Longo, Stefano B. and Rebecca Clausen. Except from "The Tragedy of the Commodity: The Overexploitation of the Mediterranean Bluefin Tuna Fishery." Organization and Environment. Reprinted by permission of Sage Publications.

1. While seemingly absurd on the surface, the general formula for capital could be said to reach its logical conclusion in M-M', or what is referred to as finance capital, money begetting more money. With this formulation, quality completely gives way to quantity.

2. The Sicilian traditional trap fishery was considered to be one of the earliest and most productive trapping systems in the region (Mather, 1995; Sará, 1998).

3. In recent times, some fisheries scientists have maintained that overfishing of juvenile ABFT, particularly those less than 1 year old and weighing as little as 4 kilograms, by modern industrial fishing has negatively affected the fishery (Mather, 1995; Safina, 2001).

4. The irony that new technologies were decreasing the need for labor in fishery was not lost on local tuna fishers who participated in this research.

5. ICCAT manages the Mediterranean bluefin fishery by determining the maximum sustainable yield (MSY) and allocating a quota or a total allowable catch (TAC) in tons to each member nation. Member nations are expected to enforce their own TACs. This is done mainly by allocating a quota for the fishing season to each vessel in a nation's fleet.

6. While there were attempts to lower the costs of labor in the modern history of the *tonnara*, this could not address the ongoing contradictions that the method of production posed for capital.

7. This phenomenon can be indicative of the precollapse stage of a fishery (Mullon, Fréon, & Cury, 2005).

8. The rate of expansion on ABFT production far exceeds the rate of population growth. Annual catches of Mediterranean ABFT increased more than 10-fold in the span of about 50 years (ICCAT, 2007).

References

Acheson, J. M. (1975). The lobster fiefs: Economic and ecological effects of territoriality in the Maine lobster industry. *Human Ecology, 3*, 183–207.

Acheson, J. M. (1988). *The lobster gangs of Maine.* Lebanon, NH: University Press of New England.

Anonymous. (2005, May). The tragedy of the commons, contd. *The Economist.* Retrieved from http://www.economist.com/node/3930586?story_id=3930586

Baran, P. A., & Sweezy, P. M. (1966). *Monopoly capital: An essay on the American economic and social order.* New York, NY: Monthly Review Press.

Benjamin, W. (1955). Theses on the philosophy of history. In W. Benjamin (Ed.), *Illuminations* (pp. 255–266). New York, NY: Harcourt, Brace, & World.

Berkes, F., Feeny, D., McCay, B. J., & Acheson, J. M. (1989). The benefits of the commons. *Nature, 340,* 91–93.

Bestor, T. C. (2001). Supply-side sushi: Commodity, market, and the global city. *American Anthropologist, 103,* 76–95.

Braverman, H. (1998). *Labor and monopoly capital: The degradation of work in the twentieth century.* New York, NY: Monthly Review Press.

Bregazzi, R. M. (2005). *The tuna ranching intelligence unit.* New Orleans, LA: Advanced Tuna Ranching Technologies.

Bregazzi, R. M. (2006). *Thunnus nostrum: Bluefin tuna fishing & ranching in the Mediterranean Sea 2004–2005.* Madrid, Spain: Advanced Tuna Ranching Technologies.

Burkett, P. (2006). *Marx and ecological economics: Towards a red and green political economy.* Boston, MA: Brill.

Calleri, N. (2006). *Un' impresa Mediterranea di pesca: I Pallavicini el le tonnare delle Egadi nei secoli 17–19* [A Mediterranean fishing company: The Pallavicini and traps of the Egadi during the 17th-19th centuries]. Genoa, Italy: Unioncamere Liguria.

Clausen, R., & Clark, B. (2005). The metabolic rift and marine ecology: An analysis of ocean crisis within capitalist production. *Organization & Environment, 18,* 422–444.

Consolo, V. (1986). *La pesca del tonno in sicilia* [Tuna fishing in Sicily]. Palermo, Italy: Sellerio Editore.

Corral-Verdugo, P., Frías-Armenta, M., Pérez-Urias, F., Orduña-Cabrera, V., & Espinoza-Gallego, N. (2002). Residential water consumption, motivation for conserving water and the continuing tragedy of the commons. *Environmental Management, 30,* 527–535.

Costello, C., Gaines, S. D., & Linham, J. (2008). Can catch shares prevent fisheries collapse? *Science, 321,* 1678–1681.

D'Amico, F. C. (1816). *Osservazioni pratiche intorno alla pesca, corso e cammino dei tonni* [Practical observations around fishing, course and path of the tuna]. Messina, Italy: Societá Tipografica.

Dietz, T., Dolsak, N., Ostrom, E., & Stern, P. (2002). *The drama of the commons.* Washington, DC: National Academies Press.

Dietz, T., Ostrom, E., & Stern, P. C. (2003). The struggle to govern the commons. *Science, 302,* 1907–1912.

Doumenge, F. (1999). La storia delle pesche tonniere [The history of tuna fishing]. *Biologia Marina Mediterranea, 6,* 5–106.

Feeny, D., Berkes, F., McCay, B. J., & Acheson, J. M. (1990). The tragedy of the commons: Twenty-two years later. *Human Ecology, 18*, 1–19.

Food and Agriculture Organization of the United Nations. (2007). *The state of the world's fisheries and aquaculture, 2006.* Rome, Italy: Author.

Foster, J. B. (1999). Marx's theory of metabolic rift: Classical foundations for environmental sociology. *American Journal of Sociology, 105*, 366–405.

Foster, J. B. (2002). *Ecology against capitalism.* New York, NY: Monthly Review Press.

Foster, J. B., Clark, B., & York, R. (2010). *The ecological rift: Capitalism's war on the earth.* New York, NY: Monthly Review Press.

Fracchia, J. (1991). Marx's *aufhebung* of philosophy and the foundations of a materialist science of history. *History and Theory, 30*, 153–179.

Fracchia, J. (2004). On transhistorical abstractions and the intersection of social theory and critique. *Historical Materialism, 12*, 125–146.

Gordon, H. S. (1954). The economic theory of a common-property resource: The fishery. *Journal of Political Economy, 62*, 124–142.

Greenberg, P. (2010, June 22). Tuna's end. *The New York Times.* Retrieved from http://www.nytimes. com/2010/06/27/magazine/27Tuna-t.html

Halpern, B. S., Walbridge, S., Selkoe, K. A., Kappel, C. V., Micheli, F., D'Agrosa, C., . . . Watson, R. (2008). A global map of human impact on marine ecosystems. *Science, 319*, 948–952.

Hardin, G. (1968). The tragedy of the commons. *Science, 162*, 1243–1248.

Hardin, G. (1974). Lifeboat ethics: The case against helping the poor. *Psychology Today, 8*, 38–43.

Hardin, G. (1998). Extensions of the tragedy of the commons. *Science, 280*, 682–683.

Heilbroner, R. L. (1986). *The essential Adam Smith.* New York, NY: W. W. Norton.

International Commission for the Conservation of Atlantic Tunas. (2007). *Report of the standing committee on research and statistics (SCRS).* Madrid, Spain: Author.

International Commission for the Conservation of Atlantic Tunas. (2010a). *Nominal catch information.* Madrid, Spain: Author.

International Commission for the Conservation of Atlantic Tunas. (2010b). *Report of the standing committee on research and statistics (SCRS).* Madrid, Spain: Author.

International Consortium of Investigative Journalists. (2010). *Looting the seas: How overfishing, fraud, and negligence plundered the majestic bluefin population.* Retrieved from http://www.publicintegrity. org/treesaver/tuna/#

Issenberg, S. (2007). *The sushi economy: Globalization and the making of a modern delicacy.* New York, NY: Gotham Books.

La Mantia, V. (1901). *Le tonnare in Sicilia* [The tuna traps in Sicily]. Palermo, Italy: Tipografia Giannitrapani.

Longo, S. B. (in press). Mediterranean rift: Socio-ecological transformations in the Sicilian bluefin tuna fishery. *Critical Sociology.* Advance online publication. doi:10.1177/0896920510382930

Longo, S. B. (2011). Global sushi: The political economy of the Mediterranean bluefin tuna fishery in the modern era. *Journal of World Systems Research, 17*, 403–427.

Mather, F. J., Mason, J. M., & Jones, A. C. (1995). *Historical document: Life history and fisheries of Atlantic bluefin tuna.* Springfield, VA: Southeast Fisheries Science Center.

MacKenzie, B. R., Mosegaard, H., & Rosenberg, A. A. (2009). Impending collapse of bluefin tuna in the Northeast Atlantic and Mediterranean. *Conservation Letters, 2*, 25–34.

Marx, K. (1977). *Capital* (Vol. 1). New York, NY: Vintage Books.

Marx, K. (1992). *Capital* (Vol. 2). New York, NY: Penguin Books.

McCay, B. J. (1998). *Oyster wars and the public trust: Property, law, and ecology in New Jersey history.* Tucson: University of Arizona Press.

McCay, B. J., & Acheson, J. M. (1987). *The question of the commons: The culture and ecology of communal resources.* Tucson: University of Arizona Press.

McEvoy, A. F. (1986). *The fisherman's problem: Ecology and law in the California fisheries, 1850–1980.* New York, NY: Cambridge University Press.

McGoodwin, J. R. (1990). *Crisis in the world's fisheries: People, problems, and policies.* Stanford: Stanford University Press.

McHugh, J. L. (1977). Rise and fall of world whaling: The tragedy of the commons illustrated. *Journal of International Affairs, 31*, 23–33.

McWhinnie, S. F. (2009). The tragedy of the commons in international fisheries: An empirical examination. *Journal of Environmental Economics and Management, 57*, 321–333.

Millennium Ecosystem Assessment. (2005). *Ecosystems and human well-being: Synthesis.* Washington, DC: Island Press.

Miyake, P. M., De la Serna, J. M., Di Natale, A., Farrugia, A., Katavic, I., Miyabe, N., & Ticina, V. (2003). *General review of bluefin tuna farming in the Mediterranean area.* Madrid, Spain: International Commission for the Conservation of Atlantic Tunas.

Mullon, C., Fréon, P., & Cury, P. (2005). The dynamics of collapse in world fisheries. *Fish and Fisheries, 6*, 111–120.

Myers, R. A., & Worm, B. (2003). Rapid worldwide depletion of predatory fishing communities. *Nature, 423*, 280–283.

Naylor, R. L., Goldburg, R. J., Mooney, H., Beveridge, M. C. M., Clay, J., Folke, C., . . . Williams, M. (1998). Nature's subsidies to shrimp and salmon farming. *Science, 282*, 883–884.

Nickler, P. A. (1999). A tragedy of the commons in coastal fisheries: Contending prescriptions for conservation, and the case of the Atlantic bluefin tuna. *Environmental Affairs, 26*, 549–576.

Normile, D. (2009). Persevering researchers make splash with farm-bred tuna. *Science, 324*, 1260–1261.

Ostrom, E. (1999). Coping with tragedies of the commons. *Annual Review of Political Science, 2*, 493–535.

Ostrom, E., Burger, J., Field, C. B., Norgaard, R. B., & Policansky, D. (1999). Revisiting the commons: Local lessons, global challenges. *Science, 284*, 278–282.

Pauly, D., Christiensen, V., Dalsgaard, J., Freese, R., & Torres, F. (1998). Fishing down marine food webs. *Science, 279*, 860–863.

Polanyi, K. (1957). *The great transformation: The political and economic origins of our time.* Boston, MA: Beacon Press.

Ponting, C. (2007). *A new green history of the world: The environment and collapse of great civilizations.* New York, NY: Penguin.

Relini, G. (2003). Fishery and aquaculture relationship in the Mediterranean: Present and future. *Mediterranean Marine Science, 4*, 125–154.

Revkin, J. (2008, November 26). The (Tuna) tragedy of the commons. *The New York Times*. Retrieved from http://dotearth.blogs.nytimes.com/2008/11/26/the-tuna -tragedy-of-the-commons/

Safina, C. (2001). Tuna conservation. In B. A. Block & E. D. Stevens (Eds.), *Tuna physiology, ecology, and evolution* (pp. 414–457). New York, NY: Academic Press.

Sarà, R. (1998). *Dal mito all' aliscafo: Storie di tonni e di tonnare* [From myth to hydrofoil: Stories of tuna and tuna traps]. Messina, Italy: Editore Raimondo Sará.

Schnaiberg, A., & Gould, K. A. (1994). *Environment and society: The enduring conflict*. New York, NY: St. Martin's Press.

Schumpeter, J. A. (1962). *Capitalism, socialism, and democracy*. New York, NY: Harper Perennial.

SELF-DOTT. (2010). *Latest news*. Retrieved from http://sites.google.com/site/self-dottpublic/

Sweezy, P. M. (1942). *The theory of capitalist development*. New York, NY: Monthly Review Press.

Tucker, R. C. (1978). *The Marx-Engels reader*. New York, NY: W. W. Norton.

Tudela, S. (2002). Grab, cage, fatten, sell. *Samudra, 32*, 9–16.

United Nations. (2005). *Millennium ecosystem assessment synthesis report*. New York, NY: Author.

Vasquez, J. C. (2010). *Governments not ready for a trade ban on bluefin tuna*. Retrieved from http://www.cites.org/eng/news/press/2010/20100318_tuna.shtml

The World Bank. (2004). *Saving fish and fishers: Toward sustainable and equitable governance of the global fishing sector* (Report No. 29090-GLB). Retrieved from http:// siteresources.worldbank.org/ INTARD/Resources/SavingFishandFishers.pdf

York, R., & Gossard, M. H. (2004). Cross-national meat and fish consumption: Exploring the effects of modernization and ecological context. *Ecological Economics, 48*, 293–302.

4

Ecological Modernization at Work? Environmental Policy Reform in Sweden at the Turn of the Century

Benjamin Vail

Currently, one of the theoretical debates in environmental sociology is whether capitalism can be rendered environmentally sustainable. Proponents of ecological modernization argue that yes, capitalism is incredibly flexible and that businesses will move toward more ecologically sustainable practices, especially with government incentives. Others, such as the authors of the previous two selections, are suspect of this view and tend to see the "treadmill of production"—capitalism's need for constant growth—as antithetical to environmental sustainability.

Benjamin Vail does not engage in this debate but asks whether Sweden's sweeping "sustainable society" policy follows the ideas of ecological modernization. In doing so, he clearly describes ecological modernization and shows how this theory has developed over time.

Sweden is widely viewed as a global leader in positive environmental practices, both in terms of public policy and business-sector activities. Throughout the 1990s and into the 2000s, Swedish society—in the realms of politics, the economy, and civil society—debated the value of sustainable development. The government decided on an ambitious long-term program to achieve a "sustainable society" by 2020. This article seeks to understand the process by which this policy decision was made—as well as its practical implications, which include potentially sweeping impacts on social and economic life in the push for environmental improvements. In pursuit of an explanation, this article asks whether the environmental sociological theory of ecological modernization describes the process of decision-making in Sweden during this time period.

The hypothesis considered here is that Swedish environmental policy reform during this period was largely consistent with the model of social change predicted (and prescribed) by ecological modernization theory (EMT). To test this hypothesis, the Swedish decision-making process is described, ecological modernization theory is introduced, and empirical evidence is presented to compare the Swedish situation with the theory's predictions.

This study gathered data through the use of key informant interviews with decision-makers in government, political parties, and environmental groups. Further information was obtained from government documents, news media accounts, and political party publications. Many sources were available in English; where sources existed only in Swedish all translations were done by the author.

Swedish Environmental Reforms
in the 1990s and Early 2000s

After several years of study and deliberation, in the late 1990s the Swedish Parliament voted to approve a new structure for national environmental policy. The purpose of the reforms was to solve environmental problems with the aim of creating a "sustainable society" within one generation. In 1998 existing environmental protection laws were consolidated into a single Environmental Code, the implementation of which was to be guided by fifteen environmental quality objectives—essentially a national "mission statement" for ecological sustainability—to be fulfilled by 2020.

The government officially said its actions were driven by the concept of sustainable development as presented in the 1987 Brundtland Report (World Commission on Environment and Development 1987), which states that development efforts should meet the needs of the present generation without compromising the ability of future generations to meet their own needs (Persson and Lindh 4).

Based on this definition of sustainable development, the government said in a "Statement of Government Policy" in 1996, "Sweden should be a driving force and a model for ecological sustainability" (Swedish Commission 2). The

Government elaborated on its understanding of sustainable development in its 1997 Spring Economic Bill and 1998 Budget Bill, stating that ecologically sustainable development involves three objectives: environmental protection, sustainable use of resources, and more efficient use of energy and resources (Persson and Lindh 5 and Sustainable Sweden, "Environmental Quality" 3). Ultimately, "the Government's primary environmental objective is to hand over a society to the next generation in which the major environmental problems have been solved" (Swedish Ministry, 2000c 6).

Under a Social Democrat-led coalition, Parliament approved two different "framework" bills designed to put this vision of a sustainable society into effect, the Environmental Code and fifteen environmental quality objectives.

. . .

In 1997, the government submitted to Parliament the first proposal for the fifteen environmental quality objectives in a bill entitled, "Swedish Environmental Quality Objectives: An Environmental Policy for a Sustainable Sweden" (Swedish Ministry, 2000c 10 and Swedish Environmental Protection Agency 2001). This bill was passed by Parliament in April 1999.

In September 1999, the government submitted details of how to achieve each objective with interim targets, monitoring strategies, and action plans. A Parliamentary committee, the Committee on Environmental Objectives, was created to study and review the environmental objectives and interim goals. In June 2000, this committee submitted its report, *The Future Environment: Our Common Responsibility.* In April 2001, the government submitted a new environmental objectives bill, *Swedish Environmental Quality Objectives: Interim Goals and Action Strategies,* to Parliament based on the committee's recommendations. This bill was passed by Parliament in November 2001. The new Environmental Code was passed by Parliament in 1998 and took effect on 1 January 1999 (Ministry of the Environment, 2000a 3).

According to Christina Lindbäck, the Director of the Division of Environmental Quality at the Environment Ministry, in the early 1990s the Swedish EPA discovered that there were about 170 environmental goals laid out in a variety of government plans. This fact had led to confusion and missed targets. Stakeholders including members of Parliament, representatives from government ministries, and NGOs and other interest groups sat on the Committee on Environmental Objectives that was appointed to propose targets, measures and strategies to fulfill the fifteen environmental quality objectives. "At the same time, the Government gave tasks to every authority in Sweden having a responsibility under each of the fifteen environmental quality objectives to do an analysis about what are the problems and to come up with proposals for how to solve these problems." Lindbäck said. . . .

The Code was created to consolidate the various laws and rules concerning the environment that were enacted piecemeal over the decades by Parliament and government agencies. The point was to rationalize environmental law to make it more comprehensible to both regulators and the regulated. The Code specified rules about land, water, and air use and protection, and was based on five fundamental principles considered to be the basis for sustainable development: protection of human health, preservation of biological diversity, minimization of use of natural resources, and protection of the natural and cultural environments (Swedish Ministry, 2000b 7).

Effective application of the Environmental Code was predicated on three general action strategies:

1. Improved efficiency in energy use, production, and transportation: energy conservation and public transportation will be promoted largely though education and economic incentives.
2. Cleaner production processes and recycling: the use of hazardous substances must be reduced and phased out and more goods recycled through education and legislation.
3. Improved environmental management practices: agricultural subsidies and more protection of natural areas are key (Committee on Environmental Objectives 11–12).

The Code was intended to facilitate action to achieve improvements in the following fifteen environmental quality objectives (Sustainable Sweden, *Environmental Quality* 4–6).

1. Clean air
2. High-quality groundwater
3. Sustainable lakes and watercourses
4. Flourishing wetlands
5. A balanced marine environment, sustainable coastal areas and archipelagoes
6. No eutrophication
7. Natural acidification only
8. Sustainable forests
9. A varied agricultural landscape
10. A magnificent mountain landscape
11. A good urban environment
12. A non-toxic environment
13. A safe radiation environment
14. A protective ozone layer
15. Limited (influence on) climate change

An Introduction to Ecological Modernization Theory

According to Thomas Nilsson of the Swedish EPA, who worked as a secretary and policy developer for the Committee on Environmental Objectives, these policies put Sweden on the "cutting edge" of international environmental reforms (Interview 5 October 2001). From a sociological perspective, ecological modernization theory (EMT) helps to explain the decision-making process of Swedish environmental reforms.

In brief, the ecological modernization point of view suggests—both as an empirical observation and as a prediction of future trends—that society is moving toward more environmentally friendly economic and social relations. Ecological modernization theorists look at the air and water quality improvements, for example, since the 1970s as proof of social progress in protecting the environment. Mol and Spaargaren state that although economic interests "still play a dominant role in production and consumption, and that they will probably always remain at least as important as—among others—ecological criteria . . . the innovation is that ecological interests and criteria are catching up with economic ones" (42).

While many authors have expounded on EMT and applied ecological modernization thinking to a variety of studies, Buttel argues that it is appropriate to focus on the writings of Mol and Spaargaren "because of all the scholars and researchers in this tradition (at least as far as the literature in English is concerned) they have done the most to articulate a distinctive theoretical argument" (Buttel, "Ecological Modernization" 58).

The origins of ecological modernization (EM) as a system of thought and social inquiry can be traced to the German sociologist Joseph Huber's work in the late 1970s (Mol and Sonnenfeld 4). Seippel says that EMT arose as a response to the radicalization of environmental thought due to the recession of the early 1980s, and also due to changes in the environmental movement, the emergence of new environmental problems, and the expanding availability of alternative discourses (289). Buttel says that EMT emerged in reaction to the ideologies and actions of 1980s radical environmental groups, as a response to the tradition in North American environmental sociology that emphasized the intrinsic nature of environmental degradation in modern society, and as a description of sustainable development efforts in developed nations ("Ecological Modernization" 59–60).

Buttel and Mol describe EMT as having moved through several "stages" of development from the 1980s through the mid-1990s and with contemporary new directions ("Ecological Modernization" 59 and "Global Economy" 2–3). Buttel writes that the "first generation" of EM thinking "was based on the overarching hypotheses that capitalist liberal democracy has the institutional capacity to reform its impact on the natural environment" ("Ecological

Modernization" 59) and that the further development of capitalist modes of production—to a kind of "green capitalism"—will result in ecological improvements. This stage tended to emphasize capitalism's ability to adapt to new conditions and was premised largely on the idea of "technical fixes" for environmental problems (see Spaargaren and Mol 334). The second generation of EM literature focused on the specific socio-political processes by which the continued social and economic development of liberal democracies—in other words, further industrialization and modernization—is hypothesized to result in ecological improvements (Buttel "Ecological Modernization" 59).

Mol and Sonnenfeld suggest that in the late 1990s a "third phase" of EMT emerged that focused on issues of private consumption, the spread of ecological modernization to non-European countries, and the influence of globalization on EM processes in individual national-states (5). This phase can be seen as a response to criticism that EMT was preoccupied almost exclusively with production processes, was Eurocentric in its orientation, and did not account for trans-national social and ecological issues (Buttel, "Classical Theory" 31–2).

Mol and Spaargaren offer a version of EMT as a theory of social change and also a political program aimed at achieving a more sustainable society (Spaargaren and Mol; Mol, "Industrial Transformations"; and Seippel 290). They assert that in contrast to other theories of social-environmental change, EMT offers a realistic, achievable vision of a re-ordering of social, economic and political relations to promote environmental improvements (Mol, "Global Economy" 9).

Ecological modernization theory makes five main claims about social-ecological changes taking place in advanced industrialized nations. The primary purpose of EMT is to explain changes in the relationships between social institutions—namely the state, market actors, and civil society—in relation to the environment. According to Mol, EMT proposes the following hypotheses:

1. While science and technology have caused environmental problems, they are also the sources of technical solutions. Preventative technologies can replace command-and-control approaches to remediate environmental problems. For example, problems such as air and water pollution can be resolved through the application of science and technology to achieve cleaner operating processes that reduce emissions from vehicles and factories.

2. Market forces and economic actors become more important as "social carriers of ecological restructuring, innovation and reform." In other words, the market encourages producers to cut costs by using more efficient technologies and by responding to consumer demand for eco-friendly products.

3. The state's role in environmental protection is transformed. Government adopts decentralized, flexible and collaborative problem-solving methods. Non-governmental organizations (NGOs), such as environmental groups, begin to play a more influential role in policy-making. And international institutions, such as the World Trade Organization and the European Union, begin to undermine the authority and ability of the traditional nation-state to determine and enforce policies by altering the meaning of sovereignty.

4. The roles and ideologies of environmental social movements change as environmental groups increasingly seek to work cooperatively with government and market actors to achieve environmental improvements. Instead of seeking to protect the environment by reducing production and consumption, for example, environmentalists try to work with government and business to make reforms. Although they will abandon their "de-modernization" ideology, these groups will continue to have a "dualistic strategy of cooperation and conflict, and internal debates on the tensions that are a by-product of this duality."

5. Society-wide shifts in discourses lead to the emergence of new ideologies characterized by concern for environmental issues. A heightened awareness of intergenerational solidarity "seems to have emerged as the undisputed core and common principle" guiding environmental reform. ("Global Economy" 5 and "Industrial Transformations" 140–2)

. . . [P]erhaps the most fundamental EMT claim is that economic actors such as manufacturers and investors will begin to take action in support of environmental protection—not in response to government command-and-control dictates or rigid regulations, but because environmental values are permeating corporate culture and because companies find it advantageous to adopt environmentally friendly practices. Mol and Spaagaren and Mol describe this process as "ecologicalization" of the economy and "economization" of ecology. In other words, science and technology make possible new market-driven fixes to environmental problems. . . .

Cleaner technologies, EMT suggests, will lead to "dematerialization" of the economy (Mol and Sonnenfeld 6). This hypothesis suggests "that for each unit of output . . . there will be progressively fewer environmental resources required as inputs into production. . . . At a highly aggregated level, dematerialization of production leads to societies and economies becoming 'decoupled' from resource use" (Buttel, "Environmental Sociology" 21). Efficiency, recycling and the use of renewable resources will reduce the need to exploit virgin natural resources and will reduce wastes, creating product "life cycles" that are environmentally benign.

Ecological modernization offers the optimistic vision of sustainable development without radical changes in the existing social-economic order. This overall view appears consistent with Swedish efforts to achieve a "sustainable society" through political and market reforms that leave the modern industrial consumer society intact.

Putting EMT to the Test in the Swedish Case

To test whether ecological modernization theory describes and explains Swedish environmental reforms, it is useful to start by asking whether evidence in the Swedish case supports Mol's five hypotheses.

The Role of Science and Technology

The Swedish example appears to provide quite strong evidence in support of Mol's hypothesis of a changing role for science and technology. The Committee on Environmental Objectives' report (2000) gave clear indications of how new technology would be necessary—and encouraged by the state—to achieve sustainability.

Improved efficiency in energy use, production, and transportation was the first action strategy declared in the Environmental Code. This policy depends on the use of new technologies such as new fuels and better engines, that simultaneously would be more efficient and reduce harmful emissions (Committee on Environmental Objectives 11).

Furthermore, the use of best possible technology was not only encouraged but mandated by the new Environmental Code. "The best possible technology is to be used for professional operations. The term *best possible technology* applies to the technology used both for the operation itself and for the construction, operation and decommissioning of the plant. An essential condition for using the best possible technology is that it must be feasible in industrial and economic terms in the line of business concerned" (Swedish Ministry, 2000b 12).

The Role of Economic Actors

There is strong evidence from this time period in Sweden supporting Mol's second hypothesis that economic actors were expected to contribute actively to environmental reform resulting in transformations in state-market relations. The government policies promoted greater efficiency in the use of resources, an outcome depending partly on new technology but also the changing habits of resource use by private individuals and corporations. For example, the concept of "Factor 10," as promoted by the United Nations, was a policy guideline. Factor 10 meant "that we must use resources, not only fossil fuels but energy and materials, on average ten times more efficiently within the next generation or two. In the view of many scientists, industrialists, and politicians, this change is essential if we are to be able to face the growing population and reduce pollution without lowering living standards" (Persson and Lindh 6).

The question of efficiency and reduced use of resources related directly to the EMT hypothesis that "ecologizing" economies tend toward dematerialization—the decoupling of production from raw natural resource inputs. There was only mixed evidence in Sweden that such a trend was taking place. One positive indicator was the fact that despite GDP growth of "approximately 43 percent in constant prices over the past 20 years, the total use of energy in industry has declined during this period" (Sustainable Sweden, "Tax Policy"). Over the same period, however, overall energy use in Sweden grew.

Perhaps the most compelling evidence for dematerialization in Sweden consisted of data showing that overall material consumption in industry had been on the decline since the late 1980s (Statistics Sweden 46). The use of non-renewable materials such as construction minerals, ore and industrial minerals and fossil fuels declined between 1987 and 1997, while the use of renewable resources remained relatively stable.

Data from Statistics Sweden, the Swedish EPA, and other sources indicate an uneven trend over the years, with a mixture of victories and losses on the "dematerialization" front.

For example, although household recycling and composting rates increased and the quantity of waste disposed in landfills decreased between 1985 and 1998, the total amount of annual municipal waste increased during this period (Statistics Sweden 15).

The amount of industrial waste produced in Sweden grew between 1993 and 1998 (Statistics Sweden 17). The per capita use of fuels decreased slightly between 1993 and 1997, but the use of non-fuel hazardous chemicals increased during the same time period, while the annual per capita use of hazardous chemical products remained about even (Swedish Environmental Protection Agency, *De Facto* 24).

There was a trend toward reduced emissions of nitrogen and phosphorus into the sea from coastal point sources between 1985 and 1997. Such reductions were very important for achieving environmental objectives such as mitigated eutrophication and improved wetlands, waterways, and coastal areas (Statistics Sweden 12).

In addition to reduced harmful emissions into Sweden's waterways, there were significant improvements in air pollution. Swedish emissions of sulphur dioxide (SO_2), a prime contributor to acid rain, declined greatly between 1980 and 1998 (Swedish Environmental Protection Agency, *De Facto* 18). Data show that the most dramatic improvements were made in the power/heating and industrial sectors. Reductions in carbon dioxide (C02) emissions mirrored those of S02 over the same time period; emissions of C02 from different sources declined between 1980 and 1999 (Statistics Sweden 52).

Despite these improvements, urban air continued to pose human health risks. Volatile organic compounds and particulate matter emitted by vehicles created smog and ground-level ozone, and caused health disorders such as asthma. Though benzene levels in urban air declined by 50 percent from 1992–1999, the levels were higher than the low-risk limit (Statistics Sweden 11). The fact that VOC emissions remained above acceptable levels was most likely a result of continuing high levels of personal auto use. But while 1998 levels of auto use were more than 10 percent higher than those in 1985, alternative forms of transportation were becoming more popular. In 1998, more than 25 percent of all journeys to and from work or school were made on foot, bicycle or public transportation (Swedish Environmental Protection Agency 13; Swedish Environmental Advisory Council 16, 18, 19).

The Swedish forestry sector appeared already to have begun to balance harvesting with environmental protection. Gustaf Aulén, an ecologist with the Södra association of Swedish forest owners, said his industry had both a "production goal" and an "environmental goal." One "important reason" why forestry companies acted to conserve nature was "increasing pressure from our customers" (Personal correspondence 8 November 2001).

There was evidence that Swedish corporate participation in certification and labeling programs was on the rise thereby suggesting that voluntary action in support of environmental improvement was catching on. The number of firms with EMAS or ISO 14001 certification grew between 1995 and 1999, from zero to over 900 (Statistics Sweden 30). In another example of industry's embrace of green labeling and ecofriendly practices, the amount of land area certified as under sustainable forestry management expanded by more than ten times between 1996 and 2000. This assessment referred to voluntary certification programs administered either by the international Forest Stewardship Council or the Pan-European Forest Certification system. Meanwhile, the amount of forested land area under public protection also grew in the 1990s from about 2.5 percent of all productive forestland in 1990 to more than 3.5 percent in 1999 (Statistics Sweden 31).

Furthermore, Sweden's use of "green taxes" based on the Polluter Pays Principle (PPP) promoted the internalization of ecological costs by corporate and individual decision-makers. The PPP mandated that any entity found to be responsible for environmental degradation, such as oil leaks or toxic emissions, was liable to pay for all costs associated with remediation of the problem. In Sweden, the PPP liability extended in the form of a tax to those who consumed goods and services such as petrol and dry cleaning. Tax reforms in 1991 began the process of imposing consumption taxes on fossil fuels and greenhouse gas emissions. Sustainable Sweden reports, "Energy taxation of motor fuels has led to noticeable improvements in urban air. The sulphur tax has helped our country meet the emissions targets for sulphur. The nitrogen oxide charge has reduced emissions from heating plants, and the energy and carbon dioxide taxes have encouraged the use of biofuels" ("Tax Policy").

. . .

The government argued that implementation of the environmental quality objectives would on balance help the national economy and enhance the performance of Swedish firms (Persson and Lindh 5). One government report asserted, "Conversion to ecologically sustainable development on a wide front can help to create growth and employment and thus promote the conditions for growth even in vulnerable regions" (Sustainable Sweden, "Environmental Quality Objectives" 22).

Thus Swedish officials echoed the EMT claim that economic rationality and ecological values need not be mutually exclusive and that eco-friendly behavior on the part of corporate and individual actors can be profitable. By the early 2000s, Swedes could interpret the energy and materials use trends as an encouraging picture of increasing efficiency and gradual environmental improvements—in other words, ecological modernization. Yet many of the changes in the marketplace were to be achieved not through ecological concern endogenous to the business community, but through economic policy instruments wielded by the state.

The Role of the State

The Swedish government certainly wanted to induce economic actors to consider environmental values. The Swedish Ministry of the Environment declared that "environmental concerns must be integrated into all decision-making. Methods must be developed in order to integrate the costs of environmental impacts into economic and social decision-making models" (Swedish Ministry, 2000c 9). The Committee on Environmental Objectives added, "Powerful policy instruments will be required, of both a normative and an informative nature. The involvement of market forces is important if efforts to reduce risk are to be pursued in a systematic way. Manufacturers' efforts to produce environmental product certificates and positive environmental labeling are examples of this" (28).

Evidence supporting the EMT assertion that the traditional role of the state will be transformed is mixed in Sweden. Mol's third hypothesis is that the government will shift from combative regulator to cooperative facilitator. This change will be accompanied by decentralization and more flexible policy-making and enforcement practices. The Swedish example appeared to validate the prediction of greater flexibility, but instead of becoming decentralized, the state expanded its power over national environmental protection and remained the prime mover in environmental protection. As shown in the previous section about economic actors, much of the impetus for market-based solutions in Sweden was expected to originate in government actions through the use of policy tools to penalize or subsidize certain behaviors.

Prime Minister Persson made perhaps the most straightforward statement of the role of the state in environmental protection: "Central government must lead the way" (Persson and Lindh 7). Sustainable Sweden added, "The task of central government in relation to the market is, inter alia, to establish clear-cut rules. The Environmental Code recently presented by the Government will lay the foundation for this work" ("Environmental Quality Objectives" 29).

The Committee on Environmental Objectives further clarified the government's role in environmental protection: "Central government will assist in this endeavor via measures taken by its sectoral agencies, by providing economic incentives and by creating other beneficial conditions for environmental work. Its task is also to ensure that laws and regulations are enacted and properly implemented. Environmental monitoring and advanced follow-up systems are further responsibilities of central government" (8).

Thus, although county boards and municipalities were responsible for the local implementation of the new policies, the central government remained the strongest force for change. Indeed, while the state sought to work with private enterprise to effect meaningful environmental reform, it also acted as a counterweight to the power of private capital. Svante Axelsson, director of Swedish Society for Nature Conservation, the largest environmental NGO in Sweden, wrote,

. . . "There is considerable potential for change through voluntary action. For example, many multinational corporations are sensitive to environmental issues. They are anxious to protect their brand reputations, of which environmental movement organizations in different regions are well aware. But the politicians are necessary as well. That which is emerging via market forces must be strengthened through political measures."

While the power and responsibility for initiating environmental policy reform remained vested in the central government, there was substantial evidence that the state was becoming more flexible and inclusive in its decision-making and enforcement practices. The green tax policy was a good example of how the state sought to use economic incentives to change behavior. According to the Committee on Environmental Objectives, "The use of economic incentives is an important means of achieving sustainable ecological development. In framing such incentives, it is important to bear in mind that they should encourage technological development and efficiency and hasten the replacement of old technologies by new ones" (19). The state's policy-making toolbox included not only taxes to discourage consumers and producers from harmful activities, but also subsidies to encourage positive changes. This was in contract to the emphasis on "end-of-pipe" pollution mandates in the 1970s and 1980s.

On the whole, the state appeared to be embracing market-based, flexible solutions to meet the environmental quality objectives. There were provisions in the Environmental Code for prosecuting violators, but the new policies emphasized preventative measures.

The Role of Non-Governmental Organizations

Mol's fourth EMT-based hypothesis is that the role and ideology of environmental social movements will change. These "subpolitical" actors will stop acting on a radical, negative "de-modernization" agenda and instead will increasingly seek to work together with the state and corporations to achieve their goals. Not only will these groups' ideologies and activities begin to change, they may become quite influential within the government, leading to the restructuring of power arrangements.

There was evidence of such a trend in Sweden. The government sought the input of environmental groups when formulating the environmental quality objectives, and the Swedish Ministry of the Environment said that "the authorities should pay attention to and support the pro-environment activities of non-governmental organizations" (Committee on Environmental Objectives 9 and Swedish Ministry, 2000c 66).

However, Gunilla Högberg Björck of the Swedish Society for Nature Conservation said that NGOS lacked the influence of business interests (Interview 8 October 2001). This may be explained in part by a trend in Sweden of decreasing public interest in environmental issues by the early 2000s. A social survey found that the Swedish public's concern for environmental issues declined during the 1990s. In 1988, 62 percent of the Swedish public said environmental issues were among their top three policy concerns, compared with only 4 percent in 1999. The study also found that environmental organizations were losing members. In 1989, 15 percent of the population said they were members of an environmental organization, compared with only 5 percent in 1999 (Lövgren and Öhngren 5).

Meanwhile, support for the Swedish Green Party was wavering, casting doubt on whether the environmental movement would continue to have a voice in Parliament. The party was seen by many as obsolete since other parties had incorporated environmental themes into their platforms. Conservative Party advisor Göran Olsson suggested that the Green Party might perish due to its own success: "Actually, it's a paradox because . . . the more they get the Social Democrats or the government to listen to them and actually propose environmental issues, the less need there is for the Green Party" (Interview October 5, 2001).

Thus, the Swedish public's interest in nature and environmental policy was waxing and waning, resulting in uncertain clout for the environmental movement. The variable strength and depth of public environmental concern relates directly to questions about discourse and ideology in Swedish society.

The Role of Discourse, Ideology, and Values

Mol's fifth EMT hypothesis is that the ecological modernization process is characterized by society-wide changes in discourses and ideologies of a pro-environment nature. There was fairly strong evidence that Swedish officials at least "talked the talk" when it came to ecological awareness and their stated intentions to act in a more environmentally friendly way. Examples of the role of discourse and ideology in Swedish environmental decision-making can be found in the political debates over the policy reforms, Swedish notions about their country's international environmental leadership, and consumers' choices to buy eco-labeled products.

While there appeared to be a certain amount of consensus within the Swedish policy arena about adopting the fifteen environmental objectives, debate raged over the question of how best to prioritize and achieve environmental improvements. Most stakeholders, including political parties, environmentalists, and business interests, agreed in principle with the environmental objectives but disagreed about how to implement the reforms.

For example, Conservative Göran Olsson said, "There is no consensus on how to get there or how fast, or other considerations or even the methods—how to do the work to get there. But since the goals are . . . such that it is practically impossible to say no. 'Do we want clean air?' Yes. It's laid out in that sense so it's very hard to say that 'No, we are opposed to clean air'" (Interview 5 October 2001).

. . . The question of proper forest management, for example, highlighted ideological differences between those who wanted state control of forests and those who wanted to educate private landowners for eco-friendly management. Genetically modified organisms, Lindbäck said, "presented another question, as did fishery policies, where you could find ideological differences about how to solve the problems. It's seldom difficult to agree on [the existence of] an environmental problem, but it's difficult to agree upon measures how to solve it" (Interview 2 October 2001).

. . . The increasing success of eco-labeled products may serve as a final example supporting Mol's hypothesis that environmental values can be seen permeating society. Gardfjell—in Lövgren and Öhngren—found that the Nordic symbol of eco-friendly products, a green swan label placed on qualifying goods, was well recognized by Swedish consumers. She found that, 'The experiences with the environmental label show that voluntary initiatives can be very significant. The environmental label has caused big breakthroughs in certain areas, but there are also commodities—for example textiles—for which the label has completely failed'. . .

Reinhard, et al. list the possibilities and limitations of using such eco-labels. The "pros" of using eco-labels include the fact that they complement other policy instruments promoting green consumption and communicate a complex message about green purchasing choices. Updating the labeling criteria leads to continuous improvement in green goods, and the requirements to use the label may be stricter than official legislation. The "cons" of using such labels include the fact that green purchasing does not reduce total consumption, the program is dependent on voluntary action by industry, not all products are suitable for eco-labeling, and products may not qualify for eco-labeling in all stages of their life cycles (Reinhard, et al. 65).

Data from Statistics Sweden show that green purchases were on the rise through the 1990s. The purchase of eco-labeled products and services as a percentage of total private consumption rose from less than 1 percent in 1995 to nearly 2.5 percent in 1998. The per capita value of purchases of eco-labeled goods and services rose from less than 500 to more than 2000 Swedish crowns (from about 50 to more than 200 in 2001 US Dollars) (32). While support for eco-labeled products fell in Norway, "the proportion of consumers strongly favouring greener products remained stable in Sweden, Denmark and Finland at around 60 percent" (ENDS Environment Daily "Norway Loses Interest").

A Critical Assessment of EMT and the Swedish Case

Empirical evidence appears to provide compelling validation of many of ecological modernization theory's claims about the characteristics of Swedish environmental policy reform. The information presented here suggests that EMT clarifies the social issues surrounding environmental policy reform in a useful way and is an applicable conceptual framework for better understanding the Swedish environmental reform decision-making process of the late 1990s and early 2000s.

However, the evidence is not an overwhelming confirmation of ecological modernization theory. Obviously, the empirical data regarding materials use and pollution can be interpreted in different ways. While some improvements are obvious and the trend is positive, one may question whether the changes are significant enough to celebrate. The question remains whether dematerialization is a clear and inevitable trend or if perhaps major changes in individual lifestyles and business practices will be necessary to achieve the environmental quality objectives.

Is technology really the magic bullet for Swedish environmental problems? Rather than achieving the vaunted goal of reducing environmental impacts through "dematerialization," critics such as Bunker, Schnaiberg, and Schnaiberg and Gould fear that more efficient production processes will instead simply make possible the use of ever greater quantities of resources (Bunker, Schnaiberg, and Schnaiberg and Gould). Thus, even cleaner and more efficient production may not necessarily lead to environmental improvements.

Even if industry was cleaning up its act and offering more green products during the 1990s, it is unclear whether businesses were acting solely or even mainly out of an ethical concern for the environment. In other words, was "ecological modernization" really taking place, in the sense that there was an emergent new relationship between humans and the natural environment?

Politically, in the Swedish case, the state consolidated its position as the first actor in environmental improvement and did not step aside to let market forces work alone. Indeed, the state choreographed the economic incentives that would make possible the "market solutions" theorized by EMT. It is through such mechanisms as green taxes and government subsidies that many of the environmental objectives are expected to be achieved, but they require substantial centralized control.

Regarding non-governmental organizations, it is possible that instead of being engaged in a collaborative policy-making process among equals, environmental groups that conform to the EMT hypothesis risk being co-opted by anti-environmental interests and may even become complicit in the green-washing of their corporate and government "partners." Rather than taking principled stands for significant reforms and fighting when necessary, environmental groups risk selling out in an effort to gain recognition within the political power structure. It is also interesting to note that EMT does not account for the possibility that anti-environmental NGOS, such as industrial trade organizations, political action committees, and think-tanks, may increase their influence. While there was no evidence for such a situation in Sweden, it is theoretically possible for anti-green NGOS to have as much, or more, power as environmental groups.

Mol's fifth hypothesis addresses changes in social discourse about environmental issues. Lindén shows how young people in Sweden today may be well educated about environmental problems and express ecological values, but their behavior generally has more environmentally negative impacts than that of their parents and grandparents. This suggests that social discourses and personal values may change, but individual and collective behavior does not necessarily become more environmentally friendly as a result. Among economic actors, the discourse still seems to be more about competitiveness and the bottom line than about saving the environment or helping future generations.

To conclude, the process of defining the issues and making decisions in the 1990s and early 2000s in support of new environmental policies did, by and large, reflect an "ecological modernization" of Swedish society. The ecological modernization perspective describes the Swedish environmental reforms, but the Swedish case does not conform one hundred percent with EMT predictions. Future research should track the implementation of the reforms agreed to in the early 2000s and continue to test the empirical evidence against EMT predictions of, and prescriptions for, environmental quality improvement.

Note

Vail, Benjamin. 2008. "Ecological Modemization at Work? Environmental Policy Reform in Sweden at the Turn of the Century." Scandinavian Studies 80(1): 85–108.

References

Aulén, Gustaf. Personal correspondence. 8 November 2001.

Björck, Gunilla Högberg. Interview. Stockholm. 8 October 2001.

Bunker, Stephen G. "Raw Material and the Global Economy: Oversights and Distortions in Industrial Ecology." *Society and Natural Resources* 9.4. (1996): 419–429.

Buttel, Frederick H. "Classical Theory and Contemporary Environmental Sociology: Some Reflections on the Antecedents and Prospects for Reflexive Modernisation Theories in the Study of Environment and Society." *Environment and Global Modernity*. Eds. Gert Spaargaren, Arthur P.J. Mol, and Frederick H. Büttel. London: Sage, 2000. 17–39.

——. "Ecological Modernization as Social Theory." *Geoforum* 31 (2000): 57–65.

——. "Environmental Sociology and the Explanation of Environmental Reform." Paper presented at the Kyoto Environmental Sociology Conference. 2001.

Committee on Environmental Objectives. *The Future Environment—Our Common Responsibility: A Summary*. Stockholm. 2000.

ENDS Environment Daily. "Norway Loses Interest in Green Consumerism." 879 (21 November 2000).

——. "Sweden Legislates for Sustainability." 984 (4 May 2001).

Karlsson, Kjell-Erik. Personal correspondence. 12 November 2001.

Karlsson, Lars-Ingmar. Interview. Stockholm. 8 October 2001.

Lindbäck, Christina. Interview. Stockholm. 2 October 2001.

Lindén, Anna-Lisa. "Values of Nature in Everyday Life: Words Versus Action in Ecological Behaviour." *Sustainability the Challenge: People, Power, and the Environment*. Eds. L. Anders Sandberg and Sverker Sörlin. New York: Black Rose Books, 1998.34–41.

Lövgren, Kerstin and Bo Öhngren, eds. "Vem bestämmer om var framtida miljö.' Seminarium pa Sigunsborg." Summary from conference at Sigtuna, Sweden November 21–2, 2000. Published 2001.

Mol, Arthur P.J. "Ecological Modernization and the Global Economy." Paper presented at the Fifth Nordic Environmental Research Conference of the Ecological Modernisation Society. 2000.

———. "Ecological Modernization: Industrial Transformations and Environmental Reform." *International Handbook of Environmental Sociology.* Eds. Michael Redclift and Graham Woodgate. London: Elgar, 1997: 138–149.

——— and Frederick H. Büttel. "The Environmental State Under Pressure." *The Environmental State Under Pressure.* Eds. Frederick H. Buttel and Arthur P.J. Mol. Oxford: Elsevier, 2002. 1–11.

——— and David A. Sonnenfeld. "Ecological Modernisation Around the World: An Introduction." *Environmental Politics* 9.1 (2000): 3–14.

——— and Gert Spaargaren. "Ecological Modernisation and the Environmental State." *The Environmental State Under Pressure.* Eds. Frederick H. Buttel and Arthur P.J. Mol. Oxford: Elsevier, 2002.

Nilsson, Thomas. Interview. Stockholm. 5 October 2001.

Olsson, Goran. Interview. Stockholm. 5 October 2001.

Persson, Goran and Anna Lindh. Government Communication 1997/98:13—Ecological Sustainability. Sundsvall, Sweden. 1997. http://www\v.sweden.gov.se/content/i/C4/29/75/a7af5i8a.pdf (Accessed 27 July 2007).

Reinhard, Ylva, et al. "Evaluation of the Environmental Effects of the Swan Eco-Label—Final Analysis." Paper presented at the Seventh European Roundtable on Cleaner Production. International Institute of Environmental Economics, Lund University, Sweden. 2001.

Schnaiberg, Allan. *The Environment: From Surplus to Scarcity.* New York: Oxford, 1980.

Schnaiberg, Allan and Kenneth Alan Gould. *Environment and Society: The Enduring Conflict.* New York: St. Martin's, 1994.

Seippel, Ornulf "Ecological Modernization as a Theoretical Device: Strengths and Weaknesses." *Journal of Environmental Policy and Planning* 2 (2000): 287–302.

Spaargaren, Gert and Arthur P.J. Mol. "Sociology, Environment, and Modernity: Ecological Modernisation as a Theory of Social Change." *Society and Natural Resources* 5 (1992): 323–344.

Statistics Sweden. *Sustainable Development: Indicators for Sweden: A First Set 2001.* 2001.

Strömdahl, Inger. Interview. Stockholm. 8 October 2001.

Sustainable Sweden. Swedish Environmental Quality Objectives. 1999.

———. Tax Policy for Ecological Sustainability. 2000.

Swedish Commission on Ecologically Sustainable Development. "Sustainable Sweden: We are on Our Way." 1998.

Swedish Environmental Advisory Council. "Green Headline Indicators: Monitoring Progress towards Ecological Sustainability." 1999.

Swedish Environmental Protection Agency. De Facto 2000: Environmental Objectives: Our Generation's Responsibility. 2000.

———. "Utveklingen av miljömälen: nyheter och bakgnmd." 2001.

Swedish Ministry of the Environment. The Swedish Environmental Code. 2000a.

. The Swedish Environmental Code: A Resume of the Text of the Code and Related Ordinances. 2000b. http://www.sweden.gov.Se/content/1/c6/o2/o5/49/6736cf92.pdf (Accessed 27 July 2007).

———. The Swedish Environmental Objectives: Interim Targets and Action Strategies: Summary of Gov. Bill 2ooo/oi:i}o. 2000c. *World Commission on Environment and Development. Our Common Future.* Oxford: Oxford UP, 1987.

World Commission on Environment and Development. *Our Common Future.* Oxford: Oxford Up, 1987.

A Tale of Contrasting Trends

Three Measures of the Ecological Footprint in China, India, Japan, and The United States, 1961–2003

Richard York, Eugene A. Rosa and Thomas Dietz

Proponents of ecological modernization theory argue that technological advances, especially ones that decrease the amount of energy and materials used in production, are key to solving many of our environmental problems. However, technological solutions often have unintended consequences that become problematic in themselves. While technologies that allow for higher levels of production with the same energy inputs would appear to be unmitigated successes, Richard York, Eugene Rosa and Thomas Dietz show that the ecological footprints—the estimated land area required for sustaining use of the environment—of China, India, Japan and the United States grew since the 1960s despite improved efficiencies. They point to the Jevons Paradox, where technological advances increase rather than decrease resource use or consumption.

Introduction

There is a considerable body of research in the world-systems literature examining the structural forces that influence national-level environmental impacts (e.g., Burns, Kick, and Davis 2003; Dietz and Rosa 1997; Dietz, Rosa, and York 2007; Jorgenson 2003; Jorgenson and Burns 2007; Jorgenson and Kick 2003; Jorgenson and Rice 2005; Roberts, Grimes, and Manale 2003; Rosa, York, and Dietz 2004; Rothman 1998; York 2007; York, Rosa, and Dietz 2003, 2004). The importance of tracking the environmental performance of nations is obvious in light of the myriad environmental problems around the globe: global warming, large-scale deforestation, desertification, loss of biodiversity, and disturbances to major geochemical cycles. A substantial variety of national-level environmental indicators have been examined in the environmental social science literature, but there is no consensus regarding which indicators are the most theoretically or substantively important. The reason for this is clear; different indicators reflect different aspects of the complex, hyper-faceted global ecology.

Our primary concern here is not with identifying which indicators are the "best" measures of human pressure on the environment, but with the proper matching of the *form* of the indicator—*total* national ecological consumption and/or pollution emissions, *per capita* ecological consumption and/or pollution emissions, or ecological consumption and/or pollution emissions *per unit of GDP* (the ecological intensity of the economy)—to various theoretical or substantive tasks. Here we use variations of the Ecological Footprint (EF) as our principal indicator for theoretical reasons explained below. Three EF variations (total, per capita, and intensity) tell fundamentally different stories about the environmental performance of nations, and it is, therefore, theoretically important to distinguish among these stories. To illustrate the differences among them, we examine temporal trends in the EF of each variation for four nations which account for a large share of the world's population, economic output, and natural resource consumption: China, India, Japan, and the United States.[1] These four nations combined account for 45% of the total global EF, indicating that what happens in these nations is particularly important for the future well-being of the planet (Loh and Goldfinger 2006:3). We first explain the EF, the environmental indicator which is our focus here. We then present analyses of the trends in the EF in these four nations, with a discussion of the substantive and theoretical implications of these trends.

The Ecological Footprint

The EF, originated by Wackernagel and Rees (1996) and further developed by them and others (e.g., Chambers, Simmons, and Wackernagel 2000; Kitzes et al. 2007), is designed to assess the demands societies place on the regenerative capacity of the biosphere. The EF has been widely used in the field of ecology and in the environmental social sciences, and is generally regarded as a reliable indicator of anthropogenic pressure on the environment (Dietz et al. 2007; Jorgenson 2003; Jorgenson and Burns 2007; Jorgenson and Rice 2005; Rosa et al. 2004; Rothman 1998; York et al. 2003, 2004). The EF is calculated, much the same way that economic consumption is, by adding up the various forms of consumption in a society—food, housing, transportation, consumer goods, and services—and the waste they generate. That consumption, similar to economic accounting, is converted into a common metric. But unlike economics, which uses prices as its key indicator of value, the EF uses productive land area as its metric. The EF is based on the recognition that land is a fundamental factor on which all societies depend, since it provides living space, products and services, and a sink for wastes. Productive land is, therefore, a justifiable proxy for the demands societies place on the environment. The EF can be interpreted as a measure of the stress a nation places on natural capital and ecosystem services. The EF can be calculated for most nations because flows and consumption of resources and the production of wastes are typically recorded with reasonable accuracy in various national accounts. Human demands on the environment, then, can be converted into the biologically productive land areas necessary to provide these ecological services.

The EF is calculated by "adding up the areas (adjusted for their biological productivity) that are necessary to provide us with all the ecological services we consume" (Wackernagel et al. 1999:377). The EF is a fairly comprehensive indicator of human pressures on natural resources and ecosystem services, since it does not ignore tradeoffs among different types of environmental exploitation (e.g., wood vs. plastic consumption). National resource consumption is calculated by adding imports and subtracting exports from production.

Because of this matching of impact to locale of consumption, the EF accounting system is particularly suitable for world-systems analyses. World-systems theorists and other scholars have focused attention on how resource extraction and consumption, as well as pollution, are geographically distributed in the world-system, where the core nations commonly consume most of the resources, while the environmental degradation associated with resource extraction and polluting industries occurs in the periphery (Arrighi 2004; Brunnermeier and Levinson 2004; Bunker 1996; Frey 1998, 2003; Grimes and Kentor 2003; Hornborg 2003; Podobnik 2002). Due to its consumption-based focus, the EF does not overlook impacts that are externalized by moving production or extraction outside national borders. It, therefore, places environmental responsibility on the nations where resources are consumed—principally in the core—rather than on the ones where they are extracted.

The types of consumption delineated above are converted into the nine types of land area that support that consumption. All nine are aggregated to arrive at the total EF. The land area types are: (1) cropland, (2) grazing land, (3) forest (excluding fuel wood), (4) fishing ground, (5) built-up land, (6) the land area required to absorb carbon dioxide emissions from use of fossil fuel, (7) fuel wood, (8) hydro-power, and (9) nuclear power. The component EF measures are weighted to take into account the fact that different types of land vary in productivity. The weighting for each type of land is scaled to its productivity relative to the worldwide average productivity of all land (including water area). For example, consumption requiring one hectare of arable land would have an EF larger than consumption requiring one hectare of non-arable land, reflecting the high productivity of arable land relative to the average productivity of all land on Earth (Wackernagel et al. 2002:9268). Built-up land is treated as arable land since cities have historically grown in agriculturally rich areas. The hydro-power component is the area taken up by the reservoirs and infrastructure associated with hydro-electric dams. Each unit of energy from nuclear power is counted at par with one from fossil energy since analyses are inconclusive about the long-term land demands of nuclear power. We emphasize that the calculation of the EF for a nation is not based on its actual land area but on the land area that would be required, at global average productivities, to support its total consumption. Therefore, nations may, as many do, have footprints that are larger than their own land areas. The data in our analyses are from the Global Footprint Network (http://www.footprintnetwork.org/) 2006 Edition and were generously provided to us by Mathis Wackernagel and are used with his permission.

Understanding Environmental Trends: National Consumption, Eco-Efficiency, and Inequality

The foundational ecological economist William Stanley Jevons (2001 [1865]) identified an important paradox that, although becoming widely known today, still remains underappreciated. He noted, in the early days of England's industrial revolution, that the increasing efficiency of coal use in production was correlated with *increasing*, not decreasing, coal consumption. This is an observation of fundamental importance since it was commonly assumed then as now that technological improvements in the resource efficiency (eco-efficiency) of production (i.e., less energy and/or materials per unit of production) would typically lead to the conservation of natural resources (e.g., Hawken, Lovins, and Lovins 1999; Reijnders 1998). In short, if changes in the production system make it so that a given amount of output can be produced with fewer inputs, it seems "obvious" that the amount of inputs should decline. However, the amount of inputs often does not decline, but instead grows because the scale of production grows faster than efficiency improves. This is Jevons's insight, and it highlights the sharp distinction between efficiency in resource use and total resource consumption. These two different indicators give two different answers to the question of environmental performance, since the most "eco-efficient" businesses, industries, or economies may be the ones consuming the greatest quantities of resources and generating the most pollution. Jevons's observation raises the possibility that, far from actually contributing to resource conservation, improvements in efficiency in many contexts may actually induce the expansion of resource consumption (Clark and Foster 2001; York 2006; York and Rosa 2003).

The distinction between efficiency and total consumption is of particular relevance to theoretical debates over the effects of economic development and technological change on the environment. Some scholars uncritically assume that advances in the material and energy efficiency of economies (e.g., where more economic capital is generated per unit of energy and/or material consumption), which are often driven by technological refinements, are indicative of environmental improvements (Andersen 2002; Fan et al. 2007; Hawken et al. 1999). This assumption is invalid from the point of view of ecosystems and biophysical processes, since the amount of economic capital generated from exploiting the environment is a separate matter from the consequences of environmental exploitation for natural capital and services. Considerable empirical evidence shows that while low-income nations often are the least eco-efficient in the sense that they use a lot of resources or produce a lot of pollution *per unit of GDP*, they are also the nations that consume the least amount of resources in *absolute* and/ or *per capita* terms (Roberts and Grimes 1997; York et al. 2003, 2004).

To illustrate the limitations of focusing on efficiency we turn to an examination of trends in the EF for China, India, Japan and the United States. In Figures 5.1–5.4 we present the trends over time in each of these nations in their total EF and their EF per unit of GDP. The latter measure we refer to as "intensity," which is the inverse of efficiency (i.e., high intensity means low efficiency). Strikingly, the trends in total EF and EF intensity illustrate how a focus on efficiency or intensity is misleading. In all nations there is a distinct trend toward declining intensity (i.e., increasing efficiency), which scholars might interpret as a sign of ecological improvements. After all, between 1961 and 2003 the EF per unit of GDP declined by a factor of 8.4, 3.2, 2.2, and 1.4 in China, India, Japan, and the United States respectively.

However, the ecologically relevant observation is that the total EF—which threatens nature's capital and services—increased quite dramatically in all of these nations over this period, by a factor of 3.9, 2.1, 2.9, and 2.9 in China, India, Japan, and the United States respectively. These findings indicate that all of these nations expanded their exploitation of the environment, while simultaneously expanding their economies even more. In other words, they used more resources while simultaneously getting more economic productivity out of each unit of resources. The improvements in efficiency (i.e., declines in intensity) were

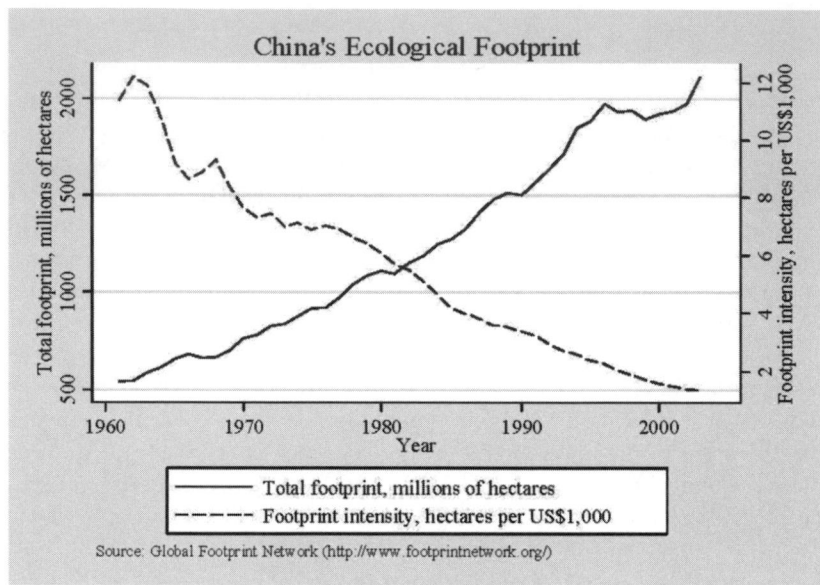

FIGURE 5.1. China's Ecological Footprint

Global Footprint Network (http://www.footprintnetwork.org/)

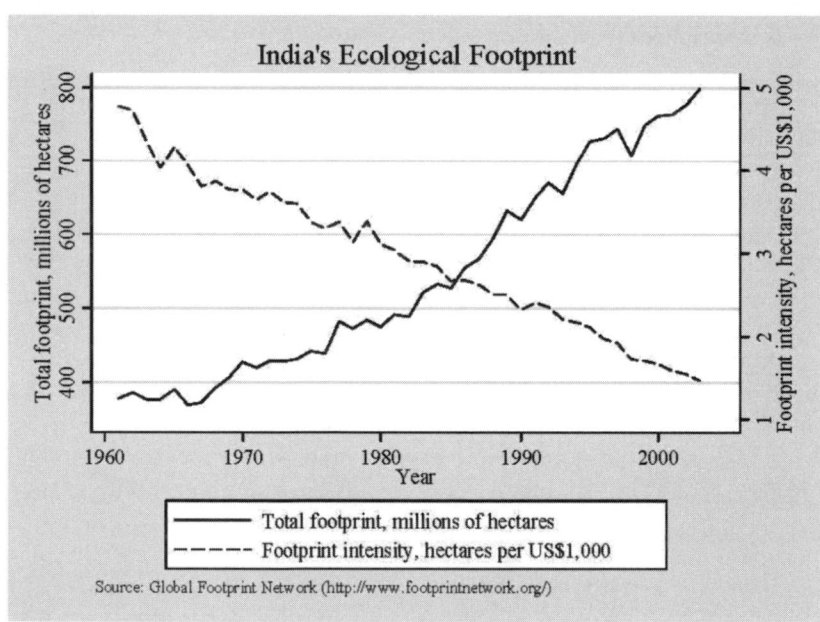

FIGURE 5.2. India's Ecological Footprint

Global Footprint Network (http://www.footprintnetwork.org/)

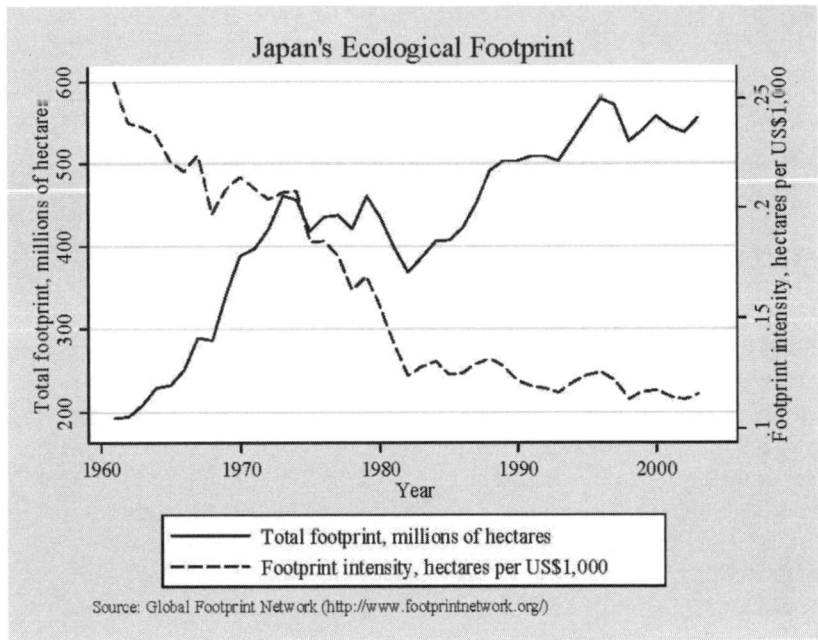

FIGURE 5.3. Japan's Ecological Footprint
Global Footprint Network (http://www.footprintnetwork.org/)

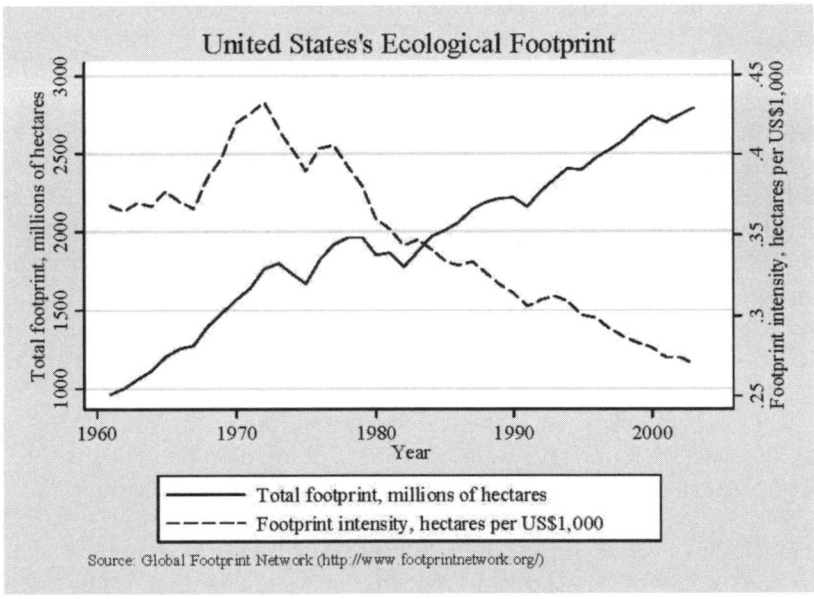

FIGURE 5.4. United States' Ecological Footprint
Global Footprint Network (http://www.footprintnetwork.org/)

clearly associated not with reductions but, rather, with steady growth in resource consumption. The two trends are likely connected in a systemic way. Following the logic of Jevons's argument, a declining ratio of EF to economic activity often translates into lower costs per unit of production—since it typically indicates fewer inputs per unit of production—making it more affordable for producers to further expand production and thereby increase their profits. China's trajectory is particularly noteworthy, for it had both the largest improvement in efficiency over the period examined here, while exhibiting the greatest increase in its total EF. In light of these considerations, it might be more appropriate to say that improvements in efficiency are an example of *economic* reform not *ecological* reform and in fact typically indicate rising environmental impacts. Thus, total impact is the most informative measure from an ecological perspective because it signals threats to nature's capital and services. In contrast, efficiency or intensity is perhaps more informative from a profit-oriented perspective. At a deeper level this difference may reflect the differences in two accounting systems: an ecological accounting system where environmental factors are the primary concern and an economic accounting system where, as externalities, environmental consequences are typically ignored.

These observations generally counter the assumption of ecological modernization theory, a prominent theory in environmental sociology, that technological transformations are the key to solving our environmental problems. Ecological modernization theorist Maurie Cohen (1997:109) argues, for example, that, "a key element in executing this [the ecological modernization] transformation is a switchover to the use of cleaner, more efficient, and less resource intensive technologies . . ." Similarly, ecological modernization proponents Fisher and Freudenberg (2001: 702) and Milanez and Bührs (2007:572) agree that the "linchpin" of the ecological modernization argument is the assertion that technological improvements can solve environmental problems. Particularly noteworthy is Andersen's (2002:1404) statement: "Because ecological modernization by definition is linked with cleaner technology and structural change . . . we can take changes in the CO_2 emissions relative to GDP as a rough indicator for the degree of ecological modernization that has taken place." In light of the findings we present here, key assumptions in ecological modernization theory appear misguided.

A third way to measure human pressure on the environment is in per capita terms. Examining per capita resource consumption removes the effects of population, assuming consumption and emissions are scaled proportionally by population size.[2] The per capita specification is perhaps most important from the perspective of global inequalities and social justice, since it allows for comparison of demands placed on the environment among the world's people and can highlight the substantial disparity in levels of consumption across nations. Figure 5.5 presents the trends in the EF per capita for the four

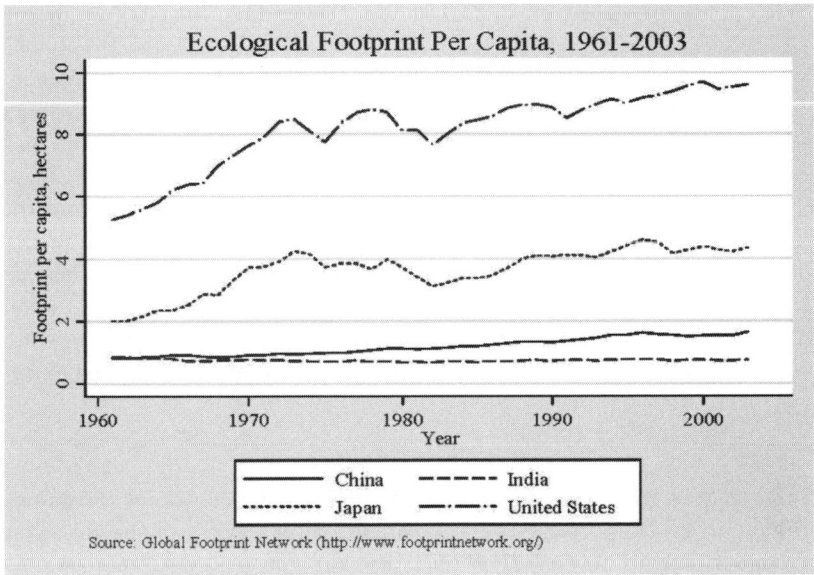

FIGURE 5.5. United States' Ecological Footprint

Global Footprint Network (http://www.footprintnetwork.org/)

nations examined here. Two observations stand out. First, while India's per capita EF stayed roughly constant from1961 to 2003, the per capita EF in each of the other three nations approximately doubled. Second, there is clearly stark inequality across nations in terms of per capita pressure on the environment. For example, in 2003 the EF per capita in the United States was approximately six times that of China and 13 times that of India. Thus, even though China and India each have very large and growing total footprints, it is clearly not because the typical person in each of those nations places a high demand on the environment relative to people in affluent nations.

In 2003, the EF intensity in both China and India was over five times greater than in the United States and about 12 times greater than in Japan. If one focused on intensity, one would conclude that the United States and, particularly, Japan are good environmental stewards relative to the two larger, poorer nations, but this would mask the fact that the average person in the both the United States and Japan have a much greater effect on the environment than the average person in either China or India.

To further explore the connections between development and environmental degradation, we statistically analyzed the connection between economic production (GDP) and the EF. . . . In all four nations the relationship between the GDP and EF is positive and inelastic (i.e., coefficients > 0 and < 1).

This indicates that as the economy of each of these nations has grown, the EF has also grown but not as fast as the economy. This type of relationship is what generates the apparently paradoxical finding discussed above where efficiency improves while the total EF grows. If an inelastic relationship such as this is hypothetically maintained indefinitely, resource consumption will continually grow while intensity declines. Thus, declines in intensity are not necessarily indicative of a move toward reductions in total consumption. It is noteworthy that the GDP coefficient is lowest in China and India, the two low-income nations, and highest in the United States, where it is close to unitary elasticity. This finding counters the common assumption that the most affluent nations will show the greatest improvements in ecological performance due to improvements in technological and other efficiencies as they continue to develop.

Conclusion

We examined trends in measures of human demands placed on nature's capital and services as indicated by three different forms of the EF—total, per capita, and per unit of GDP (intensity)—in China, India, Japan, and the United States. We found that the EF intensity of each nation's economy declined between 1961 and 2003 (i.e., the economies became more efficient in the sense that they each got more economic output per unit of EF). However, interpreting this trend as an environmental improvement is misleading because the total footprint of all four nations rose substantially over this four-decade period. Furthermore, the per capita footprint approximately doubled in China, Japan, and the United States over this period, while it remained roughly constant in India. In . . . analyses of the connection between GDP and the EF we found a positive inelastic relationship in all four nations, indicating that improvements in efficiency in each nation over this period were more than counter-balanced by increases in scale, leading the EF of each nation to grow. The key implication of these results is that improvement in efficiency is not a sign of progress toward sustainability but is paradoxically associated with increased threats to the environment.

The ecological fate of the world lies to a growing extent in India and, especially, China. Over the period examined here, China's total ecological footprint expanded four-fold to rival that of the United States. In fact, it appears that China, which builds a new coal power plant approximately every four days, has surpassed the United States to become the single largest emitter of carbon dioxide in the world (although the United States still emits much more carbon dioxide on a per capita basis) due to rapid growth in fossil fuel consumption and cement manufacturing in recent years (Cyranoski 2007; Liu and Diamond 2008). This has occurred while the carbon intensity of China's economy has declined dramatically (Fan et al. 2007), underscoring our key message here: improvements in efficiency typically do not lead to declines in environmental problems. In fact, in footprint terms China is looking more like a core nation since its footprint is larger than its land area. This is due in no small part to its vast and growing appetite for imports, such as fish, tropical wood, and manufactured goods, and to the embodied energy in these goods (Hong et al. 2007; Liu and Diamond 2005). Clearly, China's dramatic improvements in eco-efficiency and its stated commitment to tackling environmental problems have not translated into reductions in its global environmental impacts (Liu and Diamond 2008).

To achieve sustainability and avert environmental crisis the four nations we examined here and the world as a whole need to dramatically scale back their consumption of the Earth's resources. Affluent nations, like the United States and Japan, which have exceedingly high levels of per capita consumption, need to drastically reduce the demands they place on the environment and transform their political, economic, and social systems to meets people's needs without unsustainably devouring natural resources. Less affluent nations, such as China and India, need to shift their development strategies away from relentless economic expansion and focus on strategies that improve people's quality of life without escalating material consumption. It is important to note that such changes—reducing consumption in affluent nations and averting the excessive expansion of consumption in poor nations—do not necessitate inhibiting improvement of social well-being. There is ample evidence that material consumption, once beyond the level required to meet basic needs, does not have a strong association with human well-being. For example, Leiserowitz, Kates, and Parris (2005) note that in nations out of absolute poverty the association between economic development and the subjective well-being of people is very weak. Furthermore, Dietz, Rosa, and York (2007) found that there is no direct connection between environmental degradation and human well-being as measured by education and life expectancy. These findings suggest that we could further human development without worsening environmental quality if we shift our focus away from economic growth as the primary social goal and toward the enhancement of more direct features of well-being.

It is important to recognize that the size and growth of human population plays a major role in the expansion of impacts on the environment. For example, as we show here, while India's per capita EF remained roughly stable, its total EF more than doubled, tracking the growth in its population. Likewise, China has such a large total EF, rivaling that of the United States, despite still having a low per capita EF by global standards, because it has well over one billion people. Addressing the population problem can be an important part of a progressive political agenda aimed at improving quality of life since the most effective ways to reduce fertility rates include improving the status and education of women, reducing infant mortality, eliminating absolute poverty, and providing all people with access to safe, effective and affordable birth control (Cohen 1995). Thus, what is needed to reduce human impact on the global environment—the curtailing of overconsumption and the reduction of fertility rates—can be part of an agenda aimed at directly *improving* human quality of life.

In light of the continuing high levels of consumption in affluent nations, the rapid economic growth in many developing nations in recent years, and the severity of environmental problems the world faces—the most noteworthy of which may be global climate change—averting ecological crisis is arguably humanity's greatest challenge for the twenty-first century. To meet this challenge it is imperative that we move away from the unrealistically optimistic assumption that improvements in the efficiency of economies alone are likely to solve environmental problems. In the face of continued economic and population growth, that assumption is not only misleading, it is also dangerous.

Notes

Richard York, Eugene Rosa, Thomas Dietz, "A Tale of Contrasting Trends: Three Measures of the Ecological Footprint in China, India, Japan and the United States, 1961–2003," in Journal of World-Systems Research 15 (2), pp. 134–146. Reprinted by permission of American Sociological Association.

1. Based on the most recent year of the data we analyze here, the United States, China, and India have the three largest ecological footprints in the world (in that order) and Japan has the fifth largest, behind Russia. We do not examine Russia here since it has only been an independent nation since 1991. China, India, and the United States have the three largest populations in the world (in that order) and Japan has the ninth. The United States and Japan have the two largest economies in the world (in that order), China the fifth, and India the thirteenth.

2. A series of analyses have found that the population elasticity of the EF is about 1.0 (Dietz et al. 2007; Rosa et al. 2004; York et al. 2003) thus justifying the use of per capita measures.

References

Andersen, Mikael Skou. 2002. "Ecological Modernization or Subversion? The Effects of Europeanization on Eastern Europe." *American Behavioral Scientist* 45(9):1394–1416.

Arrighi, Giovanni. 2004. "Spatial and Other 'Fixes' of Historical Capitalism." *Journal of World-Systems Research* 10(2):527–539.

Brunnermeier, Smita B. and Arik Levinson. 2004. Examining the Evidence on Environmental Regulations and Industry Location. *Journal of Environment & Development* 13(1): 6–41.

Bunker, Stephen G. 1996. Raw Material and the Global Economy: Oversights and Distortions in Industrial ecology." *Society and Natural Resources* 9:419–429.

Burns, Thomas J, Edward L. Kick, and Byron L. Davis. 2003. "Theorizing and Re-thinking Linkages Between the Natural Environment and the Modern World-System: Deforestation in the Late 20th Century." *Journal of World-Systems Research* 9(2):357–390.

Chambers, Nicky, Craig Simmons, and Mathis Wackernagel. 2000. *Sharing Nature's Interest: Ecological Footprints as an indicator of sustainability.* London: Earthscan.

Clark, Brett and John Bellamy Foster. 2001. William Stanley Jevons and The Coal Question: an Introduction to Jevons's 'Of the Economy of Fuel.' *Organization & Environment* 14(1):93–98.

Cohen, Joel E. 1995. *How Many People Can the Earth Support?* New York: W. W. Norton & Co.

Cohen, Maurie J. 1997. "Risk Society and Ecological Modernization: Alternative Visions for Post-Industrial Nations." *Futures* 29(2):105–119.

Cyranoski, David. 2007. "China Struggles to Square Growth and Emissions." *Nature* 446(26):954–955.

Dietz, Thomas and Eugene A. Rosa. 1997. "Effects of Population and Affluence on CO_2 Emissions." *Proceedings of the National Academy of Sciences of the USA* 94:175–179.

Dietz, Thomas, Eugene A. Rosa, and Richard York. 2007. "Driving the Human Ecological Footprint." *Frontiers in Ecology and the Environment* 5(1): 13–18.

Fan, Ying, Lan-Cui Liu, Gang Wu, Hsien-Tang Tsai, and Yi-Ming Wei. 2007. "Changes in Carbon Intensity in China: Empirical Findings from 1980–2003." *Ecological Economics* 62(3–4):683–691.

Fisher, Dana R. and William R. Freudenburg. 2001. "Ecological Modernization and its Critics: Assessing the Past and Looking Toward the Future." *Society and Natural Resources* 14(8):701–709.

Frey, R. Scott. 1998. "The Export of Hazardous Industries to the Peripheral Zones of the World-System." *Journal of Developing Societies* 14:66–81.

———. 2003. "The Transfer of Core-Based Hazardous Production Processes to the Export Processing Zones of the Periphery: The Maquiladora Centers of Northern Mexico." *Journal of World-Systems Research* 9(2):317–354.

Grimes, Peter and Jeffrey Kentor. 2003. "Exporting the Greenhouse: Foreign Capital Penetration and CO_2 emissions 1980–1996." *Journal of World-Systems Research* 9(2): 261–275."

Hawken, Paul, Amory Lovins, and L. Hunter Lovins. 1999. *Natural Capitalism: Creating the Next Industrial Revolution.* New York: Little, Brown and Company.

Hong, Li, Zhang Pei Dong, He Chunyu, and Wang Gang. 2007. Evaluating the Effects of Embodied Energy in International Trade on Ecological Footprints in China. *Ecological Economics* 62:136–148.

Hornborg, Alf. 2003. "Cornucopia or Zero-Sum Game? The Epistemology of Sustainability." *Journal of World-Systems Research* 9(2): 205–216.

Jevons, William Stanley. 2001 [1865]. "Of the Economy of Fuel." Organization & Environment 14(1):99–104.

Jorgenson, Andrew K. 2003. "Consumption and Environmental Degradation: A Cross-National Analysis of the Ecological Footprint." *Social Problems* 50: 374–394.

Jorgenson, Andrew K. and Thomas J. Burns. 2007. "The Political-Economic Causes of Change in the Ecological Footprints of Nations, 1991–2001." *Social Science Research* 36: 834–853.

Jorgenson, Andrew K. and Edward L. Kick. 2003. "Globalization and the Environment." *Journal of World-Systems Research* 9(2):195–203.

Jorgenson, Andrew K. and James Rice. 2005. "Structural Dynamics of International Trade and Material Consumption: A Cross-National Study of the Ecological Footprints of Less-Developed Countries." *Journal of World-Systems Research* 11:57–77.

Kitzes, Justin, Audrey Peller, Steve Goldfinger, and Mathis Wackernagel. 2007. "Current Methods for Calculating National Ecological Footprint Accounts." *Science for Environment & Sustainable Society* 4:1–9.

Leiserowitz, Anthony A., Robert W. Kates, and Thomas M. Parris. 2005. "Do Global Attitudes and Behaviors Support Sustainable Development?" *Environment* 47(9): 23–38.

Liu, Jianguo and Jared Diamond. 2005. "China's Environment in a Globalizing World." *Nature* 435:1179–1186.

———. 2008. "Revolutionizing China's Environmental Protection." *Science* 319: 37–38.

Loh, Jonathan and Steven Goldfinger. 2006. *Living Planet Report 2006*. Gland, Switzerland: WWF International.

Milanez, Bruno and Ton Bührs. 2007. "Marrying Strands of Ecological Modernisation: A Proposed Framework." *Environmental Politics* 16(4):565–583.

Podobnik, Bruce. 2002. "Global Energy Inequalities: Exploring the Long-Term Implications." *Journal of World-Systems Research* 8(2):252–274.

Reijnders, Lucas. 1998. "The Factor 'x' Debate: Setting Targets for Eco-Efficiency." *Journal of Industrial Ecology* 2 (1):13–22.

Roberts, J. Timmons and Peter E. Grimes. 1997. "Carbon Intensity and Economic Development 1962–1991: A Brief Exploration of the Environmental Kuznets Curve." *World Development* 25:191–198.

Roberts, J. Timmons, Peter E. Grimes, and Jodie L. Manale. 2003. "Social Roots of Global Environmental Change: A World-Systems Analysis of Carbon Dioxide Emissions." *Journal of World-Systems Research* 9(2):277–315.

Rosa, Eugene A., Richard York, and Thomas Dietz. 2004. "Tracking the Anthropogenic Drivers of Ecological Impacts." *Ambio* 33(8):509–512.

Rothman, Dale S. 1998. "Environmental Kuznets Curves — Real Progress or Passing the Buck?" *Ecological Economics* 25:177–194.

Wackernagel, Mathis, Larry Onisto, Patricia Bello, Alejandro Callejas Linares, Ina Susana Lopez Falfan, Jesus Mendez Garcia, Ana Isabel Suarez Guerrero, and Ma. Guadalupe Suarez Guerrero. 1999. "National Natural Capital Accounting with the Ecological Footprint Concept." *Ecological Economics* 29:375–390.

Wackernagel, Mathis and William Rees. 1996. *Our Ecological Footprint: Reducing Human Impact on the Earth*. Gabriola Island, B.C: New Society Publishers.

Wackernagel, Mathis, Niels B. Schulz, Diana Deumling, Alejandro Callenjas Linares, Martin Jenkins, Valerie Kapos, Chad Monfreda, Jonathan Loh, Norman Myers, Richard Norgaard, and Jorgen Randers. 2002. "Tracking the Ecological Overshoot of the Human Economy." *Proceedings of the National Academy of Sciences of the USA* 99(14):9266–9271.

York, Richard. 2007. "Structural Influences on Energy Production in South and East Asia, 1971–2002." *Sociological Forum* 22(4):532–554.

York, Richard. 2006. "Ecological Paradoxes: William Stanley Jevons and the Paperless Office." *Human Ecology Review* 13(2):143–147.

York, Richard and Eugene A. Rosa. 2003. "Key Challenges to Ecological Modernization Theory: Institutional Efficacy, Case Study Evidence, Units of Analysis, and the Pace of Eco-Efficiency." *Organization & Environment* 16(3):273–288.

York, Richard, Eugene A. Rosa, and Thomas Dietz. 2004. "The Ecological Footprint Intensity of National Economies." *Journal of Industrial Ecology* 8(4):139–154.

York, Richard, Eugene A. Rosa, and Thomas Dietz. 2003. "Footprints on the Earth: The Environmental Consequences of Modernity." *American Sociological Review* 68(2):279–300.

PART III

Environmental Inequalities

6

Breaking the Food Chains
An Investigation of
Food Justice Activism
Alison Hope Alkon and
Kari Marie Norgaard

The three pieces in this section explore how race, class, and gender intersect with environmental issues. Since the 1980s, grassroots activists have responded to environmental inequalities by launching an effort to change community, governmental and corporate practices that endanger the health of people of color and low-income communities. These activists have experienced a wide range of successes, from resisting unwanted land uses at the local level to changing federal regulations at the national level.

In recent decades, scholarship on environment-related inequalities has flourished and new issues and ideas continue to be added to the environmental justice framework. In this next piece, Alison Alkon and Kari Norgaard describe food justice activism, which seeks to ensure access to healthy, environmentally sustainable and culturally appropriate food.

This article examines the concept of food justice through comparative case studies of two racially and spatially distinct Northern California communities. Food justice places the need for food security—access to healthy, affordable, culturally appropriate food—in the contexts of institutional racism, racial formation, and racialized geographies. Our analysis highlights the ability of food justice to serve as a theoretical and political bridge between existing work on sustainable agriculture, food insecurity, and environmental justice.

Ecology and Equity: Building Theoretical Bridges

While environmental justice advocates have long argued that low-income people and people of color suffer disproportionately from the burdens of environmental degradation, recent scholarship has also begun to emphasize the problem of disproportionate access to environmental benefits. Attention to environmental benefits helps the environmental justice movement to solidify its connection to larger democratic projects such as eco-populism (Szasz 1994), ecological democracy (Faber 1998), and just sustainability (Agyeman 2005). The sustainable agriculture movement, on the other hand, focusing primarily on the environmental benefits of fertile soil, clean water, and pesticide-free food, has often ignored the role of race in structuring agriculture in the United States (Allen 2004). Although the term sustainability includes both ecological protection and social justice by definition, sustainable agriculture activists have primarily aligned themselves with the environmental rather than environmental justice movement (Alkon 2008). Following a brief review of existing literature within sustainable agriculture and environmental justice, we offer two case studies in which activists situate their own lack of food access within historical processes of institutional racism, racial identity formation, and racialized geographies.

Bringing Social Justice Back into Sustainability

The sustainable agriculture movement has traditionally focused on technical solutions to problems of ecologically devastating food production, making use of the work of university extension agents and agroecologists. . . .

The sustainable agriculture movement consists of actors working through such diverse strategies as direct marketing initiatives (farmers markets and community-supported agriculture), urban and/or self-sufficient production (urban farms, community and backyard gardens), and policy work (food policy councils, attempts to influence the farm bill). The most prominent sectors of the movement aim to ensure the economic success of small, regional, organic farmers by encouraging consumer support for locally grown organic food.

Several scholars, however, critique the sustainable agriculture movement's ability to make sweeping social changes in the agricultural sector . . . [T]he changes advocated by the movement come through specific techniques and practices that do not disrupt the agribusiness system (Buttel 1997). As organic farming has become more popular and profitable, it has adapted many characteristics of the industrial agriculture it once sought to replace, constraining the sustainable agriculture movement's ability to advocate for progressive change (Guthman 2004). Social justice issues are also marginalized because of the emphasis on the economic success of farmers (Allen 2004). The movement's imperative that consumers pay the "true" cost of food, rather than allowing environmental costs to be externalized, and its association with fine dining and European food traditions, demonstrate its association with white privilege and affluence (Alkon and McCullen forthcoming). Sustainable agriculture, at least as it is currently practiced, cannot transform the dominant agribusiness system.

While scholarly critiques of the sustainable agriculture movement call broadly for more attention to social justice issues, the concept of food justice contextualizes disparate access to healthy food within a broader and more historicized framework of institutional racism. Because of its focus on racialized access to the environmental benefit of healthy food, food justice can link sustainable agriculture to environmental justice theory and practice.

Theorizing Food in Environmental Justice Scholarship

In the last two decades, environmental justice scholars have successfully documented the unequal distribution of environmental toxics through which low-income people and people of color bear the health burdens of environmental degradation (United Church of Christ 1987). These communities have organized numerous campaigns against the companies responsible (Allen 2003; Brown and Mikkelsen 1997; Bullard 1990; Sze 2006). Similarities in these cases shed light on an environmental justice frame (Capek 1993) or paradigm (Taylor 1997, 2000), linking distribution of environmental toxins to a culturally resonant (Gamson and Modigliani 1989) civil rights rhetoric.

While the environmental justice movement is best known for protests against site discrimination, many activists adopt a much broader approach. Often grounded in their own experiences as victims of environmental racism, activists have worked toward pollution prevention (Szasz 1994) and the internalization of the costs of production by the companies responsible (Faber 1998) so that no community should suffer the health effects of environmental toxics. Constantly looking to broaden the environmental justice frame through the inclusion of issues generally ignored by what Brulle (2000) terms the "reform" environmental movement, activists have created a complex approach incorporating the many environmental and social justice factors affecting the places where low-income people and people of color live, work and play (Alston 1991).

Despite the central importance of food to human and environmental health, and the broad-reaching frame of the environmental justice movement, the literature devotes limited attention to food access. While Gottlieb and

Fisher (1996) first highlighted an environmental justice approach to food security more than a decade ago, few environmental justice scholars have incorporated food or nutrition in their analyses. . . . The concept of food justice, offered as an extension of the more inclusive idea of environmental justice, sheds light on how the food system has been shaped by institutionalized racism.

Research Approach

Data on the West Oakland Food Collaborative (WOFC) came from three primary sources: participant observation, semistructured interviews, and a survey of customers at the West Oakland Farmers Market.[1] During 18 months of participant observation, Alkon took on a variety of roles including regular customer, volunteer gardener, researcher, and observer at the farmers market, WOFC meetings, and events and activities organized by WOFC member organizations. Copious notes were taken and later coded, allowing patterns to emerge. Eighteen in-depth interviews were conducted with WOFC participants and farmers market vendors. Interviews lasting approximately 1 hour were recorded and transcribed. The survey was administered to 100 farmers market customers over the course of 3 weeks through a sample of convenience.

Norgaard began her research in 2003 at the request of the Karuk Tribe. Tribal members had been less than successful articulating their concerns through the Federal Energy Regulatory Commission process on the relicensing of the Klamath River Hydroproject. The tribe sought to seek greater scientific backing for their claims. Data on the Karuk case study are drawn from four main sources: archival material, in-depth interviews with Karuk tribal members, Karuk medical records, and the 2005 Karuk Health and Fish Consumption Survey. The 2005 Karuk Health and Fish Consumption Survey was distributed to adult tribal members within the ancestral territory in the spring of 2005. The survey had a response rate of 38 percent, a total of 90 individuals. Additional medical data has been obtained from relevant federal, state, and county records (Norgaard 2005).

Culture and Agriculture:
The West Oakland Food Collaborative

In an old, partially refurbished Victorian home in West Oakland, now home to the Prescott Joseph Community Center, a group of activists sit around a long wood table discussing projects and strategies for the procurement of food justice. While the group is by no means entirely African American, discussions of institutional racism and inequality pervade many aspects of their work. Among other projects, those attending WOFC meetings run school and community gardens, cooking programs, and food distribution efforts focused on supplying healthy food to this low-income, predominantly African American neighborhood. The most prominent example of the WOFC's work is a weekly farmers market through which African American farmers and home-based business people sell organic produce, flowers, homemade jams, sweets, and beauty products.[2] Farmers markets are most commonly associated with the sustainable agriculture movement's promotion of small, local farmers. This market, however, emphasizes antiracism. Indeed, one market vendor described the market's primary purpose as "empowering black people."

Although the produce featured at the market is much less expensive than in wealthier neighborhoods, it struggles to attract customers unaccustomed to this kind of shopping. While the market is extremely small, it is a lively place. Customers and vendors, the majority of whom know each other by name, catch up on the week's events while shopping for the week's provisions. The farmers market celebrates African American culture through the products featured (such as black-eyed peas, greens, and yams), the music played (mostly soul and funk) and the special events celebrated (such as Black History Month and Juneteenth). The radical potential of merging racial identity formation with sustainable agriculture is recognized by one market farmer, who claims "this market fights the systems that are in place to keep down sharecroppers like my father and grandfather." Like other environmental justice efforts, the WOFC emphasizes racism and inequality, connecting environmental issues to the lived experiences of low-income people and people of color (Bullard 1990; Novotny 2000).

One of the most egregious instances of racism highlighted by the farmers market is the discrimination experienced by African American farmers. In the words of one vendor, the West Oakland farmers market is different from others because "we have black farmers . . . you don't see a lot of black farmers." WOFC members attribute the historic decline of black farmers nationwide to the United States Department of Agriculture (USDA)'s denial of loans, subsidies, and other support that enabled white farmers to transition to mechanized agriculture (Gilbert, Sharp, and Felin 2002).[3] In 1997, the USDA settled a class-action lawsuit on this issue, though black farmers and their descendents have reported difficulties claiming their portion of the settlement (Wood and Gilbert 2000). Discrimination against black farmers created an agricultural sector dominated by whites and deprived African Americans of a source of wealth and access to economic and environmental benefits.

The goal of the West Oakland Farmers Market is, in the words of one prominent WOFC member, "to connect black farmers to the black community." This view is reflected by the market's customers; a majority of those surveyed (52%) claim that support for black farmers is their most important reason for market attendance.[4]

Not only have African Americans been stripped of their abilities to produce healthy, culturally appropriate food, they are also unable to purchase similar items. WOFC members, along with food justice activists in many parts of the United States, popularize the term "food desert" in order to describe the lack of locally available healthy food (Wrigley, Margetts, and Whelan 2002). Many scholars have observed a positive correlation between the existence of grocery stores and income (Chung and Meyers 1999) and a negative one between grocery stores and the percentage of African American residents (Morland et al. 2002).

One WOFC participant, currently organizing to open a worker-owned grocery store, describes the obstacles residents face in obtaining fresh food:

> West Oakland has 40,000 people and only one grocery store. [The many] corner stores sell generic canned goods. You have that option and then the fast food chains is the other option. So what people have the option to buy is putting more and more chemicals and additives and hormones and all of these things into their bodies.

With nearly 1.5 times as many corner liquor stores as the city average (California Alcoholic Beverage Control [CABC] 2006) as well as an abundance of fast food establishments, West Oakland is typical of low-income, African American food deserts in other cities (Block, Scribner, and DeSalvo 2004; LaVeist and Wallace 2000). WOFC members describe the process through which large grocery stores closed urban locations in favor of suburban ones as "supermarket redlining," likening it to racist lending policies and further linking their own work to a broad and historicized antiracist resistance. Through food justice activism, WOFC members link their own food insecurity to institutional racism and its historic and present-day effects on the built environment (Kobayashi and Peake 2000; Massey and Denton 1998)

Not surprisingly, residents of this food desert experience high rates of diet-related health problems such as diabetes. WOFC members racialize and politicize diabetes in much the same way that environmental justice activists portray asthma (Sze 2006). In the words of one food justice activist, who recently relocated to Oakland and became involved in many of the WOFC's projects, "diabetes kills more people in our communities than crack!" (Lappe and Terry 2006) In Alameda County, African Americans, more than other racial groups,[5] are twice as likely to suffer from diabetes (CDC 2002).

WOFC members link these health disparities to the lack of locally available healthy food.

· · ·

Because this analysis ties a place-based instance of environmental injustice to a more systemic and historicized understanding of racism, the WOFC's solution focuses on local food and local economics rather than attempts to attract corporate economic development. In the words of one farmers market vendor: "I don't want Safeway or Albertsons. They abandoned the inner city. They sell poison. They pay crap wages. Independent business is the most important thing." Instead of chain grocery stores, the WOFC emphasizes "community self-sufficiency" and the ability of marginalized communities to provide, at least partially, for themselves. One WOFC participant describes the goal of her activism in the following way:

> [It's about] building a community that takes care of each other's needs. And we can self sustain outside of the dominant system. . . . We want to buy and sell from each other . . . in a way that helps us sustain our neighborhoods or our communities. That's different than consuming in a way that sustains a mega business that's separate and distinct from us.

The WOFC's projects aim to address the needs of low-income, predominantly African American, West Oakland residents through the development of local food and local economic systems.

The West Oakland Food Collaborative's food justice activism combines antiracism with the creation of a local food system. For this reason, their case offers important insights on the development of an environmental justice approach to food and its consequences for theorizing and achieving environmental justice and sustainable agriculture.

Battling Corporate River Management on the Klamath

In the Northern part of the state, the Karuk Tribe of California has mobilized its demand for food justice by lobbying the federal government to block the relicensing of four dams on the Klamath River. These dams prevent the Karuk tribe from sustaining themselves on their traditional foods, which include salmon, lamprey, steelhead, and sturgeon (Norgaard 2005). In addition to lobbying, tribal members have engaged in a variety of protest strategies including working with commercial fishermen and environmental organizations to achieve greater visibility; pleading their case at meetings of the dam's multinational corporate owners, directors, and shareholders; and participating in numerous regional protest activities.

The Klamath River dams disconnect the Karuk from their food sources in several ways. The dams degrade water quality by creating standing water where blue green algae blooms deplete oxygen and create toxic conditions downstream. Levels of the liver toxin mycrocystin were the highest recorded of any water body in the United States and 4,000 times the World Health Organization (WHO) safety limit in 2005 (Karuk Tribe of California 2006). The dams lack fish ladders or other features that would allow the passage of native salmon. When the lowest dam was built, Spring Chinook Salmon lost access to 90 percent of their spawning habitat. Around this time, most Karuk families reported the loss of these fish as a significant food source.

One tribal member describes the devastating effect of the dams on the Karuk food system as follows:

> A healthy riverine system has a profound effect on the people on the river. I have six children. If every one of those kids went down and fished and caught a good healthy limit . . . you could pretty much fill a freezer and have nice good fish all the way through the year. But now, without a healthy riverine system, the economy down here on the lower river is pretty much devastated. All the fishing community is devastated by the unhealthy riverine system.
>
> —(Ron Reed, Traditional Karuk Fisherman)

The dams and their ensuing environmental degradation have wreaked havoc on the food needs of the tribe.

The Karuk tribe articulates their right to traditional foods not only as an issue of food insecurity but of food justice. They locate their current food needs in the history of genocide, lack of land rights, and forced assimilation that have so devastated this and other Native American communities. These processes have prevented tribal members from carrying out land management techniques necessary to food attainment.

This tragic history provides context to understand the ability of the federal government to license a dam to a multinational corporation within Karuk territory. It is the dams themselves, however, that have had the most sweeping and immediate effect on Karuk food access. Until recently, Karuk people have experienced relatively high rates of subsistence living. Elder tribal members recall their first visit to the grocery store:

> I can remember first going to the store with mom when I was about in the fifth and sixth grade and going in there and it was so strange to buy, you know, get stuff out of the store. Especially cans of vegetables, like green beans and stuff; Mom used to can all that. And bread. I was about 6 years old when I saw my first loaf of bread in the store. That was really quite a change, I'll tell you.
>
> —(Blanche Moore, Karuk Tribal Member)

Traditional fish consumption for Karuk people is estimated at 450 pounds per person per year, more than a pound per day (Hewes 1973). Up until the

1980s many Karuk people, especially those from traditional families, ate salmon up to three times per day when the fish were running. Karuk survival has been directly linked to this important environmental resource.

When the dams were built, the Karuk tribe was stripped of access to much of its traditional food as well as the ability to manage the river ecosystem. In contrast to the traditional diet, present-day Karuk people consume less than 5 pounds of salmon per person per year. Self-report data from the 2005 Karuk Health and Fish Consumption Survey indicate that over 80 percent of households were unable to gather adequate amounts of eel, salmon, or sturgeon to fulfill their family needs (Norgaard 2005). As of 2006, so few fish existed that even ceremonial salmon consumption is now limited.

Like West Oakland residents, members of the Karuk tribe cannot purchase the food they once procured through a direct relationship with the nonhuman environment. Most Karuk do not believe in buying or selling salmon. Even if tribal members were willing to buy salmon, replacing subsistence fishing with store-bought salmon would be prohibitively expensive. Replacement cost analysis conducted in the spring of 2005 puts the cost of purchasing salmon at over $4,000 per tribal member per year (Stercho 2005). In the communities within the ancestral territory, this amount would represent over half of the average per capita annual income. While the Karuk are denied access to an environmental benefit because of institutional racism, they cannot replace that benefit through purchase because of poverty.

As in West Oakland, healthy, culturally appropriate food is not available within a convenient distance to tribal members. Tribal members must drive up to 40 miles each way to acquire commodity foods and up to 80 miles each way to shop at supermarkets. . . .

Because of the greatly reduced ability of tribal members to provide healthy food to their community, the Karuk experience extremely high rates of hunger and disease. Recent data from University of California at Los Angeles (UCLA)'s California Health Interview Survey (Diamant et al. 2005) show that Native people have the highest rates of both food insecurity (37.2%) and hunger (16.9%) in California (Harrison et al. 2002). The estimated diabetes rate for the Karuk Tribe is 21 percent, approximately four times the U.S. average of 4.9 percent. The estimated rate of heart disease for the Karuk Tribe is 39.6 percent, three times the U.S. average (Norgaard 2005).

Diabetes is described as a new disease among this population and is the consequence of drastic lifestyle and cultural changes (Joe and Young 1993). Tribal members account for both the severity and the sudden onset of diet-related health problems:

> Our people never used to be fat. Our people never used to have these health problems that we are encountering today. Diabetes is probably the

biggest one but not the only one. The ramifications of the food that we eat and the lives that we live. High blood pressure is another one. I have high blood pressure. My mother had diabetes. I'm borderline, I'm pretty sure. You can certainly tell that our people never used to be fat. Now you can't hardly find a skinny person around.

—(David Arwood, Traditional Karuk Fisherman)

Tribal members posit this dramatic shift as a consequence of their denied access to salmon and other traditional foods.

The Karuk tribe is the first in the nation to deploy the concept of food justice in order to link declining salmon populations caused by the dams with high incidences of diabetes and other diet-related diseases. The tribe frames declined river health and the ensuing loss of salmon as a direct result of institutional racism. The Karuk have been stripped of access to an important resource as well as the ability to manage their ancestral land. Because of cost and distance, the tribe cannot purchase what it once produced. Tribe members must rely on locally available unhealthy alternatives and commodity foods— or in too many cases, go without. Because of this process of denied access to traditional or replacement foods, diabetes researcher Kue Young (1997:164) writes that the "resolution of the major health problems of Native Americans requires redressing the underlying social, cultural and political causes of those problems." In other words, food access must be connected to the historical process of institutional racism that created food insecurity. Tribal activists make this connection through the concept of food justice.

Conclusion: Political Implications and Alliance Building

Members of the West Oakland Food Collaborative and the Karuk Tribe clearly share similar experiences. Through access to land and water, black farmers and Karuk fishermen once provided the bulk of their community's food needs. Today, West Oakland residents and Karuk tribal members live in food deserts. They cannot purchase what they once produced on their own. Activists link this lack of food access to their community's elevated rates of diabetes and other diet-related illnesses. Furthermore, both groups frame their grassroots struggles for food justice as attempts to reclaim their ability to produce and consume food.

Theoretically, food justice links food insecurity to institutional racism and racialized geography, reshaping thinking within the fields of sustainable agriculture and environmental justice. Scholars and activists in the sustainable agriculture movement have done well to challenge the corporate control of food production systems and identify resulting impacts to the long-term viability of soils and surrounding ecosystems. As food is increasingly controlled by large corporations, ecosystems suffer and communities have less control over local foods. Yet sustainable agriculture scholars and activists have not yet understood the ways that race shapes a community's ability to produce and consume food.

Moreover, a food justice framework links food access to broader questions of power and political efficacy. While many sustainable agriculture advocates and scholars implicitly assume that all communities have the ability to choose ecologically produced food, the concept of food justice can help to illuminate the race and class privilege masked by this approach. Access to healthy food is shaped not only by the economic ability to purchase it, but also by the historical processes through which race has come to affect who lives where and who has access to what kind of services. Because it highlights institutional racism and racialized geographies, food justice may therefore encourage the sustainable agriculture movement to embrace a more meaningful approach to social justice.

. . .

. . . [W]e hope the concept of food justice will contribute to environmental justice work in the following ways. In articulating a demand for access to healthy food, these cases contribute to the developing focus on racially stratified access to environmental benefits within environmental justice. Unfortunately, it is not only the extent of environmental degradation that has intensified in the past half century, but also the degree of social inequality. For this reason it will become more and more important for the environmental justice movement to place attention on access to environmental benefits. Additionally, because food is often central to communities' collective cultural identities, the concept of food justice can illuminate links between environmental justice activism and the process of racial identity formation. These dimensions address both Pellow's (2004) call for scholarly attention to process and history and Pulido's (2000) injunction to connect environmental justice to social science analyses of race.

As an issue, food justice may help environmental justice activists to galvanize a more proactive, solution-oriented approach that can complement its political pressure for government and corporate responsibility for localized epidemics and toxic pollutants. While some environmental justice organizations have moved toward a "pollution prevention" perspective, they have only begun to envision alternatives to environmental injustice conversant with traditional notions of environmental sustainability (Agyeman 2005; Pellow and Brulle 2005; Peña 2003). Because the sustainable agriculture movement has historically privileged the construction of alternative food systems over other kinds of activism, this issue can add an additional strategy to the environmental justice lexicon. Finally, it is also our hope that through the use of these case studies, activists and policymakers working on food security will understand the institutionalized nature of denied access to healthy foods in these communities.

Notes

Alkon, Alison Hope and Kari Norgaard. 2009. "Breaking the Food Chains: An Investigation of Food Justice Activism." *Sociological Inquiry* 79(3): 289–305. Reprinted by permission of John Wiley and Sons.

1. During my fieldwork, the farmers market was run by the WOFC. It had originally been founded by David Roach, whose Mo' Better Foods was one of the WOFC's member organizations. After my fieldwork, Roach became the farmers market's sole manager.

2. While the WOFC focuses on African American farmers, Mexican, Hmong, and more recently, white women farmers have also been included. Nonfarming vendors are overwhelmingly African American residents of either West Oakland, or nearby predominantly African American neighborhoods. The WOFC's promotional activities emphasize the African American farmers while treating nonblack farmers as allies. While produce sold at the farmers market and other WOFC projects need not be certified organic, recognizing that the cost of certification is often prohibitive, farmers use the phrase chemical-free to connote organic growing practices.

3. Although the decline of African American farmers took place in the rural south, it has direct bearing on African Americans living in West Oakland. Each of the African American farmers, as well as many of the other vendors, is directly descended from southern sharecroppers.

4. Other choices included good quality food, support for local farmers and small businesspeople, convenient location, and atmosphere.

5. Native Americans were not included in this data.

References

Adamson, Joni, Mei Mei Evans, and Rachel Stein. 2002. *The Environmental Justice Reader: Politics, Poetics and Pedagogy.* Tucson, AZ: University of Arizona Press.

Agyeman, Julian. 2005. *Sustainable Communities and the Challenge of Environmental Justice.* Cambridge, MA: MIT Press.

Alkon, Alison Hope. 2008. "Paradise or Pavement: The Social Construction Of The Environment In Two Urban Farmers Markets." *Local Environment: The Journal of Justice and Sustainability* 13(3):271–89.

Alkon, Alison Hope and Christie Grace McCullen. Forthcoming. "Whiteness and Farmers Markets: Performances, Perpetuations . . . Contestations?" *Antipode.*

Allen, Barbara. 2003. *Uneasy Alchemy: Citizens and Experts in Louisiana's Chemical Corridor Disputes.* Cambridge, MA: MIT Press.

Allen, Patricia. 2004. *Together at the Table: Sustainability and Sustenance in the American Agri-Foods Movement.* University Park, PA: Pennsylvania State University Press.

Alston, Dana. 1991. "*Taking Back Our Lives: A Report to the Panos Institute on Environment, Community Development and Race in the United States*." Washington, DC: Panos Institute.

Beus, C. E. and R. E. Dunlap. 1990. "Conventional Versus Alternative Agriculture: The Paradigmatic Roots of the Debate." *Rural Sociology* 55(4):590–616.

Block, Jason P., Richard A. Scribner, and Karen B. DeSalvo. 2004. "Fast Food, Race/ Ethnicity, and Income: A Geographic Analysis." *American Journal of Preventative Medicine* 27:211–17.

Brown, Phil and Edwin J. Mikkelsen. 1997. *No Safe Place*. Berkeley, CA: University of California Press. Brulle, Robert J. 2000. *Agency, Democracy, and Nature: The U.S. Environmental Movement from a Critical Theory Perspective*. Cambridge, MA: MIT Press.

Bullard, Robert. 1990. *Dumping in Dixie*. Boulder, CO: Westview Press.

Buttel, Fred. 1997. "Some Observations on Agro-food Change and the Future of Agricultural Sustainability Movements." Pp. 344–65 in *Globalising Food: Agrarian Questions and Global Restructuring*, edited by David Goodman and Michael Watts. London, UK: Routledge.

Buttel, Fred, Olaf F. Larson, and Gilbert W. Gillespie, Jr. 1990. *The Sociology of Agriculture*. New York: Greenwood Press

California Alcoholic Beverage Control (CABC). 2006. "Fact Sheet: Oakland Alcohol Retailers." Retrieved April 3, 2006 <http://Z;\Community Safety and Justice/Alcohol outlets\Website\ Factsheet_1.24.6.doc>.

Capek, Stella. 1993. "The 'Environmental Justice' Frame: A Conceptual Discussion and an Application." *Social Problems* 40:5–24.

Center for Disease Control (CDC). 2002. "National Diabetes Fact Sheet." Retrieved April 9, 2006 <http://www.cdc.gov/diabetes/pubs/figuretext.htm#fig2>.

Chung C. and S. L. Myers. 1999. "Do the Poor Pay More for Food? An Analysis of Grocery Store Availability and Food Price Disparities." *Journal of Consumer Affairs* 33:276–96.

Diamant, Alison L, Susan H. Babey, E. Richard Brown, and Theresa A. Hastert. 2005. "Diabetes on the Rise in California." UCLA Center for Health Policy Research. Retrieved March 31, 2008 <http://www.healthpolicy.ucla.edu/pubs/files/diabetes_pb_122005.pdf>.

Dunlap, Riley and William R. Catton. 1979. "Environmental Sociology." *Annual Review of Sociology* 5:243–73.

Dupris, Joseph, Kathleen S. Hill, and William H. Rodgers. 2006. *The Si'lailo Way: Indians, Salmon, and Law on the Columbia River* Durham, NC: Carolina Academic Press.

Faber, Daniel. 1998. *The Struggle for Ecological Democracy: Environmental Justice Movements in the United States*. New York: Guilford Press.

Foster, John Bellamy and Fred Magdoff. 2000. "Liebig, Marx and the Depletion of Soil Fertility: Relevance for Today's Agriculture." Pp. 43–60 in *Hungry for Profit: The Agribusiness Threat to Farmers, Food, and the Environment*, edited by Fred Magdoff, John Bellamy Foster, and Fred Buttel. New York: Monthly Review Press.

Gamson, William A. and Andre Modigliani. 1989. "Media Discourse and Public Opinion on Nuclear Power: A Constructionist Approach." *American Journal of Sociology* 95:1–37.

Gilbert, Jess, Gwen Sharp, and Sindy M. Felin. 2002. "The Loss and Persistence of Black-Owned Farms and Farmland: A Review of the Research Literature and Its Implications." *Southern Rural Sociology* 18:1–30.

Goldschmidt, Walter. [1947] 1978. *As You Sow.* Montclair, NJ: Allanheld, Osmun & Co.

Gottlieb, Robert and Andrew Fisher. 1996. "First Feed the Face: Environmental Justice and Community Food Security. *Antipode* 28:193–203.

Guthman, Julie. 2004. *Agrarian Dreams: The Paradox of Organic Farming in California.* Berkeley, CA: University of California Press.

Harrison, Gail, Charles A. DiSogra, George Manolo-LeClair, Jennifer Aguayo, and Wei Yen. 2002. "Over 2.2 Million Low Income Californian Adults are Food-Insecure, 658,000 Suffer Hunger." UCLA Center for Health Policy Research. Retrieved March 31, 2009 <http:// www.lafightshunger.org/images/hunger.pdf>.

Hewes, Gordon W. 1973. "Indian Fisheries Productivity in Pre-contact Times in the Pacific Salmon Area." *Northwest Anthropological Research Notes* 7(3):133–55.

House, Freeman. 1999. *Totem Salmon.* Boston, MA: Beacon Press.

Jackson, Jennifer. 2005. "Nutritional Analysis of Traditional and Present Foods of the Karuk People and Development of Public Outreach Materials." Orleans, CA: Karuk Tribe of California.

Joe, Jennie and Robert Young. 1993. *Diabetes as a Disease of Civilization: The Impact of Cultural Change on Indigenous People.* New York: Walter de Gruyter and Co.

Karuk Tribe of California. 2006. "Toxic Algae Threaten Human Health in PacifiCorp's Klamath Reservoirs Blooms Worse than Last Year, Little Response from Company or County." Retrieved March 31, 2009 <http://karuk.us/press/06-08-08%20 toxic%20reservoirs.pdf>.

Kobayashi, Audrey and Linda Peake. 2000. "Racism Out of Place: Thoughts on Whiteness and Antiracist Geography for the New Millennium." *Annals of the Association of American Geographers* 90(2):392–403.

Lappe, Anna and Bryant Terry. 2006. *Grub: Ideas for an Urban Organic Kitchen.* New York: Tarcher.

LaVeist T. and J. Wallace. 2000. "Health Risk and Inequitable Distribution of Liquor Stores in African American Neighborhoods." *Social Science and Medicine* 51:613–17.

Lyson, Thomas A. 2004. *Civic Agriculture: Reconnecting Farm, Food and Community.* Boston, MA: Tufts University Press.

Massey, Doreen and Nancy Denton. 1998. *American Apartheid: Segregation and the Making of the American Underclass.* Cambridge, MA: Harvard University Press.

Morland, Kimberly, S. Wing, A. Deiz Roux, and C. Poole. 2002. "Neighborhood Characteristics Associated with the Location of Food Stores and Food Service Places." *American Journal of Preventive Medicine* 22:23–29.

Norgaard, Kari Marie. (2005) "The Effects of Altered Diet on the Health of the Karuk People." Report submitted to the Federal Energy Regulatory Commission Docket #P-2082 on behalf of the Karuk Tribe of California.

Novotny, Patrick. 2000. *Where We Live, Work and Play: The Environmental Justice Movement and the Struggle for a New Environmentalism.* Westport, CT: Praeger.

Omi, Michael and Howard Winant. 1989. *Racial Formation in the United States: From the 1960s to the 1980s.* New York: Routledge.

Pellow, David N. 2004. "The Politics of Illegal Dumping: An Environmental Justice Framework." *Qualitative Sociology* 27:511–25.

Pellow, David N. and Robert J. Brulle. 2005. *Power, Justice and the Environment: A Critical Appraisal of the Environmental Justice Movement.* Boston, MA: MIT Press.

Peña, Devon. 2003. "Identity, Place and Communities of Resistance." Pp. 146–67 in *Just Sustain-abilities: Development in an Unequal World,* edited by Julian Agyeman, Robert Bullard, and Bob Evans. London: Boston, MA: MIT Press.

Pulido, Laura. 2000. "Rethinking Environmental Racism: White Privilege and Urban Development in Southern California" *Annals of the Association of American Geographers* 90(1):12–40.

Stercho, Amy. 2005. "The Importance of Place-based Fisheries to the Karuk Tribe of California: A Socio-economic Study." Master's thesis, Humboldt State University, Arcata, CA.

Szasz, Andrew. 1994. *Ecopopulism: Toxic Waste and the Movement for Environmental Justice.* Minneapolis, MN: University of Minnesota Press.

Sze, Julie. 2006. *Noxious New York: The Racial Politics of Urban Health and Environmental Justice.* Boston, MA: MIT Press.

Taylor, D. 2000. "The Rise of the Environmental Justice Paradigm." *American Behavioral Scientist* 43:508–90.

———. 1997. "American Environmentalism: The Role of Race, Class, and Gender in Shaping Activism 1820–1995." *Race, Gender & Class* 5:16–62.

United Church of Christ. 1987. *Toxic Wastes and Race in the United States: A National Report on the Racial and Socio-economic Characteristics with Hazardous Waste Sites.* New York: United Church of Christ Commission for Racial Justice.

Wilkinson, Charles. 2005. *Blood Struggle: The Rise of Modern Indian Nations.* New York: W. W. Norton and Co.

———. 2000. *Messages from Frank's Landing: A Story of Salmon, Treaties, and the Indian Way.* Seattle, WA: University of Washington Press.

Wood, Spencer D. and Jess Gilbert. 2000. "Returning African American Farmers to the Land: Recent Trends and a Policy Rationale." *Review of Black Political Economy* 27(4):43–64. Wrigley, Neil Ward, B. Margetts, and A. Whelan. 2002. "Assessing the Impact of Improved Retail Access on Diet in a 'Food Desert': A Preliminary Report." *Urban Studies* 39:2061–82.

Young, Kue. 1997. "Recent Health Trends in the Native American Population." *Population Research and Policy Review* 16:147–67.

Turning Public Issues into Private Troubles

Lead Contamination, Domestic Labor, and the Exploitation of Women

Lois Bryson, Kathleen McPhillips, and Kathryn Robinson

This reading examines government efforts to deal with contamination from lead smelters in some Australian provinces. Lead is a dangerous environmental toxin, which can cause an array of physical problems, from kidney damage to hyperactivity. Lead is especially dangerous to young children and can cause, among other things, mental retardation, brain damage, and behavior problems. However, rather than address the source of the problem (the smelters themselves), government policies have focused on individual behaviors, specifically on housecleaning, to minimize the amount of lead dust in homes. The authors, pointing to the fact that most of the homes near smelters are occupied by working-class families and most of the housecleaning is done by women, argue that the government policies are not only ineffective but are embedded in, and reproduce, unequal social class and gender relations.

Using a case study of state intervention in the industrial contamination of a residential community, this article offers a contribution to feminist analysis of the role of the state. Residents of three Australian lead smelter towns, with high levels of toxic pollution, have been given a strong message by state health authorities that their children's health could be irreparably damaged unless they adopt a strict regimen of housecleaning and child management to reduce the ingestion of lead particles by their children.

This case study of state action on a site that is classically women's domain provides insight into a "state gender regime" (Connell 1990) through examining the state "doing gender" (West and Zimmerman 1987). . . .

Unraveling the complexity of the state's role in developing and implementing its health strategy for dealing with the effects of lead pollution within smelter towns allows us to tease out some of the complexities of state intervention. How do they identify and address this health issue? Whose interests do the interventions serve? What are the impacts for different groups of women? Because the intervention is focused on mothering, we start by examining some relevant features of motherhood in contemporary Australia and its place within the wider scheme of gender relations.

Motherhood and the State Gender Regime

. . . While schools of feminist thought account in different ways for women's position and gender relations, they do not contest that motherhood involves a responsibility for family work, which falls unequally to women. Graham (1983) pointed to the bifurcated nature of caring as involving "caring about" and "caring for." In terms of parenthood, she suggested that fathers are expected to "care about" their children, and this may involve taking some responsibility for overseeing that care is provided. For mothers, the two aspects are firmly fused: They are expected to both "care about" and "care for."

Empirical studies in Australia and elsewhere of perceptions of motherhood clearly expose a dominating ideology that reflects such views of caring (Dempsey 1997; McMahon 1999; Russell 1983). . . .

Decades of research into time use confirm women's disproportionate share of the work involved in both domestic cleaning and child care relative to their male partners (Bittman and Matheson 1996; Bryson 1997; Fenstermaker Berk 1985). Women in Australia, as elsewhere, are far more likely to undertake cleaning chores and physical care of children. The Australian Bureau of Statistics (1994) found that women's share of laundry was 89 percent (90 percent if in full-time employment), their share of cleaning 82 percent (84 percent if in full-time employment), and of physical care of children 84 percent (76 percent if in full-time employment) (Bittman and Pixley 1997,

113). These tasks are central to the housecleaning regime devised by state authorities that we examine here. . . .

The Smelter Communities: Method and Background

We first became interested in the public health intervention processes in lead-affected towns when one of us (McPhillips) became caught up with the effects of lead contamination in her residential community, which bordered on Boolaroo, a smelter town in NSW [New South Wales]. McPhillips's personal experience of dealing with lead contamination became the subject of spirited debate and theorizing in our (then) shared work context—the sociology department of the local university. This led to the development of the research reported in this article.

Method

. . . In investigating the case study of Boolaroo, we collected qualitative data through direct engagement in the community; through participant observation in community activities; and through interviews with eight residents of Boolaroo, including female members of community groups (both for and against the smelter). We also interviewed personnel in the local health authority who had been involved in testing children's blood levels and in designing and implementing subsequent intervention measures.

Historical materials relating to the genesis of the political conflict over contamination in Boolaroo were available to us. These included reports in local newspapers (which had been systematically filed by the municipal library and collected by activists), reports and scholarly articles produced by the public health authorities, and a television documentary produced for the state-owned public broadcasting authority that critically recorded an intervention in 1991 intended to remove historic contamination from Boolaroo residences (Australian Broadcasting Corporation 1992). The smelter company produced regular community newsletters, which were available to us, as were the public health information brochures.

In interpreting the data relating to Boolaroo, we used a comparative perspective, drawing on the reports of similar interventions in the other Australian lead smelter towns. There are three major sites of lead production in Australia: Port Pirie in South Australia, and Broken Hill and Boolaroo in NSW [New South Wales]. . . .

. . . The critical features of the populations in all three areas affected by the pollution is that they are of low socioeconomic status with manufacturing providing predominantly male employment.

The Household Cleaning Regime

Public health authorities have systematically turned to an approach dealing with lead effects that is focused on the ways in which it is ingested, particularly by children, rather than with stopping pollution. In the vicinity of the Boolaroo smelter, for example, an attractive poster was distributed to residents, with the title "Lead: Lower the levels & protect your child" (PHU n.d.). It mentions soil, food, household dust, old paint, and the lead worker as potential sources, identifying interventions that can be made, with most of them involving an intensification of domestic labor. To avoid exposure of children to lead in household dust, parents are advised to use a wet mop instead of a broom; keep dust from children's play areas, including under beds and in closets; and remember to dust corners, along sides of windows, and behind furniture and doors. Advice to the lead worker includes the following: Keep kit bags out of reach of children; keep children away from work clothes; and clean dust from inside and outside of car, especially if driven to work. To avoid lead in food, the parents are advised to intensify domestic labor by preventing children from sucking dirty hands, fingernails, or objects; wiping surfaces before preparing food; and covering food and utensils to prevent lead dust from settling on them. The problem of contaminated soil is addressed by advice to wash children's hands before eating, especially if playing outside; to provide clean soil or sand for children to play in; and to use a nail brush under nails. The poster does not represent the source of the lead contamination in any way.

The focus on domestic-based interventions deflects attention away from the source of the pollution, which is clearly in the interests of capital. We argue that the burden of activities to ameliorate the effects of pollution falls disproportionately to women and must be counted as an aspect of the state's gender as well as class regime. The communities, which already bear the burden of toxic contamination and its attendant health, social, and economic effects, are further burdened with the responsibility of "putting things right."

The spotlight in the three smelter towns in recent years has been very much on children, even though evidence suggests that lead is a health hazard for all age groups (Alperstein, Taylor, and Vimpani 1994; Centers for Disease Control and Prevention 1991). In earlier years, the focus of official programs was on workers and also in a manner that deflected attention away from the smelting companies' practices. . . .

The 1980s and 1990s: Developing the Domestic Cleaning Regime

In the early 1980s, the South Australian health department responded to U.S. research linking impaired intellectual development with lead by undertaking a survey of the factors implicated in elevated blood lead levels of young children living within the vicinity of the smelter at Port Pirie (Landrigan 1983). Using a control sample of children with low blood lead levels, researchers found that 5 of the 16 evaluated behavioral factors were significantly associated with high lead levels. These factors were a history of placing objects in the mouth, nail biting, dirty hands, dirty clothes, and eating lunch at home rather than at school (Landrigan 1983, 8). The survey also found that higher lead levels in children were associated with the number of persons in the household working in the lead industry (cf. Donovan 1996).

However, the research also showed that none of the factors were as important as living in a contaminated environment and that living near the smelter was three times more important than anything else (Landrigan 1983, 9). Because past emissions still contaminate the atmosphere and the soil, reducing emissions was acknowledged as insufficient for dealing with the problem. More recently, public health officials recognized that the only effective way of dealing with lead contamination at smelter sites is relocating residents (Galvin et al. 1993, 377), although to our knowledge no public body has ever implemented a relocation program.

In 1984, the South Australian health department and the smelter management started an education program about the importance of personal hygiene and household cleaning. The focus was on "pathways" through which lead is ingested by children and the ways this can be minimized within the home. The general manager of smelter operations expressed the view that "given reasonable care and hygiene, then you can live with the levels of contamination from past emissions." Fowler and Grabosky (1989, 153–57) suggested that the company was "defensive and cautious" lest remedial action imply admission of legal responsibility. The company maintained public health to be a government responsibility and invested far less than the government. The South Australian government's response was restrained as well, illustrating the power of major capital by showing an unwillingness to "antagonise one of the state's largest employers" (Fowler and Grabosky 1989, 150). The government was prepared to burden working-class women, rather than business.

In 1986, another case control study examined children's blood lead levels in Port Pirie (Wilson et al. 1986). The study focused mainly on environmental issues and the implications for the smelter. It assessed behavioral differences between "cases" and "controls" and again pointed to the "pathways" for ingestion such as "biting fingernails" or "dirty clothing/hands at school." In 1988, the public health program at Port Pirie also undertook external decontamination in the yards of 1,400 homes at highest risk, and adjacent vacant blocks and footpaths were sealed (Heyworth 1990, 178). Subsequently, a "partial decontamination" of the same area was instituted, in recognition that contamination is continuous. Such a program requires a permanent cycle of treatment of the homes and vacant blocks and a continuing awareness within the community of the need for vigilance in terms of personal and home hygiene (Heyworth 1990, 183).

In 1993, after several months of remediation, including replanting tailings dumps and the implementation of housecleaning regimes, the blood lead levels had elevated in a part of the town deemed to be a nonrisk area and hence not subject to the campaign. Further investigation found the source to be stacks of lead ore left on the wharves in open piles, with dust being carried by the winds into residential areas not previously considered at risk from the smelter.

The South Australian Health Commission published a decade review of the Port Pirie program in 1993 that concluded, "Given the amount of lead contamination to which these households are exposed, changes in dust hygiene would not seem to be a realistic way to ensure lower exposures to lead by the child" (Maynard, Calder, and Phipps 1993, 25). This point, that domestic strategies are unsustainable in the long term (Maynard, Calder, and Phipps 1993, 5), had previously been made by Landrigan in 1983 and by Luke in 1991 after an extensive search of the world literature on the topic (Luke 1991, 161–67). Many people are prepared to modify their behavior in the short term, but sooner or later they revert to more comfortable habits. The report notes that because there is a constant process of recontamination, it is unrealistic to expect continuing voluntary participation of residents in programs for lead remediation. Another barrier to ongoing participation is the stigmatization that is involved if a child's blood levels are high. Parents are reluctant to have their child labeled as potentially intellectually impaired, and they themselves feel stigmatized by the implication that they have dirty houses.

Over time, parents tend to withdraw from participation in blood- monitoring programs. This can be seen as a form of resistance in situations where parents are expected to comply with surveillance of a problem that has a source external to the home and family, but they are expected to deal with the consequences. Their concerted efforts at housecleaning fail to bring the promised results, and they continue to suffer the stigmatization of the threats to their children's healthy development and the implication that they are poor housekeepers.

During the evaluations of cleaning regimes by health authorities, little attention was paid to the women involved as the cleaners, which indirectly provides us with some insight into the state gender regime. Apart from the effort and the responsibility, there is evidence that the cleaning process itself can be contaminating (Australian Broadcasting Corporation 1992; Luke 1991, 99).

Fowler and Grabosky (1989, 148) suggested that the "regulatory orientation to pollution control has been characterized by negotiation and compromise, rather than strict enforcement." Governments have been reluctant to antagonize business, and business has been motivated by a "desire to avoid the loss of a marketable product rather than environmental concern" (Fowler and Grabosky 1989, 147). State recognition of business interests as more important than smelter community residents has ultimately resulted in greater recourse to the cleaning regime. Furthermore, it is unlikely that the public health care system has the long-term capacity to maintain the level of involvement and monitoring that is required. This suggests the program is "window dressing," a project of state legitimation, which rests on the state's class and gender regime and which masks the interests that are served by de facto tolerance of levels of industrial pollution damaging to a small and easily ignored segment of the population.

Domestic Cleaning Regimes—The 1990s

A similar household cleaning regime to that developed and applied in the 1980s by public health workers in the vicinity of the Port Pirie lead smelter was subsequently put in place in the NSW smelter towns of Boolaroo and Broken Hill. The regime was formalized in 1994 by a federal agency, the Commonwealth of Australia Environmental Protection Authority (EPA), and outlined in a document published by the EPA titled *Lead Alert: A Guide for Health Professionals* (Alperstein, Taylor, and Vimpani 1994).

Lead Alert set out the "steps to minimise exposure and absorption" of lead by children. Health professionals are told to give the following advice "to parents if a child's blood lead is more than 151/2 g/dL" (Alperstein, Taylor, and Vimpani 1994, 17). Parents should ensure that children's hands and face are washed before they eat or have a nap, discourage children from putting dirty fingers in their mouths, encourage children to play in grassy areas, and wash fruit and vegetables. In terms of housecleaning, they are advised to wet dust floors, ledges, window sills, and other flat surfaces at least weekly or more often if the house is near a source point for lead; to clean carpets and rugs regularly using a vacuum cleaner; to wash children's toys, especially those used outside; and to wash family pets frequently and discourage pets from sleeping near children. The parent should ensure that the child does not have access to peeling paint or chewable surfaces painted with lead-based paint and that the child's diet is adequate in calcium and iron, which helps to minimize lead absorption. Children should be provided with regular frequent meals and snacks, up to six per day, because more lead is absorbed on an empty stomach (Alperstein, Taylor, and Vimpani 1994, 17).

The document was widely disseminated, not just in smelter communities but in situations where people had elevated blood lead levels from any source. The housecleaning regime has been promoted as a primary intervention strategy, despite the evidence from evaluations of the Port Pirie experience (as well as studies in other countries) that show it to be ineffective.

This extremely detailed cleaning regime involves an implicit threat for noncompliance, the threat of adversely affecting one's child's health and intellectual development. Because of the nature of the tasks, the responsibility for most of this work falls to mothers rather than all parents.

For communities in the vicinity of lead smelters in Australia, public health authorities recommend an even more stringent regime than that implied in *Lead Alert*. The regime suggests not vacuuming with a child in the room since the cleaning raises dust. Dusting should ideally cover what one Boolaroo mother described as "bizarre places" such as the fly wire in screen doors. Other suggested strategies include moving children's beds from under windows and putting away soft toys because they cannot be easily washed (Gilligan 1992, 4). To add to this intensification, some anxious parents intensify the regime further. The "wet dusting" or mopping over of all horizontal surfaces is done more than once a day by some mothers. In a television documentary on the subject of lead poisoning and children, women who had implemented the regime in both Boolaroo and Port Pirie expressed their frustration. "They tell you to run round with a washer after them. They are not allowed to put their fingers in the mouths"; "You do things that you just would not do"; "We must be the only housewives in New South Wales that do these tasks" (Australian Broadcasting Corporation 1992). Another mother verbalized the worry and guilt associated with such responsibility for her children's health, "You feel guilty if you just don't want to do the work . . . you think your child does not have a normal life . . . should you have more children?" (Gilligan 1992, 45).

The lead abatement program also involves the monitoring of the child's blood lead levels as the most significant means of measuring the levels of lead absorption. This means subjecting the child to frequent blood sampling and a constant measuring as to whether the family's efforts have been successful. There is constant contact for both mother and child with health and other professionals and often researchers (Australian Broadcasting Corporation 1992; Gilligan 1992, 4). The constancy of the monitoring creates the impression that the responsibility for the public health problem falls on the residents themselves (and especially on mothers), rather than the government or the corporation (see also McGee 1996, 14). The monitoring of blood lead levels also gives the impression that something is being done but actually does nothing to address the source of the contamination. In some cases, children's blood lead levels have risen after the implementation of household cleaning regimes.

A study of the effects of the lead issue on Boolaroo residents found that families of children with high blood lead levels experienced "feelings of guilt, stigma, anxiety, stress and powerlessness . . . that the difference may be due to or to be seen to be due to some action or inaction of them as parents" (Hallebone and Townsend 1993, 17). We found that in Boolaroo, health professionals regarded parental failure to present children for monitoring as evidence of irresponsibility. As with smelter workers in the 1920s, stigma is attached to those who do not conform to the cleaning standards. . . .

Not only are women enslaved by the domestic cleaning, but their children's psychological and/or emotional development is put in question. In the education booklet written by the education department for use in Boolaroo schools, the family unit is presented as the most important element in dealing with lead exposure: "Children who are supported and confident in their family unit will be better able to deal with any problems associated with the lead issue" (quoted in Mason 1992, 41).

Despite evidence of limited success in the long term, domestic cleaning regimes are becoming popular for dealing with lead contamination from gasoline. As has occurred with the smelter communities, the effect again is to shift responsibility from the polluting source to the private sphere of the family and women.

Resistance to State Interventions

The focus on housecleaning regimes as a response to children's elevated blood lead levels has the effect of stigmatizing parents and calling into question their capacity to care for their children. As noted above, mothers who have implemented the regime, however, find it very oppressive and anxiety provoking, hence many cease doing it (McGee 1996, 14). There is also resistance to the surveillance of children's blood lead levels in situations where the health authorities are not offering an effective response to the problem. The proportion of smelter-town families who continue to present their children for blood testing has declined considerably over time (Isles 1993; Maynard, Calder, and Phipps 1993, 9; Stephenson, Corbett, and Jacobs 1992; Western NSW PHU 1994).

Nevertheless, women in smelter towns have responded with active as well as passive resistance. Following the PHU's 1991 revelation of elevated blood lead levels in Boolaroo children, local residents, mainly women, formed the North Lakes Environmental Action Defence Group (No Lead). It has campaigned for action by state and local government and by the smelter to counter the high levels of lead pollution. . . .

No Lead has addressed the issue of lead contamination by refocusing public attention on the responsibilities of the government to regulate the industry and the industry's responsibility to reduce toxic emissions. They have found themselves in direct conflict with the company's public relations strategists who have attempted to downplay their political significance as legitimate representatives of community interest. No Lead has been able to successfully work with environmental groups like Greenpeace and has achieved some success in refocusing government attention on Boolaroo. For example, a Parliamentary

Select Committee set up in 1994 resulted in a management plan that placed more responsibility on the smelter and the local government in limiting the effects of plant emissions, although it reinforced the emphasis on housecleaning regimes (NSW Parliament 1994).

Other women in Boolaroo have actively resisted government interventions intended to ameliorate the exposure of children to lead, which they see as stigmatizing their children as intellectually limited or themselves as poor housekeepers. The most significant of these was the 1992 resistance by the Parents and Citizens Association to a temporary closure of the local school for remediation. The parents questioned whether the school was indeed contaminated or if the contamination was any more significant than that which they experienced in their homes. They rejected the implication that the school posed a threat to their children's intellectual development, citing cases of local children who had succeeded academically. The women involved in this public protest expressed a fear that the school would be closed forever, once the children had been relocated. McPhillips (1995, 48) commented that the issue brought out the "deep-felt suspicion that this section of the local community held for government bureaucracies." That is, they do not see the public authorities as acting in their interests and resist the authorities' efforts to intervene in the situation. In this case, the women's resistance was successful, and the remediation was carried out while the school was routinely closed for summer holidays.

Conclusion: Lead Levels, Public Health Strategies, and State Gender Regimes

The strategy promoted by public health authorities for smelter towns, rather than dealing with the source of the pollution, turns this public issue into a private family matter. In appearing to do something, the state selected a remediation strategy that has been repeatedly proven to be ineffective. Research from many countries (Luke 1991) persistently shows that the major issue is one of proximity to the smelter and the level of emissions, with past pollution also a critical factor. There is a continuing history of failure of the smelting companies to own the pollution problem they cause and to deal with it. Profit levels, rather than health concerns, have historically taken precedence, with the state mediating the corporations' interests. The state historically has facilitated the shifting of the focus of responsibility for the problem to the relatively powerless. Now the blame is laid on working-class women, whereas early in the twentieth century, it was directed toward recently arrived male immigrant workers, although women were indirectly implicated.

The official remediation strategy does not fall in a gender-neutral way on both parents. It relies for its implementation on additional daily caring labor being undertaken by mothers of children deemed "at risk" and thus on the basis of a traditional understanding of the responsibilities associated with motherhood. In addition, it relies for compliance on the mothers' emotional commitment to their children's health, a situation with great potential to engender feelings of guilt and to stigmatize those who "fail." The exploitation of these working-class women's unpaid caring labor is not only an example of the state "doing" gender but a recent form of "doing" class as well. Brown and Ferguson (1995, 161) noted that:

> when activists discover that local industry values its bottom line or international reputation more highly than it does the health of children in the community, this realization violates the trust that the women toxic waste activists have placed in the ideal of corporate citizenship and governmental protection.

Working-class mothers are the target of a burdensome housecleaning regime that absorbs their labor but at the same time effectively shifts responsibility for ensuring the pollution does not damage their children's health away from the corporation and the state. This strategy reflects a state gender regime that involves material exploitation in the form of reliance on women's labor in a manner that serves powerful interests and ideological exploitation through the manipulation of the women's sense of maternal responsibility.

The structural features of class and gender do not, of course, account for the whole story. Residents are not duped nor have they have been silent on the matter. The women as individuals resist or reject the recommended regime and have been at the forefront of organized community resistance strategies. Women organized into community-based pressure groups have had limited success in directing attention back onto the smelter as the source of the toxic pollution and away from their responsibility as domestic carers for the health of their children.

This case study raises specific questions about where the responsibility lies for the health of residents of smelter communities. But it also illuminates class and gender relations in contemporary Australia and the manner in which the state is engaged in the reproduction of class and gender difference.

Note

Bryson, Lois, Kathleen McPhillips, and Kathryn Robinson. 2001. "Turning Public Issues into Private Troubles: Lead Contamination, Domestic Labor, and the Exploitation of Women's Unpaid Labor in Australia." *Gender & Society* 15(5): 755–72.

References

Alperstein, G., R. Taylor, and G.Vimpani. 1994. *Lead alert: A guide for health professionals.* Canberra, Australia: Commonwealth Environmental Protection Agency.

Australian Broadcasting Corporation. 1992. *Living with lead.* Television documentary screened on *Four Corners,* 14 September.

Australian Bureau of Statistics. 1994. *How Australians use their time.* Canberra: Australian Bureau of Statistics.

Bittman, Michael, and George Matheson. 1996. *"All else in confusion": What time use surveys show about changes in gender equity.* SPRC Discussion Paper Series No. 72. Sydney: Social Policy Research Centre.

Bittman, Michael, and Jocelyn Pixley. 1997. *The double life of the family: Myth, hope, and experience.* Sydney: Allen and Unwin.

Brown, P., and F. Ferguson. 1995. "Making a big stink": Women's work, women's relationships, and toxic waste activism. *Gender & Society* 9:145–72.

Bryson, Lois. 1997. Citizenship, caring and commodification. In *Crossing borders: Gender and citizenship in transition,* edited by Barbara Hobson and Anne Marie Berggren. Stockholm: Swedish Council for Planning and Co-ordination of Research.

Centers for Disease Control and Prevention. 1991. *Preventing lead poisoning in young children.* Atlanta, GA: U.S. Department of Health and Human Services.

Connell, R. W. 1990. The state, gender, and sexual politics. *Theory and Society* 19:507–44.

Dempsey, Ken. 1997. *Inequalities in marriage: Australia and beyond.* Melbourne: Oxford University Press.

Donovan, John. 1996. *Lead in Australian children: Report on the national survey of lead in children.* Canberra: Australian Institute of Health and Welfare.

Fenstermaker Berk, Sarah. 1985. *The gender factory: The apportionment of working American households.* New York: Plenum.

Fowler, R., and P. Grabosky. 1989. Lead pollution and the children of Port Pirie. In *Lead pollution: Fourteen studies in corporate crime or corporate harm,* edited by P. Grabosky and A. Sutton. Milson's Point NSW, Australia: Hutchinson.

Galvin, J., J. Stephenson, J. Wlordarczyk, R. Loughran, and G. Wallerm. 1993. Living near a lead smelter: An environmental health risk assessment in Boolaroo and Argenton, New South Wales. *Australian Journal of Public Health* 17:373–78.

Gilligan, B., ed. 1992. *Living with lead: A draft plan for addressing lead contamination in the Boolaroo and Argenton areas, NSW.* Lake Macquarie, Australia: Lake Macquarie City Council.

Graham, Hilary. 1983. Caring: A labor of love. In *A labor of love: Women, work and caring,* edited by Janet Finch and Dulcie Groves. London: Routledge and Kegan Paul.

Hallebone, E., and M. Townsend. 1993. Who bears the weight of lead in society? A social impact assessment of proposed changes to the national guidelines for blood lead levels. Technical appendix 3. In *Reducing lead exposure in Australia: An assessment of impacts,* vol. 2, edited by Mike Berry, Jan Garrard, and Deni Greene. Canberra, Australia: Department of Human Services and Health.

Heyworth, J. S. 1990. *Evaluation of Port Pirie's environmental health program.* Master of Public Health diss., Adelaide University, Adelaide, Australia.

Isles, Tim. 1993. Boolaroo blood-lead tests show no change. *Newcastle Herald,* 13 July.

Landrigan, P. J. 1983. *Lead exposure, lead absorption and lead toxicity in the children of Port Pirie: A second opinion.* Adelaide: South Australian Health Commission.

Luke, Colin. 1991. A study of factors associated with trends in blood lead levels in Port Pirie children exposed to home based intervention. Master of Public Health diss., Adelaide University, Adelaide, Australia.

Maguire, Paul. 1994. Green buffer "best way" to cut lead poisoning in young children. *Newcastle Herald*, 3 June.

Mason, Chloe. 1992. Controlling women, controlling lead. *Refractory Girl* 43:41–42.

Maynard, E., I. Calder, and C. Phipps. 1993. *The Port Pirie lead implementation program: Review of progress and consideration of future directions (1984–1993)*. Adelaide: South Australian Health Commission.

McGee, T. 1996. Shades of grey: Community responses to chronic environmental lead contamination in Broken Hill, NSW. Ph.D. diss., the Australian National University, Canberra.

McMahon, Anthony. 1999. *Taking care of men: Sexual politics in the public mind*. Cambridge, UK: Cambridge University Press.

McPhillips, K. 1995. Dehumanising discourses: Cultural colonisation and lead contamination in Boolaroo. *Australian Journal of Social Issues* 30:41–55.

NSW Parliament. 1994. *Report of the select committee upon lead pollution*. Vol. 1. December.

Public Health Unit. n.d. Hunter Area Health Service. Poster.

Russell, Graeme. 1983. *The changing role of fathers?* St. Lucia, Australia: University of Queensland Press.

Stephenson, J., S. Corbett, and M. Jacobs. 1992. Evaluation of environmental lead abatement programs in New South Wales. In *Choice and change: Ethics, politics and economies of public health. Selected papers from the 24th Public Health Association of Australia conference, 1992 Canberra*, edited by Valerie A. Brown and George Preston. Canberra: Public Health Association of Australia.

West, C., and D. H. Zimmerman. 1987. Doing gender. *Gender & Society* 1:125–51.

Western NSW Public Health Unit. 1994. *Risk factors for blood lead levels in preschool children in Broken Hill 1991–1993*. Dubbo, Australia: Western New South Wales Public Health Unit.

Wilson, D., A. Esterman, M. Lewis, D. Roder, and I. Calder. 1986. Children's blood lead levels in the lead smelting town of Port Pirie, South Australia. *Archives of Environmental Health* 41:245–50.

Addressing Urban Transportation Equity in the United States

Robert D. Bullard

Robert Bullard, longtime environmental activist and scholar, argues that transportation is crucial to environmental justice. Automobile transport, with its attendant sprawl development, exorbitant use of fossil fuels and production of CO2 emissions, is a major contributor to environment-related health problems such as asthma and also a host of environmental ills. Auto transport in the United States is subsidized by the government, which pays for roads and other infrastructure upon which cars depend. Such investments tend to disproportionately benefit the middle and upper classes, while poor urban communities often depend on public transportation, which is less well supported by our government.

In the United States, all communities do not receive the same benefits from transportation advancements and investments.[1] Despite the heroic efforts and the monumental social and economic gains made over the decades, transportation remains a civil rights issue.[2] Transportation touches every aspect of where we live, work, play, and go to school, as well as the physical and natural world. Transportation also plays a pivotal role in shaping human interaction, economic mobility, and sustainability.

Transportation provides access to opportunity and serves as a key component in addressing poverty, unemployment, and equal opportunity goals while ensuring access to education, health care, and other public services. It is basic to many other quality-of-life indicators such as health, education, employment, economic development, access to municipal services, residential mobility, and environmental quality (Bullard and Johnson 1997, 8–9; Lewis 1997, xi–xii).

Transportation equity is consistent with the goals of the larger civil rights movement and the environmental justice movement. Transportation investments, enhancements, and financial resources have provided advantages for some communities, while transportation decision making has made other communities disadvantaged.

Race and class dynamics operate to isolate many low-income and people of color central-city residents from expanding suburban job centers. Transportation dollars have fueled suburban highway construction and job sprawl. Some transportation projects have cut wide paths through low-income and people of color neighborhoods, isolated residents physically from their institutions and businesses, disrupted once stable communities, displaced thriving businesses, contributed to urban sprawl, subsidized infrastructure decline, created traffic gridlock, and subjected residents to elevated risks from accidents, noise, spills, and explosions from vehicles carrying hazardous chemicals and other dangerous materials.[3] The continued residential segregation of people of color away from suburban job centers (where public transit is inadequate or nonexistent) may signal a new urban crisis and a new form of "residential apartheid."[4]

Old Wars, New Battles

In 1896, the U.S. Supreme Court wrestled with this question of the different treatment accorded blacks and whites. In *Plessy v. Ferguson,* the Supreme Court examined the constitutionality of Louisiana laws that provided for the segregation of railroad-car seating by race (Franklin and Moss 1974, 540–552). The court upheld the "white section" and "colored section" Jim Crow seating law, contending that segregation did not violate any rights guaranteed by the U.S. Constitution.[5]

On December 1, 1955, in Montgomery, Alabama, Rosa Parks ignited the modern civil rights movement. Mrs. Parks refused to give up her bus seat to a white man, in defiance of local Jim Crow laws. Her action sparked new leadership around transportation and civil rights. Mrs. Parks summarized her feelings about resisting Jim Crow in an interview with sociologist Aldon Morris in 1981: "My resistance to being mistreated on the buses and anywhere else was just a regular thing with me and not just that day."

Follow the Dollars

Transportation spending programs do not benefit all populations equally (Bullard and Johnson 1997, 7). By following the transportation dollars in metropolitan regions, one can tell who is "important" and who is not. The lion's share of transportation dollars is spent on roads, while urban transit systems are often left in disrepair. Nationally, 80 percent of all surface transportation funds is earmarked for highways and 20 percent is earmarked for public transportation.[6] Public transit has received roughly $50 billion since the creation of the Urban Mass Transit Administration in the early 1960s, and roadway projects received more than $205 billion between 1956 and the early 1990s (Dittmar and Chen 1995).

Generally, states spend less than 20 percent of federal transportation funding on transit. The current federal funding scheme is biased against metropolitan areas. The federal government allocated the bulk of transportation dollars directly to state DOTs (Puentes and Bailey 2003). Many of the road-building fiefdoms are no friend to urban transit. Just less than 6 percent of all federal highway dollars are suballocated directly to the metropolitan regions. Moreover, thirty states restrict use of the gasoline tax revenue to funding highway programs only (Puentes and Prince 2003). Although local governments within metropolitan areas own and maintain the vast majority of the transportation infrastructure, they receive only about 10 percent of every dollar they generate? Disparate transportation outcomes can be subsumed under three broad categories of inequity: procedural, geographic, and social.

Procedural Inequity

Attention is directed to the process by which transportation decisions may or may not be carried out in a uniform, fair, and consistent manner with involvement of diverse public stakeholders. Do the rules apply equally to everyone?

Geographic Inequity

Transportation decisions may have distributive impacts (positive and negative) that are geographic and spatial, such as rural versus urban versus central city. Some communities are physically located on the "wrong side of the tracks" and often receive substandard transportation services.

Social Inequity

Transportation benefits and burdens are not randomly distributed across population groups. Generally, transportation benefits go to the wealthier and more educated segment of society, while transportation burdens fall disproportionately on people of color and individuals at the lower end of the socioeconomic spectrum. Intergenerational equity issues are also subsumed under this category (Bullard, Johnson, and Torres 2001, 965). The impacts and consequences of some transportation decisions may reach into several generations.

In summary, heavy government investment in road infrastructure may be contributing to an increase in household transportation costs. Lest anyone dismiss transportation as a tangential issue, consider that Americans spend more on transportation than any other household expense except housing. On average, Americans spend nineteen cents out of every dollar earned on transportation expenses (Jakowitsch and Ernst 2003; Floyd 2003, 1C). They spend more on transportation than they do on food, education, and health care. The nation's poorest families spend more than 40 percent of their take-home pay on transportation. This is not a small point since African-American households tend to earn less money than whites. Nationally, African-Americans earn only $649 per $1,000 earned by whites (Thomas 2002, 1–2). This means that the typical black household in the United States earned 35 percent less than the typical white household.

Erasing Transportation Inequities

In general, most transit systems have tended to take their low-income and people of color "captive riders" for granted and concentrated their fare and service policies on attracting middle-class and affluent riders out of their cars. Moreover, transit subsidies have tended to favor investment in suburban transit and expensive new commuter bus and rail lines that disproportionately serve wealthier "discretionary riders." Almost 40 percent of rural counties in this country have little or no public transportation, and "[i]n areas with populations from one million and below, more than half of all transit passengers have incomes of less than $15,000 per year" (Bogren 1990).

In urban areas African-Americans and Latinos constitute more than 54 percent of transit users (62 percent of bus riders, 35 percent of subway riders, and 29 percent of commuter-rail riders) (Pucher and Renne 2003, 49 and 67). Nationally, only about 5.3 percent of all Americans use public transit to get to work (Garrett and Taylor 1999, 11). African-Americans are almost six times as likely as whites to use transit to get around (Pucher and Renne 2003, 67). Urban transit is especially important to African-Americans since more than 88 percent live in metropolitan areas and more than 53 percent live inside central cities (Cantave and Harrison 2001).

Lack of car ownership and inadequate public transit service in many central cities and metropolitan regions with a high proportion of "captive" transit dependents exacerbate social, economic, and racial isolation, especially for low-income people of color residents who already have limited transportation options. Nationally, only 7 percent of white households do not own a car, compared with 24 percent of African-American households, 17 percent of Latino households, and 13 percent of Asian-American households (Pucher and Renne 2003, 49–77). People of color are fighting to get representation on transportation boards and commissions, and to get their fair share of transit dollars, services, bus shelters and other amenities, handicapped accessible vehicles, and affordable fares.

Rosa Parks could not sit in the front or back of a Montgomery bus today, since that city dismantled its public bus system—which served mostly blacks and poor people (Stolz 2000). The cuts were made at the same time that federal tax dollars boosted the construction of the region's extensive suburban highways. The changes in Montgomery took place amid growing racial geographic segregation and tension between white and black members of the city council. The city described its actions publicly as fiscally necessary, even as Montgomery received large federal transportation subsidies to fund renovation of nontransit improvements.

Suburban Sprawl and Health

In *Sprawl City: Race, Politics, and Planning in Atlanta*, the authors documented that government-subsidized sprawl has substantial social equity, civil rights, and health implications. Sprawl-fueled growth is widening the gap between the haves and the have-nots. Suburban sprawl is fueled by the "iron triangle" of finance, land use planning, and transportation service delivery.[7] Sprawl has clear social and environmental effects.[8] The social effects of suburban sprawl include concentration of urban core poverty, closed opportunity, limited mobility, economic disinvestment, social isolation, and urban/suburban disparities that closely mirror racial inequities (Blackwell 2001, 1273–1277). The environmental effects of suburban sprawl include urban infrastructure decline; increased energy consumption; automobile dependency; threats to public health and the environment including air pollution, flooding, and climate change; and threats to farmland and wildlife habitat (Ehrenhalt 1999, A23).

Many jobs have shifted to the suburbs and communities where public transportation is inadequate or nonexistent. The exodus of low-skilled jobs to the suburbs disproportionately affects central-city residents, particularly people of color, who often face more limited choices of housing location and transportation in growing areas. Between 1990 and 1997, jobs on the fringe of metropolitan areas grew by 19 percent versus 4 percent job growth in core areas (Bullard, Johnson, and Torres 2004). While many new jobs are being created in the suburbs, the majority of job opportunities for low-income workers are still located in central cities.

Suburbs are increasing their share of office space, while central cities see their share declining. The suburban share of the metropolitan office space is 69.5 percent in Detroit, 65.8 percent in Atlanta, 57.7 percent in Washington, D.C., 57.4 percent in Miami, and 55.2 percent in Philadelphia (Lang 2000). Getting to these suburban jobs without a car is next to impossible. It is no accident that Detroit leads in suburban "office sprawl." Detroit is also the most segregated big city in the United States (Farley et al. 1993, 1–2; Powell 2003, H12), and the only major metropolitan area without a regional transit system. In Detroit, the Motor City, only 2.4 percent of metropolitan Detroiters use transit to get to work (U.S. Department of Transportation 2004).

Transportation-related sources account for more than 30 percent of the primary smog-forming pollutants emitted nationwide and 28 percent of the fine particulates. Vehicle emissions are the main reason 121 air quality districts in the United States are in noncompliance with the 1970 Clean Air Act's National Ambient Air Quality Standards. More than 140 million Americans—of whom 25 percent are children—live, work, and play in areas where air quality does not meet national standards (American Public Transportation Association 2003). Emissions from cars, trucks, and buses cause 25 to 51 percent of the air pollution in the nation's nonattainment areas. Transportation-related emissions also generate more than a quarter of the greenhouse gases.[9]

Improvements in transportation investments and air quality are of special significance to African-Americans and other people of color who are more likely to live in areas with reduced air quality when compared with whites. National Argonne Laboratory researchers discovered that 57 percent of whites, 65 percent of African-Americans, and 80 percent of Latinos lived in the 437 counties that failed to meet at least one of the EPA ambient air quality standards in 1992 (Wernette and Nieves 1992, 16–17). A 2000 study from the American Lung Association shows that children of color are disproportionately represented in areas with high ozone levels. Additionally, 61.3 percent of black children, 69.2 percent of Hispanic children, and 67.7 percent of Asian-American children live in areas that exceed the 0.08 ppm (parts per million) ozone standard, while only 50.8 percent of white children live in such areas (American Lung Association 2000).

Reduction in motor vehicle emissions can bring about marked health improvements. For example, the Centers for Disease Control and Prevention (CDC) reports that "when the Atlanta Olympic Games in 1996 brought about a reduction in auto use by 22.5 percent, asthma admissions to ERs and hospitals also decreased by 41.6 percent" (Jackson and Kochtitzky 2001, 3). The CDC researchers also concluded that "less driving, better public transport, well designed landscape and residential density will improve air quality more than will additional road ways." Excessive ozone pollution contributed to

86,000 asthma attacks in Baltimore, Maryland; 27,000 in Richmond, Virginia, and 130,000 in Washington, D.C. (Abt Associates for the National Campaign Against Dirty Power October 1999, 31).

Air pollution from vehicle emissions causes significant amounts of illness, hospitalization, and premature death (Fischlowitz-Roberts 2002). A 2002 study in *The Lancet* reports a strong causal link between ozone and asthma (McConnell et al. 2002, 386–391). Ground-level ozone may exacerbate health problems such as asthma, nasal congestions, throat irritation, respiratory tract inflammation, reduced resistance to infection, changes in cell function, loss of lung elasticity, chest pains, lung scarring, formation of lesions within the lungs, and premature aging of lung tissues (Ozkaynak et al. 1996, 2–7).

A 2001 CDC report "Creating a Healthy Environment: The Impact of the Built Environment on Health" (Fischlowitz-Roberts 2002), points a finger at transportation and sprawl as major health threats. Air pollution claims seventy thousand lives a year, nearly twice the number killed in traffic accidents. Although it is difficult to put a single price tag on the cost of air pollution, estimates range from $10 billion to $200 billion per year (Bollier 1998, 9). Asthma is the number one reason for child hood emergency room visits in most major cities in the country, with the hospitalization rate for African-Americans three to four times the rate for whites (Ozkaynak et al. 1996, 2–7). African-Americans are three times more likely than whites to die from asthma (Centers for Disease Control 2000, 58).

Getting sick is complicated for the nation's uninsured. Blacks and Hispanics are most at risk of being uninsured; blacks and Hispanics now constitute 52.6 percent of the 43 million Americans without health insurance (Mills and Bhandari 2003, 7). Nearly half of working-age Hispanics lacked health insurance for all or part of the year prior to being surveyed, as did almost one-third of African-Americans. In comparison, one-fifth of whites and Asian-Americans ages eighteen to sixty-four lacked coverage for all or part of the year (Collins et al. 2002).

In addition to health and environmental reasons for the United States to move our transportation beyond oil-powered vehicles to more secure and sustainable alternatively fueled ones, there are compelling energy security and economic strength reasons to invest in clean fuels technology. The United States has more than 217 million cars, buses, and trucks that consume 67 percent of the nation's oil. Transportation-related oil consumption in the United States has risen 43 percent since 1975 (Under wood 2001). The United States accounts for almost one-third of the world's vehicles. With just 5 percent of the world's population, Americans consume more than 25 percent of the oil produced worldwide with almost 60 percent of our oil coming from foreign sources (Underwood 2001).

Conclusion

Transportation is a basic ingredient for quality-of-life indicators such as health, education, employment, economic development, and access to municipal services, residential mobility, and environmental quality. Transportation continues to be a civil rights issue. Improvements in transportation investments and air quality are of special importance to low-income persons and people of color who are concentrated in the nation's most polluted urban centers. Transportation investments, enhancements, and financial resources, if used properly, can bring much-needed revitalization to urban areas.

The environmental justice movement has set out clear goals of eliminating unequal enforcement of the nation's environmental, public health, housing, employment, land use, civil rights, and transportation laws. Transportation is a key ingredient in any organization's plan to build economically viable and sustainable communities. State Departments of Transportation and metropolitan planning organizations have a major responsibility to ensure that their programs, policies, and practices do not discriminate against or adversely and disproportionately impact people of color and the poor.

Notes

Bullard, Robert D. "Addressing Urban Transportation Equity in the United States," in *Breakthough Communities: Sustainability and Justice in the Next American Metropolis*, Pavel, M. Paloma, ed. Foreword by Carl Anthony, pp. 490–59, 2009 Massachusetts Institute of Technology. Reprinted by permission of The MIT Press.

1. See Preface to *Just Transportation: Dismantling Race and Class Barriers to Mobility*, eds. R. D. Bullard and G. S. Johnson (Gabriola Island, B.C.: New Society Publishers, 1997), pp. xiii-xiv and 7.

2. See Foreword by J. Lewis in *Just Transportation: Dismantling Race and Class Barriers to Mobility*, eds. R. D. Bullard and G. S. Johnson (Gabriola Island, B.C.: New Society Publishers, 1997), pp. xi-xii. See also M. Garrett and B. Taylor. 1999, "Reconsidering Social Equity in Public Transit," *Berkele)' Planning Journal* 13 (1999): pp. 6–10. Available at http:ffwww.ced.berkeley.edufpubs.bpj/ backissues13.html or http:ffwww.uctc.netfpapersf701.pdf. "The incongruence between transit ridership patterns and subsidy policies has both social and special consequences that can potentially reinforce existing patterns of racial, ethnic, and economic segregation."

3. See D. Kong, "Filipino Americans Work to Preserve Heritage," *Honolulu Star-Bull* (December 26, 2002). Available at http:f/starbulletin.com/2002/12/26/news/fstory8 .html. "By the 1930s, Stockton was home to the largest Filipino population outside the Philippines. But a cross-town freeway cut through the neighborhood in the early 1970s, and the once-vibrant enclave is now just a shadow of what it was."

4. See R. D. Bullard, "Introduction: Anatomy of Sprawl," in *Sprawl City: Race, Politics, and Planning in Atlanta*, eds. R. D. Bullard, Glenn S. Johnson, and Angel O. Torres (Atlanta: Island Press, 2000), pp. 3–4. "Apartheid-type employment, housing,

development, and transportation policies have resulted in limited mobility, reduced neighborhood options, decreased residential choices, and diminished job opportunities for African-American and other people of color who are concentrated in cities."

5. *Plessy v. Ferguson.* 1896. 163 U.S. 537, at 548. "[W]e think the enforced separation of the races, as applied to the internal commerce of the state, neither abridges the privileges or immunities of the colored man, deprives him of his property without due process of law, nor denies him the equal protection of the laws, within the meaning of the fourteenth amendment."

6. See T. W. Sanchez, R. Stolz, and J. S. Ma, "Moving to Equity: Addressing Inequitable Effects of Transportation Policies on Minorities," a joint report of the Civil Rights Project at Harvard University and the Center for Community Change (2003). Available at http:ffwww.civilrightsproject.ucla.edufresearchf transportationftrans_paper03.php. See also Surface Transportation Research and Development Needs for the Next Century, Testimony Before the House Committee on Science, Subcommittee on Technology (April 23, 1997). Hank Dittmar, Executive Director, Surface Transportation Policy Project, notes that "highway and vehicle research . . . account for more than 80% of available funding."

7. See W. W. Buzbee, "Urban Sprawl, Federalism, and the Problem of Institutional Complexity," *Fordham Law Review* vol. 68, no. 112 (October 1999):57–136. "Providing that the main strategy of TEA-21 is to avoid patronage driven transportation decisions by mandating a more open and participatory planning process as a condition for receipt of federal dollars."

8. Ibid., describing the social and environmental deterioration in the Atlanta area due to sprawl.

9. Testimony Before the Senate Finance Committee, Statement of J. S. Cannon, on behalf of INFORM, Inc. (July 10, 2001).

PART

Social Construction of the Environment— Identity, Emotions and Community

Wild Horses and the Political Ecology of Nature Restoration in the Missouri Ozarks

J. Sanford Rikoon

One of the core concepts of sociology is the "social construction of reality"—the idea that we shape our understanding of reality through our interactions with each other. Sociologists promote the view that our ideas about nature are necessarily embedded in our personal experience, sociopolitical history, and cultural context. The next three selections reveal different ways in which humans create meanings around "environment" and "nature" and how those meanings are shaped and contested. The authors show that different social actors may have more or less power to impose on others their own stories or understandings about the natural world. In the first article, J. Sanford Rikoon analyzes a conflict between the National Park Service and the Missouri Wild Horse League over how to manage horses on the range. Rikoon explains how the National Park Service managers and scientists defined the horses as a "feral" nonnative species that was introduced by humans and should be removed. The Missouri Wild Horse League, on the other hand, defined the horses as "wild" animals that represented an important part of the unique ecological history of that region; the league argued, therefore, that the horses should be allowed to continue to roam. This study shows how the differences in the way groups define nature has to do with the collective identities of those groups; and the question of who gets to do the defining has to do with the groups' relative access to political, financial, and other resources.

Introduction

In May of 1990, the National Park Service (NPS) announced its intention to remove small bands totaling around 25 free-roaming horses from the Ozark National Scenic Riverways (ONSR) in south-central Missouri. Immediately following the appearance of a brief NPS press release in the weekly newspaper in Eminence, near the Park's headquarters, community residents began voicing their opposition to the NPS, politicians, and the media. Within six months, local citizens united under the banner of a new group called the Missouri Wild Horse League (MWHL). Resistance by the anti-removal advocates took the form of protests and demonstrations, news releases, a series of litigation challenges, and appeals to state and federal legislators. Legal efforts resulted in a temporary restraining order from a federal judge in St. Louis in late 1990 and a permanent injunction against NPS action from the US District Court in Cape Girardeau in 1992. The Park Service in turn was successful the following year in overturning the injunction before the US Circuit Court of Appeals in St. Louis (Wilkins et al., 1991 and Wilkins et al., 1992). Although legally entitled to remove the horses, the agency refrained from taking any action as it contemplated the potential fallout from heightened media attention and a rising tide of Federal legislative proposals to curb its powers.

After three years of efforts in the US Congress, Bill Emerson (R-MO, 8th District) finally put an end to the conflict with an amendment to the 1996 Omnibus Parks and Public Lands Management Act. Emerson's rule prohibited the NPS from carrying out its 1990 decision and further enjoined the agency to "protect free roaming horses living within the boundaries" of the OSNR and ordered the agency to provide "adequate pastures to accommodate the free-roaming horse herd" (Omnibus Parks, 1996). The congressman's success thus finished off a conflict that had endured through five years of state and federal legislative attention, four years of legal arguing in federal courts, and six years of oftentimes intense and acrimonious encounters between the NPS and local citizens.

Environmental conflicts are at their heart issues about power to decide everything from the definition of nature to access to natural resources and, as a consequence, to reap whatever tangible and intangible spoils go with such victories. As Congressman Emerson's amendment reveals, the power of who gets to decide who decides is often paramount in a theater where the actors range, as in this case, from the local to the national and where the appropriate public (and not so public) arenas range from pastures along the Current River to committee hearing rooms on Constitution Avenue.

This essay focuses on competing cultural constructs about the object of the conflict—the horses themselves. Specifically, it examines the discourses and narratives of the National Park Service and local residents active in the MWHL to understand how each framed the wild horses in relation to both nature and culture, to examine the meaning that the horses had in terms of preferred landscapes, and to reveal how these meanings reflected the social identities of the actors themselves (Nygren, 1999). These are epistemological issues because they require us to ask about the process through which knowledge is created and evaluated, and how particular understandings of the world relate to organized and specific systems of logic, belief, and authority (Raedeke and Rikoon, 1998).

Social Constructions of Landscapes

... Resolutions of environmental conflicts in most public arenas require a decision about whose construction of the environment should be protected, and whose construction should be discounted. In these contexts, settlement rarely depends on any objective measure of whose construct is "better," but rather on which competitor has the greater power—usually political and economic power—to influence the decision-makers. The results, of course, have critical implications not only for the evolution of environmental policy but also for the protection of local people, livelihoods, and culture bound up with access to and use of physical resources. Conflicts over the protection or restoration of landscapes, natural resources, and species are not isolated or simple struggles over defining nature or the landscape. In many cases, conflicts between groups with competing views and interests in the environment embody wider social and economic power relationships and struggles over the control of finite resources. Victory in any environmental conflict results not only in the legitimation and ascendance of one type of knowledge over another, but also in the domination of particular social groups and cultural systems because knowledge itself is part of the cultural systems embedded in social groups. In other words, controversies over physical resources—including the conflict over Ozark wild horses discussed in this essay—can be viewed as social struggles played out in the form of environmental conflict.

Feral or Wild: National Park Service Understandings of Feral Horses

The Park Service perspective, as expressed in both legal arguments and personal interviews with NPS staff, characterize the horses as exotics, literally species in the wrong place or habitat. The first and major line of reasoning for this world-view is formalized agency rules and regulations. The concept of "exotic" in NPS discourse developed out of an ecosystem management philosophy and set of guidelines harking back to the so-called Leopold Report, which in 1963 recommended that "biotic associations within each park be maintained, or where necessary recreated, as nearly as possible in the condition that prevailed when the area was first visited by the white man" (Leopold et al., 1963). The NPS implemented this perspective as an agency-wide mandate for designated "natural zones," including the horses' habitat area in the ONSR, through the 1970 General Administration Act and the 1978 Redwoods Amendment. In essence, the changes shifted the orientation of NPS management from a more recreationalist and conservationist approach to one firmly wedded to an ecosystem preservation ideology and the science of ecology. The authorities in this latter system are the ecologists, biologists, and other scientists who determine the nature of native habitats (Zimmerer, 1996). Adherents of this perspective understand the world through generalized laws and principles developed in the institutional and research contexts of the natural sciences; their constructions of the landscape are not embedded in the local social or cultural contexts in which habitats are located (Forbes, 1999 and Watts, 2000).

Exotic species are of no use to protectors of a "natural area" who, in this case, view the horses as intruders. Consequently, NPS narratives about the landscape contain scant references to the horses, except to establish their recent historical origins and "unnatural" introduction that places them outside of nature and therefore labels them as candidates for removal. Texts that mention the horses are typically couched in impersonal tones with a distant and objective rhetoric:

> The original ownership of the horses is not known. The present small band is believed descended from a pair of horses released in the 1950s. The original group may have been supplanted by additional release in subsequent years. As feral stock, introduced by human action, the horses are not considered native species. (US Department of Interior, 1991)
>
> I've seen the horses a number of times. I don't know if you've seen them, but you wouldn't know they're wild horses. They're like any horse out in the field. You can get fairly close to them. If someone wasn't sitting there to point it out—They talk about them being a draw to the visitor. I don't necessarily think that's true because unless someone was pointing the horses out to you as wild, as far as you know they're just like horses in any pasture. They don't look any different [laughs]. Need to paint a big "W" on the side [laughs]. (Interview with Ben Clary, Superintendent of the OSNR)

These narratives mark the horses as marginal to the NPS mission to preserve "nature" and further highlight the animals' position in NPS belief systems as neither native nor truly wild. Interestingly, the connection of the horses to culture, which is so important to local constructions, disqualifies them from being characterized in NPS worldviews as either "wild" or a legitimate "wilderness" species. The Park Service's preservationist ideology conceives the landscape as an object to be "wildernized" by removing any connection to culture. NPS employees code these meanings through the particular descriptors used to characterize the horses and through the maintenance of skepticism to local narratives. The horses are rarely termed "wild" but typically are characterized as "feral," a designation that suggests their danger to other species. NPS constructions seldom recognize narratives from local residents, area legends, or information from oral histories. When such perspectives are mentioned, the references include such vague disclaimers as "is believed" and "are known to." This rhetoric serves as signifiers of local understandings of the landscape that the NPS considers suspect because these experiences remain non-validated by professional expertise.

The composite NPS "master" narrative about the horses is grounded in the experimental and universalizing cultural framework of a positivistic science. Relevant knowledge is collected at field sites, tested in laboratories, aggregated in computer models, and transmitted within the group through formal educational channels and conduits. "Natural" landscapes are bounded by the "natural" laws of energy, climate, geology, hydrology, and other physical systems as these are "discovered" by experts. Park Service officials understand the world through their commitment to the principles of a scientific ecosystem management, and several park officials involved with the wild horse case said that they were "bound by science" (and regulation) to make the decisions that they did. The overall process then is deterministic rather than emergent, and deductive rather than inductive.

Visions of nature are often connected to the self-identities of groups (Bell, 1994, Forbes, 1999 and Nygren, 2000). The social communities within the NPS most central to the agency's constructions of "natural" landscapes are those of the wildlife biologists, ecologists, and other physical and biological scientists. As Robbins (2002) emphasizes, institutionalized knowledge at all scales and levels are an important part of most stories, and certainly the knowledge system of "scientists" are socioculturally embedded. In this case, ecological science adherents have over the years developed a holistic, albeit temporally and spatially limited, ecosystem-based cultural framework reflecting their understandings of the world. It is this framework through which NPS staffers evaluate knowledge and make management decisions. In relation to the horse conflict, the Park Service considered themselves as "honor bound rule upholders" working on behalf of ecosystem integrity and the larger public good (typically defined as "national" rather than "local"). Such views indicate a belief that humans are the protectors of an integrity that exists outside of themselves and can be objectively assessed.

One important product of this kind of thinking is the development of "natural" ecosystems narratives at odds with either humanistic or social science understandings of cultural or human ecology. Park management decision-makers have been socialized to accept a value system that characterizes natural ecosystems devoid of any human contamination as good, and human intrusions on those ecosystems as bad (a stance that oddly places most homo sapiens—other than the managers themselves—outside any "natural sphere"). According to this orientation, resource professionals are managing for nature; they are nature protectors. In its strictly preservation narrative, an idealized nature is associated with the past, specifically a pre–European immigration past, while culture and human activities have become associated with modernity and the present. Thus nature is depicted in NPS narratives as something that must be "wildernized," "demodernized," and managed apart from, rather than connected to, human communities. The attempt to remove the wild horses and the controversy that followed are consequences of this attempt to "naturalize" the ONSR.

A second product of this way of organizing the world is faith in what might be called a progressive linearity of ecological education, and a concomitant belief that a lack of education is the major obstacle standing between people's resistance and acceptance of NPS decisions. According to this orientation, resistance to ecological ideas comes from lack of ecological understanding; hence, NPS employees usually believe that with patience and education, people who resist will over time come to see and accept the perspective of science and the authority of scientists. In a rather direct letter to Congressman Emerson, a wildlife biologist commented:

> The decision of the National Park Service to remove livestock from the park is the only sound and sensible policy it could adopt. There exists a wealth of research literature on the consequences of allowing exotic plants and species to occupy native systems. The literature argues powerfully that exotic plants and animals have a high potential for causing serious and irreversible damage to native areas.
>
> As in science generally, the field of conservation biology is studded with cases where 'common sense,' meaning what an uninformed individual thinks is reasonable, is directly contrary to what sound science suggests.
>
> I recognize that political capital can be generated for arguing the locally popular yet biologically disastrous position that the horses should remain. I would urge you to consider the evidence more thoroughly. You

may not understand the issues, but just as a patient with a tumor is liable to trust the physician who recommends the treatment, I urge you to recognize that it is as wise to reject the evidence from conservation biology as to reject the medical evidence regarding treatment for a tumor.

—Letter to Congressman Emerson, September 9, 1994, from a
faculty member of a campus of the state university system

The NPS narratives invoke a set of standards established through the cultural frameworks of biologists and ecologists and disavow any significance to the cultural meaning systems of local residents. While the ONSR, like most Park Service sites, includes personnel and activities concerned with area cultural resources, NPS epistemology disassociates these horses from culture (or, more accurately, a culture worth conserving) in two ways. First, the agency tends to prioritize cultural units using the same time perspective they attach to "good" species and "bad" species. As Howell (1994, p. 122) notes, the more removed a human activity is from the present, the more compatible it is with the NPS mission: "Over the years its preservationist ethic led the Park Service to separate nature from culture and to value historical over contemporary cultural expressions." NPS narratives fix the horses' origin in the very recent past and this modern pedigree is inconsistent with their notion of "true" Ozark heritage and history. Second, the dominant NPS view of Ozark history and heritage rarely extends to the conservation of contemporary physical artifacts whose cultural significance to local residents is largely intangible and, in many respects, anti-NPS. Indeed, to many MWHL members, the wild horses have come to symbolize the struggle of a people who perceive their recent history as one of disempowerment and disenfranchisement at the hands of government and external forces.

Local Resident Understandings of Wild Horses

In contrast to the academic and science-based foundations of the belief and value systems of NPS employees, local residents' views of the horses and their importance to the landscape are based on knowledge generated through immediate personal experience and local culture and filtered through collective interpretations of their Ozark past and anxieties about their future. In effect local constructions exchange the sanitizing lens of the institutional relations and the community of physical and biological scientists as moral authorities for the praxis of everyday life and the experience of past and future generations. Opponents' narratives of the horses, in contrast to NPS discourse, are embedded in discussions of the area's culture and history, contain many references to community places and people, and are related in personalistic styles.

Local knowledge of the horses themselves is based on direct encounters and personal sightings. The resulting narratives describe the horses and human encounters with them in great detail and suggest a much more developed human-nature intimacy than is apparent in the NPS narratives.

> We were over there on V Highway by Two Rivers. We rode up in the field and there was all three herds. Now they were not together. There was one little herd and then over about thirty yards another. And then out there about 50 or 60 yards was the other herd. And that was all of them, to my knowledge, except two little yearling studs that had been kicked out . . . . And I'd give anything to have had a movie camera. When we rode up, the wind was a-blowing and we come up on the wrong side for them to smell us or hear us either. And we just rode out on the edge of that field and set there watching them. And then all of a sudden one of them look up and seen us. Man, he throwed his head up and snorted, whinnied. He just whistled, whistled through his nose. Then they all took that look. So here comes that first bunch. They are running up there always looking us over. And then here comes the other bunch running up and lined up with them. And then here comes the third bunch.
>
> —Author interview with Jim Smith

> I'm real fond of the two white mares in that one bunch that spends a lot of time by the old Thomas place. Sometimes I wouldn't know those two apart. They're old. They're like thirteen, fourteen years old. I know that because I saw them as colts and for a while there I couldn't tell one from the other. And there's a gray mare with 'em and I'd always know her. And there's a white crooked necked mare. And that bunch has got three, kind of roanish grays in there. And then they got two colts. One of them has a blaze face and it's been turning white.
>
> —Author interview with Russ Noah

Local attachments to the wild horses are often intensely personal because of individual and social connections to sighting the horses that are free to roam the area, "owned" by no one. Some Ozarkers tell of regular Sunday afternoon family outings to look for the animals; others would ride out periodically or during particular seasons to check the herds.

> Well, my little girl got killed when she was fifteen. And then the other boy is twenty-five now. The girl was the one that (pause)—that's one reason that I (pause) have been so hard wanting them [wild horses] to stay here.

When she was little, like nine or ten years old, we rode a lot. We rode a lot. She got a big thrill out of them. She always wanted to go see them.

—Interview with Bill Smith

In fact, my great uncle, and granddad, my dad—their horses in the wintertime when they wasn't using them, they'd turn 'em out. And they'd go back on Jerktail Mountain on the Big Glade and winter back up there. And they'd be with the wild horses and sometimes it take 'em a month or two. When they got ready to go to plowing and working the field and stuff in the spring they'd have to go and get those horses. They kept a bell on one of their horses so they could hear em. And every once in a while during the winter when they wasn't doing anything they'd ride back there and call 'em up and feed them, especially that old bell horse. She was the herd leader. If they kept her gentle enough they could catch her. Then when they'd ride back they would catch her and lead her to the house with the rest of the herd. Her bunch would follow, you see. And a lot of the times that's the way they'd get em. Catch theirs back, you know. Somebody would get around and cut theirs out and when they took that old bell—cause them horses, you stayed with that bell. They'd cut 'em out and herd 'em a little bit and then they'd go and follow and follow 'em to the house. You can't hardly run 'em and catch 'em period. It's like trying to catch a deer out in the woods, you know.

—Author interview with Jim Thomas

Local social constructions of the landscape also include diverse legends of the horses' origins. Almost all of these texts establish an older pedigree for the bands still in the ONSR. Whether or not the actual date of the wild horses' origin is more recent or more remote, such stories establish in local tradition a connection of the horses with previous generations and experiences.

I've heard lots of stories about those wild horses. There's some that tell you that those horses date back to the Civil War and before. Wild horses of the Ozark hills were caught and trained and used for cavalry mounts. Then the settlers and the farmers they used them to clear and till and work their fields and such. I don't know how they did that but that's what they had and they did it. And then the timber used them to skid the logs, great big logs sometimes, from the forests around here and that's what they used to build our houses and our farms.

—Author interview with Alan Akers

Well, there have always been wild horses. I grew up in the Ozarks. We had wild horses when I was a kid and I'm 77 years old. But like I said, we had open range and I used to drive the cattle in when I was a little kid and I'd run into a herd of wild horses then. They'd be a running around and they'd scare me. I'd be kind of afraid of 'em.

—Author interview with Elmo Thompson

Elmo Thomspon's reference to "open range" keys a critical meaning of the horses—the horses' connection of locals to a series of events that have changed Ozark people and life forever. In many of the Ozarker narratives, and especially in the discourses of longer-term residents, the horses are closely linked to the closure of the open range and, by extension, to the erosion of a cherished and traditional Ozark lifestyle due to the intrusions of the values, regulations, and lifestyles of outsiders. While the region had previously coped with a number of menaces, including the cultural hegemony and resource exploitation of timber companies around the turn of the twentieth century, families had withstood previous external threats through the operation of a strong informal economy, use of available natural resources (including those now in the protected OSNR), and access to and use of a public commons in the form of an open range comprised largely of undeveloped forest and meadow areas. The current older generation is steeped in a tradition of open range, and even the official NPS history of the ONSR area (Stevens, 1991, p. 29) notes that the "southern hillmen . . . fervently believed in open range." Although agricultural mechanization diminished open range customs in southern Missouri following World War II, the practice continued in parts of the Missouri Ozarks, especially in the region in and around the ONSR, until the late 1960s, or past the date of the park's establishment. Shannon County (the site of Eminence) was the last county in Missouri, and one of the last in the nation, to use open range practices. In the stories of removal opponents, the wild horses are products and tangible reminders of the open range era and express the essence of the philosophy of open range in which inhabitants adapt to, rather than change, the environment. In particular, the open range connotes an earlier, and pre-government, era of Ozark lifestyle based on a system of individual freedom to use the land, and a strong community in which individuals shared a basic social trust and system of communal resource use.

Well, you see, most people around here it's just kind of part of the heritage. It's the only wild horses in the state of Missouri, you know. And now they call 'em feral horses. And I guess maybe any horse at sometime or another has become a tame horse. But these horses there's not one live horse in that bunch that I know of that's ever been touched, you know.

And I mean when I was a boy it was open range. There was always horses that people—that didn't really belong to anybody. And then when the range closed there was some of these horses left and they're still here.

—Author interview with Bill Smith

They've (wild horses) originated out of domestic horses. Back in the 20s and 30s there was people that lived up and down the Jacks Fork and Current River and every little old holler almost had a family living there—and of course, there was a lot of sawmill work back then and that's about all there was to do really. But then when the Great Depression come along a lot of those folks just simply starved out and had to leave here and go to work somewhere. And at that time, see, they had open range. And those people would run their stock outside, especially what they wasn't using. They'd keep their milk cows up and their buggy horse or their horse that they was riding and using, you know—keep them up where they could catch 'em and get to 'em and use 'em. But, the other they just let run out in the wild. And everybody had their own brand and their own mark on their animals and they left 'em and they just made it.

—Author interview with Jim Smith

Narrators opposed to the horses' removal tell their stories with pride and emotion. A self-described "old-timer" named Matt Hunt, who is also acknowledged by many residents as the local "expert" on the horses, says that he has seen and heard of the wild horses throughout his life. He claims that "removing those horses from the Park Service grounds would be like tearing the last page out of a history book" (Author interview with Matt Hunt). Like long-time Ozark residents, the horses are a product of the mountainous geography and complex social and economic processes that created them. But perhaps unlike the locals, the wild horses are survivors and symbols of what the locals would like to be.

By defining the wild horses as cultural objects and invoking meanings involving family and the communal action associated with the practice of open range grazing, residents closely associate themselves materially and ideologically with the wild horses and their plight. The wild horses are not simply a product of the open range, but in their "wildness" they are a last tangible reminder of an idealized lifestyle characterized by freedom, community, and self-control. The close of open range represents an example of how Ozarkers believe outside pressures have affected, and continue to affect, their unique institutions and lifestyles. As with many resource dependent communities with a relatively recent history of geographic and cultural isolation, the Ozarks have been tremendously impacted over the past three decades by outsiders, especially government agencies, environmental organizations, and tourists (Stevens, 1991). Beginning with the creation of the ONSR in the mid-1960s, resident peoples in the region have witnessed land condemnation and a host of restrictions on their economic and recreational activities in the name of ecological restoration, protection, and management. The ONSR itself was the second NPS site (after Yellowstone) in the country whose creation required the acquisition of private lands and the use of eminent domain. And since then, as Brady (1991 and Brady, 1994) and other researchers (Rikoon and Goedeke, 2000) have pointed out, the history of NPS–local resident relationships is marked by numerous attempts (some successful and some not) at cultural and social intervention on the part of the federal agency.

As a result of this history, many long-term residents have come to associate the Park Service, and the government in general, as an immensely powerful force whose legacy has been the loss of local control, freedom, and power over their lives and livelihoods. The same values are associated with both the wild horses and an idealized Ozarker identity. Importantly, local visions of the horses and strategies of self-identity are deeply intertwined in constructions of the landscape. These links were made dramatically clear in the 1990s at events such as wild horse benefit shows where t-shirts and ball caps emblazoned with the phrase "wild and free let 'em be" referred to the protesters' own idealized identity as much as that of the horses. Local residents came to symbolically identify with the plight of the horses, and they linked treatment of the horses with their own treatment at the hands of the government. This is no inappropriate stretch of imagination—both groups are marginalized, both groups are powerless. In the end, if the Park Service would consider the wild horses as species *non grata* and ticket them for removal, is it not also possible to believe that local people fear their own futures in the region are marked by a similar precariousness?

Implications for Ecosystem Management

In summary of the preceding discussion of competing cultural constructions of this landscape, NPS texts speak in terms of ecosystem generalities and principles, present a unidimensional discourse of an idealized landscape devoid of human-nature interaction apart from management activity, and characterize the horses as an anonymous intruding species. In contrast, local residents' depictions are expressed in terms of experiential events and specific encounters, tell of the horses in a personalized and detailed rhetoric, present a more complex and symbiotic human-nature relationship, and relate the horses' experiences to their own Ozark history and heritage. In regard to symbol formation, the horses represent a secular intrusion to the NPS, a symbol of contemporary human culture that mars their sacred scientific ecosystem vision of an ideal nature landscape. To removal opponents, the entire conflict has served to elevate the horses from a secular and largely taken for granted status to a more sacred status as symbols of residents' own lost, or in jeopardy, regional identities and the long and continuing struggle between many locals and the NPS/outsiders.

The two competing visions concerning the free-roaming horses on the Ozark landscape reflect continuing and contrasting notions about the relationship between nature restoration and resource use. Ecosystem management of public nature parks in the U.S. stresses the goals of preservation and restoration. Local communities and resident peoples have increasingly contested the dominant NPS ethic of preservation, as exemplified in Yellowstone National Park, but the relationship between nature preservation and nature use is unresolved. For the Park Service, the notion of being an agency protecting a national public good remains strong. Local site managers have realized that some balance is needed in terms of local use of the park. They are inclined, however, to regard local uses as "special interests" that must be placated to maintain good public relations, but they are inclined to regard such compromises as fundamentally opposed to agency interests.

Local opponents to the wild horse removal accept a conception of nature as wilderness. But in this case the horses are part of that nature in that they are "wild" and run "free." As opposed to NPS self-identification as naturalists or environmentalists, many local citizens define themselves as conservationists who champion a dynamic and interactive human-nature relationship. Their narratives of the landscape focus more heavily on issues of resource use and the conservation of resources linked to the maintenance of local livelihoods and cultural and social traditions. They argue to the Park Service that the Ozarks are not Yellowstone. In the words of local trail-rider Kathy Thomas, "we don't want to be made into another Yellowstone; we live here." Instead, they call for a "common sense" approach to nature and ascribe a concomitant lack of common sense to the Park Service. This view is most overt in a host of narratives about Park Service regulations, local resistance, and conflicts between local traditional uses of the landscape and the Park Service's impositions of what can and cannot be done in the ONSR.

Blaikie (1995, p. 209) notes that "only by acknowledging multiple views, understanding the politics of how actors present their views and pursue their projects, can current scientific and conservation thinking be literally brought down to earth." The Ozark wild horse conflict is at first glance a disagreement between NPS officials and local citizens regarding whether or not a small band of horses should be removed. However, in a deeper context it represented a fundamental and symbolic conflict about social and political power and who should have it. There are certainly many justifications for the Park Service's imperative to protect nature (as they define "nature" and "the natural") and to engage in restoration activities. Yet, when protected areas such as the Ozark Riverways are created and managed without the involvement and interest of people in the area, there are costs involved—not only to the protected area itself, but also in terms of the loss of regional identity and missed opportunities for cultural conservation and livelihood sustenance. The struggle over the wild horses in the Ozark Riverways reveals the many disjunctures that result from the dichotomous categories used by conservation professions (Rikoon, 1996). The small bands of horses that continue to roam the region are oblivious, of course, to the categories that humans use to describe them. But the thirst to categorize the landscape into dichotomies of nature and culture, tangible and intangible, and exotic and indigenous may exclude more than they include. It is into these kinds of conceptual gaps that the horses fall, and certainly it is this kind of marginality issue with which many of their protectors often self-identify. . . .

It seems so obvious today to argue that local communities can and should be more involved in the policy and program decisions that affect the ecosystems in which they live, although even this lesson learned over decades of international development and protection failures is under renewed scrutiny (Chapin, 2004). But too often the knowledge and needs of local residents remain discounted in the US by more powerful outsiders who feel themselves possessors of a privileged knowledge of the world. Such perspectives, however, ultimately defeat themselves by alienating the very people whose support is crucial if the environment is to be protected in a sustainable way (Cronon, 1996a and Cronon, 1996b). As Berry (1987, p. 43) notes, "The only thing we have to preserve nature with is culture." In the case of the resolution of the Ozark wild horse controversy, the final verdict had very little to do with wild horses and community empowerment and a lot to do with the Republican Party's 1996 Contract with America. In a rather ironic twist, the horse controversy became a symbol used by the Republican Party, including Congressman Emerson, to depict the excesses of an overbearing, misdirected, and intrusive government bureaucracy (Author interview with Bill Emerson). The horses are now protected, but this outcome was not the result of an effort to empower local communities and their culture; rather it was the end result of a political slap on the wrist given to an agency that legislators felt should be directing its resources to more "important" concerns.

Note

Rikoon, J. Sanford. 2006. "Wild Horses and the Political Ecology of Nature Restoration in the Missouri Ozarks." *Geoforum* 37: 200–211.

References

Bell, M.M., 1994. *Childerley: Nature and Morality in a Country Village*, University of Chicago Press, Chicago.

Berry, W., 1987. *Home Economics*. Northpoint, San Francisco.

Blaikie, P., 1995. Changing environments or changing views? A political ecology for developing countries, *Geography* 80 (348), pp. 203–214.

Bradley, K., 1997. Unfinished business: Missouri's Natural Streams Campaign and the changing conditions of environmental action/research. Ph.D. Dissertation, University of Missouri-Columbia.

Brady, E., 1991. Mankind's thumb on nature's scale: trapping and regional identity in the Ozarks. In: B. Allen and T. Schlereth, Editors, *Sense of Place: American Regional Cultures*, University Press of Kentucky, Lexington, pp. 58–73.

Brady, E., 1994. "The river's like our back yard": tourism and cultural identity in the Ozark National Scenic Riverways. In: M. Hufford, Editor, *Conserving Culture: A New Discourse on Heritage*, University of Illinois Press, Urbana, pp. 138–151.

Chapin, M., 2004. A challenge to conservationists, *WorldWatch* 13 (6), pp. 17–24.

Cronon, W., 1996a. The trouble with wilderness: a response, *Journal of Environmental History* 1, pp. 52–53.

Cronon, W., 1996b. Introduction: in search of nature. In: W. Cronon, Editor, *Uncommon Ground: Rethinking the Human Place in Nature*, W. W. Norton, New York, pp. 23–56.

Forbes, A.A., 1999. The importance of being local: villagers, NGOS, and the World Bank in the Arun Valley, Nepal, *Identities* 6 (2–3), pp. 319–344.

Fairhead, J., and M. Leach., 1994. Contested forests: modern conservation and historical land use in guinea's ziama reserve, *African Affairs* 93, pp. 481–512.

Goedeke, T., 2005. Devil, angel or animal: the social construction of otters in conflict over management. In: Herda-Rapp, A., Goedeke, T. (Eds.), *Mad about Wildlife: Looking at Social Conflict over Wildlife*. Brill Academic Publishers, Leiden.

Howell, B.J., 1994. Linking cultural and natural conservation in National Park Service policies and programs. In: M. Hufford, Editor, *Conserving Culture: A New Discourse on Heritage*, University of Illinois Press, Urbana, pp. 122–137.

Leopold, A.S., S.A. Cain, C. Cottram, I.N. Gabrielson, and T.L. Kimbell, 1963. Report on wildlife management in the national parks, *National Parks Magazine* (October) (insert).

Nygren, A., 1999. Local knowledge in the environment-development discourse: from dichotomies to situated knowledges, *Critique of Anthropology* 19 (3), pp. 267–288.

Nygren, A., 2000. Environmental narratives on protection and production: nature-based conflicts in Río San Juan, Nicaragua, *Development and Change* 31 (4), pp. 807–830.

Omnibus Parks and Public Lands Management Act, 1996. US Congress. 1996. Public Law 104–333, Sec. 803.

Raedeke, A.J., and J.S. Rikoon, 1998. Competing knowledge systems and agricultural decision-making, *Agriculture and Human Values* 14, pp. 145–158.

Raedeke, A.J., J.S. Rikoon, and C.H. Nilon, 2000a. Factors affecting landowner participation in ecosystem management: a case study in South-Central Missouri, *Wildlife Society Bulletin* 29 (1), pp. 195–209.

Raedeke, A.J., J.S. Rikoon, and C.H. Nilon, 2000b. Ecosystem management and landowner concern about regulations: a case study in the Missouri Ozarks, *Society and Natural Resources* 14 (1), pp. 77–94.

Rikoon, J.S., 1996. Imagined culture and cultural imaging: the case of the USDA-SCS 'Harmony' campaign, *Society and Natural Resources* 9, pp. 583–597.

Rikoon, J.S., and T. Goedeke, 2000. *Challenging Environmentalism: The Failed Effort to Establish the Ozark Highlands Man and the Biosphere Reserve.* The Edwin Mellen Press, New York and Cardiff.

Robbins, P., 2002. Obstacles to a first world political ecology? Looking near without looking up, *Environment and Planning* 34, pp. 1509–1513.

Stevens, D.L., 1991. *A Homeland and a Hinterland: the Current and Jacks Fork Rivers.* National Park Service, Omaha.

U.S. Department of Interior, 1991. National Park Service, 1991. *Environmental Assessment for Removal of Feral Horses, Ozark National Scenic Riverways, Missouri.* National Park Service, Omaha.

Watts, M., 2000. Contested communities, malignant markets, and gilded governance: justice, resource extraction, and conservation in the tropics. In: C. Zerner, Editor, *People, Plants, and Justice: The Politics of Nature Conservation*, Columbia University Press, New York, pp. 21–51.

Wilkins, Richard and Ronald Smotherman v. Secretary of the Interior, 1991. United States District Court, Eastern District Missouri, Southeastern Division, Case Number S91-31-C(5).

Wilkins, Richard and Ronald Smotherman v. Secretary of the Interior, 1992. United States Court of Appeals, Eighth Circuit, Case Number 92-2871.

Zimmerer, K.S., 1996. Discourse on soil loss in Bolivia: sustainability and the search for socioenvironmental middle ground. In: R. Peet and M. Watts, Editors, *Liberation Ecologies: Environment, Development, Social Movements*, Routledge, London, pp. 110–124.

10

People Want to Protect Themselves a Little Bit

Emotions, Denial, and Social Movement Nonparticipation

Kari Marie Norgaard

Citizen action is an important way to bring about social and environmental change. But such action depends not just on the perceived existence of a problem but also on people's understandings of that problem and their emotional responses to it. Kari Marie Norgaard looks at the failure of a community in Norway to take action on global climate change. Given that Norway's weather has already been measurably affected by climate change and given Norwegians' relatively high level of knowledge about this issue, Norgaard asks why many Norwegians avoid participation in social action. Norgaard argues that part of the answer lies in the negative emotions—feelings of fear, guilt, helplessness, and so forth—that this issue elicits. Her case study documents how community members engage in collective avoiding of the topic because it makes them unhappy or uncomfortable. Collectively, they seek to distance themselves from the problem. While Norgaard focuses on climate change, her argument may be useful in thinking about many different environment-related problems.

. . . Global climate change is arguably the single most significant environmental issue of our time. Scientific reports indicate that global warming will

have widespread ecological consequences over the coming decades including changes in ecosystems, weather patterns, and sea level rise (IPCC 2001).
Impacts on human society are predicted to be widespread and potentially
catastrophic as water shortages, decreased agricultural productivity, extreme
weather events, and the spread of diseases take their toll. Potential outcomes
for Norway include increased seasonal flooding, decreased winter snows and
the loss of the gulf stream that currently maintains moderate winter temperatures, thereby providing both fish and a livable climate to the northern
region. In Norway public support for the environmental movement as well
as public awareness of, and belief in, the phenomenon of global warming
have been relatively high. In Bygdaby the weather was noticeably warmer
and drier than in the past. Yet, in spite of the fact that people were clearly
aware of global warming as a phenomenon, everyday life went on as though
global warming, and its associated risks, was not a possibility. Despite the
apparent heaviness and seriousness of the issue, it was not discussed in the
local newspaper, or the strategy meetings of local political, volunteer or
environmental meetings I attended. Aside from casual comments about the
weather, everyday life went on as though global warming, and its associated
risks—did not exist. Instead, global warming was an abstract concept, that
was not integrated into everyday life. Mothers listened to news of unusual
flooding as they drove their children to school. Families watched evening
news coverage of failing Hague climate talks followed by American made sit-
coms. Few people even seemed to spend much time thinking about it. It did
not appear to be a common topic of either political or private conversation.
How did people manage to outwardly ignore such significant risks? Why did
such seemingly serious problems draw so little response?

   The people of Bygdaby are not unique. Despite the extreme seriousness
of global warming, the pattern of meager public response in the way of social
movement activity, behavioral changes or public pressure on governments
exists worldwide. Public apathy on global warming has been identified as a
significant concern by environmental sociologists (e.g., Kempton et al. 1995,
Dunlap 1998, Rosa 2001, Brechin 2003). Existing literature emphasizes the
notion (either explicitly or implicitly) that information is the limiting factor in
public non-response. Yet the people I met were generally well informed about
global warming. They expressed concern frequently, yet this concern did not
translate into action.

   Over time I noticed that conversations about global warming were emo-
tionally charged and punctuated with awkward pauses. The people I spent
time with and interviewed raised a number of emotional concerns including
fear of the future and guilt over their own actions. During an interview, Eirik
described the complexity of the issue:

We go on vacation and we go shopping, and my partner drives to work every day. And I drive often up here to my office myself. We feel that we must do it to make things work on a practical level, but we have a guilty conscience, a bit of a guilty conscience.

. . . It became further apparent that community members had a variety of tactics for normalizing these awkward moments and uncomfortable feelings— what Arlie Hochschild calls practices of emotion management (1979, 1983, 1990). This paper describes how the presence and management of unpleasant and troubling emotions associated with global warming worked to prevent social movement participation in this rural Norwegian community.

In Bygdaby the possibility of global warming was both deeply disturbing and almost completely invisible, simultaneously unimaginable and common knowledge. The people I spoke with *did* believe global warming was happening, expressed concern about it, yet lived their lives as though they did not know. . . .

Methods: An Ethnography of the Invisible

The observations in this paper are based on one year of field research including 46 interviews, media analysis, and eight months of participant observation. The people I spent time with lived in a rural community of about 14,000 inhabitants in western Norway. Because my research question concerned why people were *not* more actively engaged with the issue of global warming, gathering information required a number of strategies to minimize the tendency for people to begin talking about global warming because it was a topic they knew I found interesting. I kept the specific focus of my research vague, telling people that my work was on issues such as "political participation" and "how people think about global issues." . . . As a participant observer I attended to the kinds of things people talked about, how issues were framed, and especially noted topics that were not discussed. I watched regional television news and read the local and national newspapers. I paid particular attention to beliefs, emotions and cultures of talk with respect to global warming, i.e., whether it was discussed, if so how it came up, how people seemed to feel talking about it. . . . I interviewed as wide a variety of people as I could find. Those I interviewed ranged in age from 19 to early 70s. Respondents were from a variety of occupations, and from six of the nine active local political parties. . . .

. . . I attempted to minimize the degree to which respondents felt a moral pressure to provide a particular answer by first listening to see whether global warming was volunteered as an issue. If global warming was not raised (as it often was not), I asked what people thought about the recent weather (which was widely described as abnormal), and followed with more specific questions such as when they first began thinking about global warming and whether they spoke about global warming with family or friends.

Why Norway?

Despite the salience of my questions to the situation in all Western nations, a case study set in Norway is particularly useful. Anyone who begins to talk about movement non-participation, denial and political action in the U.S. immediately encounters a host of relevant questions: "Do people really know the information?" "Is global warming really happening? I thought it was still controversial." "Do people really have enough time and money to spare that we can consider it denial that they are not acting?" "People in the U.S. are apathetic in general, why would it be any different on this issue?" Each of these are valid questions that complicate an analysis like mine. Yet each of these factors is either absent or minimized in Norway: Norway has one of the highest levels of GDP of any nation and a fifty year history of welfare state policies that has redistributed this wealth amongst the people (UNDP 2004). In terms of political activity, Norwegians again are exemplary. High percentages of Norwegians vote and are active in local politics. When it comes to information and knowledge, Norwegians are a highly educated public. Norway and Japan are tied for the highest level of newspaper readership in the world. Furthermore, in contrast to the situation in the U.S. (Gelbspan 2004), Norwegian media did raise the issue of global warming in their coverage of the unusual weather, and described potential future weather scenarios and impacts. Although there were certainly skeptics about global warming in Bygdaby, such skepticism is much less than in the United States where large counter campaigns have been waged by industry (McCright and Dunlap 2000, 2003). Finally, Norwegians have been proud of their relationships to nature, environmentalism and leadership on global environmental issues including global warming (Eriksen 1993, 1996). If any nation can find the ability to respond to this problem, it must be in such a place as this, where the population is educated, cared for, politicized and environmentally engaged.

Research in Norway is also unique due to the particularly strong contradiction between professed values and the nation's political economy. In Norway there is strong identification with humanitarian values and a heightened concern for the environment (Reed and Rothenberg 1993). Yet as the world's sixth largest oil producer, Norway is one of the nations of the world that has benefited most from oil production. The presence of high levels of wealth, political activity, education, idealism and environmental values together with a petroleum based economy made the contradiction between knowledge and action particularly visible in Norway.

"Bygdaby" was selected because its size allowed me access to a wide cross section of the community, and the fact that residents spoke a dialect I was able to understand. The presence of a nearby lake (that failed to freeze) and ski area (that opened late) were not conditions I selected for, but ones that nonetheless added to the visibility and salience of global warming for community members.

The Winter of 2000–2001 in Bygdaby

Global warming was clearly salient for Norwegians on both the local and national levels during the time period of my research. A number of unusual weather events took place in the fall and winter that year. Most tangible was the very late snowfall and warmer winter temperatures in Bygdaby. Temperatures for the community as reported by the local newspaper showed that average temperature in the Bygdaby region on the whole was warmer than in the past. In fact, as of January 2001 the winter of 2000 was recorded as the second warmest in the past 130 years. Additionally, snowfalls arrived some two months late (mid- to late January as opposed to November). As a result of these conditions, the ski area opened late, with both recreational and economic effects on the community, and the ice on the lake failed to freeze sufficiently to allow ice fishing, once a frequent activity. In fact, not only did the local ski season start late, the downhill ski area opened with 100% artificial snow—a completely unprecedented event. A woman who was walking on the lake drowned when the ice cracked and she fell through, although this sort of accident could have happened in the spring of any year when the ice normally broke up.

The topic of global warming was also very visible in the media. In addition to weather events, a number of national and international political events brought global warming to Bygdabyingar's minds. In November, several thousand miles to the South, the nations of the world held climate meetings at the Hague. Both the King and Prime Minister mentioned global warming in their New Year's Day speeches. Three weeks later on January 22, 2001, the United Nations Intergovernmental Panel on Climate Change released a new report on climate. In March U.S. President George Bush declared that following the Kyoto Protocol was not in the economic interests of the United States and flatly rejected it. Each of these events received significant attention in the regional and national press. . . . Indeed I was continually impressed with the level of up to date information that people had regarding global warming. Here is an excerpt from a focus group that I conducted with five female students in their late teens the week after the climate talks at the Hague failed. Note that these young women are aware of the failed talks, are familiar with (and critical of) the fact that Norway is required to decrease carbon dioxide emissions 5% by the year 2008, and that they feel that global warming is a real issue, observable in their immediate surroundings:

Kari: What have you heard about global warming?

Siri: I have heard about the conference, I became a bit afraid when they didn't reach agreement. . .

Trudi: Our Minister of Environment! In 2008 we will decrease our emissions by five percent (General laugher)

Mette: That will help!

Kari: And is it something that you feel is really happening, or . . .(Several speaking at once)

Mette: Now it is incredible, five degrees Celsius is, you know, really strange . . . mmm, Ja-

Siri : (Interrupting) There should be snow [now].

Trudi: It comes in much closer for us. It is here . . . You notice it. You know, it's getting worse and worse . . . Last year there was snow at this time of year. And actually that is the way it should have been for quite some time now.

A Series of Troubling Emotions

Although the sense that people fail to respond to global warming because they are too poorly informed (Read et al. 1994, Kempton et al. 1995, Dunlap 1998, Bord et al. 1998, Brechin 2003), too greedy or too individualistic, suffer from incorrect mental models (Bostrom et al. 1994) or faulty decision making processes (Halford and Sheehan 1991), underlies much of the research in environmental sociology, the people I spoke with expressed feelings of deep concern and caring and a significant degree of ambivalence about the issue of global warming. People in Bygdaby told me many reasons why it was difficult to think about this issue. In the words of one man, who held his hands in front of his eyes as he spoke, "people want to protect themselves a bit." Community members described fears associated with loss of ontological security, feelings of helplessness, guilt and the associated emotion of fear of "being a bad person" . . . .

Not only were these emotions unpleasant in themselves, the feelings that thinking about global warming raised went against local emotion norms. . . . Emotion norms in Bygdaby (and Norway generally) emphasized the importance of maintaining control (beholde kontroll) and toughness (å være tøff), and for young people, being cool (kult)—especially in public spaces. Adults, especially men and public figures, faced pressures to be knowledgeable and intelligent. In some settings, especially for educators, there was an emotion norm of maintaining optimism. Educators described balancing personal doubts and deep feelings of powerlessness with the task of sending a hopeful message to students. When I spoke with Arne, a teacher at the local agricultural school:

> I am unfortunately pessimistic. I just have to say it. But I'm not like that towards the students. *You know, I must be optimistic when I speak with the students.*

Note that Arne's use of the phrase "you know" highlights the sense that this reality, the need to be optimistic with students, is taken for granted, incontestable. . . .

Risk, Modern Life and Fears Regarding Ontological Security

> Automobile and plane crashes, toxic chemical spills and explosions, nuclear accidents, food contamination, genetic manipulation, the spread of AIDS, global climate change, ozone depletion, species extinction and the persistence of nuclear weapons arsenals: the list goes on. Risks abound and people are increasingly aware that no one is entirely safe from the hazards of modern living. Risk reminds us of our dependency, interdependency and vulnerability (Jaeger et al. 2001, 13).

One day in mid-December my husband and I, disappointed with the lack of snow in Bygdaby, decided to take the train a few hours away to a neighboring community. The temperature was about minus five and the sun was shining brightly on the bare fields surrounding our house as we loaded our skis into the taxi and headed down the road to the train. "Do you like to ski?" I asked our driver? "Oh yes, but I don't do much of that anymore," he replied. "When I was a kid we would have skis on from the first thing in the morning to the end of the day. There was so much more snow back then. When you think of how much has changed in my fifty years it is very scary."

Global warming threatens biological conditions, economic prospects and social structure (IPCC 2001). At the deepest level, large scale environmental problems such as global warming threaten people's sense of the continuity of life, what Anthony Giddens calls ontological security (1984, 1991). What will Norwegian winters be like without snow? What will happen to farms in the community in the next generation? . . .

Feelings of Helplessness—"You have to focus on something you can do"

I think that there are a lot of people who feel that no matter what I do I can't do anything about that anyway.

As Hege Marie, a student in her late teens described, a second emotion that the topic of global warming evoked was helplessness. The problem seemed so large and involved the cooperation of people in so many different countries. Governments were unable to reach agreement. Perhaps entire economic structures would have to change. Thus it is not surprising that rather than feeling that there was much that could be done, Liv, a woman in her late sixties, pronounced that, "we must take it as it comes," and Gurid told me, "you have to focus on something you can do or else you become completely hopeless."

Fear of Guilt

Thinking about global warming was also difficult because it raised feelings of guilt. Members of the community told me they were aware of how their actions contributed to the problem and they felt guilty about it.

> So many times I have a guilty conscience because I know that I should do something, or do it less. But at the same time there is the social pressure. And I want for my children and for my wife to be able to experience the same positive things that are normal in their community of friends and in this society. It is very . . . I think it is a bit problematic. I feel that I could do more, but it would be at the expense of, it would create a more difficult relationship between me and my children or my partner. It really isn't easy.

Guilt was also connected to the sense of global warming as an issue of global inequity: Norwegian wealth and high standard of living are intimately tied to the production of oil. Given their high newspaper readership and level of knowledge about the rest of the world, community members were well aware of these circumstances. This understanding contrasted sharply with the deeply ingrained Norwegian values of equality and egalitarianism (Jonassen 1983, Kiel 1993), thus raising feelings of guilt.

Fear of "Being a Bad Person"— Identity: Self and National Images

Another source of concern that comes with awareness of global warming is the threat it implies for individual and national self-concepts. . . .

Norwegian public self-image includes a strong self-identification of being environmentally aware and humanitarian (Eriksen 1993, 1996). Norwegians have been proud of their past international leadership on a number of environmental issues including global warming. Stereotypical characterization of Norwegians describes a simple, nature loving people who are concerned with equality and human rights (Eriksen 1993, 1996). Yet Norway has increased production of oil and gas threefold in the last ten years. Expansion of oil production in the 1990s contributed significantly to the already high standard of living, making Norway one of the countries in the world that has most benefited from fossil fuels. In 2001 Norway was the world's sixth largest oil producer and the world's second largest oil exporter after Saudi Arabia (MoPE 2002). Information about global warming—such as Norway's inability to reach Kyoto reduction quotas, increasing carbon dioxide emissions and government expansions of oil development—makes for an acute contradiction between the traditional Norwegian values and self-image and the present day economic situation in which high electricity use, increasing consumption and wealth from North Sea oil make Norway one of the larger per capita contributors to the problem of global warming. . . . For Norwegians, information on global warming not only contradicts their sense of being environmentally responsible. As a problem generated by wealthy nations for which people in poor nations disproportionately suffer, knowledge of global warming also challenges Bygdabyingar's sense of themselves as egalitarian and socially just. . . .

A Cultural Tool Kit of Emotion Management Strategies

If the emotions of fear, guilt, hopelessness or "fear of being a bad person" worked against social change in Bygdaby, how might this have happened? In Bygdaby there were active, observable moments which, although fleeting, pointed to the role of emotions in the generation of non-participation as an active process—what Nina Eliasoph calls the *production* of apathy (1998). If what a person feels is different from what they want to or are supposed to feel they may engage in some level of *emotional management* (Hochschild 1979, 1983, 1990, Thoits 1996). While the act of modifying, suppressing or emphasizing an emotion is carried out by individuals, emotions are being managed to fit social expectations, which in turn often reproduce larger political and economic conditions. . . . In the case of global warming in Bygdaby, emotions that were uncomfortable to individuals were also uncomfortable because they violated norms of social interaction in the community. And at least some of these emotion norms in turn normalized Norway's economic position as a significant producer of oil.

　. . . In Bygdaby people managed the unpleasant emotions described in the previous section by avoiding thinking about them, by shifting attention to positive self-representations, and—especially in terms of the emotion of guilt—by framing them in ways that minimized their potency. When it came to the strategy of framing and of shifting attention to positive self-representations, community members had available a set of "stock" social narratives upon which to draw, many of which were generated by the national government and conveyed to the public through the media. . . .

Ann Swidler uses the metaphor of "tools in a tool kit" to describe the set of resources available to people in a given culture for solving problems (1986). Using this metaphor I will briefly describe how these culturally available strategies served as tools that were used to achieve selective attention and perspectival selectivity—and thereby to manage thinking in such a way as to manage emotions.

Selective Attention

Selective attention can be used to decide what to think about or not to think about, screening out for example painful information about problems for which one does not have solutions (e.g., "I don't really know what to do, so I just don't think about that"). Strategies of emotion management in the form of selective attention were primarily aimed at managing the emotions of fear and helplessness. Here I describe the techniques of controlling exposure to information, focusing on something you can do and not thinking too far into the future.

"We Can't Dig Ourselves into Depression, Right?":
Controlling Exposure to Information

. . . Community members described feelings of uncertainty as being easily evoked by too much information, thus adhering to the emotion norms of maintaining optimism and control required managing exposure to information on global warming. Educators and activists in particular had to be careful not to become overwhelmed in order to continue their work:

> No, but you can't—you know I feel that in a way the philosophy of all this is happening so fast. *I do as much as I can,* and *we can't focus on what's painful.* We don't go in and have meetings and talk about how gruesome everything is. We talk about how it is and *can't dig ourselves down into depression, right?*

Another activist described how she reads very little of the details, that it is in fact "better not to know everything." People were aware that there was the potential that global warming would radically alter life within the next decades, and when they thought about it they felt worried, yet they did not go about their days wondering what things would be like for their children, whether these could be the last years farming could take place in Bygdaby, or whether their grandchildren would be able to ski on real snow. They spent their days thinking about more local, manageable topics. Mari described how, "you have the knowledge, but you live in a completely different world." . . .

"I don't allow myself to think so far ahead"

There is a lot of unrest in the country. There is a lot that is negative. Then I become like—yeah, pfff! But when someone has something that they are working on, in relation to that you are trying to influence—then it's like, okay to be optimistic after all. But I think that this can just explode around us, and so it is well that *I don't allow myself to think so far ahead.*

The most effective way to manage unpleasant emotions was to turn your attention to something else, as Lise, a young mother describes in the above passage, or by focusing attention onto something positive, as she also describes. . . .

Focusing on Something You Can Do

Similar to the strategies of controlling exposure to unpleasant information and not thinking too far ahead was the strategy of focusing on something that you could do. . . . Peter, a local politician, describes how global warming is a theme that "everyone is interested in" but which does not receive attention on the local level because there "isn't so much that you can do."

Yes, it is of course a theme that everyone is interested in, but locally it isn't discussed much because . . . well climate change, you know there isn't so much you can do with it on a local level, but of course everyone sees that something must be done . . .

Peter's comments are similar to the earlier passage with Lise who describes both the need for optimism and the underlying hopelessness that global warming raised.

Perspectival Selectivity

Unpleasant emotions of guilt and those associated with a "spoiled identity" could be managed through the cognitive strategy of perspectival selectivity. Perspectival selectivity, "refers to the angle of vision that one brings to bear on certain events" (Rosenberg 1991, 134). Euphemisms, technical jargon and word changing are used to dispute the meanings of events such as when military generals speak of "collateral damage" rather than the killing of citizens. Stanley Cohen writes, "Officials do not claim that 'nothing happened' but what happened is not what you think it is, not what it looks like, not what you call it" (2001: 7). Here I describe two "stock" social narratives that were frequently used to change the angle of vision one might bring to the facts about Norway's role in the problem of global warming.

"Amerika" as a Tension Point

Bygdabyingar knew an amazing number of facts about the U.S. References to the U.S. appeared in numerous conversations I participated in and overheard while in Bygdaby. I use the Norwegian spelling of the word to indicate that I am talking about a stereotypical Norwegian view of the U.S., what Steinar Bryn calls Mythic America (Bryn 1994). There are many stereotypical images of the U.S. in Norway, but to me what is most interesting is not the images themselves but how they were used.

Stories about "Amerika" were often told in strategic moments to deflect Norwegian responsibility and shortcomings and to support notions of Norwegian exceptionalism (we may not be the best, but we aren't anything as bad as they are). For example, in late April of 2001 U.S. President Bush made the infamous statement that he would not sign the Kyoto Protocol on the grounds that it was, "not in the U.S. economic interests." Many Bygdabyingar took the opportunity to tell me of their criticism of this position. Bush's comment was widely repeated and discussed in the Norwegian press and in public commentary. Here the statement was used in a motivational speech by a local young woman on May 1, 2001:

> The Kyoto agreement is about cutting carbon dioxide emissions by 5 percent. And even that ridiculous pace was too much for the climate-hooligan George W. Bush in the United States. The head of the USA's environmental protection department said that "We have no interest in meeting the conditions of the agreement." Well, that may be so. But it is other countries that will be hit the hardest from climate change . . .

Yet despite widespread criticism of the United States for taking such a position, this is essentially the same move that the Norwegian government made in dropping national emissions targets, increasing oil development, taking a leading role in the development of the carbon trading schemes known as the Kyoto and Clean Development Mechanism and shifting the focus from a national to an international agenda (Hovden and Lindseth 2002). In this context, criticizing the poor climate record of the U.S. directs attention away from Norway's shifting behavior, sending the message that at home things are not that bad. . . .

"Norway Is a Little Land"

A second narrative, "Norway is a little land" deflected troubling information and emotions connected to Norway's role in global warming with the subtext that, "we are so few, it doesn't really matter what we do anyway." While it often conveyed a genuine sense of powerlessness, this discourse also worked to let people off the hook, creating the sense of "why bother." During a conversation about his opposition to Norway joining the European Union, Joar, a Bygdabyingar in his early 50s explained how this emphasis on Norway's size, while in some sense true, is also a strategic construction:

> **Kari:** But what kind of a role do you think that Norway should take internationally?
>
> **Joar:** *Well, we are of course a very small country, almost without meaning,* if you think economically we are completely uninteresting.
>
> **Kari:** But Norway has lots of oil compared with other countries.
>
> **Joar:** Yeah, yeah, okay. We are in fact almost at the level of Saudi Arabia. *But it [is] of course an advantage to be meaningless.* It doesn't really matter for us to argue, *they don't bother to get mad at us, because we are so meaningless.* And in that connection, we are a bit you know, peaceful, right. We have been involved in both the Middle East and . . . (here he refers to the Oslo Accords and his second example is not spoken, just given as a gesture of the hand for emphasis).

Note that as the conversation continues he uses Norway's small economy as the example of why it "is meaningless." When I asked him about Norway's oil, he suddenly "remembers" the fact that Norway is, after Saudi Arabia, the second largest oil exporter in the world. Then he explains the strategic advantage of being "meaningless," that other countries don't bother to get upset with Norway. At the end of the passage he adds to the construction of Norway as a nation not worth getting upset with by drawing on the sense of Norway as a "peaceful nation" (referring to the peace prize) and their involvement in the Oslo Accords. In being small, meaningless and peaceful, he is constructing in our conversation a sense of Norwegian innocence that is very prevalent.

The phrase "Norway is a little land" gives the sense that they are doing "their part" and turns blame back onto those who are "worse," especially the United States, as described earlier. It serves to imply that, "the problem isn't really us. We, in fact, are innocent." . . .

Discussion: Emotions, Emotion Management and the "Production of Apathy"

Non-response to the possibility of global warming may seem "natural" or "self-evident"—from a social movement or social problem perspective not all potential issues get translated into political action. Yet with a closer view we can understand non-response as a *social process*. Things *could have been* different. Community members could have written letters to the local paper articulating global warming as a political issue, they could have brought the issue up in one of the many public forums, made attempts to plan for the possibility of what the future weather scenarios might bring, put pressure on local and national leaders, decreased their automobile use, asked for national subsidies to cover the economic impacts of the warm winter, or engaged their neighbors, children, and political leaders in discussions about what climate change might mean for their community in the next ten and twenty years. Indeed in other parts of the world things *were* different. The severe flooding in England that fall was linked to global warming by at least some of the impacted residents. People from affected communities in England traveled to the climate talks at the Hague to protest. More recently, three cities in the United States have initiated a lawsuit against the federal government over global warming. Bygdabyingar could have made a similar move—rallied around the lack of snow and its economic and cultural impacts on some level, any level, be it local, national or international. But they did not.

Most of the emotions Bygdabyingar felt in conjunction with information on global warming: fear, guilt and concern over individual and collective identity could have motivated social action. Perhaps in some cases these emotions did generate actions, but they did not generate many. . . .

. . . [E]motions of fear and helplessness contradicted emotion norms of being optimistic and maintaining control. These emotions were particularly managed through the use of selective attention: controlling one's exposure to information, not thinking too far into the future and focusing on something that could be done. Although the range of emotion management techniques appeared to be used across the community, I found these strategies used with more frequency by educators, men and public figures. The emotion of guilt and the fear of being a bad person or desire to view oneself and the collective community in positive light contrasted not only with specific local emotion norms surrounding patriotism, but also the general social psychological need to view oneself in a positive light (i.e., manage identity). Guilt and identity were managed through the use of perspectival selectivity: by emphasizing Norway's small population size and that no matter what they did, Norwegians were not as bad as the "Amerikans."

Conclusion: Emotions, Denial and Social Movement Nonparticipation

Emotions can be a source of information (Hochschild 1983) and an impetus for social action (Jasper 1997, 1998, Polletta 1998), but my observations in Bygdaby suggest that the desire to avoid unpleasant emotions and the practice of emotion management can also work against social movement participation. Although not normally applied to environmental issues, research on the sociology of emotions is highly relevant to understanding community member's reactions to global warming. While current work in environmental sociology has emphasized the "information deficit model" (Buckeley 2000), my ethnographic and interview data from a rural Norwegian community do not support this interpretation. Instead this research indicates community members had sufficient information about the issue but avoided thinking about global warming at least in part because doing so raised fears of ontological security, emotions of helplessness and guilt, and was a threat to individual and collective senses of identity. Rather than experience these unpleasant emotions, people used a number of strategies including emotion management to hold information about global warming at arm's length.

Emotions played a key role in denial, providing much of the reason why people preferred not to think about global warming. Furthermore, the management of unpleasant and "unacceptable" emotions was a central aspect of the process of denial, which in this community was carried out through the use of a cultural stock of strategies and social narratives that were employed to achieve selective attention and perspective selectivity. Thus movement non-participation in response to the issue of global warming did not simply happen, but was actively produced as community members kept the issue of global warming at a distance via a cultural tool kit of emotion management techniques.

Note

Norgaard, Kari Marie. 2006. "'People Want to Protect Themselves a Little Bit': Emotions, Denial, and Social Movement Nonparticipation." *Sociological Inquiry* 76(3): 372–396.

References

Bostrom, Ann, M. Granger Morgan, Baruch Fischoff, and Daniel Read. 1994. "What Do People Know About Global Climate Change? I: Mental Models." *Risk Analysis* 14(6): 959–970.

Bord, Richard, Ann Fisher, and Robert O'Connor. 1998. "Public Perceptions of Global Warming: United States and International Perspectives." *Climate Research* 11(1): 75–84.

Brechin, Steven. 2003. "Comparative Public Opinion and Knowledge on Global Climatic Change and the Kyoto Protocol: The U.S. versus the World?" *International Journal of Sociology and Social Policy* 23(10): 106–134.

Bryn, Steinar. 1994. *The Americanization of Norwegian Culture.* Doctoral Dissertation, Department of Philosophy, University of Minnesota.

Buckeley, Harriet. 2000. "Common Knowledge? Public Understanding of Climate Change in Newcastle, Australia." *Public Understanding of Science* 9: 313–333.

Cohen, Stanley. 2001. *States of Denial: Knowing About Atrocities and Suffering.* Polity Press, 2001.

Dunlap, Riley. 1998. "Lay Perceptions of Global Risk: Public Views of Global Warming in Cross National Context." *International Sociology* 13(4): 473–498.

Eliasoph, Nina. 1998. *Avoiding Politics: How Americans Produce Apathy in Everyday Life*. Cambridge: Cambridge University Press.

Eriksen, Thomas Hylland. 1993. "Being Norwegian in a Shrinking World." Pp. 11–38 in Anne Cohel Kiel (ed.), *Continuity and Change: Aspects of Contemporary Norway*. Oslo: Scandinavia University Press.

———. 1996. *Norwegians and Nature*. From Official Government website. Retrieved May 10, 2006. www.dep.no/odin/english/p30008168/history/032005-990490/dok-bu.html.

Gelbspan, Ross. 2004. *How Politicians, Big Oil and Coal, Journalists, and Activists Are Fueling the Climate Crisis—And What We Can Do to Avert Disaster*. Basic Books.

Giddens, Anthony. 1991. *Modernity and Self Identity: Self and Society in the Late Modern Age*. Cambridge: Polity Press.

———. 1984. *The Constitution of Society*. Cambridge: Polity Press.

Halford, Grame, and Peter Sheehan 1991. "Human Responses to Environmental Changes." *International Journal of Psychology* 269(5): 599–611.

Hochschild, Arlie 1990. "Ideology and Emotion Management: A Perspective and Path for Future Research." Pp. 108–203 in Kemper, T. D. (ed.), *Research Agendas in the Sociology of Emotions*. Albany: State University of New York Press.

———. 1983. *The Managed Heart: The Commercialization of Human Feeling*. University of California Press.

———. 1979. "Emotion Work, Feeling Rules and Social Structure." *American Journal of Sociology* 85: 551–575.

Hovden, Eivind, and Gard Lindseth. 2002. "Norwegian Climate Policy 1989–2002." Pp. 143–168 in William Lafferty, Morton Nordskog, and Hilde Annette Aakre (eds.), *Realizing Rio in Norway: Evaluative Studies of Sustainable Development*. University of Oslo.

IPCC (Intergovernmental Panel on Climate Change). 2001. *Climate Change 2001: Synthesis Report*. Cambridge: Cambridge University Press for the IPCC.

Jaeger, Carlo, Ortwin Renn, Eugene Rosa, and Thomas Webler. 2001. *Risk, Uncertainty and Rational Action*. London: Earthscan.

Jasper, James M. 1998. "The Emotions of Protest: Affective and Reactive Emotions in and Around Social Movements." *Sociological Forum* 13(3): 397–424.

———. 1997. *The Art of Moral Protest*. University of Chicago Press.

Jonassen, C. 1983. *Value Systems and Personality in a Western Civilization: Norwegians in Europe and America*. Columbus: Ohio State University Press.

Kempton, Willet, James S. Bister, and Jennifer A. Hartley. 1995. *Environmental Values in American Culture*. Cambridge, Mass: MIT Press.

Kiel, Anne Cohel. 1993. *Continuity and Change: Aspects of Contemporary Norway*. Oslo: Scandinavia University Press.

McCright, Aaron M., and Riley E. Dunlap. 2003. "Defeating Kyoto: The Conservative Movement's Impact on U.S. Climate Change Policy." *Social Problems* 50(3): 348–373.

———. 2000. "Challenging Global Warming as a Social Problem: An Analysis of the Conservative Movement's Counter-Claims." *Social Problems* 47 (4):499–522.

MoPE (Norwegian Ministry of Petroleum and Energy) 2002. *Environment 2002: The Norwegian Petroleum Sector Fact Sheet* Oslo. Oilje og energidepartmentet.

Polletta, Francesca. 1998. "It Was Like a Fever . . . Narrative and Identity in Collective Action." *Social Problems* 45: 137–159.

Read, Daniel, Ann Bostrom, M. Granger Morgan, Baruch Fischoff, and Tom Smuts. 1994. "What Do People Know About Global Climate Change? II Survey Studies of Educated Lay People." *Risk Analysis* 14: 971–982.

Reed, Peter, and David Rothenberg. 1993. *Wisdom in the Open Air: The Norwegian Roots of Deep Ecology*. Minneapolis: University of Minnesota Press.

Rosa, Eugene. 2001. "Global Climate Change: Background and Sociological Contributions." *Society and Natural Resources* (14)6: 491–499.

Rosenberg, Morris. 1991. "Self-processes and Emotional Experiences." Pp. 123–142 in Judith Howard and Peter Callero (eds.), *The Self-Society Dynamic: Cognition, Emotion and Action*. Cambridge University Press.

Swidler, Anne. 1986. "Culture in Action." *American Sociological Review.* 51: 273–286.

Thoits, Peggy. 1989. "The Sociology of Emotions." *Annual Review of Sociology* 15: 317–342.

———. 1996. "Managing the Emotions of Others." *Symbolic Interaction* 19: 85–109.

United Nations Development Programme (UNDP). *United Nations Human Development Report 2004: Cultural Liberty in Today's Diverse World.* Data on Norway. Retrieved May 10, 2006. hdi.undp.org/reports/global/2004/.

Community Economic Identity

The Coal Industry and Ideology Construction in West Virginia

Shannon Elizabeth Bell and Richard York

Sometimes it is difficult to garner support for environmental initiatives that involve polluting or environmentally exploitative industries because workers fear losing their jobs if those industries are in any way threatened. However, what happens when environmentally damaging industries employ fewer and fewer people, even while maintaining environmentally exploitative practices? Shannon Bell and Richard York argue that the coal industry in West Virginia has worked to instill a sense of cultural identity around coal mining in hopes that community members will feel attached to the industry even though it now provides fewer jobs than in the past. Using this case, the authors show that ideological manipulation is a means by which those in power attempt to hold on to that power.

In the wake of industrialization and "postindustrialization," natural-resource extraction has played a diminishing role in the economies of affluent nations. Although the United States, like other countries of the Global North, has continued to consume vast quantities of natural resources, the contribution of extractive industries to total employment and to total national economic production—as typically measured by gross domestic product—has been declining for decades. This decline primarily has been due to mechanization and to imports of raw materials from the Global South. This national-level pattern has manifested itself across the United States in a variety of communities that historically were closely connected to extractive industries, such as timber and mining. Due to this legacy, many rural communities are left with an identity tied to a particular extractive industry, even though that industry no longer provides many jobs or plays a dominant role in the local or regional economy. This tendency for many in a community to identify with an industry that was *historically* important in the local economy, but that may not be any longer, is regularly exploited by extractive industries to maintain their political influence, which is often used to avoid government regulations aimed at ensuring the protection of the environment and public health.

. . . [W]e document how the contribution of extractive industries to the economies of communities around the nation has declined dramatically while these extractive industries continue to create large-scale environmental problems. In particular, with the massive job losses that are the typical outcome of the "treadmill of production" (Schnaiberg 1980), the bond that has historically maintained the loyalties of many rural communities to extractive industries has been dramatically weakened, if not destroyed. One of our key aims is to help determine why some communities continue to support industries that cause harm—for example, by degrading the environment—while providing few (and declining) benefits, such as reliable high-paying jobs. To illustrate the processes we discuss, we provide an empirical assessment of how the coal industry in West Virginia attempts to suppress political opposition to the destructive effects of coal mining by actively working to maintain and reinforce the centrality of coal to the identity of the state and local communities.

The Treadmill of Production and the Legitimation Process

The "treadmill of production" model is one of the most influential and important theories in the environmental sociology literature (Buttel 2004; Foster 2005; Foster and York 2004). First introduced by Allan Schnaiberg (1980) in order to explain why environmental degradation in the United States had grown dramatically since World War II, the treadmill of production model argues that ecological destruction is intrinsic to capitalist (as well as some other) modes of production. Schnaiberg contended that the economic boom following World War II led to increased production and profits, which were invested in the development of new production technologies. These technologies came with large operating expenses that needed to be financed, however, and industries responded to these fixed costs by further increasing production so as to increase profits. The increase in production led to an escalating need for natural resources, which were extracted at greater rates and used in ways that "substantially increased both the volume of production waste and the toxicity of wastes" (Gould, Pellow, and Schnaiberg 2004:300). This pattern of increasing extraction and degradation in order to generate greater and greater profits has become the central operating framework of the global market. It is widely held that the treadmill of production, along with the ecological degradation it generates, is unavoidable unless the relations of production under corporate capitalism are changed (Buttel 2004; Foster 2005; Foster and York 2004; Gould et al. 2004; Schnaiberg 1980).

The effects of the treadmill of production are not limited to the ecological, however; displaced workers are another result. "Improvements" in technology lead to an increase in "worker productivity," which accelerates the treadmill, "producing higher production and profits with fewer workers" (Gould et al. 2004:306). This pattern, where jobs decline even while production expands, is clearly visible in the case of natural-resource extraction industries, particularly timber and mining. . . .

. . . [A]s Figure 1 reveals, while coal production increased dramatically in West Virginia from the late 1970s to the 1990s, coal-mining employment declined substantially, as it has generally done in the postwar era. This trend was not limited to West Virginia; as Figure 2 shows, national-level data on coal production and employment reveal an even starker negative association, where production rose as jobs declined. As the above evidence indicates, a pattern exists among extractive industries: consistent with treadmill of production theorizing, even when production increases in these industries, employment levels decrease.[1]

Gould et al. (2004) draw attention to an important intersection between ecological degradation and jobs: Historically, those individuals who are the most affected by industrial pollution and environmental damage also typically have been dependent on the jobs within the polluting industries. Pollution and degradation have become "geographically and socially removed" from the middle class, which has the money to move upstream and upwind from the contamination and destruction, while blue-collar workers have been "induced and/or coerced" to live in close proximity to pollution, in part due to the lower housing prices in these areas (298). Thus, many of the people suffering the most acute costs of ecological degradation are some of the least likely to fight against the treadmill processes because of their economic dependence on the destructive industries. Furthermore, many will even fight *for* the companies polluting their communities or destroying their ecosystems because they fear further job losses if environmental regulations are tightened. This system works to discourage mobilization against these industries, while at the same

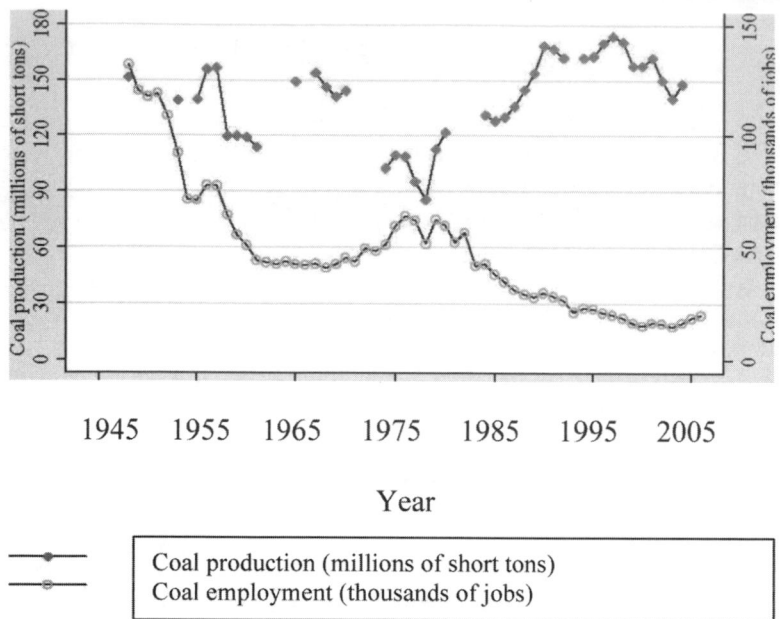

FIGURE 1. West Virginia Coal Employment and Production

Sources: Workforce West Virginia (2000a, 2000b, 2001, 2002, 2003, 2004, 2005, 2006, 2007), Energy Information Administration's Annual Coal Report (2002, 2004, 2006), and United States Census Bureau's Statistical Abstract of the United States (1961, 1971, 1981, 1991, 1994, 2000, 2005).

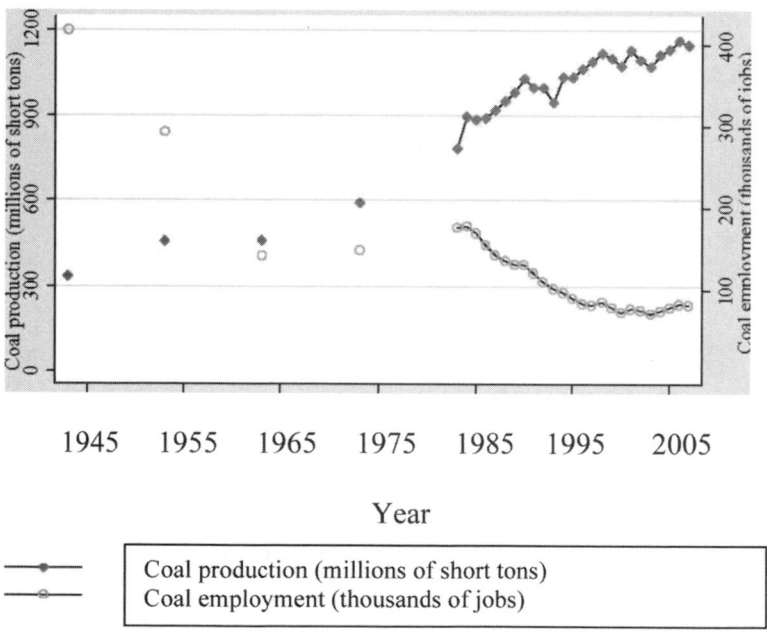

FIGURE 2. United States Coal Employment and Production

Source: National Mining Association (2008).

time producing an arsenal of workers that can be mobilized to create a coun termovement for the industry in opposition to any efforts to impose stricter environmental regulations and disrupt treadmill processes.

However, when there is a large-scale reduction in jobs, and employment no longer connects an industry to the community it pollutes, why do communities continue to support industry, even though industrial practices have detrimental social and environmental effects? . . . We argue that public acquiescence to the wishes of industry is in part achieved by industries' calculated efforts to reconstruct a bond with the communities they degrade, attempting to replace the employment connection between industry and community with a constructed ideology of dependency and economic identity.

Critical traditions, from Marxism to feminism, have often emphasized how ideology is employed to further the interests of those in power by mystifying the nature of social relations and the causes of oppression. . . . [A]nalyses of how culture and ideology are manufactured and manipulated in order to further elite interests have become a central part of research on the power structure (Habermas 1975; Herman and Chomsky 2002; Lukes 1974; Mann 1970; Mészáros 1989).

The work of Jürgen Habermas, the most renowned heir to the tradition of the Frankfurt School, is particularly relevant to our analysis. He clearly recognized the ecological threats created in capitalist societies and the social challenges that accompany these threats. . . .

. . . The argument that we develop below is that owners and managers of extractive industries actively construct, maintain, and amplify community economic identity in order to ensure that certain ideologies dominate in communities that historically depended on natural-resource extraction, thereby averting a legitimation crisis. Maintaining and reinforcing community economic identity is critical to avoiding a legitimation crisis, for, as Habermas argued, "traditions can retain legitimizing force only as long as they are not torn out of interpretive systems that guarantee continuity and identity" (Habermas 1975:71).

Industry efforts at legitimation via ideology manipulation can be understood as part of what Habermas (1984, 1987) has identified as the colonization of the "lifeworld" (the realm of everyday, lived experience where people find meaning from culturally grounded traditions of interpretation). Habermas observed that in modern societies, particularly capitalist ones, the lifeworld is increasingly invaded by the overarching social system. For example, the marketing industry aims to define what our goals in life should be (consumption—our life's purpose becomes to accumulate mass-produced goods, and people come to see themselves as "consumers"), and the state aims to define key features of our identity (nationalism/patriotism—people come to identify as, for example, Americans, rather than as community members, human beings, etc.). The efforts of extractive industries to lure the public into identifying with industry are part of this same process, where logging and mining, for example, come to be seen not simply as sources of employment but rather as key features of individuals' and communities' identities—that is, workers often come to identify first and foremost as loggers or miners, and communities come to identify as logging or mining communities . . .

The Historical Roots of Dependency

As the second-leading coal producer in the United States (behind Wyoming), and the top coal-producing state in Appalachia, West Virginia's historical ties with the coal industry have strongly influenced the economic, political, and social structures of the state. . . .

Numerous scholars have referred to Central Appalachia as an "internal colony" (Gaventa 1978; Lewis and Knipe 1978; Weller 1978) or an "internal periphery" (Walls 1978) created to provide cheap resources to fuel the rest of the country. Both of these models point to outside interests' exploitation of the resources of Central Appalachia through the subjugation and domination of its people. Part of this continued domination has been achieved through corporate ownership of the majority of the land,[2] effectively blocking other industries from entering the region in an attempt to maintain this part of Appalachia as a mono-economy. As Lewis and Knipe (1978) assert, "it is advantageous for coal mining to operate in isolation without competing companies" because the extraction process is tied to a particular location and the work is hazardous and strenuous (19).

A cheap workforce was the foundation of early mining, and it was essential for the coal barons to remove the Appalachian people from their land in order to "turn them into a docile workforce" (Haynes 1997:49). Another method to ensure a cheap—and captive—workforce was the establishment of company towns. In the late 1800s and early 1900s, men were recruited into the state by the tens of thousands to work in the booming mining industry. The population skyrocketed during this period, and hundreds of company towns and coal camps, which were completely owned and controlled by the coal companies, sprang up throughout Central Appalachia. In these towns, the coal companies owned the houses, the streets, the schools, the water systems, the churches, the recreational facilities (if there were any), the doctor's office, and the company store, which was the only store in the town where one could buy groceries, furniture, clothes, and other goods. In addition, most coal companies paid their employees in "scrip," their own monetary system redeemable only within that particular company's town (Lockard 1998). The use of scrip ensured that the miners and their families were unable to travel outside the town to buy fundamental supplies and that the company store was able to charge monopolistic prices for its goods. The company store system and the other company-supplied services for which miners were charged, such as tool sharpening, health care, and housing rent, were "a key mechanism . . . for increasing company profits" (Cook 2000:192) . . .

Since the 1980s . . . there has been a shift in the Appalachian coalfields' economy, threatening the coal industry's stranglehold on the region. During the 1980s, the Appalachian coalfields saw a diversification in the region's economy, wherein service sector jobs replaced mining jobs as the leading source of employment and earnings (Maggard 1994; Miewald and McCann 2004). Increased mechanization in the coal mines and the advent of mountain-top removal coal mining have drastically reduced the number of mining jobs throughout Central Appalachia, and West Virginia in particular (Burns 2005). As mining jobs have continued to drop off, service-sector jobs have risen, calling into question the coal industry's status as the "backbone" of the state.

Coal and the West Virginia Economy

The $3.5 billion coal contributed to West Virginia's gross state product in 2004 represented only 7 percent of the total gross state product, ranking behind retail trade ($4.0 billion), real estate and rentals ($4.6 billion), health care and social assistance ($4.8 billion), and government ($8.4 billion) (U.S. Department of Commerce 2005). Furthermore, mining's contributions to the West Virginia state product declined from the late 1990s into the 2000s (Witt and Fletcher 2005), and its contributions are forecast to continue declining over the next thirty years (Witt and Leguizamon 2007) . . .

As Figure 1 shows, coal employment in West Virginia has steadily declined since the 1940s. This reduction in mining jobs has caused a massive exodus from the state: Since 1950, West Virginia has experienced a net out-migration of 40 percent of its population (West Virginia Health Statistics Center 2002).[3] In 1948 there were 131,700 coal miners in the state, while in 2006 there were only 20,100. This represents a more than five-fold reduction in the number of jobs even after controlling for the decline in the population . . .

The decline in mining jobs since the mid-twentieth century was not because of a decline in the scale of coal production, since, although it swung up and down over this period, coal production was about the same at the beginning of the twenty-first century as it was in the late 1940s (see Figure 1). Job losses were clearly due to the ongoing processes of the treadmill of production where workers are replaced by machines. Changes in coal-extraction practices meant that the same amount of coal could be extracted in the twenty-first century by employing only one-sixth the workers required in the mid-twentieth century. Coal *was* a central part of the building of West Virginia's economy. However, with the advent of the continuous mining machine, the longwall mining machine, and most recently, mountaintop removal mining, a vast workforce of coal miners is no longer needed . . .

As discussed above, treadmill of production theory posits that increases in productivity will typically lead to escalating ecological degradation. The Appalachian coal case is no exception. Technological advances in the methods of coal extraction and processing have had growing impacts on the health, safety, and livelihoods of people living in the coalfields. Below we briefly describe some of the most serious environmental consequences of coal mining so as to clarify the reasons that resistance to the coal industry has emerged and, consequently, industry efforts to further the ideology of the coal industry have intensified.

Environmental Consequences of Coal Mining

Mountaintop removal coal mining and the resulting valley fills have spurred a great deal of controversy within "coal communities" and the larger region. This form of coal extraction has become widespread throughout Central Appalachia, particularly in southern West Virginia and eastern Kentucky. Under the mountains in these areas lie thin layers of low-sulfur coal, which are extremely valuable and are too narrow to be mined by more traditional methods of deep mining. In order to reach this coal, mining operations must remove the "overburden" (which includes the tops of mountains, forests, etc.) to expose the coal seam below. Surplus volume of broken rock, called "excess spoil," is generated through this mining technique and must be disposed of. Typically, it is dumped in valleys that are adjacent to the surface mines, creating "valley fills" (United States Environmental Protection Agency 2003) . . .

Among its many consequences, mountaintop removal mining leads to flooding. In the steep mountain terrain of southern West Virginia, most homes have been built in the valleys next to creek banks. When the mountains above these homes are deforested and flattened, there is nothing left to stop the rain from washing down the mountainsides. Thus, flooding has destroyed the homes of numerous coalfield residents. . . .

Another major environmental problem associated with mining stems from "coal-sludge dams" (also termed "slurry impoundments"). Before coal is sent to market for processing, it must be cleaned in order to reduce sulfur and noncombustible materials present in the coal. The waste generated by the cleaning process is called coal slurry (or "sludge") and consists of "water, fine particles derived from the coal, and chemicals used in coal washing" (Orem 2006). This black chemical sludge is either stored in huge impoundments on the surface of flattened mountaintops or injected into abandoned underground coal mines (Orem 2006). There are currently 111 coal-sludge impoundments in West Virginia (Coal Impoundment Location and Information System 2005).

Many of these enormous black lakes are situated on mountaintops directly above small communities.

Sometimes these impoundments leak, and even completely give way . . .

A . . . recent coal-slurry disaster occurred in 2000 in Martin County, Kentucky. The impoundment collapsed, spilling 250 million gallons of coal waste (20 times greater than the Exxon Valdez oil spill), polluting more than 70 miles of West Virginia and Kentucky waterways, killing wildlife, and razing habitat. Homes were destroyed by the thick, black sludge. Although there was little national media coverage, the EPA called it "one of the worst environmental disasters in the history of the Southeastern United States" (Eades 2000). Forty-five other slurry impoundments in West Virginia are considered to be at high risk for failure, and thirty-two are at moderate risk (Eades 2000).[4]

Not all coal waste ends up in sludge impoundments. Instead, some coal operations inject the slurry underground into abandoned coal mines. This method of "disposal" creates an entirely new set of problems including well water contamination and the health problems it can lead to, such as liver and kidney cancers, colitis, skin disorders, and organ failure (Orem 2006; Wells 2006) . . .

Flooding and coal-slurry impoundments and injections are only the beginning of the many ways in which coal adversely affects the environment and residents of the southern coalfields. Damage from blasting; respiratory problems from coal dust; accidents caused by overweight, speeding coal trucks; and the loss of hunting grounds and homesteads are a few more of the consequences of coal for these rural communities. Even the laws that are in place to protect the land and people, such as the Clean Water Act, have been largely ignored by many coal companies, as evidenced by the fact that coal giant Massey Energy was charged with 4,633 violations of the Clean Water Act between January 2000 and December 2006 (Associated Press 2007).

The people living in coal-mining regions of Appalachia have found themselves in a conflicted situation. Most people living in the coalfields have been dependent, at some point in their lives, on the industry that is now destroying their homes, health, and safety. While many are affected by irresponsible mining, until recent years most residents have remained silent while the coal industry has continued to dominate this region. However, due to the seriousness of the environmental problems generated by the coal industry, a grassroots movement has steadily grown in numbers and power within Central Appalachia over the past decade. The Coal River Mountain Watch, Ohio Valley Environmental Coalition, Citizens Coal Council, Kentuckians for the Commonwealth, the Sludge Safety Project, and the newly emerged college movement Mountain Justice are just a few of the organizations that have been engaging in forms of resistance and direct action. Staging nonviolent protests, generating publications, lobbying the legislature, filing lawsuits, blocking new mining permits, and working with filmmakers and journalists to expose the devastation coal has caused to the environment and rural communities are a few of the strategies these organizations have utilized to hold the coal industry accountable.

Industry Ideology: The Birth of the "Friends of Coal"

According to coal analyst Richard Bonskowski (2004), the grassroots efforts at resistance described above are in part responsible for the recent small decline in coal production within West Virginia, as well as Appalachia as a whole. In particular, efforts relating to litigation and permitting delays for new mountaintop-removal mines and stricter enforcement of coal-truck weight limits and license fees have been especially influential. However, the coal industry has not stood idly by in the face of these challenges. This became especially apparent in the coal industry's strategy to win one of the most contentious legislative debates in West Virginia in recent years: coal-truck weight limits. Through its efforts to win this battle, the West Virginia Coal Association constructed a countermovement to the environmental justice movement, calling the organization it created the "Friends of Coal," which has engaged in elaborate framing efforts to maintain and amplify coal's status as the economic identity of West Virginia.

In 2002, in response to a series of recent deaths from accidents involving overweight coal trucks (some that were more than double the legal limit), Delegate Mike Caputo (D-Marion) introduced a bill in the West Virginia legislature to increase enforcement of the truck weight limits. Coal industry–supporting legislators quickly introduced retaliatory legislation that would raise maximum legal weight limits for coal trucks from 80,000 pounds to 132,000 pounds (with a 5 percent variance) (Nyden 2002). Neither bill passed, but legislative efforts on both sides continued to stir controversy in the state.

During the summer of 2002, as the coal truck debate was raging, board members and officers of the West Virginia Coal Association held a strategic planning meeting to discuss ways that they could improve public relations (Shanghai Zoom Intelligence Co., Ltd. 2006). The outcome of that meeting was the birth of the "Friends of Coal," which was to be a "grassroots organization" that would be "dedicated to informing and educating West Virginia citizens about the coal industry and its vital role in the state's future" (Friends of Coal 2007). As West Virginia Coal Association President Bill Raney explained,

> For many years . . . we have claimed that coal represents many more West Virginians beyond the thousands directly employed by the industry. Friends of Coal clearly indicates that this is the case. . . . With Friends of Coal, we are making an effort to count, organize and mobilize these

people. It's time to clearly demonstrate to public officials, to media representatives and to the general public, just how many lives are touched in a positive way by the coal industry. (Shanghai Zoom Intelligence Co., Ltd. 2006)

In addition, according to *Coal Leader: Coal's National Newspaper,* "One of the aims of the new organization 'Friends of Coal' is to reverse the perception that coal mining has declined in importance in West Virginia and the country" ("Friends of Coal" 2003). While the Friends of Coal boasts that it is a "grassroots organization," its funding comes from the member companies of the West Virginia Coal Association (Hohmann 2005). Furthermore, Raney was paraphrased as stating that the campaign is an effort to "remove 'impediments' to coal mining" (Wire Reports 2002), clearly stating the agenda of the organization.

In January 2003, the West Virginia Coal Association contracted with the West Virginia–based firm Charles Ryan Associates "to provide public relations, advertising and internet services for Friends of Coal" (Shanghai Zoom Intelligence Co., Ltd. 2006). . . .

. . . Since 2003, the organization has launched a full-scale campaign within West Virginia to reconnect the people of the state to an industry that can no longer truly be characterized as the "lifeblood" of the economy. The focus of our empirical analysis is on the activities that this organization undertakes and the messages it imparts to West Virginians. We argue that the underlying strategy of the Friends of Coal is to attempt to counter the coal industry's loss of citizens' employment loyalties by constructing an ideology of dependency and identity through a massive public relations campaign.

Data and Methods

In order to uncover the main strategies that the Friends of Coal uses in its attempt to reconstruct a bond between the coal industry and West Virginia communities, we use two approaches: content analysis and field observations. Data for our content analysis were gathered from four different sources: (1) regional and national newspaper articles during the period 2002–2007 that mention the Friends of Coal, (2) articles referencing the Friends of Coal in *Coal Leader: Coal's National Newspaper* during the period 2003–2006, (3) the Friends of Coal website, accessed once in 2005 and then again in 2007, and (4) the West Virginia Coal Association Website (the parent organization for the Friends of Coal), accessed in 2008. . . .

We undertook the coding process in an inductive manner, first reading through the documents and then creating (1) a list of *actions* that the Friends of Coal has taken since its inception during the summer of 2002; and (2) a list of *themes and messages* that it is attempting to impart to the West Virginia public.

In addition to our content analysis, we utilized observations from the first author's field research in southern West Virginia during the summers of 2006 and 2007. These observations were gathered as a part of a larger project examining the social impacts of the coal industry on rural communities and the resistance movement that has risen up to hold the coal industry accountable for irresponsible mining practices. Data for this larger project include 20 in-depth interviews with randomly selected individuals living in a coal town in Boone County, West Virginia (Bell 2009); 25 interviews with activists involved in the environmental justice movement in Central Appalachia; and four months' worth of field notes spanning two summers, written while engaging in participant observation as a volunteer with a grassroots environmental justice organization in Boone County and while living in two different coal towns during the summers of 2006 and 2007. While we do not explicitly utilize the interview data here, general knowledge gained from the interviews and the field observations inform our analysis.

Results

Through the coding process, we found that the Friends of Coal's main strategy to reconstruct a bond between the coal industry and West Virginia communities centers on attempting to present coal mining as the defining feature of the state. The statement "It is likely that no state and industry are as closely identified with one another as West Virginia and coal," which appeared on the Friends of Coal website in 2005, imparts exactly the message this organization hopes West Virginians will come to believe, despite the coal industry's declining contribution to employment in the state. The coal industry works to create (or re-create) and maintain its standing as the "identity" of West Virginia. Through our content analysis and field observations, we found that the Friends of Coal employs two strategies to do this: (1) by appropriating West Virginia cultural icons; and (2) by creating a visible presence in the social landscape of West Virginia through stickers, yard signs, and sponsorships.

Strategy 1: The Appropriation of West Virginia Cultural Icons

Even before securing Charles Ryan Associates as their public relations firm, the Friends of Coal recruited a spokesperson. Don Nehlen, popular retired football coach of the West Virginia University Mountaineers and recent inductee into the College Football Hall of Fame, quickly became the face of the Friends of Coal. Nehlen was soon joined by two other spokespersons: retired Marshall University football coach Bobby Pruett and, in 2006, professional bass fisherman Jeremy Starks. In addition, retired Air Force General "Doc" Foglesong has appeared in at least one television commercial speaking on behalf of the Friends of Coal. Each of these spokespersons represents important West Virginia cultural icons, which also reflect the historic and present hegemonic masculinity of the region. We define cultural icons as those representations of cultural or regional identity that resonate with individuals of a particular area or community.

The winner icon. Coaches Nehlen and Pruett together represent the two Football Bowl Subdivision (formerly Division 1) teams in the state and thus represent the two sets of football fans that exist in West Virginia: the Mountaineers fans (West Virginia University) and the Thundering Herd fans (Marshall University). In a state of only 1.8 million, these two football teams are important cultural icons. Through securing the two coaches with the most wins in the history of these two teams, the Friends of Coal has attempted to appropriate football—and winning—as a part of its identity. To further this end, in 2006 Friends of Coal became the corporate sponsor of a seven-year football series, called the "Friends of Coal Bowl," which pits the Mountaineers and the Thundering Herd against each other. This is particularly relevant because, until 2006, the two teams had played only once since 1923. College football fans in West Virginia have been waiting for many years for the two in-state rivals to play each other. After four match-ups, the Friends of Coal Bowl is a raging success in the state, further solidifying the Friends of Coal as an integral component of college football in West Virginia.

The Friends of Coal further reinforces this connection between the coal industry and football through two 30-second television commercials promoting the Marshall University Thundering Herd and the West Virginia University Mountaineers. The first commercial begins with a chorus singing, "When we go down deep through the dark today, we come up with the light for America." Next, the narrator announces, "Champions are born of hard work and determination, and just like the Thundering Herd, coal miners are a championship team. During this 2008 season, the Friends of Coal honor our coal miners and our Thundering Herd—all champions indeed." Then, the chorus concludes the commercial by singing, "Coal is West Virginia!"[5] The second commercial is similarly worded, praising coal miners and the West Virginia University Mountaineers for both being "championship team[s]," making the Friends of Coal's message difficult to miss.

The Friends of Coal have also added NASCAR driver Derek Kiser to this "winner" icon by becoming his primary corporate sponsor. Kiser now drives a race car with the "Friends of Coal" logo prominently placed across the hood. Thus, through associating itself with the winning football coaches and the winning NASCAR driver, the Friends of Coal sends the message that the coal industry is a winner, too.

The provider and defender icon. The provider icon and the defender icon are closely intertwined within Friends of Coal propaganda. This becomes particularly apparent in two Friends of Coal television commercials. In the first of these commercials, called "American Hero," retired Air Force General "Doc" Foglesong narrates as images of (male) coal miners hard at work flash across the screen:

> DOC: You could say the West Virginia coal miners are modern-day pioneers. Men and women of courage, pride and adventure, who safely go where no one's been before and harvest the coal that powers our nation. . . . In fact, if these miners didn't produce coal, our nation would be in trouble. More than half of the nation's electricity is generated by coal. West Virginia is the national leader in underground coal-mining production, and America needs that energy—today more than ever. So if you know a West Virginia coal miner, say "Thanks." Not that he or she is doing it for the thanks. They're doing it for their family and for our future. I'm retired Air Force General Doc Foglesong. Friends of Coal salute [*sic*] the pioneering spirit of the West Virginia coal miner. Why not join us and do the same?

Within the text of this commercial the coal *industry* becomes synonymous with the coal *miner*. Thus, the coal industry is presented as a provider—both for West Virginia's families and for the nation's energy demands. As Doc states, "America needs that energy—today more than ever," and it is the West Virginia coal industry that is to thank for meeting those energy demands . . .

Underlying this commercial is . . . the image of the West Virginia coal industry (as represented through the face of the coal miner) as "defender" of our country: "If these miners didn't produce coal, our nation would be in trouble." Furthermore, the choice of a retired military general as the narrator of this commercial is particularly telling of the messages that the Friends of Coal seeks to present: The coal industry defends the "American way of life" just as the military does. Thus, coal is more than an energy source—it is a *patriotic* energy source . . .

Through appropriating the cultural icon of the provider and defender as being ultimately represented within the workers of the coal industry, the Friends of Coal is able to again construct a connection between the increasingly isolated coal industry and the local communities. The coal industry's approach fits with Habermas's (1975) observation that efforts at legitimation typically draw on existing cultural institutions, providing continuity with tradition. The coal industry, in its development of the provider and defender icon—linking coal to the military, a symbol of patriotism and strength—is clearly trying to imbed coal mining in deep cultural traditions. It connects its legitimation efforts with those of the state, which has long worked to build the image of the military as a noble institution on which all Americans depend.

The outdoorsman icon. Hunting and fishing are important traditions to many West Virginians. Many West Virginians pride themselves on being avid outdoorspeople, a value that often stands in contradiction to the destructive ecological practices of the coal industry. Mountaintop removal mining has caused the destruction of vast tracts of land once used for hunting, digging ginseng root, morel gathering, and collecting other types of medicinal herbs such as black cohosh, bloodroot, and mayapple. Many streams in which West Virginians used to swim and the fish habitat they provided have been buried under valley fills or polluted with acid mine drainage and coal waste. Thus, the Friends of Coal needed to address this contradiction to make the coal industry appear to also value the outdoors, as a large number of West Virginians do. This they attempted to accomplish by becoming the primary corporate sponsor of professional bass fisherman Jeremy Starks and by bringing him on as an official spokesperson for the Friends of Coal in 2006. Adding even more to his credentials as an "environmentally conscious" spokesperson for the Friends of Coal is the fact that Starks serves as a representative on the Bass Angler Sportsman Society's (BASS) "conservation team," which meets with government officials to discuss conservation issues.

Starks appears in two 60-second Friends of Coal television commercials, the first alongside Nehlen and Pruett and the second on a stream bank fishing with five children. In the first commercial, Starks, Nehlen, and Pruett are fishing from Starks's 21-foot bass boat, which has a panoramic photo of West Virginia mountains and the "Friends of Coal" logo emblazoned across its side. As the three of them fish in a West Virginia stream, they discuss the West Virginia coal industry:

NEHLEN:	Thousands of tons of coal are mined in this area.
STARKS:	And scientific tests have shown
PRUETT:	That the water is clean, clear, and a strong provider for wildlife. And the coal mining industry is proud of that.
NEHLEN:	And of their role in making sure that it stays that way.

. . .

From the mouth of self-proclaimed conservationist Jeremy Starks, we are assured that coal extraction and a clean environment can coexist.[6] We are even told that the coal industry actually *improves* water quality! It is through this assertion that the Friends of Coal attempts to identify itself as the quintessential West Virginia "outdoorsman."

Through appropriating some of the most potent cultural icons of the region, such as football, the military, race-car driving, the accomplished outdoorsman, and the working-class provider, the Friends of Coal has attempted to amplify the connection between West Virginia and coal so that this industry appears to be more than a provider of jobs; it embodies all of the characteristics of the archetypal West Virginian.

. . .

Strategy 2: Becoming Pervasively Visible within the Social Landscape of West Virginia

The second major way in which the Friends of Coal endeavors to become the identity of West Virginia is through its attempts to be seen virtually *everywhere* in the state and penetrate the lifeworld. The organization accomplishes this in three major ways: (1) distributing hard-hat stickers, window decals, buttons, yard signs, and ball caps at nearly every major public event; (2) sponsoring events, community improvement projects, scholarships, and any other venue that provides an opportunity for the Friends of Coal logo or name to be in the public's attention; and (3) entering the school system through the Coal Education Development and Resource (CEDAR) Program of southern West Virginia.

The Friends of Coal logo. Reflecting the Friends of Coal's goal to pervade the visual landscape with its presence, Warren Hylton, West Virginia Coal Association board member (quoted in Shanghai Zoom Intelligence Co., Ltd. 2006), asserted, "This logo will be the visible proof that there are Friends of Coal all over West Virginia. . . . The more you see of this symbol, the more you can be sure our message is getting across." The Friends of Coal has made concerted efforts to distribute its stickers, hats, buttons, and yard signs widely throughout West Virginia, and even into other Appalachian states. . . .

Friends of Coal sponsorships. Connected to the wide distribution of Friends of Coal logos is the extensive list of events, places, and services that the Friends of Coal has sponsored in the five years since its inception. . . . Friends of Coal's massive campaign to have its name attached to everything from soccer fields to auto fairs to the capital city's Fourth of July celebration to volleyball games to theater performances is a clear attempt to broaden its base of support to those individuals who may not care about football or fishing and who may not come from a working-class background. Through appearing to sponsor everything and anything, the Friends of Coal gives the impression that the coal industry is still acting as the backbone of the state, regardless of whether it provides many jobs or contributes significantly to public services. Thus, these diverse sponsorships serve to perpetuate an ideology of dependency: Without the coal industry, West Virginians would not only be without jobs, they would also be without sporting events, soccer fields . . . , cultural events, and community centers.

Coal education in the schools. In his study of social cohesion in liberal democracies, Mann (1970) found that the most common form of "manipulative socialization" by the state does not attempt to *change* the values of the working class, but instead seeks to *perpetuate* the values that hinder the working class from interpreting "the reality it actually experiences" (437). This insight fits with our observation that the coal industry actively works to maintain and amplify its status as the state's economic identity in order to prevent the working class from recognizing the coal industry's role in the economic and environmental degradation of coalfield communities. Furthermore, Mann (1970) cites studies that reveal the school system's crucial role in the manipulative socialization of children, particularly those from working-class families. In this same way, the coal industry, with the blessing of the state, endeavors to socialize school children in the southern coalfields to an "understanding of the many benefits the coal industry provides in daily lives" through the CEDAR Program, which consists of special coal-education materials and curricula created by the West Virginia Coal Association (West Virginia Coal Association 2007).

. . .

Conclusions

The drive for profit accumulation is a defining feature of capitalism and is central to the treadmill of production. This drive has always generated a fundamental tension, however, because activities that increase profits also frequently degrade the environment and undermine social wellbeing. These circumstances create legitimation problems for the owners of the means of production. The machinations of the treadmill have been particularly apparent in regions that historically depended on extractive industries, such as mining and timber, as the mainstay of their economies. In an effort to increase profits, industries in the post–World War II era accelerated the mechanization of production, leading to the dual consequences of displacing workers and increasing environmental degradation. In the aftermath of these transformations in production practices, many rural communities were left with polluted environments and high unemployment due to a decline in industry jobs. The social and environmental costs of production led to the public's growing opposition to industry's often unrestrained access to natural resources. This rising tide of protest, challenging the power of industry, has increasingly led to industry backlash, where extractive industries struggle to cling to their power, despite their declining contribution to the economy and employment.

Our aim here has been to address a lacuna in the treadmill of production theory by incorporating theoretical concepts from the neo-Marxian tradition on the legitimation process so as to further our understanding of how industry gains compliance from substantial segments of the public. One of the ways that industry maintains its power is to actively construct ideology that furthers its interests—an observation made by Marx, but developed further by a line of critical scholars, including Lukács, Gramsci, Horkheimer, Adorno, and Habermas. Here, we examined a manifestation of this in "postindustrial" America. The changes in coal production in West Virginia illustrate how industry works to maintain community loyalty when it no longer serves as a major source of employment. When the number of jobs it provided declined due to changing mining practices, the coal industry faced a legitimation crisis that challenged its hold on political power. The industry response to this challenge has been to engage in cultural manipulation, attempting to construct a pro-coal ideology that shapes community economic identity. Key strategies for furthering this process center on the appropriation of West Virginia cultural icons and the infusion of coal-industry ideology into a variety of social arenas. The intended effect of these efforts has been to (re)construct the identity of West Virginia as both economically dependent on coal and culturally defined by coal, the latter being part of what Habermas identified as the colonization of the lifeworld. The West Virginia case illustrates processes that likely occur elsewhere in the nation, such as in the historically timber-dependent communities in the Pacific Northwest. Analyses of ideology construction by the economic elite may, therefore, help shed light on a variety of social and economic processes occurring throughout the United States and around the world.

Notes

Bell, Shannon Elizabeth and Richard York. 2010. "Community Economic Identity: The Coal Industry and Ideology Construction in West Virginia." *Rural Sociology* 75(1): 111–143.

1. The overall consequences of corporate capitalism for the economy and employment structure are, of course, more complicated than the treadmill model may suggest. New types of jobs (e.g., information technology) may be created as other types of jobs (e.g., mining) disappear, so that the net effect of the treadmill may not always be *overall* job losses. However, the pattern described by the treadmill model does generally hold when focusing on manufacturing and extractive industry jobs.

2. The Appalachian Land Ownership Task Force's (1983) study of land ownership patterns in 80 counties in Central and southern Appalachia found that 72 percent of the 13 million acres of surface land in the study were owned by absentee owners, and of the top 50 private owners, 46 were corporations. This pattern is even more dramatic in the highest coal-producing regions of Appalachia: four of the five counties with the most corporately held land are in the coalfields of southern West Virginia, and in those counties nearly 90 percent of the land is owned by corporations.

3. However, West Virginia's population declined by only about 10 percent over this period due to natural increase.

4 Slurry impoundments are not limited to the coal preparation process. Coal burned at coal-fired power plants generates coal fly-ash slurry, which is stored in impoundments. In December 2008, 1.1 billion gallons of coal fly-ash slurry broke through an impoundment at the Tennessee Valley Authority (TVA) Kingston Fossil Plant in Harriman, Tennessee, contaminating a branch of the Emory River and approximately 300 acres of the surrounding land (U.S. Environmental Protection Agency 2009).

5. The West Virginia Coal Association Website claims that the song featured in this television commercial was the coal industry's theme music 25 years ago. The chorus—"Coal is West Virginia"—has been made into a cell phone ringtone that is available for downloading from the Website (West Virginia Coal Association 2008).

6. This message is one that is being promoted through the coal industry's "Clean Coal" campaign, which many argue is nothing more than an advertising scheme to counter coal's reputation as a "dirty" fossil fuel.

References

Bell, S.E. 2009. "'There Ain't No Bond in Town Like There Used to Be': The Destruction of Social Capital in the West Virginia Coalfields." *Sociological Forum* 24(3):631–57.

Bonskowski, R. 2004. "EIA Coal Statistics, Projections, and Analyses: What They Say about Changes in the Coal Industry." Presented at spring meeting of SME Central Appalachian Section, April 15–17. Retrieved December 3, 2007 (www.eia.doe.gov/cneaf/ coal/page/f_p_coal/coalstats.ppt).

Bonskowski, R., W. Watson, and F. Freme. 2006. "Coal Production in the United States: An Historical Overview." Energy Information Administration. Retrieved December 3, 2007 (http://www.eia.doe.gov/cneaf/coal/page/coal_production_review.pdf).

Burns, S.L.S. 2005. "Bringing Down the Mountains: The Impact of Mountaintop Removal Surface Coal Mining on Southern West Virginia Communities, 1970–2004." PhD dissertation, Department of History, West Virginia University, Morgantown, WV.

Buttel, F. 2004. "The Treadmill of Production: An Appreciation, Assessment, and Agenda for Research." *Organization and Environment* 17(3):323–36.

"CEDAR of Southern West Virginia." 2005. *Coal Leader: Coal's National Newspaper*, September. Retrieved February 3, 2009 (http://www.coalleader.com/).

Coal Impoundment Location and Information System. 2005. "Listing of Coal Impoundments: West Virginia." Wheeling Jesuit University. Retrieved December 6, 2006 (http://www.coalimpoundment.org/locate/list.asp).

Cook, S.R. 2000. *Monacans and Miners: Native American and Coal Mining Communities in Appalachia*. Lincoln, NE: University of Nebraska Press.

Eades, R. 2000. "Brushy Fork Slurry Impoundment—A Preliminary Report." Ohio Valley Environmental Coalition. Retrieved January 3, 2006 (http://www.ohvec.org/issues/ slurry_impoundments/articles/brushy_fork.pdf).

Energy Information Administration, Office of Coal, Nuclear, Electric, and Alternate Fuels. 1995. *Longwall Mining*. Washington, DC: U.S. Department of Energy. Retrieved December 15, 2008 (http://tonto.eia.doe.gov/ftproot/coal/tr0588.pdf).

Energy Information Administration. 2002, 2004, 2006. "U.S. Coal Production by Coal-Producing Region and State." *Annual Coal Report*. Retrieved December 2, 2007 (http://www.eia.doe.gov/cneaf/coal/page/acr/backissues.html).

Foster, J.B. 2005. "The Treadmill of Accumulation: Schnaiberg's Environment and Marxian Political Economy." *Organization and Environment* 18(1):7–18.

Foster, J.B. and R. York. 2004. "Political Economy and Environmental Crisis: Introduction to the Special Issue." *Organization and Environment* 17(3):293–94.

Freudenburg, W.R., L.J. Wilson, and D.J. O'Leary. 1998. "Forty Years of Spotted Owls? A Longitudinal Analysis of Logging Industry Job Losses." *Sociological Perspectives* 41(1):1–26.

"Friends of Coal." 2003. *Coal Leader: Coal's National Newspaper*, March. Retrieved November 3, 2007 (http://www.coalleader.com/).

Friends of Coal. 2005. "Homepage." Retrieved February 9, 2005 (http://www. friendsof coal.org/).

———. 2007. "Welcome Friends of Coal," *Friends of Coal*. Retrieved December 1, 2007 (www.friendsofcoal.org).

Gaventa, J. 1978. "Property, Coal, and Theft." Pp. 141–59 in *Colonialism in Modern America: The Appalachian Case*, edited by H.M. Lewis, L. Johnson, and D. Askins. Boone, NC: Appalachian Consortium Press.

Gould, K.A., D.N. Pellow, and A. Schnaiberg. 2004. "Interrogating the Treadmill of Production: Everything You Wanted to Know about the Treadmill but Were Afraid to Ask." *Organization and Environment* 17(3):296–316.

Gramsci, A. 1971. *Selections from the Prison Notebooks*. New York: International Publishers.

Habermas, J. 1975. *Legitimation Crisis*. Translated by T. McCarthy. Boston, MA: Beacon.

———. 1984. *The Theory of Communicative Action*. Vol. 1, Reason and the Rationalization of Society. Translated by T. McCarthy. Boston, MA: Beacon.

———. 1987. *The Theory of Communicative Action*. Vol. 2, Lifeworld and System: A Critique of Functionalist Reason. Translated by T. McCarthy. Boston, MA: Beacon.

Haynes, A. 1997. *Poverty in Central Appalachia*. NewYork: Garland.

Herman, E.S. and N. Chomsky. 2002. *Manufacturing Consent: The Political Economy of the Mass Media*. NewYork: Pantheon.

Hohmann, G. 2005. "Capitol Rallies to Reflect Divergent Opinions on Coal." *Charleston Daily Mail*, March 20, p. 1A.

Horkheimer, M. and T.W. Adorno. 1972. *Dialectic of Enlightenment*. Translated by John Cumming. New York: Herder and Herder.

Lewis, H.M. and E.E. Knipe. 1978. "The Colonialism Model: The Appalachian Case." Pp. 9–31 in *Colonialism in Modern America: The Appalachian Case*, edited by H.M. Lewis, L. Johnson, and D. Askins. Boone, NC: Appalachian Consortium Press.

Lockard, D. 1998. *Coal: A Memoir and Critique*. Charlottesville, VA: University Press of Virginia.

Lukács, G. [1923] 1972. *History and Class Consciousness*. Translated by R. Livingstone. Cambridge, MA: MIT Press.

Maggard, S.W. 1994. "From Farm to Coal Camp to Back Office and McDonald's: Living in the Midst of Appalachia's Latest Transformation." *Journal of the Appalachian Studies Association* 6(1):14–38.

———. 1999. "Gender, Race, and Place: Confounding Labor Activism in Central Appalachia." Pp. 185–206 in *Neither Separate nor Equal: Women, Race, and Class in the South*, edited by B.E. Smith. Philadelphia, PA: Temple University Press.

Mann, M. 1970. "The Social Cohesion of Liberal Democracy." *American Sociological Review* 35(3):423–39.

Marx, K. and F. Engels. 1991. *The German Ideology*. New York: International Publishers.

Mészáros, I. 1989. *The Power of Ideology*. New York: New York University Press.

Miewald, C.E. and E.J. McCann. 2004. "Gender Struggle, Scale, and the Production of Place in the Appalachian Coalfields." *Environment and Planning A* 36:1045– 64.

National Mining Association. 2008. "Trends in U.S. Coal Mining 1923–2007." Retrieved February 8, 2009 (http://www.nma.org/pdf/c_trends_mining.pdf).

Orem, W.H. 2006. "Coal Slurry: Geochemistry and Impacts on Human Health and Environmental Quality." U.S. Geological Survey, Eastern Energy Resources Team. PowerPoint Presentation to the Coal Slurry Legislative Subcommittee of the Senate Judiciary Committee, West Virginia Legislature, November 15.

Schnaiberg, A. 1980. *The Environment: From Surplus to Scarcity*. New York: Oxford University Press.

Shanghai Zoom Intelligence Co., Ltd., China Energy Competitive Intelligence Provider. 2006. "Making Friends: West Virginia Coal Needs You." *Coal and Electric Power— April News*, April 14. Retrieved November 3, 2007 (http://www.zoomchina.com .cn/new/ content/view/4301/197/).

State of West Virginia. 2007. *Executive Budget Fiscal Year 2008*. Vol.1, *Budget Report*. Retrieved August 20, 2007 (http://www.wvbudget.gov/report/WVBudget ReportFY2008.pdf)

Stockman, V. 2006. "Jack Spadaro: Former Top MSHA Safety Trainer Fights the Tragic Consequences of Mountaintop Removal Mining." *Appalachian Voice*, Spring. Retrieved December 14, 2009 (http://www.appvoices.org/index.php?/site/voice_ stories/ jack_spadaro1/issues/151/238).

U.S. Census Bureau. 1961, 1971, 1981, 1991, 1994, 2000, 2005. "Mining and Mineral Products." *Statistical Abstract of the United States*. Washington, DC: Government Printing Office.

U.S. Department of Commerce, Bureau of Economic Analysis. 2005. "Gross State Product in Current Dollars, 2004." Retrieved February 10, 2005 (http://www.bea.gov/ bea/ newsrel/gspnewsrelease.htm).

U.S. Department of the Interior, Bureau of Land Management. 1994. Rangeland Reform Environmental Impact Statement. Washington, DC.

U.S. Environmental Protection Agency. 2003. Chapter 3: "Affected Environment and Consequences of MTM/VF." *Draft Environmental Impact Statement: Mountaintop Mining/ Valley Fills in Appalachia*. Retrieved December 4, 2006 (http://www.epa .gov/region3/ mtntop/eis.htm).

——. 2005. *Mountaintop Mining/Valley Fills in Appalachia Final Programmatic Environmental Impact Statement*.RetrievedSeptember28,2007(http://www.epa.gov/ region03/ mtntop/ p.4).

——. 2009. "EPA to Oversee Cleanup of TVA Kingston Fossil Fuel Plant Release." News release from Region 4. Retrieved May 14, 2009 (http://www.epa.gov/ region4/ kingston/index.html).

Walls, D.S. 1978. "Internal Colony or Internal Periphery? A Critique of Current Models and an Alternative Formulation." Pp. 319–49 in *Colonialism in Modern America:*

The Appalachian Case, edited by H.M. Lewis, L. Johnson, and D. Askins. Boone, NC: Appalachian Consortium Press.

Weller, J. 1978. "Appalachia: America's Mineral Colony." Pp. 47–55 in *Colonialism in Modern America: The Appalachian Case*, edited by H.M. Lewis, L. Johnson, and D. Askins. Boone, NC: Appalachian Consortium Press.

Wells, L.A. 2006. "Lawsuits Muddy Water Project." *Appalachian News-Express*, August 13. Retrieved August 13, 2006 (http://www.newsexpresssky.com/articles/2006/07/30/top_story/01water.txt).

West Virginia Bureau of Employment Programs, Workforce West Virginia. 2005. "Monthly Report on the Civilian Labor Force, Employment and Unemployment Data." Retrieved February 11, 2005 (http://www.wvbep.org/bep/lmi/TABLE2/T205west.HTM).

West Virginia Coal Association. 2007. "CEDAR." Retrieved February 12, 2009 (http://www.wvcoal.com/cedar.html).

———. 2008. "'Coal Is West Virginia' Hits the Airwaves." (July 3, 2008). Retrieved February 14, 2009 (http://www.wvcoal.com/news/wvcoal-news/344-qcoal-is-west-virginiaq-hitsthe-airwaves.html).

West Virginia Health Statistics Center, West Virginia Bureau for Public Health, Department of Health and Human Resources. 2002. "A Look at West Virginia's Population by Decade, 1950–2000." Retrieved February 10, 2005 (http://wvdhhr.org/bph/oehp/ hsc/briefs/eight/default.htm).

West Virginia State Treasurer's Office. 2007. "Quarterly Distributions: 25% Portion Distributed to Municipalities." *Coal Severance Tax Distributions*. Retrieved August 20, 2007 (http://www.wvsto.com/Tax+Distribution/Coal+Severance+Tax.htm).

Wire Reports. 2002. "Nehlen to Pitch for Coal Group; Ex-WVU Coach Calls Industry 'Vital' to State's Future." *Charleston Daily Mail*, December 13, p. 2C.

Witt, T.S. and M. Fletcher. 2005. *Tourism and the West Virginia Economy*. Bureau of Business and Economic Research, West Virginia University. Retrieved August 18, 2007 (http://www.be.wvu.edu/bber/publications.aspx#).

Witt, T.S. and J.S. Leguizamon. 2007. *Tourism and the West Virginia Economy*. Bureau of Business and Economic Research, West Virginia University. Retrieved August 18, 2007 (http://www.be.wvu.edu/bber/publications.aspx#).

Workforce West Virginia. 2000a, 2001, 2002, 2003, 2004, 2005, 2006, 2007. "West Virginia—Employment and Wages." West Virginia Bureau of Employment Programs. Retrieved February 11, 2008 (http://www.wvbep.org/bep/lmi/DEFAULT.HTM).

———. 2000b. "West Virginia Nonfarm Payroll Employment, by Industry, Annual Averages 1939–1999." West Virginia Bureau of Employment Programs. Retrieved February 11, 2008 (http://www.wvbep.org/bep/lmi/e&e/nf_39-99.htm).

PART

V

Perspectives on Disaster

Silent Spill
The Organization of an Industrial Crisis
Thomas D. Beamish

The two pieces in this section are sociological explorations into the causes and consequences of disasters. While these two readings are about oil spills, it is important to note that environmental sociologists investigate the social causes and consequences of all types of disasters—from major storms (like Hurricane Katrina) to nuclear meltdowns.

Thomas Beamish examines one of the biggest oil spills in U.S. history—the spill at Guadalupe Dunes in California. While some environmental tragedies happen in a flash, like the Exxon Valdez spill near Alaska and the BP oil spill in the Gulf of Mexico, much environmental destruction happens slowly over many years. As Beamish shows, the cleanup at Guadalupe Dunes came late; the original problem had been allowed to mushroom into a total disaster over many years of inaction. Beamish, in his investigation of the systemic and institutional underpinnings of this long-term event, argues that the extent of this disaster was exacerbated by both the slowness in which it occurred and the style of decision making that takes place in particular kinds of organizations.

There's a strange phenomenon that biologists refer to as "the boiled frog syndrome." Put a frog in a pot of water and increase the temperature of the water gradually from 20°C to 30°C to 40°C . . . to 90°C and the frog just sits there. But suddenly, at 100°C . . . , something happens: The water boils and the frog dies. . . . Like the simmering frog, we face a future without precedent, and our senses are not attuned to warnings of imminent danger. The threats we face as the crisis builds—global warming, acid rain, the ozone hole and increasing ultraviolet radiation, chemical toxins such as pesticides, dioxins, and polychlorinated biphenyls (PCBs) in our food and water—are undetectable by the sensory system we have evolved.

—Gordon and Suzuki 1990

U nderneath the Guadalupe Dunes—a windswept piece of wilderness 170 miles north of Los Angeles and 250 miles south of San Francisco—sits the largest petroleum spill in US history. The spill emerged as a local issue in February 1990. Though not acknowledged, it was not unknown to oil workers at the field where it originated, to regulators that often visited the dunes, or to locals who frequented the beach. Until the mid-1980s, neither the oily sheen that often appeared on the beach, on the ocean, and the nearby Santa Maria River nor the strong petroleum odors that regularly emanated from the Unocal Corporation's oil-field operations raised much concern. Recognition, as in the frog parable, was slow to manifest. The result of leaks and spills that accumulated slowly and chronically over 38 years, the Guadalupe Dunes spill became troubling when local residents, government regulators, and a whistleblower who worked the field no longer viewed the periodic sight and smell of petroleum as normal. . . .

I first heard of the Guadalupe spill on local television news in August 1995. (My home was 65 miles from the spill site.) The scene included a sandy beach, enormous earth-moving machinery, a hard-hatted Unocal official, and a reporter, microphone in hand, asking the official how things were proceeding. The interplay of the news coverage and Unocal's official response caught my attention more than anything else. The representative asserted that Unocal had extracted 500,000 gallons of petroleum from a large excavated pit on the beach just in view of the camera. The newscaster ended the segment by saying (I paraphrase) "It's nice that Unocal is taking responsibility to get things under control." This offhand remark about responsibility set me to thinking about the long-term nature of the spill and about why it had not been stopped sooner, either by Unocal managers or by regulators.

A few months later, a colleague and I drove to the beach. My colleague, a geologist who was familiar with the area, had suggested that we visit the Guadalupe Dunes for their scenic beauty. We walked the beach and the dunes that border the oil field, alert for signs of the massive spill. The pit that Unocal had recently excavated had been filled in. The only hint of the project that remained was a small crew that was driving pilings into the sand to support a steel wall intended to stop hydrocarbon drift (movement of oil on top of groundwater) and the advancing Santa Maria River, which threatened to cut into an underground petroleum plume and send millions more gallons into the ocean.

Unocal security personnel followed along the beach, watching suspiciously as we took pictures. In fact, the spill was so difficult to perceive (only periodically does the beach smell of petroleum and the ocean have rainbow oil stains) that my impressions wavered. Was this really a calamitous event? The whole visit was imbued with the paradox of beauty and travesty.

Under my feet was the largest oil spill in California, and most likely the largest in US history. . . . Yet the "total amount spilled" continue to be, as one local resident noted in an interview, a matter of "political science." There is still controversy over just how big this spill really is. The smaller of the two estimates . . . (8.5 million gallons) comes from Unocal's consultants. State and local regulatory agencies do not endorse it (Arthur D. Little et al. 1997). The estimates quoted most often by government personnel put the spill at 20 million gallons or more, which would make it the largest petroleum spill ever recorded in the United States.

At first glance, it seems strange that so many individuals and organizations missed the spillage for so many years; "passivity" seems to be the word that best characterizes the personal and institutional mechanisms of identification and amelioration. It is also clear that the Guadalupe spill is very different from the image of petroleum spills that dominates media and policy prescriptions and the public mind: the iconographic spill of crude oil, complete with oiled birds and dying sea creatures.

The Guadalupe Dunes spill is only the largest *discovered spill*. Representing an inestimable number of similar cases, it exemplifies a genre of environmental catastrophe that portends ecological collapse.

Describing his impression of the spill in a 1996 interview, a resident of Orcutt, California, explained why he remained unsurprised by frequent diluent seeps: "When you grow up around it—the smell, the burning eyes while surfing, the slicks on the water—I didn't realize it could be a risk. It was normal to us." In a 1997 interview, a local fish and game warden—one of those initially responsible for the spill's investigation—responded this way to the question "Why did it take so long for the spill to be noticed?": "It is out of sight, it's out of mind. I can't see it from my back yard. It is down there in Guadalupe, I never go to Guadalupe. You know, I may have walked the beach one time, but I never saw anything. It smelled down there. What do you expect when there is an oil field? You know, you drive by an oil production site; you are bound to smell something. You are bound to."

In the days and weeks after my initial visit to the dunes, I wondered why the spill had gained so little notoriety. Beginning my research in earnest, I visited important players, attended meetings, took official tours of the site, and followed the accounts in the media.

What makes the Guadalupe spill so relevant is that it represents a genre—indeed a pandemic—of environmental crises (Glantz 1999). Collectively, problems of this sort—both environmental and non-environmental—exemplify what I term *crescive troubles*. According to the *Oxford English Dictionary*, "crescive" literally means "in the growing stage" and comes from the Latin root "crescere," meaning to "to grow." "Crescive" is used in the applied sciences to denote phenomena that accumulate gradually, becoming well established over time. In cases of such incremental and cumulative phenomena (particularly contamination events), identifying the "cause" of injuries sustained is often difficult if not impossible because of their long duration and the high number of intervening factors. Applied to a more inclusive set of social problems, the idea of crescive troubles also conveys the human tendency to avoid dealing with problems as they accumulate. We often overlook slow-onset, long-term problems until they manifest as acute traumas and/or accidents (Hewitt 1983; Turner 1978).

There are also important political dimensions to the conception of crescive troubles. Molotch (1970), in his analysis of an earlier and more infamous oil spill on the central coast of California (the 1969 Santa Barbara spill), relates a set of points that resonate with my discussion. In that article, Molotch examines how the big oil companies and the Nixon administration "mobilized bias" to diffuse local opposition, disorient dissenters, and limit the political ramifications of the Santa Barbara spill. Two of his ideas have special relevance: that of the *creeping event* and that of the *routinization of evil*. A creeping event is one "arraigned to occur at an inconspicuously gradual and piecemeal pace" that in so doing diffuses consequences that would otherwise "follow from the event if it were to be perceived all at once" (ibid., p. 139). . . .

Our preoccupation with immediate cause and effect works against recognizing and remedying problems in many ways. It is mirrored in the way society addresses the origin of a problem and in the way powerful institutional actors seek to nullify resistance and diffuse responsibility. The courts and the news media, for instance, often disregard the underlying circumstances that led to many current industrial and environmental predicaments, focusing instead on individual operators who have erred and pinning the blame for accidents on their negligence (Perrow 1984; Vaughan 1996; Calhoun and Hiller 1988). Yet this ignores the systemic reasons why such problems emerge. In short, most if not all of our society's pressing social problems have long histories that predate their acknowledgment but are left to fester because they provide few of the signs that would predict response—for example, the drama associated with social disruption and immiseration. . . .

The inability of our current remedial systems, policy prescriptions, and personal orientations to address a host of pressing long-term environmental threats is frightening. There are, however, numerous examples of disconnected events—seemingly unrelated individual crises recognized after the fact—that have received widespread public attention. Through national media coverage, images of ruptured and rusting barrels of hazardous waste bearing the skull and crossbones have become icons that fill many Americans with dread (Szasz 1994; Erikson 1990, 1994). But these are only the end results of ongoing trends that have been repeated across the country with less dramatic consequences. In view of the startling deterioration of the biosphere, much of which is due to slow and cumulative processes, more attention should be devoted to how such scenarios unfold. . . .

My specific intent is to uncover how and why the Guadalupe spill went unrecognized and was not responded to even though it occurred under unexceptional circumstances. The industrial conditions were quite normal, and the regulatory oversight was typical. It would seem that there was nothing out of the ordinary, other than millions of gallons of spilled petroleum. This is, in part, why the spill is so instructive. It represents a perceptual lacuna—a blank spot in our organizational and personal attentions. . . .

Why didn't local managers report the seepage, as the law requires? How did field personnel understand their role? How could pollution of such an enormous magnitude be left so long before receiving official recognition and action? Why did the surrounding community take so long to react? . . .

The reality that surrounds crescive circumstances is characterized by polluters who are unlikely to report the pollution they cause, authorities who are unlikely to recognize that there is a problem to be remedied, uninterested media, and researchers who take interest only if (or when) an event holds dramatic consequence. In short, all those who are in positions to address crescive circumstances are disinclined to do so. Forms of degradation that lack direct and immediate impact on humans, dramatic images of dying wildlife, or other archetypal images of disaster tend to be downplayed, overlooked, and even ignored.

The national print media certainly mirrored the propensity to ignore the Guadalupe spill (Hart 1995). Over the period 1990–1996, the national press devoted 504 stories to the *Exxon Valdez* accident and only nine to the Guadalupe spill.

In a 1996 interview, a reporter for the *Santa Barbara News Press* offered his opinion as to why the Guadalupe spill had received little public attention until 1993. His view resonates with three of the four social factors articulated above (social disruption, stakeholders, and media fit):

> We didn't see black oily crude in the water and waves turning a churning brown. We didn't see dead fish and dead birds washing up. We didn't see boats in the harbor with disgusting black grimy hulls. This is largely an

> invisible spill. It took place underground. . . . Because it was not so visual, especially before Unocal began excavation for cleanup, I think that it just didn't capture the public. . . . But after Unocal began excavations, driving sheet pilings into the beach, scooping out massive quantities of sand, setting up bacteria eating machines, burning the sand. It began to dawn on people the magnitude of this thing, but again it wasn't in their back yards, Guadalupe is fairly remote. . . . And it's not a well-to-do city [the city of Guadalupe]—comparatively, anyway, with the rest of our area. . . . So I don't think it really sparked the public interest as much as it could have or would have if it was . . . a surface spill. . . .

Central to my research were field interviews with members of the local oil industry, government regulators, community members, and environmental activists. These interviews were tape recorded, transcribed, and systematically analyzed. In addition to the interviews, there were many spontaneous conversations—in hallways, in office waiting rooms, in the homes of those that were the intended interviewees—with individuals I had not originally contacted or planned to meet. Though not recorded, these conversations should not be seen as any less important than the others. I also pursued ethnographic context, recording scores of informal conversations concerning the spill. I accumulated and analyzed a substantial collection of archival materials, and I have followed media portrayals of the spill closely since 1989. . . .

In its early stages (from 1953 until 1978 or 1979), the leakage at the Guadalupe field was not troubling, nor was there anyone to whom to report it. Because it was part of routine fieldwork, it received little attention. According to those who read the meters that tracked the coming and going of the diluent, "many times there were little leaks; that was just normal" (field worker, telephone interview, 1996). A worker quoted in a local newspaper went so far as to say that "diluent loss was a way of life at the Guadalupe oil field" (Friesen 1993). Dumping hundreds of gallons of diluent into the dunes, as long as it was done a gallon at a time, was an ordinary part of production. This is not a great leap of reason; oil work obviously involves oil. Until the 1970s, Unocal sprayed the dunes with crude oil to keep them from shifting and thus to make field maintenance and transportation easier. If spraying crude oil over the dunes was unproblematic, why would diluent leaks, which were largely invisible as soon as they hit the sand, be unsettling? Although workers mention that they became alarmed in the 1980s when puddling diluent periodically appeared as small ponds on the surface of the dunes, the chronic leaks themselves evoked little attention. In brief, at Guadalupe the normalcy of spilling oil of all kinds (crude oil, lubricants, and diluent) worked to blunt perceptions of the leaks as problematic. The leaks were an expected part of a day in the life of an oil worker. According to the *Telegram-Tribune* (Greene 1993b): "A backhoe [operator] at the field . . . for 12 years . . . cited 'an apparent lack of concern about the immediate repair of leaks or the detection of leaks.' Diluent lines would not be replaced unless they had leaked a number of times or were a 'serious maintenance problem. . . .' Although workers checked meters on the pipelines and looked for leaks if there was a discrepancy, often a problem wasn't detected until the stuff flowed to the surface' said . . . a field mechanic."

By both historical and contemporary accounts, oil spills have long been a common occurrence in oil-held operations. This seems to have been especially the case at fields operated by Union Oil. But this does not help us understand why, once field personnel recognized the spillage as a significant problem, they denied it and failed to report it (as specified by state and federal law) for 10 years or more. A first step in understanding why workers failed to report their spill to the authorities once it had "tipped" toward becoming a grievous problem requires us to attend to the vocabulary, the structure, and the enactment of work and how these factors not only molded workers' perceptions of the leaks but also kept them from reporting outside their local work group.

The "Company Line," 1978–1993

Organizationally, oil work at the Guadalupe field was arranged, like work in many traditional industrial settings, around a hierarchical seniority system. Recruitment and promotion were internally derived, meaning the field workers relied on their immediate foremen and supervisors for instruction, guidance, and ultimately, future chances at success (promotion, salary increase, choice of shifts, and so forth). . . . This organizational structure helps to explain Unocal employees' silence about the Guadalupe spill after it was recognized as a threat. Even when the leaks began to look more like a bona fide spill, the rank-and-file workers were insulated from reporting it themselves by their position within the field's hierarchy and their immediate responsibilities. Reporting outside the work group was management's domain.

A Unocal field worker I interviewed in 1997 articulated his experience of the change from a normal to a problematic spill as follows: "You come up and you see a clamp [on a] diluent [pipe]line. It is leaking. You tighten it up, you change it, you . . . fix it and it . . . has made a puddle. That is not something you would turn in. When it went into the ocean . . . and you see the waves break and they weren't breaking white [but] brown water, there is a problem. [That happened] sometime in the 1980s. . . . We all knew right then . . . we had some kind of problem. Well, we all kind of estimated it could be rather large considering that this field had been here so long before we ever got there." Corroborating this worker's impressions, another worker quoted in the *Telegram-Tribune* (Greene 1993b) remembered finding large concentrations of diluent that were no longer the "leaks" that had created them but looked more like a typical "oil spill": "In 1980 a large puddle of diluent that had saturated the sand and bubbled up to fill a spot 5 to 10 feet wide. . . ." He told investigators that he and his co-workers realized at the time there were problems with the diluent system "even though management seemed to ignore the problems."

By this time, the problems brought on by "normal operating procedures" were obvious and destructive. This became especially apparent in the mid-1980s, when accelerated spillage periodically slowed oil production at the field (Greene 1992b, 1993a; Rice 1994). Yet, instead of self-reporting the spillage, the field workers turned to denial and secrecy. . . .

In view of the hierarchy in the field, they were not responsible; their managers were. The hierarchical insulation from responsibility thus helped to keep workers who watched diluent spill into the dunes from feeling obligated to do something about it. When relieved of making decisions, people tend to cede their personal responsibility to those who are in control (Milgram 1974; Asch 1951). . . .

The field's hierarchy had five major levels. A new worker began as a utility man, then worked his way up to pumper and then to field mechanic. If able, with long enough tenure at the field he could become a foreman. Over the foremen were the field supervisors, who headed operations at specific fields; over them was a superintendent who oversaw Guadalupe and another oil operation in the area. . . .

The culpability of all those at the field, but especially the superintendent, supervisors, and field foremen, coupled with the field's organizational characteristics, meant that explicit knowledge concerning the scope and scale of the leaks stayed inside the local operation. "Each field is its separate own little field," said a field worker interviewed in 1997. "We were kind of out in the middle of nowhere. So once we reported to our superior [a field foreman] then he has to report it to the field supervisor, who has to report to the regional superintendent, who then reports it to Los Angeles. Somewhere along the line I think it stopped. I think that it stopped with the field supervisor." This field worker was describing a loosely *coupled* organizational arrangement—one with organizational units that are "somehow attached, but [whose] attachment may be circumscribed, infrequent, weak in its mutual affects, unimportant, and/or slow to respond" (Weick 1976, p. 3). In this case, the slack that existed at the local field between workers and between workers and managers and the loose organizational coupling that existed between the local field and corporate offices (including environmental divisions) were reflected in the technical division of responsibilities, in the authorities of office, and in the expectations placed on each. A great deal of flexibility existed between these units as long as certain goals were met. In this case, petroleum continued to be produced and sent out at an acceptable rate. In view of the local field's autonomy and field personnel's collective interest in remaining a viable production unit, not telling outsiders about the spill made a great deal of sense. . . .

The long-term nature of the Guadalupe spill made it especially problematic for all those who worked the field for any length of time. Liability for it was diffuse—indeed, organization wide. For those in the lower echelons, going outside the proscribed line of command to report the spill created triple jeopardy: Not only would they risk being personally associated with an organizational offense; they also would have been informing on co-workers and endangering their careers by implicating their superiors. One does not succeed within a vertically organized work setting by "ratting out" one's superiors or co-workers. Fear of social and organizational reprisal was evident in my discussions with field personnel, in California wardens' accounts of their interactions with subpoenaed field personnel, and in local newspapers' stories such as Greene 1993b: "Current employees contacted for this story were surprised and dismayed their names would become public because of what they told the state investigators. They worried about their superiors and co-workers at Unocal finding out."

Workers at the Guadalupe field did not want to go over the head of their field foreman, their supervisor, or their superintendent. A field worker, interview by telephone in 1997, said: "There is somebody above you and someone above them and someone above them. One thing that you don't want to do is break the chain of command . . . that causes friction." Informing might have affected how many hours of work one received, one's chances of promotion, and ultimately whether or not one would keep a well-paying job. . . .

A Culture of Silence

Local managerial power and organizational routines did not wholly determine behavior at the field. The normative framework that prevailed there was also attributable to the subculture of oil-field work and to individual workers' agency. . . .

To understand more fully why workers kept quiet about a spill they knew was patently illegal while field managers covered it up and lied to authorities about its origins, we must look beyond matters of hierarchy and seniority. We must look at individual motivations and at the social glue that bound workers to their work group. In short, we must look at the dominant social milieu at the oil field in order to see how social relations between workers played into the initial normalization of the spill and how they reinforced the intra-organizational conditions that discouraged self-reporting. Taken separately, both structural and cultural explanations would predict that self-reporting was unlikely; together, they make self-reporting appear a dubious regulatory strategy. . . .

Social Ties and Field Secrets

Workers at Guadalupe inherited and developed a set of norms and beliefs about what were and were not appropriate in-group behaviors. This is a normal part of group unity. Moreover, that this unity led to the coverup of an ongoing petroleum spill becomes more understandable (even if socially inexcusable) when we address the threat it posed to each individual at the field and to the local outfit as a whole. . . .

. . . [P]ressure to keep the spill a secret, based in a de facto culture of silence was observable in how field workers reacted when they found out that one of them had called the authorities. (. . . the first admission came in an anonymous telephone call to state officials in February of 1990.) When interviewed in 1997, the field worker who initially blew the whistle related being overheard by the field office's secretary and described the secretary's reaction to his phone call as follows:

I got on the phone in the office. I say [to the health department official], "Okay, I'll talk to you later," and I hear his click, and I'm still on the phone, and I hear another click. The secretary eavesdropped and heard my conversation. She came in, and she started yelling at me, "What are you doing! We will all lose our jobs!" And I said, "Not if we didn't do anything! If it isn't ours, why would we lose our jobs? We are not going to lose our jobs!" We knew [about the spill]. But I never thought it would come to the point where they would shut everything down. What I thought would happen is they would isolate the problem and go on producing.

. . . Individuals, in protecting themselves from association with the spill, also collectively shielded the organization from harm, at least in the short term. The threats of a shutdown of the field and a loss of jobs and the social pressure to remain silent kept workers from reporting the spill. (Once the spill was "discovered" by regulators, Unocal's corporate headquarters did shut the field down, and all the workers were either transferred or laid off.)

Moreover, breaking with one's peers and eliciting an out-of-group admission about what was (initially at least) a "normal" part of production was also unlikely for a set of more socially relevant reasons. Even once the spill had accumulated and became noticeable, reporting it would mean informing on co-workers and facing their opinions. Once his identity became known at the site, the whistleblower was ostracized by many of his fellow workers. . . .

Inter-Organizational Location as Amplification

In conjunction with the organizational location of workers relative to one another and to management and with the culture of silence that characterized the field, the Guadalupe field's structural isolation from outside interference (both physically and organizationally from regulatory authorities and Unocal's head offices) and the corporate incentives worked against self-reporting. Like many other corporations, Unocal was not a monolithic undifferentiated body with a single objective or universally shared knowledge. In organizational form, Unocal consisted of loosely coupled upstream corporate offices, production units, and downstream refinery and vending segments. Insulation from outside interference amplified the power that field routines and the local production culture had over individual perceptions and over field workers' choices.

Because the Guadalupe field was largely autonomous from its head offices, its day-to-day domestic affairs were largely internal. A report of an incident had to go to the top before making its way to outside authorities. Because the information stopped in the field's chain of command, it never made it out of the field, where action could be taken to stem it. This is not a claim that Unocal headquarters could not have known about the spill if they had wanted to investigate it. The argument forwarded here is more passive: Headquarters was interested only in specific information from Unocal's extraction divisions, and this information tended to consist of production quotas rather than of information as to whether environmental matters were being addressed. Again, Unocal, as a corporation, seemed to care little about how local operations performed their production as long as the fields continued to produce profits. . . .

Had efficiency included not wasting diluent, a case could be made that the loss of diluent into the dunes would have been a sign to those on the outside that something was amiss. In this instance, Unocal's head offices may have taken a more active interest if dollars were being lost. Had hundreds of thousands of gallons of refined petroleum product been purchased from an external source and subsequently lost, it would seem expensive and hard to cover up. But spilling was considered a part of producing oil at Unocal's operations, and it also was rather normal for others in the industry. Furthermore, it was considered largely an internal affair. The diluent used at the site beginning in the early 1950s originated at Unocal's refinery situated at the edge of the Guadalupe Dunes, literally a part of the Guadalupe field's production infrastructure. Oil extracted from the Guadalupe field was piped to the Nipomo refinery for initial separation. Diluent, as a by-product of this refining process, was then pumped back to Guadalupe for use. At Guadalupe, diluent was stored at a number of tank farms; from there it was transferred via pipeline to individual extraction wells. If production was consistent, lost diluent would not be missed, especially in view of the normality of spilling and the shoddy records that were being kept (because the price of refining was internal). Losing diluent cost the local operator little (at least, relative to getting caught or facing the prospects of personally reporting it), as long as crude oil was being produced at the expected rate. On the other hand, if the field supervisor reported the spills (which had "tipped" toward the obvious in the 1980s) he would have known that he had a big monetary and criminal problem on his hands. It would have tarnished his personal record, reflected badly on Unocal's image as a whole, potentially shut down the local operation, and presented the possibility of criminal prosecution. What is more, the potential fines for having not reported the spill are significant. . . .

Two examples of the penalties associated with pollution of this sort illustrate the predicament that field managers confronted when deciding whether to report the spill. The federal Clean Water Act specifies that violators can be fined between $5000 and $50,000 a day per violation for being "knowingly" negligent. Estimating the potential fines involved for this single act would require starting with the date of the amendment's passage (in 1973) and calculating daily fines up to 1990 (when Unocal ceased using diluent at the field). The estimate ranges from $31,025,000 to $310,250,000. Likewise, under California's Proposition 65 (a citizen-sponsored "right to know" act passed in 1987) Unocal was also liable for not reporting its release of petroleum into local river and ocean waters frequented by recreationalists. Proposition 65 caps fines against violators at $2,500 per person per exposure day. These are but two examples.

Moreover, the field supervisor and superintendent personally stood to lose thousands of dollars in potential bonuses that were paid for meeting corporate expectations. Field supervisors received incentives in the form of commendations, quick advancement, and end-of-the-year bonuses for keeping production costs down and petroleum yields high. High production costs would have resulted from capital outlays for such items as Guadalupe's pipeline infrastructure. Much as in the system that prevailed in the Soviet Union into the 1980s, costs were "hidden" by a reward system that recognized only production goals and the accompanying steady income stream. Thus, the primary goal was keeping production high, not worrying about diluent costs that (at least on paper) were trivial, being locally internalized. According to a Unocal supervisor interviewed in 1997 for this research, why it took 38 years for the spill to be reported by field managers was rather easy to understand: "Unocal [did not report the spill] to the public because local managers received financial incentives to keep costs low. The corporate culture of the production outfits saw spills as a normal part of their routine." Although this was not the only reason that local Unocal managers would continue to spill, it certainly provided a strong incentive not to report it or stop the leakage at the field once it had become organizationally ominous. Only negative personal and organizational repercussions would have resulted if local managers reported the spill. As a latent product of the pressures articulated thus far, spilling and not reporting makes a great deal of sense from the production side of the equation. . . .

In brief, organization-sponsored complicity, the culture of silence, and the inter-organizational isolation of the field combined to make reporting of the Guadalupe spill improbable until the accumulation of diluent had gotten so bad that neither insiders (field personnel) nor outsiders (regulators) could fail to recognize it, a society of environmentalists was there to be concerned about it, and the insistent local media were eager to report on it. These are all factors that society can ill afford to either count on or wait for. . . .

. . . The predominantly social, cultural, and structural explanations I have put forth are powerful in part because of the nature of industrial regulation in the United States, where it has been left to corporate actors to report their own excesses. There is little interdiction, investigation, or active following up of problems by government authorities until a situation is so dire that a coverup is impossible to sustain. Thus, outside of personal motivation on the part of a worker, a foreman, or a supervisor to report a leak, there is little (aside from morals) that would impel anyone in a company to do so. And that is a slippery slope that takes us back inside the social dynamics that characterized the normative and cognitive institutions that characterized Unocal's local field operations. . . .

Note

Beamish, Thomas D. 2002. *Silent Spill: The Organization of an Industrial Crisis.* Cambridge, MA: MIT Press.

References

Arthur D. Little Inc. in association with Furgro West, Headley and Associates, Marine Research Specialists, and Science Applications International Corp. 1997. Guadalupe Oilfield Remediation and Abandonment Project.

Asch, S. 1951. "Effects of Group Pressure upon the Modification and Distortion of Judgments." In *Groups, Leadership, and Men*, ed. H. Guetzkow. Carnegie Press.

Bensman, J. and I. Gerver. 1963. "Crime and Punishment in the Factory: The Function of Deviancy in Maintaining the Social System." *American Journal of Sociology* 28: 588–598.

Brown, P., and E. Mikkelsen. 1990. *No Safe Place: Toxic Waste, Leukemia, and Community Action*. University of California Press.

Calhoun, G., and H. Hiller. 1988. "Coping with Insidious Injuries: The Case of Johns-Manville Corporation and Asbestos Exposure." *Social Problems* 35, no. 2: 162–181.

Dinno, R. 1999. *Protecting California's Drinking Water from Inland Oil Spills*. Planning and Conservation League, Sacramento.

Elliston, F., J. Keenan, P. Lockhart, and J. Van Schaick. 1985. *Whistleblowing: Managing Dissent in the Workplace*. Praeger.

Erikson, K. 1990. "Toxic Reckoning: Business Faces a New Kind of Fear." *Harvard Business Review* 90: 118–126.

Erikson, K. 1994. *A New Species of Trouble: The Human Experience of Modern Disasters*. Norton.

Friesen, T. 1993. "Criminal Charges May Be Eliminated against Unocal." *Five Cities Times-Press-Recorder*, December 7.

Garfinkel, H. 1956. "Conditions of Successful Degradation Ceremonies." *American Journal of Sociology* 61: 420–424.

Glantz, M., ed. 1999. *Creeping Environmental Problems and Sustainable Development in the Aral Sea Basin.* Cambridge University Press.

Glazer, M. 1987. "Whistleblowers." In *Corporate and Governmental Deviance*, ed. M. Ermann and R. Lundman. Third edition. Oxford University Press.

Gordon, A., and D. Suzuki. 1990. *It's a Matter of Survival.* Harvard University Press.

Greene, J. 1992b. "Unocal: A Leaky Environmental Record." *Telegram-Tribune*, August 5.

Greene, J. 1993a. "Unocal Spills May Have Gone Unreported." *Telegram-Tribune*, July 1.

Greene, J. 1993b. "Unocal Workers Confirm Leaks." *Telegram-Tribune*, June 17.

Hart, G. 1995. "How Unocal Covered Up a Record-Breaking California Oil Spill." In *The News That Didn't Make the News and Why*, ed. C. Jensen. Four Walls, Eight Windows.

Hawkins, K. 1983. "Bargain and Bluff: Compliance Strategy and Deterrence in the Enforcement of Regulation." *Law and Policy Quarterly* 5, no. 1: 35–73.

Hewitt, K., ed.1983. *Interpretations of Calamity: From the Viewpoint of Human Ecology.* Allen & Unwin.

Milgram, S. 1974. *Obedience to Authority.* Harper & Row.

Molotch, H. 1970. "Oil in Santa Barbara and Power in America." *Sociological Inquiry* 40 (Winter): 131–144.

Perrow, C. 1984. *Normal Accidents: Living with High Risk Technologies.* Basic Books.

Pratt, J. 1978. "Growth or a Clean Environment? Responses to Petroleum-related Pollution in the Gulf Coast Refining Region." *Business History Review* 52, no. 1: 1–29.

Pratt, J. 1980. "Letting the Grandchildren Do It: Environmental Planning during the Ascent of Oil as a Major Energy Source." *Public Historian* 2, no. 4: 28–61.

Rice, A. 1994. "Endless Bummer." *Santa Barbara Independent*, March 17.

Skillern, F. 1981. *Environmental Protection: The Legal Framework.* McGraw-Hill.

Szasz, A. 1994. *Ecopopulism: Toxic Waste and the Movement for Environmental Justice.* University of Minnesota Press.

Turner, B. 1978. *Man-Made Disasters.* Wykeham.

Vaughan, D. 1996. *The* Challenger *Launch Decision: Risky Technology, Culture, and Deviance at NASA.* University of Chicago Press.

Weick, K. 1976. "Educational Organizations as Loosely Coupled Systems." *Administrative Science Quarterly* 21, March: 1–19.

Weick, K. 1995. *Sensemaking in Organizations: The Mann Gulch Disaster.* Sage.

Wolf, S. 1988. *Pollution Law Handbook: A Guide to Federal Environmental Law.* Quorum Books.

Yeager, P. 1991. *The Limits of the Law: The Public Regulation of Private Pollution.* Cambridge University Press.

The BP Disaster as an *Exxon Valdez* Rerun

Liesel Ashley Ritchie, Duane A. Gill, and J. Steven Picou

Unlike the Guadalupe Dunes oil spill described by Beamish, which moved in slow motion, the BP oil spill in the Gulf of Mexico was fast-moving and immediately dramatic in its impacts. While some sociological studies focus on the social organization of how a disaster occurs, others examine the results or consequences for human societies. Using lessons learned from the Exxon Valdez disaster, Liesel Ashley Ritchie, Duane A. Gill and J. Steven Picou reflect on the consequences of human-made disasters for communities; for example, the authors show how communities such as those along the Gulf Coast and those affected by the Exxon Valdez spill often suffer economically, as they are dependent on resources and a clean environment for income-generating activities such as fishing or tourism.

On April 20, 2010, eleven people were killed when the Deepwater Horizon drilling rig exploded. Owned by Transocean Ltd. and contracted to BP, the rig burned in the Northern Gulf of Mexico until it eventually collapsed, leaving a breached wellhead gushing an estimated 55,000 barrels of oil per day. Some 185 to 205 million gallons of crude oil were released before the wellhead could be capped in July and permanently sealed in September, nearly five months after the initial explosion.

As this environmental disaster unfolded, the nation witnessed the riveting reporting of oil penetrating the marshes and washing ashore on white sandy beaches. At the same time, individuals and communities who depend on the Gulf of Mexico worried about the economic and socio-cultural effects as well as how to get compensated for damages.

Over a year later, there is no more 24-hour CNN coverage. If one were to rely solely on media accounts, it might seem that the Deepwater Horizon disaster is over. One *New York Times* from February 1, 2011 read: "Report Foresees Quick Gulf of Mexico Recovery"—yet the article goes on to say, "The 39-page report acknowledges that any definitive assessment at this point is impossible, and that fully understanding the spill's ecological effects will take years." Not surprisingly, more pressing national and international events have caught the media's attention. Most Gulf waters have been reopened for fishing, seafood is being tested and deemed safe for human consumption, and beaches are being declared clean and, in fact, inviting. Still, economic and social upheaval will likely leave the communities along the Northern Gulf of Mexico (the Gulf) in disarray for the foreseeable future.

Indeed, lessons learned from 21 years of social science research on community impacts of the 1989 *Exxon Valdez* oil spill (EVOS) suggest this recent environmental disaster is far from over. If the BP disaster follows the EVOS script, we can anticipate some of the problems in store for residents of Gulf communities. The severity of the disaster depends on how the natural and social environments interrelate and the amount of damage to the ecosystem. We know that social and psychological stress are heightened by the uncertainty that comes from toxic contamination. The complexities of local and regional economies and the upheaval created by a temporary economic boom created by cleanup operations also contribute to the disaster. Finally, as injured parties seek compensation for damages from this environmental disaster, many are further traumatized by impersonal bureaucratic structures and protracted litigation processes.

It is especially difficult for people who have not experienced an environmental or "technological" disaster to fully understand what people and communities along the Gulf are going through. Among both researchers and in the general public, there is a broad tendency to distinguish between "natural" disasters and "technological" or "environmental" disasters. It is perhaps most useful to think about disasters as being on a continuum, with "natural" disasters at one end of the continuum and human-caused disasters at the other. While these events' qualities and characteristics overlap in terms of their social impacts, what we typically refer to as "natural" disasters such as tornadoes, earthquakes, and hurricanes, are considered "Acts of God." There is no one to blame and, in most cases, communities are able to come together to rebuild and move on. At the other end of the continuum, technological disasters such as Chernobyl, Dhopal, and the more recent BP oil spill are triggered by human error. These tend to result in long-term community disruption and chronic psychological stress.

As Michael Edelstein has noted, "outsiders" don't understand why environmental disaster survivors can't just move on. And if outsiders can't understand, they are less likely to offer support, and that further impedes community recovery. It is our hope that the past can offer some lessons in how best to approach long-term recovery in the Gulf.

Community Ties to the Environment

Sociologists Steve Kroll-Smith and Steve Couch's ecological-symbolic approach to disasters asserts that community recovery and interpretive processes are influenced by the type of environment damaged and the community's relationship to that environment. Renewable resource communities (RRCs) like those affected by the EVOS in Alaska are particularly vulnerable to the effects of an environmental disaster. They depend on renewable natural resources for their social, cultural, and economic existence. As noted by Steve Picou and Duane Gill, sociologists who have studied the EVOS for more than 20 years, understanding environment-social relationships between these aspects of life in RRCs is essential to understanding the often ignored human side of environmental disasters.

The fishing community of Cordova, Alaska—located on Prince William Sound and considered "ground zero" for the EVOS—is a prime example of how the fate of an RRC is tied to its natural environment. Although more than 20 years have passed since the supertanker *Exxon Valdez* ran aground, only 10 of 26 resources/species are classified by the EVOS Trustee Council as having recovered from the contamination of the oil spill. The herring biomass has yet to returned to a level where harvesting is viable—a critical problem for the fishing fleet and community that once depended heavily on the revenues associated with the short, but highly profitable, herring season each spring. Despite Exxon's claims that the herring population's crash following the spill had nothing to do with its oil, a substantial body of recent research indicates otherwise. In short, academics have documented long-term impacts of the toxic crude oil for the Prince William Sound ecosystem. Among these is the persistence of volatile levels of *Exxon Valdez* oil in intertidal regions, on beaches, and in salmon streams, as well as significant declines in local fisheries.

Particularly for commercial fishermen and Alaska Natives in Cordova and other oiled communities, the consequences of EVOS-related environmental degradation have been significant. These include empirically documented elevated levels of collective trauma, social disruption, economic uncertainty, community strain, and psychological stress. Notably, the chronic community impacts of the EVOS are directly tied not only to the actual loss of various types of resources, but also to the threat of the *future* loss of resources.

It is in this context that we consider the situation for communities along the Gulf in the aftermath of the Deepwater Horizon blowout. This disaster damaged marine ecosystems and resources—the extent of which has yet to be fully realized. Additionally, the dispersants used to mitigate the impacts of the spill threaten several "at-risk" industries along the northern Gulf. Commercial and recreational fishing, tourism, and other enterprises tied to natural resources have already suffered severe economic losses and the threat of loss continues. In particular, there remains uncertainty regarding the recovery of shrimp, oysters, crab, and other fish. As in Alaska, there are Native American groups such as the Houma in Louisiana with strong cultural ties to the natural environment that was threatened or damaged by the oil and dispersants.

Data collected in communities along the Gulf of Mexico in the months since the BP spill reveal high levels of psychological stress among groups that rely on renewable natural resources for their livelihoods, as well as concerns related to health as a result of exposure to the oil and dispersants. In Alabama, for example, we found that the strongest predictors of stress were family health concerns, commercial ties to renewable resources, and concern about economic future, economic loss, and exposure to the oil. Unfortunately, the experiences of Gulf communities resonate with the ongoing narratives of Alaskans over two decades following the EVOS.

Invisible Trauma

In the late 1980s, anthropologist and physician Henry Vyner wrote about the psychological effects of environmental contamination—"invisible trauma." Similar issues are addressed by Michael Edelstein in *Contaminated Communities: The Social and Psychological Impacts of Residential Toxic Exposure*. One of the primary concerns regarding environmental impacts and ultimately, how these impacts affect communities and groups has to do with ecological damage that is difficult to detect. Even more challenging is assessing damage that may not emerge until years after initial contamination. A January 2011 report by the Harte Research Institute for Gulf of Mexico Studies at Texas A&M University-Corpus Christi concluded: "Realistically, the true loss to the ecosystem and fisheries may not be accurately known for years, or even decades." According to a 2005 National Research Council study, determining ecosystem recovery in the aftermath of an event such as the BP spill is more challenging than assessing initial impacts.

In a milieu of general uncertainty regarding the range and scope of environmental contamination, there is also confusion about the nature and extent of health-related impacts, economic impacts, and social impacts. Social impacts are particularly detrimental when they are the result of chronic, long-term uncertainty and social disruption often associated with technological disasters.

The Money Spill

The complexity of the coastal economy along the Northern Gulf of Mexico far exceeds that of the region affected by the EVOS in Alaska. To date, the diverse yet intertwined oil and gas extraction economies, tourism or "beach" economies, and commercial fishing economies have all experienced both direct and indirect impacts of the BP oil spill. The temporary Federal moratorium on deepwater drilling hurt Louisiana communities dependent on the oil and gas industry for their livelihoods. Many areas in Alabama and Florida were hit by declines in tourism because potential visitors were concerned about oiled beaches and toxic waters unsuitable for swimming, as well as restrictions on recreational marine boating and sport fishing. And similar concerns related to the safety of seafood from the Gulf have been far-reaching, shaking consumer confidence and causing disruptions to the commercial fishing industry, including seafood harvesting, processing, and distributing. This hurts markets that were already mired in the process of rebounding from the effects of Hurricanes Katrina and Rita in 2005. From this perspective, the economic recovery of coastal communities is strongly related to perceptions of seafood consumers and tourists around the country—which further confounds community recovery.

Conversely, in the weeks and months after the Deepwater Horizon blowout there was considerable social and economic disruption associated with the "money spill"—large amounts of money that were spent on oil mitigation and clean-up efforts. As was the case in the *Exxon Valdez* disaster, in which those who made money on clean-up efforts were referred to as "spillionaires" and "*Exxon* whores," the money spill and ensuing economic disruption along the Gulf fostered problems in many communities. In media accounts and in our own interviews, some residents expressed frustration with perceived inequalities in chances to work on the Vessels of Opportunity program. For example, some locals felt shut out by the contracting process, growing particularly agitated in cases where they saw people from outside the area having their boats hired. Unequal access to resources associated with the money spill pitted family, friends, and neighbors against each other.

As in the wake of the EVOS, this money spill contributed to social upheaval and the emergence of a "corrosive community." This term, coined by environmental sociologists Bill Freudenburg and Timothy Jones in the 1990s, refers to post-disaster social environments in which social relationships are altered, social support breaks down, and civil order is disrupted. Notably, corrosive communities typically emerge following human-caused disasters, rather than in the context of natural disasters. If experience with the EVOS is any indication, this damage to social networks and the long-term potential for diminished social capital—trust and social ties—is very real. Loss of social capital may further increase stress levels, affecting overall community well-being. In addition, there is a strong possibility for outmigration from coastal communities over the long term as a result of declining economic conditions related, at least in part, to the BP spill. In Alabama, one-third of our survey sample indicated a desire to move from their community. Should this occur, communities will lose not only social capital, but also human capital.

Impersonality and Collective Stress

Although separated by more than 20 years, both the EVOS and the BP oil disasters highlight critical issues of recreancy (blame), responsibility, and loss of trust in corporations and government. These are characteristic of human-caused disasters. In the months following the Deepwater Horizon blowout, frustration and anger over accountability, lack of transparency, and finger-pointing over who was responsible escalated in coastal states and the halls of Washington. Following the Exxon playbook, BP continues to downplay the amount of oil that was released into the Gulf and tries to spread the blame to Halliburton for a faulty cement job and Transocean for operating an unsafe rig. This corporate posturing sets the stage for BP to minimize financial responsibility for resulting environmental, economic, and social damages.

Relative to the grounding of the *Exxon Valdez*, public responses to the rig explosion suggest higher levels of perceived complicity and corruption between BP and the former Minerals Management Service (now the Bureau of Ocean Energy Management, Regulation, and Enforcement). More than two decades of data regarding attitudes toward government, big business, and the U.S. legal system in the context of the EVOS show that that beliefs about trust and blame are related to frustration, anger, alienation, and stress. Given this empirical evidence, we can expect these or similar outcomes to escalate over time among Gulf Coast residents.

Corporations like Exxon and BP aren't designed to react to the demands of being responsible for a disaster. When it comes to dealing with claimants and the public, their corporate cultures and bureaucratic structures seem impersonal and insensitive. Government bureaucracies and our justice system are not much better in responding to survivors of environmental disasters. Interacting with the impersonality of corporate and government bureaucracies and engaging with the legal system not only exacerbates existing stress, it creates new stress for victims.

In the months since the BP disaster, the financial claims process has, indeed, become a bureaucratic and legal obstacle, as well as a source of contention and stress. Despite the unprecedented establishment of a $20 billion escrow fund to compensate those affected by the spill, the Governor of Alabama has characterized the process as "extortion." In March 2011, eleven months into the cleanup, the Gulf Coast Claims Facility reported that of 155,000 claims applications submitted for full or interim payments, just 25 percent had been processed. Many people filing claims have expressed frustration and anger with the futility of the process. With its pronouncements to pay "legitimate" claims and to make survivors "whole," BP's public relations campaign since shortly after the explosion on the Deepwater Horizon rig has also mirrored that of Exxon's in 1989. Similarly, President Obama's remark that the compensation funds represent "an important step towards making the people of the Gulf Coast whole again" hasn't instilled confidence among those who lived through the EVOS. As one Alaskan recently put it: "That's lawyer speak for 'we're going to pay out as little as possible.'"

Litigation as "Secondary Trauma"

Minimal financial support from the BP claims process has caused many who believe that they've incurred unpaid losses to resort to litigation. This, too, is reminiscent of the predicament in which many commercial fishermen in Alaska found themselves after the EVOS. Following the EVOS, and now in the wake of the BP disaster, it is apparent that there are some things that are not valued or even considered in the calculation of damages. How does one calculate the value of the base of a food chain—plankton, larval fish, and many bottom dwelling organisms—species that are difficult to see with the naked eye? How do we assign value to a way of life that is lost to human-caused environmental contamination? In the case of the EVOS, Alaska Native claims of damage to their cultural heritage and subsistence practices were dismissed in Federal Court. Moreover, actual damage claims did not include losses incurred after the case went to trial in 1994. Shortly after going to trial, the multi-million dollar herring fishery collapsed and, to this date, has not recovered.

BP spill-related litigation will be delayed until 2013 and is likely to result in protracted legal processes for literally thousands of Gulf Coast residents. Research tells us that this will prolong the social impacts of the disaster, leaving most plaintiffs with a lack of closure. With the precedent set by *Baker v. Exxon*, which took almost two decades to wind through the U.S. judicial system, we can anticipate prolonged litigation-related stress for those involved. If it follows the pattern documented in Alaska, this "secondary trauma" could prove to be as stressful as the initial disaster itself. Coupled with other long-term, chronic social impacts previously discussed we can expect high levels of stress among individuals, groups, and communities to continue, just as with the EVOS. If damage awards through the BP claims process remain contentious and redress through the courts is delayed, mental health problems and community disruption will persist for decades along the Gulf Coast.

Disasters like the BP oil spill are what Kai Erikson, a sociologist who studies social consequences of catastrophic events, describes as a "new species of trouble" that "scare human beings in new and special ways, . . . [and] . . . elicit an uncanny fear in us." And as German sociologist Ulrich Beck suggests, these events also represent risks that are a major feature of contemporary society. The cumulative impacts of hurricanes Katrina, Rita, and Wilma in 2005, Ivan in 2004, and now the BP oil spill disaster are intensified by the current global economic crisis and our reliance on fossil fuels. Together, these stressors take a toll on various forms of community capital, including financial, human, social, built, political, natural, and cultural capital.

Like the EVOS, and environmental disasters in general, the BP oil spill will continue to reveal "contested" scientific evidence concerning ecological damages, emerging secondary traumas such as the claims process and litigation, and serious community conflict and mental health problems. Given what we know about the trajectory of economic and social recovery for survivors of the EVOS more than 20 years ago, the situation in Gulf communities warrants close monitoring and attention by researchers, mental health care providers, policy-makers, and perhaps most importantly, the public at large.

Note

Ritchie, Liesel Ashley, Duane A. Gill, J. Steven Picou. 2011. "The BP Disaster as an *Exxon Valdez* Rerun." *Contexts* 10:30.

References

Beck, Ulrich. 1992. *Risk Society: Towards a New Modernity*. London, England: SAGE Publications, Inc.

Edelstein, Michael. [1988] 2004. *Contaminated Communities: The Social and Psychological Impacts of Residential Toxic Exposure*. Boulder, CO: Westview Press.

Edelstein, Michael. 2000. "Outsiders Just Don't Understand." Pp. 123–42 in *Risk in the Modern Age: Social Theory, Science and Environmental Decision-Making*, edited by M.J. Cohen. New York: St. Martin's Press, Inc.

Exxon Valdez Oil Spill Trustee Council (EVOSTC). 2010. *Update on Injured Resources and Services, 2010*. Anchorage, AK: *Exxon Valdez* Oil Spill Trustee Council [November]. http://www.evostc.state.ak.us/Universal/Documents/Publications/2010IRSUpdate.pdf

Exxon Valdez Revisited: Rights and Remedies. 2009. *University of St. Thomas Law Journal* 7:1.

Freudenburg, William R. and Robert Gramling. (2011). *Blowout in the Gulf. The BP oil spill disaster and the future of energy in America*. Cambridge, MA: The MIT Press.

Freudenburg, William R. and Timothy Jones. 1991. "Attitudes and Stress in the Presence of Technological Risk: A Test of the Supreme Court Hypothesis." *Social Forces* 69(4):1143–68.

Gill, Duane A., J. Steven Picou, and Liesel A. Ritchie. Forthcoming. "The *Exxon Valdez* and BP Oil Spills: A Comparison of Initial Social and Psychological Impacts." *American Behavioral Scientist*.

Kroll-Smith, J. Stephen and Stephen R. Couch. 1991. "What is a Disaster?" An Ecological Symbolic Approach to Resolving the Definitional Debate." *International Journal of Mass Emergencies and Disasters* 9:355–66.

Picou, J. Steven and Duane A. Gill. 1997. "Commercial Fishers and Stress: Psychological Impacts of the *Exxon Valdez* Oil Spill." Pp. 211–36 in *The* Exxon Valdez *Disaster: Readings on a Modern Social Problem*, edited by J.S. Picou, D.A. Gill, and M. Cohen. Dubuque, IA: Kendall-Hunt.

Picou, J. Steven, Cecelia Formichella, Brent K. Marshall and Catalina Arata. 2009. "Community Impacts of the *Exxon Valdez* Oil Spill: A Synthesis and Elaboration of Social Science Research." Pp. 279–307 in Stephen R. Braund and Jack Kruse (eds.). *Synthesis: Three Decades of Social Science Research on Socioeconomic Effects Related to Offshore Petroleum Development in Coastal Alaska*. MMS OCS Study Number 2009–006. Minerals Management Service, Alaska, OCS Region, Anchorage, AK.

Ritchie, Liesel Ashley. 2004. *Voices of Cordova: Social Capital in the Wake of the* Exxon Valdez *Oil Spill*. Ph.D. Dissertation. Department of Sociology, Anthropology, and Social Work. Mississippi State University. Available at http://www.colorado.edu/hazards/research/voicesofcordova_ritchiedissertation.pdf

Ritchie, Liesel Ashley and Duane A. Gill, D.A. 2007. "Social Capital Theory as an Integrating Framework for Technological Disaster Research." *Sociological Spectrum* 27:1–26.

Vyner, Henry. 1988. *Invisible Trauma: The Psychological Effects of Invisible Environmental Contaminants*. Lexington, MA: Heath.

PART

Globalization

14

The Unfair Trade-off
Globalization and the
Export of Ecological Hazards
Daniel Faber

Globalization is the process by which technological, communications, and political changes have intensified the worldwide exchange of money, goods, people, and culture. In this piece, Daniel Faber discusses how globalization has also accelerated the exchange of ecological hazards between nations. Due to imbalances between countries in terms of national-level environmental governance and due to weak global structures of environmental governance, this exchange has led to a worldwide system of environmental "in" justice, in which affluent nations (where environmental laws are relatively strict) export ecological hazards to poor nations (where environmental laws are relatively weak). The poorer countries (often referred to as "the global South") have limited capacity to adequately evaluate and manage the risks associated with such hazards; transnational corporations are thus endangering people's health and environments in many areas of the world. Faber suggests that only by achieving greater social governance over trade, lending institutions, and regulatory bodies can the process that leads some national and corporate leaders to sacrifice human and environmental health in order to compete in the world economy be overcome.

The Global Ecological Crisis

... The creation of modern global communications and transportation systems, and the development of advanced infrastructure in the newly industrializing countries, are granting industrial capital the geographic mobility to take advantage of more favorable business climates abroad. This is especially true in the countries of East Asia and the global South with large supplies of cheap and highly disciplined wage laborers, abundant natural resources and energy supplies, tax advantages, and weaker environmental regulations. The commodities and surplus-profits produced by the factories are then exported back into the United States and other advanced capitalist countries. The pollution, however, remains behind. Even worse, the toxic waste, industrial pollution, discarded consumer goods, and other forms of "anti-wealth" produced in the United States are also becoming increasingly mobile, and end up in the "pollution havens" of the Third World. Prior to the invention of environmental protection laws in the United States and elsewhere, it was not necessary (let alone cost-effective) to export environmental problems to other countries. This is no longer the case. . . .

Dumping on the Third World: The Export of Ecological Hazards and Environmental Justice

... The worsening ecological crisis in the global South is directly related to an international system of economic and environmental stratification in which the United States and other advanced capitalist nations are able to shift or impose the environmental burden on weaker states. In fact, one of the primary aims of U.S. economic planners is to cut costs by displacing environmental problems [externalities] onto poorer Southern nations—countries with little power in global environmental policy decision-making institutions. Lawrence Summers, former Undersecretary of the Treasury of International Affairs and key economic policy-maker under the Clinton administration [and former President of Harvard University], is infamous for writing a 1991 memo as a chief economist at the World Bank that argued,

> Just between you and me, shouldn't the World Bank be encouraging more migration of the dirty industries to the LDCs [less developed countries]? . . . I think the economic logic behind dumping a load of toxic waste in the lowest wage country is impeccable and we should face up to that. . . . I've always thought that under-populated countries in Africa are vastly under-polluted.

The Summers memo reflects the "thinking" of many U.S. policy makers aligned with the interests of U.S. multinational corporations: that human life in the Third World is worth much less than in the United States. If the poor and underemployed masses of Africa become sick or die from exposure to pollution exported from the United States, it will have a much smaller impact on the profits of international capital. Aside from the higher costs of pollution-abatement in the United States, if highly-skilled and well-compensated American workers fall prey to environmentally-related health problems, then the expense to capital and the state can be significant. Although morally reprehensible, under the capitalist system it pays business to shift pollution onto the poor in the less developed countries.

Given the willingness of undemocratic governments in the global South to trade-off their environmental protection for economic growth, the growing mobility of capital (in all forms) is facilitating the export of ecological problems from the advanced capitalist countries to the third world and sub-peripheral states. This *export of ecological hazard* from the United States and other Northern countries to the less developed countries takes place: (1) . . . in the form of foreign direct investment (FDI) in domestically-owned hazardous industries, as well as destructive investment schemes to gain access to new oil fields, forests, agricultural lands, mining deposits, and other natural resources; (2) . . . with the relocation of polluting and environmentally hazardous production processes and polluting facilities owned by transnational capital to the South; (3) . . . as witnessed in the marketing of more profitable but also more dangerous foods, drugs, pesticides, technologies, and other consumer/capital goods; and (4) . . . with the dumping of toxic wastes, pollution, discarded consumer products, trash, and other forms of "anti-wealth" produced by Northern industry.

Hence, corporate-led globalization is facilitating the displacement of ecological hazards from richer to poorer countries. Although a few international agreements (such as the Basel Convention) have been put into place, they are for the most part ineffective at stemming the transfer of hazards. Since few peripheral countries have the ability to adequately evaluate and manage the risks associated with such hazards, the export practices of transnational corporations are increasing the health, safety, and environmental problems facing many peripheral countries. . . .

Antigreen Greenbacks: The Export of Ecologically Hazardous Investment Capital

. . . Since the mid-1970s, the U.S. regime of environmental regulation has resulted in stricter laws, increased delays due to permitting, and higher costs related to pollution control technology, liability and insurances cases, and worker health and safety. These costs are especially significant for companies involved in the production of heavy metals, asbestos-containing products, copper and lead smelting, and leather tanning, and has led these industries to relocate overseas. On the other hand, the competition for foreign investment among the developing countries is fierce, and combined with the imposition of structural adjustment policies by the International Monetary Fund (IMF) and World Bank on indebted developing countries, more and more nations are opening themselves up to increased FDI by weakening environmental standards.

. . . As a consequence, the rate of growth in hazardous industries in the developing countries is now greater than the overall industrial growth in those same countries, indicating that the cost advantages stemming from weaker environmental protection is attracting investment. Again, this trend began in the late 1970s, just as environmental regulations became more stringent in the United States and other advanced capitalist countries.

China: The New Economic Superpower, or Ecological Nightmare?

. . . Although China has excelled in providing low-quality consumer goods, the country is now ramping up to create more advanced industries, adding state-of-the-art capacity in cars, specialty steel, petrochemicals, and microchips. So, while American petrochemical makers have invested in little new capacity inside the United States over the past decade, over 12,000 workers are constructing a $2.7 billion petrochemical complex in Nanjing, China. This facility will be among the world's biggest, most modern complexes for making ethylene, the basic ingredient in plastics. Constructing such a plant in China offers sizable cost advantages over rival facilities in the United States, Europe, and Japan due to the lower environmental costs of doing business. The Chinese government allows industry to freely pollute the air, water and ground, which (combined with the low cost of labor) easily allows industry to undercut the prices charged by companies abiding by strict standards elsewhere in the world. However, the economic incentives offered to foreign capital to invest in China, including few controls over pollution and worker health and safety violations, have created an ecological nightmare. As stated by the journalists Joseph Kahn and Jim Yardley,

> Environmental woes that might be considered catastrophic in some countries can seem commonplace in China: industrial cities where people rarely see the sun; children killed or sickened by lead poisoning or other types of local pollution; a coastline so swamped by algal red tides that large sections of the ocean no longer sustain marine life. China is choking on its own success.

The magnitude of this ecological crisis is apparent in a 2007 draft report by the World Bank and China's State Environment Protection Agency. The study finds that 750,000 people die prematurely in China each year, mainly from air pollution in the large cities. . . . Incredibly, only 1 percent of the country's 560 million city dwellers breathe air considered safe by the European Union. And air quality is getting worse. The central government's most recent report put the cost of air pollution at $64 billion in 2004.

Of the twenty most polluted cities in the world, according to the World Bank, sixteen are located in China. About one-third of China's lakes, rivers, and coastal waters are so polluted that they pose a threat to human health, according the Organization for Economic Cooperation and Development. As a result, 300 million Chinese don't have access to clean drinking water, resulting in 60,000-odd premature deaths a year. Acid rain falls over 30 percent of the country. Industrial pollution is so extensive that the country's birth defect rate is triple that of the developed nations. At least a million Chinese babies born each year have birth defects. As acknowledged in the World Bank report, China's poor are disproportionately affected by these environmental health burdens. The World Bank puts the cost of China's pollution at 8 percent of GDP, although some economists say it as high as 10 percent of GDP, which is equal to the country's rate of economic growth. Fed up with the pollution, a number of environmental riots have erupted in China in recent years, and are likely to become more numerous in the future.

Africa's Black Gold: Investing in Repression and Environmental Injustice

. . . Nigeria has seen huge investments of U.S. capital to develop the oil fields, and is now the eighth leading exporter of oil in the world (and the largest oil producer in Africa). More than $300 billion in oil has been exported since 1975. Petroleum companies such as Chevron and Royal Dutch Shell have invaded the oil-rich Niger Delta, home to the Ogoni people, and one of the most populated regions in all of Africa. At the invitation of a brutally repressive Nigerian government, the international oil companies ignore standard environmental protection measures in order to cuts costs and maximize profits. Enjoying a complete lack of government oversight, the oil companies have created what the European Parliament calls "an environmental nightmare" for the Ogoni people. A constant barrage of oil spills—an average of 300 per year—have significantly contaminated waterways and groundwater, killed fish and other wildlife on which the local people are dependent, and decimated the resource base of numerous subsistence economies in the region. Petroleum pollution in Ogoni streams is 680 times greater than European Community permissible levels. Leaking pipes have also caught fire, exploded, and killed hundreds of people. Toxic wastes dumped in unlined pits litter the countryside, while continuous gas flares pollute nearby villages with 35 million tons of CO_2

a year (76 percent of natural gas in the oil producing areas is flared, compared to 0.6 percent in the United States, along with 12 million tons of methane, which is more than any nation on earth). Local crops will not grow, and acid rain pervades the area.

As the ecological crisis emerged full force in the early 1990s, the Ogoni people organized peaceful protests to raise international awareness of their plight. In response to awareness such actions were generating around the world, the [then] military government reacted with extreme repression. In November of 1995, Ken Saro-Wiwa, the leader of the Movement for the Survival of Ogoni People—a highly respected and renowned playwright in the international community—and eight other Ogoni leaders, were arrested on trumped-up treason charges. They were immediately tried by a military tribunal, found guilty, and executed. Despite the military's unfounded allegations, the world knew the "Ogoni 9" were killed for organizing peaceful protests against the country's large oil exporter, Royal/Dutch Shell. As stated in a recent report, "Shell failed to use its substantial influence with the Nigerian government to stop the execution. Indeed, Shell has publicly admitted that it had invited the Nigerian army to Ogoni land, provided them with ammunition and logistical and financial support for a military operation that left scores dead and destroyed many villages." In defense of the company and the military regime following the execution, Naemeka Achebe, the general manager for Shell Nigeria, stated, "For a commercial company trying to make investments, you need a stable environment . . . Dictatorships can give you that. Right now in Nigeria, there is acceptance, peace, and continuity."

In response to the repression, Nigerian villagers have brought suit in U.S. court against Chevron alleging that the company supported military attacks on protesters in the Niger Delta. A Human Rights Watch investigation uncovered Chevron's use of a covert Nigerian security force known as the "kill-and-go" squad against the movement. In the trial, Chevron stated that the incident was "regrettable" but resulted from attempts by protesters to take control of weapons held by security personnel. Although the company was cleared of direct liability in 2004, the judge in the case noted that a reasonable juror could reason that the company had indirect responsibility, and could be liable for reparations due to its "extraordinarily close relationship" with Chevron Nigeria. In August of 2007, another judge allowed claims of wrongful death and other human rights suits to proceed. . . .

Global Pollution Havens: The Export of Ecologically Hazardous Industry

. . . In the age of corporate-led globalization, free trade and neo-liberal economic policies are encouraging countries to lower wages and environmental standards in order to cuts costs and achieve a comparative advantage in the world economy. By pitting various nations against one another in this "race to the bottom" phenomenon, in which countries lower environmental regulations in order to gain a competitive edge, multinational corporations have acquired greater and greater power vis-a-vis the nation-state. With the increased international mobility of industrial capital, various governments [at all levels] are pressured to reduce the financial burden of environmental regulations, taxation policy, labor rules, and consumer product safety requirements upon industry. Otherwise, the manufacturer will simply pick up and move to another part of the world where the business climate is more favorable. The state is left with little choice but to grant such concessions if the jobs and other economic benefits are to be preserved.

Over the last three decades, those U.S.-based industries most heavily impacted by environmental regulations, including lead smelting, dye and chemical manufacturing, asbestos-related production, pesticides, textiles, copper smelting, vinyl chloride, etc., have moved to other countries with weaker rules and enforcement. American companies often make no secret of the fact that more stringent environmental regulations are a major factor in relocating facilities abroad. As stated by the U.S. corporation Chemex, "As a result of tougher environmental regulations . . . many North American [mineral oil] refineries have ceased operations. Recognizing an opportunity, Chemex redirected its focus to the procurement of quality used refineries" for export to developing countries. This process is now accelerating, as double standards in worker and community health protection become more commonplace in the world, especially in the less developed countries of the Caribbean, Africa, Latin America, and especially Asia. According to a United Nations study, over half of the transnational firms surveyed in the Asia-Pacific region adopt lower standards in comparison to their country of origin in the North. As a result, the increased mobility of U.S. capital is serving to relocate many of the worst public health risks and environmental injustices associated with "dirty industry" to the global South. . . .

Mexico: Environmental Troubles South of the Border

. . . Since the passage of the North American Free Trade Agreement (NAFTA) in 1994, Mexico's environmental problems have worsened throughout the country. NAFTA is a free trade agreement that reduces tariffs and other barriers to trade among Mexico, Canada, and the United States. Aided by the agreement, dirty industries are moving out of the United States to Mexico, where environmental standards are lax, unions are weak, and worker health and safety concerns are ignored. Along the 2,100-mile U.S.-Mexico border running from the Pacific Ocean to the Gulf of Mexico, there are more than

2,000 factories, or *maquiladoras*, including U.S. companies, involved in textiles and clothing, chemicals, and electronics. A 1991 U.S. Government Accounting Office study even found that several Los Angeles furniture manufacturers relocated to Mexico after the establishment of stringent air pollution restrictions in California (80 percent of these businesses cited environmental costs in their decision to move).

The explosive growth of the *maquiladoras* is creating an ecological disaster along both sides of the border. Factories big and small generate huge volumes of pollution (some 87 percent of *maquiladoras* use toxic materials in their production processes). Reports show that industrial waste is seldom treated before it is discharged into rivers, arroyos, the Rio Grande, or the ocean. *Maquiladoras* also generate a substantial amount of hazardous waste, including dangerous solvents such as trichloroethylene, acids, heavy metals like lead and nickel, paints, oils, resins, and plastics. Over 65 percent of such waste is unaccounted for in either the United States or Mexico. The situation is growing worse because NAFTA no longer requires TNCs to return waste to the United States for proper disposal. . . .

Buyer Beware: The Export of Ecologically Hazardous Commodities

In the era of corporate-led globalization, dangerous pesticides and other chemicals, biotechnology, drugs, and other consumer products that are highly restricted in the United States are still manufactured here and routinely exported to other nations. American corporations know that there is little government oversight or public pressure to inspect and regulate such products in overseas markets, and that significant profits are to be made from shipping their hazardous products to unsuspecting consumers all around the world. This process has been underway for many decades, but is accelerating with the expansion of world trade.

One of the most hazardous commodities exported by the United States to the rest of the world are pesticides. Roughly a billion pounds of pesticides are exported each year, or *45 tons per hour*. Tragically, American policy makers have done little to stop the export of pesticides forbidden in the United States. Under the Federal Insecticide, Fungicide and Rodenticide Act (FIFRA), EPA does not review the health and environmental impacts of pesticides manufactured for export only, or what are termed "never registered" pesticides. The most recent figures available indicate that nearly 22 million pounds of these exported pesticides are banned or severely restricted for use in the United States, an average of more than 22 tons per day. Furthermore, an average rate of more than 30 tons per day of "extremely hazardous" chemicals, as rated by the World Health Organization, are also exported. Nearly 1.1 billion pounds of known or suspected carcinogenic pesticides were exported by the United States between 1997 and 2000, an average rate of almost 16 tons per hour. As a result, many pesticides that the Environmental Protection Agency (EPA) has judged too dangerous for domestic use, as well as pesticides never evaluated by the EPA, are regularly shipped from U.S. ports.

. . . The most dangerous U.S. chemical exports are often destined for Third World countries where the prevailing working conditions—a lack of protective equipment, unsafe application and storage practices, inadequate training of pesticide applicators—greatly magnify the health risks for agricultural workers and their families. In fact, about 57 percent of these products are shipped to the developing world, while most of the remaining chemicals are shipped to ports in Belgium and the Netherlands for reshipment to developing countries. As a result, poisonings continue to mount. The World Health Organization (WHO) estimates that three million severe pesticide poisonings occur each year, and, of these, a minimum of 300,000 people die, many of them children. Some 99 percent of these cases occur in developing countries.

The Global Circle of Poison

The people of the global South are not the only ones being poisoned by pesticides exported from the United States. Third World agricultural exports contaminated with pesticides come back to the United States and other Northern countries in a vicious "circle of poison." Although the U.S. environmental movement was successful in legally restricting or prohibiting the use of many hazardous chemicals such as DDT in the 1970s, multinational corporations continue to manufacture and export these same pesticides to the Third World. The circle of poison closes when U.S. citizens consume Third World exports contaminated with the pesticides. For instance, imports of Chilean grapes, Canadian and Mexican carrots, Mexican broccoli and tomatoes, Argentine and Hungarian apple juice, and Brazilian orange juice are found to have worse levels of pesticide contamination than U.S.-grown crops.

Food and Drug Administration (FDA) data shows that food imports from developing countries are often contaminated with pesticides banned or restricted for health reasons in the United States, including a violation rate of 40.8 for all imports of Guatemalan green peas; 18.4 percent for Mexican strawberries; and 15.6 percent for Mexican lettuce. FDA inspections of Chinese imports have also caught dried apples preserved with a cancer-causing chemicals; frozen catfish laden with banned antibiotics; scallops and sardines coated with bacteria, and mushrooms laced with illegal pesticides. These were among the 107 food imports from China that the FDA detained at U.S. ports in April of 2007, along with more than 1,000 shipments of tainted Chinese dietary supplements and other products.

Both U.S. and foreign corporations know that exporting tainted products into the United States poses little risk of being caught by an underfunded and understaffed Food and Drug Administration. FDA testing of food imports (and domestic products) is infrequent and restricted to only a few choice chemicals. Since 1997, FDA officials have examined just 1.5 percent of all food imports, while shipments skyrocketed from more than 4 million entries in 1997 to more than 15 million in 2006. Under assault from the Bush administration and the polluter-industrial complex, the FDA's regulatory affairs staff is getting leaner—it shrank from a high of 4,003 full-time employees in the 2003 fiscal year to 3,488 in 2007. As a result, noncriminal foreign and domestic inspections carried out by FDA's Center for Food Safety and Applied Nutrition staffers amounted to 9,038 in 2005, down from 11,566 just two years earlier.

In the few instances where testing is done, FDA health standards are inadequate. In some cases, consumption of a single food item contaminated with chemicals at levels allowed by FDA, such as DDT in fish, would expose the consumer to more than 50 times the daily intake levels considered "safe" by the EPA. Persistent organic pollutants such as DDT and PCBs are implicated in a breast cancer epidemic that impacts an estimated 2,044,000 women in the United States, and claims about 40,000 lives each year. In fact, a person eating the USDA's recommended five servings of fruits and vegetables per day will eat illegal pesticides at least 75 times per year. In contrast, the average consumer has to eat about 100 pounds of fresh fruits and vegetables in order to eat from a shipment tested for pesticides by the FDA. This means that the average American is at least 15 times more likely to eat an illegal pesticide than to eat from a shipment tested by the FDA. A form of *toxic trespass*, these dangerous chemicals are invading the bodies of U.S. citizens, and are linked to various types of cancers, learning disabilities and autism, immune system suppression, central nervous disorders, damage to reproductive systems, and numerous other disorders. According to the U.S. Centers for Disease Control (CDC), the American people carry a "body burden" of the pesticides chlorpyrifos (Dursban) and methyl parathion that dramatically exceed acceptable thresholds for chronic exposure. . . .

Dumping on the Third World: The Export of Pollution and Hazardous Waste

The United States is the single largest producer of hazardous wastes in the world. Each year the United States produces some 238 million tons. Meanwhile, the costs of hazardous waste disposal in the United States has grown from $15 per ton in 1980 to over $250 per ton, while the costs of incineration has increased over three-fold to between $1,500 and $3,000 per ton. Although capital has looked to reduce expenses by locating hazardous waste dumps and facilities in poor communities of color throughout the United States, there is also a growing incentive to export wastes to developing countries. The disposal costs per metric ton of hazardous waste in Africa, for instance, has historically hovered around $40–$50 per ton (and in the case of an agreement between the Gilbraltar-based company and the Benin Republic government, for as low as $2.50 per ton). These costs are so low because regulations governing toxic waste disposal are virtually nonexistent in developing countries.

The incentive to cut disposal costs by exporting toxics to the global South is also strong among other advanced capitalist countries. Hundreds of cases involving hundreds of millions of pounds of hazardous waste being exported from the advanced capitalist countries to the South have been documented over the last two decades. As if emboldened by the words of former World Bank chief economist Lawrence Summers, "I've always thought that under-populated countries in Africa are vastly *under*-polluted," dump sites of toxic waste from Western nations can be found throughout Africa, from Senegal to Nigeria, to Zimbabwe, Congo, and even South Africa. In some years, West Africa alone has imported up to 300 million tons of toxic waste from some 24 industrialized countries.

A Toxic Terror in the Ivory Coast

The devastating impacts of hazardous waste trade in Africa and the global South is illustrated by case of the *Proba Koala* in the Ivory Coast. Exemplary of the growing integration of capital on a global scale, the *Proba Koala* was a Korean-built, Greek-managed, Panamanian-flagged tanker chartered by the London branch of a Swiss trading corporation whose fiscal headquarters are in the Netherlands—the multibillion dollar Dutch global oil and metals trading company called Trafigura Beheer BV. The ship had been acting as a storage vessel for unrefined gasoline. In the summer of 2006, the Trafigura had explored disposing of the ship's "washings" after a routine cleaning of the storage hull with caustic soda in Amsterdam. However, due to the $300,000 or more cost estimate for disposing of the waste in that city, the company instead elected to take the ship to the Ivory Coast, even though there are no facilities capable of handling high-level toxic wastes. Upon arrival, the captain of the *Proba Koala* contacted a local company called Compagnie Tommy to dispose of the waste for a mere $15,000, representing a huge savings for Trafigura.

On August 19th of 2006, the *Proba Koala* offloaded 528 tons of the washings onto more than a dozen tanker trucks. The washings were a toxic alkaline mix of water, gasoline, and caustic soda, which gave off many poisonous chemicals, including hydrogen sulfide. After loading up, Compagnie Tommy simply waited until after midnight. Under the cover of darkness, the tanker trucks fanned out to dump the waste in 18 public open-air sites around the country's main city of Abidjan. These sites included the city's main garbage dump, a roadside field beside a prison, a sewage canal, and several neighborhoods. In a scene eerily reminiscent of the Bhopal disaster, citizens throughout the city awoke at night to an overpowering stench that burned their eyes and made it hard to breathe. By morning, nausea, vomiting, diarrhea, nose bleeds, stomach aches, chests pains, and breathing difficulties were affecting thousands of people. Tests later showed the sludge contained excessive levels of mercaptans and hydrogen sulfide, a potent poison that can quickly paralyze the nervous system, and cause blackouts, respiratory failure and death. More than 100,000 Abidjan residents sought medical treatment, and 69 were hospitalized as a result of the dumping. Fifteen people died. The spreading illnesses sparked violent demonstrations from a population convinced that government corruption was to blame for the dumping. The political furor ultimately forced the prime minister and his government to resign in September of 2006 (though many were later reinstated). Nevertheless, this mass resignation is unprecedented in the history of the Ivory Coast, and symbolizes the anger among the African people that their home would be used as a dumping ground by the advanced capitalist nations.

Limitations of the Basel Convention for Controlling Global Dumping of Toxic Waste

In 1989, some 118 countries signed onto the Basel Convention on the Transboundary Movement of Hazardous Wastes and Their Disposal. Enacted in 1992, the treaty was designed to better regulate the movement of hazardous waste between nations. Unfortunately, there were problems left unaddressed. For one, the Convention did *not* prohibit waste exports to any location except Antarctica, and instead merely required a notification and consent system known as "prior informed consent" (PIC). As such, if a nation did consent to accept hazardous wastes for disposal, but did not have the capacity to control and monitor such wastes in a safe and environmentally sound manner, then the prior informed consent rule was meaningless. In addition, a number of key nations, including the Ivory Coast and the United States, undermined the agreement by failing to ratify the main amendment to the Basel Convention. The Convention also did not adequately address the dumping of toxic products and materials through industrial recycling programs. Nevertheless, despite these problems, the Basel Convention established a new international norm that views the export of hazardous wastes from the North to the South as an unacceptable act of ecological imperialism.

Immediately after the adoption of the Convention, the international environmental movement and less developed countries went to work on overcoming its limitations. Over the course of the 1990s, their actions proved successful. The Convention has subsequently been strengthened through the adoption of hundreds of decisions, a protocol, an amendment, and the amendment of annexes. Of these agreements, the Basel Ban is the most important, as it puts into place a global ban on the export of hazardous wastes from members of the Organization for Economic Co-operation and Development (OECD) to non-OECD countries. It has, without question, in the words of the Basel Action Network, "transformed the Basel Convention from a control regime, to a no exceptions, environmentally-justified trade barrier to hazardous waste."

Unfortunately, even as a non-Party, the United States has vociferously opposed improvements to the Basel Convention. In fact, since the very beginning of the Basel negotiations, both Republican and Democratic administrations alike have joined with the polluter-industrial complex to strongly oppose the concept of a no-exceptions waste trade ban. Furthermore, the United States is attempting to redefine what constitutes hazardous wastes, including efforts to avoid the Basel Convention for the management of end-of-life American ships or to de-list certain types of electronic wastes. . . .

Recycling "Trash for Cash"

In the new millennium, a new wave of waste trade is developing in the form of various "trash for cash" or recycling schemes of post-consumer products. Loopholes in the rules allow waste transfers to legally continue under the auspices of recycling. These exported wastes take the form of used car (lead acid) batteries, cell phones, plastics, heavy metals, old ships laden with asbestos, and lead scrap, which is shipped from the United States to southern China, India, Pakistan, the Philippines, Malaysia, and Taiwan for "recycling." In January of 1993 alone, for instance, the United States sent over 1,985 tons of plastic waste to India. These new types of waste products are becoming a far more serious form of toxic dumping in comparison to the export of toxic chemicals.

. . . Electronic waste (or E-waste) is perhaps the most rapidly growing waste problem in the world. According to the United Nations, about 20 million to 50 million tons of E-waste is generated worldwide annually. Such waste contains toxins like lead, mercury, and other chemicals that can poison waterways, the land, or air (if burned). The United States, which uses most of the world's electronic products and generates most of the E-waste, is able to significantly reduce disposal costs by shipping E-wastes to the developing countries, especially Asia. In addition to U.S. efforts to undermine the Basel Convention, the U.S. government has also intentionally exempted E-wastes from the Resource Conservation and Recovery Act (RCRA). In short, the export of E-waste to developing countries serves as an economic escape valve for American industry. Rather than designing products that are less toxic and that can be more easily rebuilt and reused, American business maximizes profits by building products with very hazardous components with a short life span. Some 20 million computers become obsolete each year in the United States, generating some 5 to 7 million tons of E-waste.

In the era of corporate-led globalization, toxic wastes disposal is running "downhill" on the path of least resistance. About 80 percent of the E-waste handled by traders is exported to Asia, and 90 percent of that is destined for China, where environmental regulations are weak and poorly enforced. E-waste today contains a witches' brew of toxic substances such as lead and cadmium in circuit boards; lead oxide and cadmium in monitor cathode ray tubes (CRTs); mercury in switches and flat screen monitors; cadmium in computer batteries; polychlorinated biphenyls (PCBs) in older capacitors and transformers; and brominated flame retardants on printed circuit boards; plastic casings, cables, and polyvinyl chloride (PVC) cable insulation.

The open burning, acid baths, and toxic dumping around recycling centers releases vast quantities of pollution. Lead levels in drinking water are 2,400 times higher than what the World Health Organization considers to be safe in the Guiyu region of China. Similar environmental problems can be found in India and Pakistan recycling operations. As in the United States, poor communities surrounding the plants bear the greatest health impacts from these operations. . . .

A Better World Is Possible?

In the era of neo-liberalism and corporate-led globalization, environmental justice (EJ) movements in the both the United States and the global South have a mutual interest in developing coordinated strategies. The growing ability of multinational corporations and transnational financial institutions to evade environmental safeguards, worker/community health and safety regulations, and dismantle unions and the social safety nets in the United States is being achieved by crossing national boundaries into politically repressive and economically oppressive countries. And in this context, abetted by "free trade" agreements and economic liberalization enforced by the WTO, various nationalities and governments are increasingly being pitted against one another to attract capital investment by dismantling labor and environmental laws seen as damaging to profits. In this respect, corporate-led globalization is weakening the power of the EJ movement to win concessions from the state and American industry.

At the same time, any potential victory by a community of color in the United States against the disposal of toxic incinerator ash in their own locality is quite limited if the result is the transport and disposal of the same waste in a poor West African community. If multinational corporations flee to the Third World to avoid environmental regulations and liability in the North, then the actions of U.S. environmentalists may be indirectly exacerbating environmental injustices elsewhere in the world. Stringent environmental standards must be applied to all nations in order to foster global environmental justice. A reworking of established "free trade" agreements in favor of more positive "fair trade" agreements are an important first step in the struggle to defeat neo-liberal economic policy. Such a "fair trade" agreement would establish minimum standards or "floors" for regulations rather than "ceilings." In other words, rather than a "race to the bottom," whereby the nation with the weakest environmental regulations sets the standard "ceiling" which all trading partners must accept, a transnational EJ movement must work for a series of mandatory strong standards that apply to all nations. Such a regulatory harmonization process would privilege nations with the strictest environmental laws as establishing a standard "floor" to which all other countries must comply if trade is to be conducted between them.

. . . The implementation of new international agreements and treaties to address the environmental injustices fostered by corporate-led globalization cannot be piecemeal in approach. Strong baseline standards around particular issues is not enough. Agreements must be comprehensive in nature, taking into account *all* of the interconnected processes by which ecological hazards are displaced and transferred between countries, and especially between the North and South. For instance, in response to the Basel Convention (and Basel Ban), there is evidence that as dirty industries are deterred from exporting hazardous wastes abroad, many factories are relocating from their home bases in the United States to more permissive investment locations in the poorer countries. Once relocated, industry is able to take advantage of the less stringent environmental regulations to more cheaply dispose of hazardous waste directly inside the new country. As a result, the intent of the Basel Ban will be defeated.

Unless comprehensive international rules are also put into place to govern foreign direct investment in "toxic" industries, hazardous wastes may still wind up in other countries via this alternative route. The migration of dirty industries to maquiladora zones in Mexico are a strong example of the migration process. . . . [T]here are signals that a new transnational EJ movement devoted to tackling the export of ecological hazards to poor communities of color inside and outside of the United States is beginning to take shape. The Southwest Network for Economic and Environmental Justice (SNEEJ), and the Environmental Health Coalition (EHC), for instance, are placing pressure on multinational corporations and government agencies to clean-up pollution along the U.S.-Mexico border. In addition, a coalition of Canadian, U.S., and Mexican organizations have successfully expanded right-to-know legislation in Mexico, including the establishment of a Pollutant Release and Transfer Register that is similar to those in Canada and the United States. Although still in its infancy, the rise of an environmentalism of the poor in the global South and new transnational networks of EJ organizations in the North are among the most promising vehicles for curbing the ecological horror stories brought about by corporate-led globalization.

In the short run, only by achieving greater social governance over trade and lending institutions and regulatory bodies can the process that leads different countries to sacrifice human and environmental health in order to compete in the world economy be overcome. This includes efforts to reestablish popular control over the United Nations as a counterweight to the WTO. . . . [I]nstitutions, including transnational corporations and large banks, the International Monetary Fund and the World Bank, the United Nations, and the General Agreement on Trade and Tariffs (GATT), must be opened up to greater public participation in decision-making. The anti-globalization movement, in the form of the International Forum on Globalization (IFG), has prepared alternative proposals for building a more just and sustainable international system that ends corporate dominance over the world economy. These IFG proposals include a system of unified global economic governance under a restructured United Nations. In the long run, however, even bigger transformations are necessary. . . .

Note

Faber, Daniel. 2008. "Chapter 4: The Unfair Trade-off: Globalization and the Export of Ecological Hazards." In *Capitalizing Environmental Injustice: The Polluter-Industrial Complex in the Age of Globalization*. New York: Rowman & Littlefield.

15

Driving South
The Globalization of Auto Consumption and Its Social Organization of Space
Peter Freund and George Martin

As Daniel Faber's piece illustrated, the development of a global economy is among the most important trends of the last several decades. Aided by heavy governmental support for transportation infrastructures, such as roads, wealthy countries became completely dependent on auto transport by the middle of the twentieth century. Now the automobile culture is spreading throughout the world. Freund and Martin explore the effects that the automobile is having on the organization of social space in poorer countries. The authors show that poorer countries face challenges in their attempts to adopt the automobile culture, including a lack of automobile infrastructure and the high costs of importing oil. Because of these challenges, pollution, health problems, dangers to pedestrians and bicyclists, and the loss of green space are exacerbated.

Introduction

Since its introduction over a century ago, the automobile has become an icon of freedom, progress, and modernity throughout the world. Auto ownership is used as an indicator of economic development; it is the leading mass-produced durable good in the world. In developed countries, it has become the dominant transport modality; in parts of the U.S. it is the *only* viable means of everyday mobility. Most significantly, the attainment of individualized auto consumption for the great majority of populations in places like the U.S. has structured general perceptions of what is the most desirable and the most practical means of mobility. This attainment is made material by the now-embedded public infrastructures necessary for private auto use, from roads to regulating bureaucracies.

Countries of the South are rapidly adopting Western modes of consumption such as mass auto ownership as a path to economic development. Between 1993 and 1997, vehicle registrations rose by 40 percent in the North, compared to 61 percent in the South. But what kind of development is it?

> But what, then, should we mean by development? And how do we measure higher living standards? Are the living standards of a family in Bangkok raised, for example, when their cash income rises enough so that they can purchase an automobile—when the pleasure of car ownership is offset by the loss of free time caused by the need to work more hours, or even take a second job, to pay for the car and all its attendant costs, by the longer commuting time caused by other motorists exercising their freedom, by lung cancer, by the generalized urban blight of jammed roads, car parks, petrol stations, used-car lots, drive-in fast-food franchises, brown skies and howling car alarms? Is this a higher standard of living?

It is the replication of auto transport, etched in concrete and asphalt, that is the embodiment of a dream to which many in the world aspire. However, the auto represents more than transport. Its mass consumption has transformed the physical structure of landscapes, contributed to atmospheric, soil, and water degradation, and shaped, often in negative ways, the social organization of communities.

It is important, when considering these changes, not to see them as a product of "the automobile" but rather as a consequence of the way its use is promoted and organized, as part of an auto-centered transport *system*. This system includes a vast material infrastructure of roadways, repair facilities, auto supply shops, gas stations and service facilities, motels and tourist destinations, storage spaces, and an extensive social infrastructure of bureaucracies for the control of traffic, the education of drivers, and the regulation of drivers, vehicles, and fuels (among other things).

In addition to their dependence on elaborate infrastructures and to their increasing scale of use, autos have qualitative features that maximize their use of space; they require multiple, dedicated spaces. Spaces have to be allocated not only in driveways, but also on roads, in parking lots, and at work sites. All of these spaces are difficult to use for any purpose other than temporary car storage; at other times they are vacant. Fundamentally, in auto-centered transport oystems (ACTS) the auto is not only the dominant mode of transport; its use commands the disposition of much public space, which it wastes much more than it employs.

The emergence of auto-centered systems and their hegemony over public space in many parts of the world is not only a testament to the success of a particular technological form and a system for organizing its use, including the social life around it, but also to the extreme way in which capitalism has come to structure consumption. As a *mode of consumption,* auto-centered transport is a highly individualized, privately-owned form which is heavily subsidized by the state. The relationships among the auto, the environment, and capitalist economy revolve around the use of a technology which is the central durable commodity in the mature capitalist economy. This mode of consumption—not just the auto itself—is being diffused to countries in the South, a diffusion that has accelerated in the global, neoliberal 1990s.

The Globalization of Auto Hegemony

While auto production and consumption became worldwide phenomena at the end of the 20th century, great variation in the concentration of ownership remains. . . . [J]ust three nations in the world—the U.S., Germany, and Japan—account for 53 percent of world vehicle production and 49 percent of consumption, while they have only eight percent of world population. Their domination of auto production and consumption is a major factor in their supremacy over the world economy. Despite the ongoing economic restructuring based on technological advances in computers, electronics, and telecommunications, the auto-oil industrial complex retains a leading position in the global economy; in 1997, it accounted for six of the world's 10 largest business firms.

Auto densities in the world range from a high of 1.3 persons per vehicle in the U.S. to a low of 12,913 persons per vehicle in Afghanistan. For purposes of analysis, the nations of the world can be sorted into three groups by their degree of auto-centered transport systems (ACTS):

1. The counties with the most developed ACTS feature three or less persons per vehicle, in a total of 38 places. The most populous among these places are the U.S., Japan, Germany, Italy, the UK, and France. Africa and Central and South America have no developed ACTS, but several oil-rich nations in Asia—Brunei, Kuwait, and the United Arab Emirates—do have developed ACTS. In places with the most developed ACTS, autos dominate the cities, auto-induced urban sprawl is considerable, and the countrysides have become auto-dependent.

   In the nation with the most developed ACTS, the U.S., we can speak of the emergence of *hyperautomobility*—characterized by very high auto density (highlighted by the specialization of vehicles within households) and by very high auto use (indicated by increasing trips and distances, but with decreasing vehicle occupancy). The hyperautomobile U.S. is different from the other nations with the most developed ACTS. While U.S. cities average 54 percent more autos per person than European cities, auto use is even more pronounced. Auto kilometers per year per person average 143 percent more in U.S. cities than in European cities.

2. The mid-range ACTS countries have 4–50 persons per vehicle, in a total of 70 places. The most populous mid-range ACTS nations are Russia, Brazil, Mexico, Turkey, and Thailand. Mid-range ACTS countries include all of the former centrally planned economies of Eastern Europe and most of South America, as well as Israel, South Korea, and Taiwan. In these places with mid-range ACTS, the cities are also auto-dominated, but auto-induced urban sprawl is not yet pronounced and cities maintain a moderate level of transport diversification. The countrysides retain a mix of motorized and non-motorized transport.

3. Finally, the least developed ACTS countries have more than 50 persons per vehicle, in a total of 50 places. All these are in Africa or Asia, with the exception of the following nations in the Americas: Bolivia, Cuba, El Salvador, Guatemala, Haiti, and Honduras. The most populous nations are China, India, Indonesia, Pakistan, Bangladesh, and Nigeria. In these countries with the least developed ACTS, cities have been penetrated by autos but retain considerable diversity of transport modalities, while the countrysides are virtually auto-free. There is little or no auto-induced urban sprawl. . . .

In many respects, car troubles are an urban phenomenon, and this is starkly illustrated in the growing transport problems of the megacities of the South. Autos have been increasing at relatively high rates in many Asian, African, and Latin American cities, so that these cities at first glance resemble those of the North—featuring super highways and super traffic congestion. However, there are several significant differences in the current status of auto transport in cities of the North and the South:

1. In the South, auto transport has not become a mass phenomenon; it is largely restricted to the relatively small elite and middle class sectors, which constitute a small minority of the population.

2. Because auto transport is the privilege of a minority in Southern cities, these cities retain a more diversified transport modal split relative to the North. The working and poor classes of Southern cities depend on public transport (where available) and upon non-motorized transport, especially cycling, walking, and animal power.

3. Because many of the nations of the South are relatively poor and debt-laden, the public costs of auto transport come at a greater social price than they do in Northern cities. Principal among these costs is the provision of an adequate sociomaterial infrastructure, including roadways and regulating bureaucracies. The development of infrastructure lags behind the introduction of the car in Southern cities. Infrastructures for walking and other non-motorized forms of transport are even less developed than auto infrastructures. For instance, over 70 percent of Jakarta's roads have no sidewalks. Mass transit is similarly neglected as scarce resources are diverted to subsidize ACTS. One of the more dramatic illustrations of this uneven development is the relatively high toll in roadway-related human carnage in Southern nations.

4. Related to this infrastructure issue is a special problem for many Southern nations: They have to import oil to operate autos. Since autos can run without an adequate material and social infrastructure but not without oil, the oil-poor nations of the South are further disadvantaged, as their meager resources can be sapped by oil import costs.

. . . [S]ince auto markets in the developed nations have matured, the great potential for new markets exists in the South. The greatest increases in new car sales from 1997 to 2005 are forecast to be in China, India, and the Philippines. For auto makers such a trend is hopeful, yet the globalization of auto-centered transport represents an immeasurable ecological threat and badly aggravates already existing social inequities in access to transport. In short, ACTS are neither sustainable nor equitable.

The growth of auto-centered transport in the South thus brings into sharp relief issues of social inequality, the inappropriate use of transport technology, and the limits of globalizing such an energy-and-resource intensive and environmentally unfriendly system. The ideal of a motorized world built in the image of Southern California is simply not physically and economically feasible on a global scale.

The continuing diffusion of ACTS into the South is a major contributor to the South's growing ecological problems. The environmental problems of autocentric transport in the South, especially air, soil, and water pollution, have been well documented. Here, our focus is on the social organization of space promoted by auto-centered transport.

Modes of Consumption and the Social Organization of Space

In considering the diffusion of auto-centered transport systems, it is important to emphasize the sociomaterial aspects of consumption, of which two are central. First the resource (including especially land) and energy-intensive nature of auto-centered transport systems is at the core of the social and ecological problems that these systems cause. In the 1990s, the environmental problems caused by such systems have become global issues (e.g., global warming). Second, most central for our analysis is the impact of auto-centered transport as a mode of consumption on the *social organization of space.*

While the negative aspects of the diffusion of the auto are obvious enough in countries of the North, in the poorer and less developed South they are gravely aggravated. Surface transport (in this case the auto) has been described by some as an "engineering industry" that is not carried out inside a factory but outside in public space. In the South, just as the economic and technological development of the means of production is uneven, so is the development of the modes of consumption. Uneven development here means that the spatial and other contradictions of auto-centered transport are accentuated in countries of the South.

What are being exported to the South are not only technological forms that originated in the North, but consumerism, mainly modeled on that of the U.S. In this evolving model of consumerism, the auto is the transport commodity for local elites and is rapidly becoming the "privileged means of urban transportation." These newly emerging auto consumption patterns have influenced urbanization and drained scarce public resources in the South.

One looming consequence of the diffusion of such a mode of consumption to the South revolves around issues of sustainability or what some have called the "China factor." What happens to space in the form of arable land if, for instance, auto transport was to be adopted by all 1.2 billion Chinese? Total vehicle production increased by 152 percent between 1991 and 1998 in China and its mix changed as well. While the proportion of passenger cars was only six percent in 1991, it rose to 31 percent in 1998.

While arable land is not in scarce supply in many Northern countries, in many nations of the South it is.

> China, which has almost exactly the same land in area as the U.S., has four times as many people living on it. Since such a large proportion of China is desert or mountains, its population is crammed into dense concentrations around the great river valleys. As a result, the country must feed more than one-fifth of the world's population on less than one-fifteenth of its farmland.

Does it make sense for China to pave over arable land or land usable for dwelling spaces? Other countries of the South face similar problems, especially Egypt, Bangladesh, and Indonesia. For example, each year in Indonesia, 250 square kilometers of agricultural land, forest, and wetland become roads and urban spaces, displacing large numbers of people.

The use of land by autos reflects the great social inequality that exists in the South. In developing countries in general—and in Brazil in particular—transport and traffic policies, coupled to economic and social policies, have crystallized remarkable differences between those with and without access to private transport. Most decisions have a common objective: to adapt space to the use of the automobile for selected social groups.

In the North, the disenfranchisement of poor people, people displaced by freeways, people with disabilities and older people and children is one harsh feature of auto-centered systems. In the South, such disenfranchisement is amplified, particularly in African and Latin American cities in which alternative modalities are underdeveloped and human-powered vehicles are not as widespread as in many Asian cities.

In the less developed auto-centered systems of the South, spatial contradictions and their impact on safety are glaring, since the possibilities of technological fixes (e.g., resources for more benign organizations of traffic) are not available, and the technical potentials of mass automobility have not been realized. While road deaths in the developed countries are down to less than five per 10,000 vehicles per year, in the developing countries the picture is quite different: 40 deaths per year per 10,000 vehicles in India, 77 in Bangladesh, and 192 in Ethiopia. Transport space is in poor condition and it disenfranchises and is unsafe for the great majority who are not auto users. Traffic control is poor, as are mass transit alternatives. . . .

In South Africa, extremes of wealth and poverty contribute to one of the world's worst safety records. Luxury cars mix with overcrowded trucks (used as buses), donkey carts, cows, and pedestrians to produce a deadly combination. Black townships do not have sidewalks, adequate lighting, or pedestrian overpasses on the roads through which affluent-owned high-powered vehicles race. For most blacks, transport (even now, in post-apartheid society) in cities is confined to public transport. Whites travel mostly by auto: one out of two white South Africans owns a car; only one of 100 blacks do. South Africa, unlike many other countries of the South, has a developed transport infrastructure—but one which excludes modalities other than the automobile.

The growing space demands of auto owners are also degrading public places, the urban commons, in cities of the South; for example, the principal plaza in Mexico City. What used to be a popular and pleasant place to walk and socialize is now "filled with deafening traffic and the air is blue with car exhaust—trying to walk is more dangerous than driving." Another example is Bangkok. Once called the "Venice of Asia," the city has paved over its canals; still, gridlock and pollution grow. . . .

Autocentric transport demands massive public investment of land and resources for its infrastructures. The public purses of most nations of the South are not big enough to make these investments. In many cities of the South, the result is traffic congestion on an unprecedented level, congestion that carries great inefficiency costs in the transport of goods as well as workers. For example, in Sao Paulo, the lack of an adequate subway system and of well-developed auto infrastructures has produced perhaps more traffic noise, air pollution, and congestion than in any other city in the world. However, consistent with their positions of power and their orientations to technologies of the North, wealthy Paulistanos are buying themselves out of this morass—by purchasing helicopters. At over 400, the fleet of private helicopters is the biggest of any city in the developing world, trailing only the fleets of New York City and Tokyo. The social class contradictions of such uneven development is highlighted by the fact that "it is easier for a wealthy person to buy a helicopter than it is for a working class person to buy a car." . . .

. . . Poor people, particularly poor rural women, have an unequal transport burden. In effect, they are invisible to transport planners mainly concerned with large scale economic activity and with motorized traffic.

In many countries of the South where other modalities are in pervasive and intensive use (e.g., bicycles in Chinese cities), these modalities are being pushed to the side and increasingly marginalized. Human-powered vehicles such as rickshaws and bicycles are seen by the middle classes and elites as archaic and as impeding the smooth flow of motorized traffic. In Bombay and Jakarta, such vehicles have been banned and in Manila they have been removed from the main roads. Transport planners dislike large amounts of mixed traffic and their bias is to eliminate any obstacles to motorized traffic. Calcutta, despite a shortage of revenues, is investing in a huge new road infrastructure complete with flyovers, motor ways, and the rest. These structures will exclude the cycle rickshaws which are a source of jobs for many of Calcutta's poor. In Bangladesh approximately 1.25 million people are directly involved with driving and maintaining rickshaws, while five million people depend on them for subsistence. Rickshaws are not part of government planning and in a government report, they were described as "slow moving" vehicles that should eventually be eliminated and replaced by automobiles and trucks.

Transport Policy and Change

Governments in Southern countries are eagerly adopting the auto as the primary means of transport. Automobility is viewed as a sign and a means of economic development. Malaysia's experience with its government's "National Car Project" in the 1980s is an example of the huge costs involved in developing an auto industry. The auto is an up-market product that costs more than the average Malaysian house. In addition to sinking funds into production of the car, the government built new auto infrastructures, while cutting expenditure for rail and bus transport. Despite this public investment, the Malaysian car faces immense challenges. Local critics argue that the experience demonstrates the folly of such industrial mega-projects for developing nations.

While most cities in the South have allowed free rein to the auto, some have restricted its use. One successful example of diversifying transport in the South is Curitiba, Brazil, a city of 1.6 million. Beginning in the 1970s, the city adopted a series of transport-related measures, including improved bus transit, cycle ways and pedestrian ways, and integration of transport and zoning policies, in which higher densities were encouraged along major arterials and a mix of jobs, homes, and services were included in local areas. Additional policies have included traffic calming schemes and in-fill, in which new development is sited in abandoned land in the existing city rather than sprawling outward. Several improvements have been attributed to these policies, including the facts that Curitiba's rate of accidents per vehicle is now the lowest of Brazilian cities and its fuel consumption per vehicle is 30 percent less than in other Brazilian cities of its size. Finally, residents of Curitiba spend about 10 percent of their incomes on transport, one of the lowest such rates in Brazil. This is despite the fact that the city's auto ownership rate is high by Brazilian standards, second only to Brasilia's. Various grassroots projects, such as those sponsored by the Institute for Transportation and Development Policy, are trying to develop and sustain transport diversity, especially those modalities that are less energy-and-resource intensive and are useful to poor people, women, and people with disabilities. "Afri Bike," for instance, promotes bicycles as development tools, sponsoring an urban-based center where vendors can lease load-carrying bikes. . . .

Mobility is a growing problem for poorer people in the South. There, the increasing cutbacks in the public sector because of debt repayment, coupled with population growth in urban areas that outdistances the availability of public transport, deprives many people of any form of mobility except walking. . . .

Not only do many Southern governments subsidize auto transport and the auto industry at the expense of alternatives, so, too, do banks. Non-motorized forms of travel such as improved bicycles (e.g., using light metal) and carts have received virtually no subsidies. Alternative transport, which local elites view as "backward," is sacrificed to the auto. Yet, in the South, bicycles are a source of jobs and foreign exchange, and generate small-scale entrepreneurial activities such as vending, scrap collecting, and delivery services. Moreover, their manufacture and maintenance are labor-intensive enterprises.

Because of government support for the wholesale introduction of auto technology many Southern cities have become caricatures of the most auto-centered cities in the U.S. Cities such as Caracas have almost unimaginable journeys to and from work (up to seven hours per day), elaborate freeways without adequate feeder arterials that result in massive congestion, and highways that stop abruptly at the edges of old city centers because of lack of space. These cities could hugely benefit from improved bus service, bicycle and jitney use, and other less energy- and-resource intensive modes of transport.

Conclusion

The automobile and its socioenvironmental consequences revolve around its dual aspects as a transport *system* and a *mode of consumption*. When speaking of development, one is not simply talking about technological diffusion, but also the diffusion of consumption patterns. In countries of the South, the automobile has spread to local elites and is beginning to dominate (especially urban) space and to drive other modalities out. Just as with the diffusion and globalization of a mature capitalist mode of production, so too the diffusion of a mature capitalist mode of consumption takes place in an uneven fashion.

A consumption mode of transport characterized not only by auto hegemony but by auto dependence is increasingly proving itself to be a form of unsustainable development and a socially destructive mode of consumption. Its diffusion to countries of the South aggravates its problematic social and environmental consequences in the short term. Even in the long term, if countries of the South could fully develop an auto-centered transport system such as that which exists in North America, the results would be disastrous in terms of the impact on the ambient environment and, above all, on social space. Deconstructing the taken-for-granted notion that autocentric transport is "progress" can lead us to reconsider such general questions as what is the "good life" and what constitutes material prosperity, and what kind of transport investments and planning need to be made—in the *North*, not only the South.

What distinguishes the auto from other consumer goods (including other durable goods) is that while the latter may also be energy-and-resource intensive, the car's pervasive and intensive use requires a great deal of *space*. The bulk of this space, furthermore, is the most desirable *public* space (e.g., in urban centers). The auto appropriates valuable public space and, particularly in countries of the South, makes this space virtually unusable for other non-motorized modalities (including walking). In this way, the adoption of auto-centric transport can spearhead a more general development of capitalist consumption, i.e., the car provides a material inlay for Western consumerism. For example, in Venezuelan cities, auto-centered consumption patterns have been the catalyst in privatizing public space and in individualizing consumption.

The auto is a private consumer good that is (in the North as well as South) heavily subsidized by the state. Scarce public resources go into highways and the infrastructures that automobiles need in order to be intensively and pervasively used by a minority of citizens in the South. Yet little is invested in ameliorating the impact of emerging automobility on social and physical environments. Technical fixes (e.g., systems of traffic control) and educational campaigns for safety are not nearly as developed as in countries of the North. There, the systemic limits to emission control and accident prevention are being reached, with further significant reductions only possible through social changes—changes in travel patterns and modal splits, both of which lead to a consideration of the re-organization of space.

As a means of empowering the mass of the population and contributing to a more sustainable form of transport, a *diversity* of modalities should be developed and subsidized. Non-motorized vehicles can be appropriate technologies, not only for countries of the South, but also in the North (e.g., countries like Denmark and the Netherlands). Mass transit and non-motorized transport need to be valorized and taken seriously in technological development (e.g., new metal alloys, solar power). Developing such modalities can represent a move "back to the future." Asian cities, particularly those of China, could benefit a great deal from such a shift in development policy.

Contemporary auto technologies do not co-exist well with other uses of their spaces. Highways built for autos are not hospitable for walkers and cyclists. Even motorized public transit like buses find it difficult to use auto-centered space. For example, effective bus transit requires frequent stopping for on- and off-loading passengers. For this reason, local buses are unable to make full use of auto highways. In the North, where auto-centered transport has matured, other modalities have been pushed aside, especially in the U.S. It will be difficult to re-engineer social space in the U.S., so that other modalities can be effectively used—even if the political will were present. In cities of the South, diversification in transport still remains, but it is gradually being pushed aside as auto consumption rises. While the South could profit from the negative lesson of the North and preserve (and modernize) their transport diversification, it is not happening. So far the neoliberal global development model has been too powerful.

. . . Transnational corporations based in Western Europe, North America, and Japan view the South—especially the so-called emerging market countries—as fast-growing, potentially vast markets for their commodities, as their own markets become saturated with goods and tend to stagnate. These corporations and the nation-states of the North are trying to globalize the way of life that evolves from automobility in general and to help develop the material infrastructure for the use of automobiles in the South in particular. The auto industry, petrochemicals, and other sectors dependent in part or whole on mass automobility are clamoring for a greater play in the South. Mass motorization in the South, it is thought, is the answer to excess productive capacity and profit shortfalls in the North.

While it is easy for countries of the North to tout sustainable development (having reaped the dubious benefits of unsustainable development), the countries of the South suffer the most. It is thus the North that needs to take the initiative in "greening" both production and consumption. This is because the North has done the most damage to the environment (especially as imperialists and neo-imperialists in exploiting resources in the South); has the material resources to make needed changes (some have termed the countries of the North post-scarcity societies); and as a model for development (particularly the U.S.) has the moral obligation to provide an example of a greener and socially less destructive way of life.

Whether or not there can be a greening of consumption in the North *or* the South depends on planning the global market place, shifting production to less energy-and-resource intensive consumer goods, encouraging more sustainable and socially democratic modes of consumption—in all countries of the world.

Note

Freund, Peter, and George Martin. 2000. "Driving South: The Globalization of Auto Consumption and Its Social Organization of Space." CNS, 11, no. 4: 51–71. 1.

PART VII

Science, Risk and Knowledge

Risk Society and Contested Illness

The Case of Nuclear Weapons Workers

Sherry Cable, Thomas E. Shriver,
and Tamara L. Mix

As the pieces in this section illustrate, many sociologists believe it is important to think critically about science and knowledge production and to understand and show how scientific endeavors are, at their heart, social endeavors—that science itself is a social construct.

Sociologists sometimes refer to modern society as a "risk society"—one that is organized around hazards that people themselves create. In a risk society, the distribution of societal risks may become as important to quality of life as the distribution of wealth. Risk societies rely on complex production technologies; the management, policy making, and general understanding of these technologies require multiple specialized experts. The reliance on experts leads to both the unintentional and intentional restriction of citizens' access to information about environmental hazards. The ability of citizens to protect themselves from risks is related to their ability to access and understand information. This article explores these issues as they manifest at the Oak Ridge Nuclear Reservation, a key installation of the federal nuclear weapons complex. The authors examine the conditions under which managers and other institutional authorities withhold technical knowledge from the public and dispute workers' claims of environmental illness.

Contemporary societies consciously invite exposures to environmental hazards that pose unique risks to human health. Beck (1992, 1995, 1996) uses the term "risk society" to describe societies organized around the environmental hazards created by modern agricultural and industrial production technologies. Risks derive from hazards deliberately "induced and introduced by modernization itself" (Beck 1992:21) through technologies developed to generate increased capital accumulation. Since about 1945, production technologies have relied significantly on radioactive substances, heavy metals, and synthetic organic chemicals—substances scientifically demonstrated to be associated with specific human ailments (Cable, Hastings, and Mix 2002; Commoner 1972; Schnaiberg 1980).

A society's reliance on risky and complex production technologies elevates experts to prominence in private and public decision-making arenas. It also restricts citizens' access to information about environmental hazards. Information restriction occurs, often unintentionally, because technologies require multiple specialized experts who create abstract knowledge systems that are incomprehensible to the majority of citizens (Giddens 1991). Intentionally restricted access, on the other hand, derives from private and public institutions' close control over scientific knowledge related to economic production. Private institutions, such as corporations, guard knowledge as a proprietary commodity, and the state withholds certain information for ideological and security reasons. Without full access to information, citizens cannot assess specific risks and make informed decisions about where they work and live, nor are they prepared to protect themselves from the risks they cannot avoid.

Without resources to protect themselves from exposures, people inevitably get sick. How does the risk society respond to claims that illnesses are caused by the production technologies that define the age? Research shows that individuals who attribute their symptoms to environmental exposures and turn for aid to their physicians, employers, and political leaders frequently receive little support. Instead, they find themselves embroiled in public conflict. We refer to illnesses that "engender major scientific disputes and extensive public debates over environmental causes" (Brown et al. 2003:213) as contested environmental illnesses. . . .

In this article, we build on the risk society thesis to advance understanding of authorities' contestations of disease claims linked to risky production materials. We draw on documents, observations, and in-depth interviews with 124 residents, workers, and activists in East Tennessee to investigate the public dispute over the environmental illness claims of nuclear weapons workers. Attention centers on Oak Ridge Nuclear Reservation, a key installation of the federal nuclear weapons complex. Under what conditions do institutional authorities contest environmental illness claims of known diseases? Which authorities contest illness claims? And how is institutional power exercised to withhold technical knowledge from the public? Such questions, which make up the core of our analyses, contribute to sociological scholarship on environment, illness, and workplace power dynamics, but also to broader social scientific concerns pertaining to knowledge and open, democratic discourse.

Risk Society and Contested Environmental Illnesses

Contemporary Ecological Hazards

... Since the 1990s, "risk society" is the tag most commonly used for reference to postwar societal changes (Beck 1992, 1995, 1996; Eder 1996; Gare 1995; Giddens 1990, 1999; Habermas 2001; Jameson 1991). Beck (1992) argues that contemporary societies' wealth is inextricably linked to environmental hazards—surplus capital is complemented by surplus dangers to human health. He writes: "In the risk society, the unknown and unintended consequences [of production] come to be a dominant force in history and society" (p. 22). Fearing such consequences, citizens often question the premier roles of science and technology in directing economic expansion. Giddens (1999) illuminates the nature of unintended consequences by stressing the differences between industrial societies' natural, acts-of-the-gods risks, such as flood and famine, and the risk society's decidedly anthropogenic, deliberately assumed risks, such as exposures to radiation and synthetic pesticides. Risk analysts depict societies as dominated by knowledgeable experts whose technological choices carry ecological threats that are deliberately borne for the anticipated benefits of increased capital accumulation. But the risks are not equally distributed in society. Politically powerful private-sector groups who make technological decisions advocated by the experts in their hire reap significant benefits, yet the costs—adverse health effects—disproportionately affect the general public. ...

The most extensive production technologies of the risk society are those associated with the Cold War's nuclear arms race and with the petrochemical industry. The nuclear arms race increased reliance on production technologies that use materials associated with serious human health problems, such as uranium, mercury, cyanide, nickel, chromium, and beryllium. The petrochemical industry's postwar expansion replaced many naturally occurring materials used in agriculture and manufacturing with synthetic organic compounds. Fabricated as artificial combinations of amino acids, petrochemicals have no corresponding enzymes to help them biodegrade. Consequently, they accumulate in food webs, where they pose constant threats to life. The emergent technologies of genetic engineering and nanotechnology continue the risk society's trend of introducing unnatural substances to the natural environment.

Ubiquitous health threats inevitably bring illnesses—eventually. Because contemporary risks have a long latency period, technologies' toxic byproducts sleep as ticking timebombs in many communities. The first bombs began exploding in the 1980s when citizens confronted health threats in their workplaces and communities (Bullard 2000; Cable and Cable 1995; Cole and Foster 2001; Nelkin and Brown 1984). Many people now complain of illnesses that they attribute to hazardous exposures. Symptoms include multiple chemical sensitivities, immune system deficiencies, tremors, chronic fatigue, memory loss, unexplained rashes, chronic headaches, tumors, and clinical depression. These illnesses are now so frequently reported that researchers refer to them as "environmental" illnesses—a commonality portending that, in the near future, the defining characteristic of risk societies may well be widespread environmental illnesses. . . .

Analytic Frame and the Case of Nuclear Weapons Workers

Risk societies are accompanied by citizens' claims of environmental exposure–induced illnesses, as well as contestations of those claims by corporate, government, and medical authorities. These authorities often prioritize organizational needs over citizens' needs in the service of profit, power, and ideology. Contestation denies the ill access to needed services and benefits. . . .

. . . One of the three original Manhattan Project sites, the Oak Ridge facility produced the enriched uranium that fueled the Hiroshima bomb. Throughout the subsequent Cold War, workers continued to handle hazardous materials as they developed the hydrogen bomb, enriched uranium to weapons- and commercial-grade levels, researched the use of radioisotopes, and manufactured components for nuclear weapons systems.

This case is itself opportune for three significant reasons. First, the nuclear weapons industry is emblematic of the risk society's production technologies that use hazardous substances. The chief production substances used at the Oak Ridge Nuclear Reservation were mercury, cyanide, uranium, and beryllium.

Second, Oak Ridge workers' claimed illnesses are known diseases. Medical experts have scientifically established links between exposures to weapons production materials and adverse health effects. Exposures to mercury, particularly in vapor form, are associated with tremors, respiratory problems, emotional instability, sleeplessness, memory loss, muscle weakness, headaches, and numbness. Acute and chronic cyanide exposures may cause headaches, palpitations, convulsions, skin disorders, nasal irritation, and tremors. Radioactive exposures are associated with malignant effects such as cancers of the bone, liver, thyroid, and lung, and with nonmalignant effects such as degenerative changes and impaired function of bone marrow, kidneys, lungs, and the eyes. Beryllium is associated with life-threatening respiratory problems, including lung cancer. Institutional acknowledgment of these known associations between exposures and specific diseases is manifested in federal regulations for worker safety.

Third, records of hazardous exposures, which can be used to demonstrate the exposure-illness link for a particular individual, are more likely to be maintained for workers than for the general public. The public's protection from exposures consists of Environmental Protection Agency (EPA) regulations on toxic emissions that establish standards for air, water, and land quality. Emissions records are required of organizations, but exposure records for members of the public are not. In contrast, workers are protected from exposures by the Occupational Safety and Health Administration (OSHA). OSHA regulations establish limits on workers' hazardous exposures and also impose requirements for worker safety that include regular monitoring of workers' exposures and maintaining accurate individual exposure records. Exposure records constitute a database for connecting individuals' exposures to their illnesses.

We use the following questions to guide our case study analysis: What was the institutional context for nuclear weapons workers' hazardous exposures and claims of known illnesses? Without the ambiguous climate created by the etiological uncertainty of presumed diseases, what was the basis for authorities' contestation of workers' claims of known illnesses? What powers specific to the contesting institutions were used to dispute illness claims, and what particular tactics did authorities use to contest workers' claims of known diseases?

Data and Research Strategy

We collected data in a multiyear effort through in-depth interviews, document analysis, and observation. Our primary data source is indepth interviews with 124 respondents. . . .

. . . The sample is predominantly white, evenly split in terms of gender, and 29 percent lived in Oak Ridge since at least early childhood. The bulk of the respondents are employed as professionals (30.6 percent), technicians (25 percent), and laborers (15.3 percent). Because of the way we selected respondents, the majority believe that exposures to weapons production materials had caused illnesses. . . . Over half of the respondents work at the Reservation, and 25 respondents (20.2 percent) claim illnesses from exposures to weapons production materials.

. . . Nearly all [the ill respondents] are white, and 65 percent are female . . . 64 percent lived in Oak Ridge since at least early childhood, and 32 percent spent adulthood as Oak Ridge residents. One ill respondent is a lifelong resident of nearby Knoxville, but his father worked for decades at the Reservation.

The respondent himself had been a Reservation employee for three years. Ill respondents worked predominantly as technicians (44 percent) and laborers (24 percent). Most (96 percent) were either Reservation workers (76 percent) or lived with Reservation workers as children or spouses (20 percent). All 25 ill respondents report that their illness claims were contested.

We checked interview data for verification against documents including local and regional newspapers (*The Oak Ridger*, the *Knoxville News-Sentinel*, and the *Nashville Tennessean*), local historical accounts of Oak Ridge, documents obtained from the Department of Energy (DOE) Reading Room and through Freedom of Information Act requests, State of Tennessee public documents, and personal correspondence between physicians and patients and among activists. Additionally, we engaged in observation at various government-sponsored and activist-sponsored public meetings in venues such as the American Museum of Science and Energy and the Oak Ridge Visitors' Bureau.

The Institutional Context of Workers' Contested Illness Claims

The Oak Ridge Nuclear Reservation is a part of the nuclear weapons production complex in which the DOE supervises the design, construction, assembly, and disassembly of nuclear warheads at 17 major sites in 13 states (Ehrlich and Birks 1990). Conforming to the principle that the government must not compete with private enterprise, the sites are managed by more than 70 corporations, including Union Carbide, General Electric, Westinghouse, Martin Marietta, Lockheed, and Monsanto. Employing about 12,000 workers, the Oak Ridge Reservation maintains the nation's largest stock of fissile materials. The central institutional context for the contested illness claims of nuclear weapons workers is the DOE. But the DOE delegates authority to its Oak Ridge Office (ORO) for supervision of local operations in coordination with corporate management authorities. Consequently, both the federal and the local organizational contexts are critical factors in Reservation workers' exposures and illness claims.

The DOE and the Federal Nuclear Weapons Complex

The Manhattan Project was initiated in 1942 as one of three research and production facilities constructed by the U.S. Army to produce the world's first atomic bomb. National security demanded that project operations remain secret. All employees, from physicists to janitors, worked under a security system known as compartmentalization. Originally established to limit interaction among scientists, the system was refined in wartime to restrict the flow of all information to a "need-to-know" basis. Workers were prohibited from discussing any aspect of their jobs on penalty of forfeiting their security clearances. Revocation of security clearance meant that the worker was suspended without due process pending an investigation; conviction would bring imprisonment. As a result, most workers remained as uninformed about the Manhattan Project's mission as the public—until the second bomb exploded over Nagasaki. The government then released the Smyth Report, a semi-technical account of the scientific developments that culminated in the military use of atomic energy.

The motives of key actors for releasing the Smyth Report varied, revealing a fundamental contradiction that remains unresolved: the withholding of information from citizens by a democratic government. Author and physicist Smyth's motivation was shared information. In the report's summary, he states that the further development and use of atomic bombs should be determined in a public process:

> In a free country like ours, such questions should be debated by the people and decisions must be made by the people through their representatives. . . . The people of the country must be informed if they are to discharge their responsibilities wisely (Smyth 1945:13.7 8)

Smyth's objective was in sharp contrast to pronouncements by Secretary of War Henry Stimson and Manhattan Project Director General Leslie Groves. Stimson (1945) hoped that the report would "backfire reckless statements by independent scientists after the demonstration of the bomb." He said, "If we could be sure that these could be controlled and avoided, all of us would much prefer not to issue such a paper." In the foreword to the report, Groves emphasized the need for strict limits on the release of information because of national security requirements, and he warned that public requests for further information were inappropriate and violators would be subject to the Espionage Act.

Secrecy prevailed; the Cold War began as the heated war ended. Political tensions with the USSR heightened security concerns, which were manifested in the dramatic enlargement of the weapons complex in pursuit of a superior nuclear arsenal. Stringent secrecy norms imposed at weapons production sites exceeded wartime restrictions on information flow to the point of contradicting the constitutional imperative to preserve an open democratic government safeguarded by checks and balances. The 1946 Atomic Energy Act, which transferred control of nuclear weapons production from military to civilian authorities via the Atomic Energy Commission (AEC), contradicted constitutional mandates by authorizing the agency to function with only minimal congressional surveillance. The act, "prevented the American people and their elected representatives from participating in atomic policy making. It also created an echelon of decision makers who were, in the main, accountable only to themselves" (Udall 1994:174).

Kinsella and Mullen (2007:74) describe contradiction in government responsibilities as a paradox: "Citizens must be informed participants in atomic matters, while national security limits their access to information." The AEC embodied the paradox and initiated the government's perennial dilemma of simultaneously promoting and regulating nuclear energy. Kinsella and Mullen describe the government's control of information as the deliberate attempt to constrain public knowledge about nuclear matters so as to contain democratic public discourse. They label these efforts "discursive containment" (Kinsella 2001; Kinsella and Mullen 2007).

Congress periodically challenges discursive containment, but with mixed results. Legislators perceived that the 1946 Administrative Procedures Act, originally designed to open government to the public, was routinely manipulated by the executive branch to withhold information, rather than to distribute it (Rosenbloom 2003). They passed the 1966 Freedom of Information Act (FOIA), mandating that federal agencies provide information about their activities to the public upon request. But the FOIA's first exemption prohibits agencies from providing information in records authorized as secret in the interest of national defense or foreign policy (5 U.S.C. 552 [b] [1] 2002). Legislators again challenged the principle of secrecy when criticisms that the AEC favored research and development over safety and regulation led them to pass the 1974 Energy Reorganization Act. It replaced the AEC with two new agencies: the Nuclear Regulatory Commission, charged with regulating commercial nuclear energy matters, and the Energy Research and Development Administration (ERDA), designed to promote nuclear energy. In 1977, ERDA's responsibilities were transferred to the newly established DOE, which is now responsible for nuclear weapons production facilities.

In the 1980s, residents of communities hosting weapons facilities challenged nuclear secrecy . . .

. . . The federal government avoided a crisis with the 1993 announcement of DOE's new "openness policy." In accordance with this policy, the DOE declassified and released volumes of highly technical information—so technical that the EPA subsequently developed the Technical Assistance Program to provide grants that enable communities to hire expert help in interpreting DOE documents. But the massively increased flow of technical information failed to produce a more informed public. This failure is seen in the Final Report of the United States Senate Commission on Protecting and Reducing Government Secrecy (1997). The commission concluded that secrecy is a form of government regulation, that excessive secrecy has significant consequences for the national interest when policy makers are not fully informed, and that the government is not held accountable for its actions.

DOE officials maintained discursive containment while appearing to address criticisms about the public's right to know. Kinsella and Mullen (2007) point to the need for technological expertise in interpreting information as critical to continued discursive containment. By shifting the emphasis from the provision of information to the need for expert interpretation of the information, DOE officials limited the range of voices that could legitimately speak about hazardous exposures . . . .

The ORO [Oak Ridge Office] and Corporate Management

The Oak Ridge Nuclear Reservation consists of three large facilities. K-25 is a gaseous diffusion plant for uranium enrichment (closed in 1985), X-10 is a national research laboratory, and Y-12 fabricates warhead components. During the war, the plants and the town were managed by the U.S. Army. The entire site was enclosed by barbed-wire fencing and the gates were guarded by armed soldiers. Only at the war's end was it revealed that the Reservation had produced the enriched uranium for the Hiroshima bomb. The Reservation's postwar mission changed little because the subsequent nuclear arms race demanded increased production. In 1946, when control of the plants and the town was transferred to the AEC, agency authorities wanted to relinquish control of the town and urged residents to incorporate. The residents agreed in 1959 only after the federal government promised to subsidize town revenues (Cable, Shriver, and Hastings 1999). The AEC managed the Reservation until the 1974 creation of the shortlived Energy Research and Development Administration, which was eliminated with the 1977 establishment of the DOE. Local supervision was implemented through DOE's Oak Ridge Office and contracted corporate management. Weapons production remains the town's sole economic base.

In 1983, rumors of a secret government study to investigate mercury releases from Y-12 led a local journalist to file a FOIA request. The report he received documented management's 1977 discovery of significant off-site mercury contamination. The journalist's published stories forced DOE officials to acknowledge that 2.4 million pounds of mercury had been unintentionally released from Y-12 between 1950 and 1977. A subsequent congressional investigation concluded that the DOE "released incomplete and misleading information about mercury to the public" and had "used national security as a convenient shield behind which the non-sensitive but politically volatile data on the quantity of mercury releases could be buried and obscured" (Cable et al. 1999).

In 1989, the Reservation was placed on the EPA's Superfund list. More than 700 separate contaminated sites, totaling 5,000 acres, were identified. The list included 247 buildings, some the size of auto plants, contaminated with radiation and other toxic substances; 56 waste burial grounds, contaminated with solvents, lubricants, chemicals, uranium, mercury, strontium, thorium, tritium, and substances still classified as secret; and 52 settlement ponds with chemicals, metals, and PCBs (Thomas, Frank, and Paine 1997).

A handful of residents began claiming illness from exposures to the known hazards and formed a citizens' organization. Mobilization was hampered by members' periodic health setbacks and harsh criticisms from neighbors. The ill citizens were particularly overwhelmed by the flow of documents released by the DOE. Respondents described the difficulties in collecting, reading, and interpreting the highly technical information. Documents were shipped from site to site on a tight timetable, and each load remained in place only briefly. Activists were forced to photocopy the documents quickly and examine them later. The documents were housed in the public library, which had regulations prohibiting their removal from library premises and stringently restricted patrons' use of the sole photocopier.

Workers increasingly claimed exposure-induced illnesses in the mid-1990s. In 1995, ORO created a cyanide working group as part of a study by the National Institute of Occupational Safety and Health. Group members met regularly, on site and on the clock, for discussions led by Reservation physicians. Although discouraged from meeting alone off site, many members did so, and in 1996 the support group morphed into an activist organization: the Coalition for a Healthy Environment. . . .

The Contestation of Nuclear Workers' Illness Claims

Workers' long-time silence about hazardous exposures and illnesses should not be construed as ignorance—workers were keenly aware that they were exposed to hazards and sometimes knew which substances they were exposed to. When the institutional and organizational context changed enough to allow public voicing of concerns, workers spoke out about their illnesses. But their claims of known diseases, although associated with ORO-documented exposures to hazardous substances, were contested by government, corporate, and medical authorities.

Workers' Exposures to Risky Technologies

Respondents offered graphic descriptions of their exposure experiences. An African American woman with multiple cancers, who moved to Oak Ridge in 1944, described her wartime exposures on a job cleaning up radioactive materials at shift's end:

> We had to wear meters all the time. And we had to have goggles over our eyes and over our ears and over our mouths. And you had to go out every

time the bell rang and catch air for about 10 minutes. And I would forget to go out! They would come back and I'd be done stayed overtime—that's what I believe made me sick. One time I see this man come in there to pick up his tube [respirator] without his goggles on—without his eyes covered up. Blood come out of his eyes, nose, mouth, ears—everywhere! He didn't live—he died on his way there [to the hospital]. That hot stuff eat him up.

Postwar improvements increased worker safety, but exposures remained routine. A female machinist who began work in 1974 and is now plagued with memory lapses, thyroid problems, and extreme fatigue emphasized management's forceful control: "They told you what to do, you did it, and that was it." She described an example of her exposures:

We would have to go down to the burial ground do some jobs there. That's when we would see the uranium burning up out of the ground. There would be areas that looked like little lava pits! I mean, [it was] just oozing up . . . it looked like a heavy cream oozing up out of the ground. I said, "What's all that?" and they said, "That's all the junk that we buried here for years."

Perhaps the most striking example showing the routine nature of hazardous exposures was related by a female whose exposures occurred after the implementation of rigid compliance rules associated with the Reservation's listing as a Superfund site. As stipulated by EPA requirements, all hazardous wastes stored on the Reservation had to be sampled, analyzed, and characterized for proper disposal. The severely ill worker described her job as a trained hazardous waste sampler:

It wasn't anything for us to do 700 samples in a 16-day period just two people for the whole plant! We would get requests like, "It looks like ice cream salt," but it was actually something that had been used in an experiment. We didn't know what it was . . . we were given orders to go sample and, after we took it to Analytical Chemistry and they had a chance to analyze, then we would know what was in it. To keep from having a big hassle, a lot of times they would tell us, "This is only distilled water just have to have it checked because I have to," and then it would come back [from chemical analysis] as tritium or whatever in it.

Workers described a broad range of symptoms including thyroid problems, chronic fatigue, rashes, memory loss, dizziness, respiratory problems, and vision and hearing loss. . . .

A worker whose position in the plant's fire department took him into nearly all of the Reservation's buildings described his deteriorating condition from cyanide exposures:

> I couldn't drive my own vehicle. When it got to that point and I couldn't drive, I had to have help with a lot of things. I couldn't remember how to get back home. I started having to have somebody drive me from that point on.

Ill workers resented not being adequately informed about occupational risks. The hazardous waste sampler quietly stated: "We didn't know what we were dealing with—we were just a sampling tool. We were more or less expendable."

Contestation Tactics and Corporate Management

Although DOE supervision of Reservation production activities was implemented through ORO, corporations contracted for on-site management were directly responsible for staffing, managing, and supervising Reservation workers. Consequently, workers' illness claims were contested by corporate management authorities who used three tactics: denial of individual exposures, refusal to allow access to health records, and reassignment to unfavorable job tasks.

Corporate management contested illness claims by denying that a worker was exposed to the substance as claimed. A pollution prevention technician who worked for two years in one of the most heavily polluted K-25 buildings tested positive for cyanide poisoning. She regularly "rationalized away" her health problems before recognizing them in a written description of cyanide poisoning. When she spoke with her plant supervisors, expecting their support, she was stunned at their denial that cyanide was even present in her work environment. She exclaimed:

> The managers were saying there was no cyanide out there! I write monthly reports to DOE, and I've got at least three or four projects that have got "cyanide" in the title! Don't tell me there is no cyanide out there!

Even claims based on substantiated evidence of links between an individual's specific exposures and subsequent illness were subject to denial by the management. A Y-12 machinist, whose 1993 diagnosis of beryllium disease was the fifth such Reservation case, reported that corporate manager Lockheed originally planned to contest his beryllium exposure case in court:

> Lockheed's attorneys were planning to contest the fact that exposure to beryllium could cause asthma, even though it was documented in my

medical report by one of the world's experts on beryllium disease! It was a matter of record that that's what caused my problems, yet they were going to contest it!

Other claims were contested through management's refusal to permit workers access to their own on-site medical records. A security officer with heavy metal poisoning expressed his determination to force the release of information on medical tests ordered and performed on him at the Reservation:

> Me and my lawyer are currently filing a new FOIA—I want every record they got on me! I want to know what they did with every drop of blood that come out of me, or any other biological samples they may have taken from me. If they were aware that we were being exposed to this stuff—there's not much of a way that they could not have been aware of it. For years, I wondered why they didn't do the tests for heavy metals and things on us. You work in a uranium enrichment plant—why in the world would you not look for uranium?

Some respondents who were able to retrieve their medical records reported that information about their exposures was deleted or falsified. A respondent related an anecdote about a friend who requested his radiation exposure history when he learned that several of his work group members had died of cancer. The records were finally provided eight months after the request, and they indicated his employment for time periods in which he was not employed and showed no exposures for periods when he knew he was exposed.

In preemptive strikes against future illness claims, corporate authorities reassigned complaining workers to unfavorable tasks. A K-25 process operator who questioned management's procedural compliance was reassigned to the steam plant "because it was a whipping post—if you caused too much trouble over on the cascade or something, that's where you ended up because it was so nasty."

Contestation Tactics by Reservation Employed and Contract Physicians

Two sets of Oak Ridge physicians were distinguishable by their organizational contexts. One set consisted of physicians engaged by ORO to work at the Reservation, conducting workers' annual physical examinations, treating accidental exposures, and performing monitoring tasks such as administering blood tests and examining the dosimeters that measured individuals' radioactive exposures. The other set of physicians was made up of local, private-care physicians who were part of an unorthodox medical establishment in which the sole hospital, a nonprofit organization, wholly owned a for-profit subsidiary that contracted with nearly all Oak Ridge physicians. The subsidiary owned the medical practices, including nursing and clerical staffs, office space, equipment, and phone and computer services, and hired the physicians on annually renewable contracts. The operations of both the nonprofit hospital and the for-profit subsidiary were overseen by a board of directors on which ORO and corporate management officials routinely served.

This structural setting was highly conducive for transforming independent medical authorities into captive professionals (Daniels 1969). . . . Reservation and contract physicians at Oak Ridge were likely pressured to adopt corporate management's norm of contesting workers' illness claims. Physicians contested claims through three tactics: failure to inform workers of their medical test results, discrediting of peers who legitimated workers' illness claims, and derogation of patients.

Reservation physicians contested illness claims by failing to inform workers of the test results. A laundry room supervisor described what happened when she received the results of her two subordinates' annual examinations, which showed high levels of cyanide:

> They [medical services] made it a point to tell me that I was not to let them know that there was a problem, because "we don't want to concern anybody—we don't want to upset anybody!" I was just to send the workers down to do theirs over and check it again. Management said, "Keep your mouth shut." Not in those words, but that's what they were telling me.

Workers described situations in which Reservation and contract physicians contested their illness claims by discrediting peers who legitimated them. A female mechanic, for example, was initially informed by Reservation physician Dr. A that her test results indicated cyanide poisoning, only to have his word repudiated by Reservation physician Dr. B:

> I got to feeling so bad that I went up to see Dr. [A] again, but they wouldn't let me see him. They gave me Dr. [B]. I said to him, "I need a cyanide urinalysis test." He said: "That's a bunch of bullshit! That is a crock! And we know who started it." And he pushed his head over to Dr. [A]'s office.

Dr. Bill Reid provides the most striking and well-documented example of contract physicians discrediting a peer. Reid, an oncologist, was actively recruited by the hospital's subsidiary in 1992. Concerned about high incidences of unusual symptoms among his patients and reasoning that the illnesses might be related to hazardous exposures at the Reservation, he contacted ORO authorities to request a list of his patients' most likely exposures. Reid tested and treated his patients for conditions such as heavy metal poisoning. He described his patients' predicaments to us:

> Their symptoms are so vague that they just get written off. All the flags are up that would normally bring studies, bring clinical work. But they [ORO] have been about to kill anybody doing anything. Most of the people are dying long before they get cancer—of infections and other problems.

Although Reid's patients were gratified to receive sympathetic care that confirmed their own suspicions, his peers retaliated by discrediting him. They publicly vilified him as a drug addict and a medical incompetent, subjected him to a punitive peer review, suspended his hospital privileges, and warned at least one of his staff members that if she continued to work for Reid, she would never find employment again in the county. Reid was eventually vindicated in the peer review, but the subsidiary refused to renew his contract, and he was forced to leave Oak Ridge.

When workers were informed of abnormal medical test results, they were frequently blamed for their own symptoms by Reservation and contract physicians who attributed the negative results to workers' personal habits rather than occupational exposures. A materials handler applying for disability followed instructions to retrieve her medical records from her physician and deliver them to X-10's medical department. She described her exchange with the department's head:

> When I took them the medical results, he said, "Some of these are just a little bit out and—I tell you—heavy drinking can cause these tests to be abnormal." I told him that I don't drink. He said, "I'm just saying, heavy drinking on the weekends can cause these tests to be abnormal." I told him, I don't drink period! He said, "I'm just saying, heavy drinking can cause these test results. We have a lot of information, but not enough data we need more data!" He said it three times!

Many workers reported that their physicians summarily dismissed their questions about possible links between their illnesses and occupational exposures and treated them instead for depression and similar emotional disorders. A worker said quietly: "A lot of doctors don't believe me. It's like—'This guy is crazy! There's nothing wrong with him.' I've actually had the doctors label me psycho—'He's crazy!'" . . .

Discussion and Conclusions

Risk societies are characterized by multiple contradictions and by a lopsided concentration of power. They produce unprecedented wealth but pose known unique hazards. They rely on the logic of science yet hold scientists captive to organizational and production goals. Risk societies are fueled by the informed, private determination of risks whose consequences are borne by the uninformed public. Power in risk societies is concentrated in the same institutions and organizations that reap the greatest rewards from the system: risk authorities retain the power to define risks, direct production technologies, control the dissemination of both scientific knowledge and personal data, and perpetuate—even accelerate—the risk society. The implications of the risk society for less powerful social actors appear bleak. The public is involuntarily exposed to singularly hazardous substances about which they are deliberately kept ignorant. When inevitable illness claims point to the cause as the very wellsprings of the risk society's wealth, their claims are forcefully rejected. Workers are on the front lines of this relatively powerless, exposed, and uninformed public. They are the risk society's canary in the coal mine. . . .

Corporate management authorities, Reservation-employed physicians, and contract physicians contested workers' illness claims using a combination of their own and federal resources. Corporate management used information control in tactical denials that an individual had been exposed to a specific hazard, and to refuse a worker's access to health records maintained by the corporation. They wielded power in tactical reassignments of troublesome workers to unfavorable tasks. Illness claims could not be legitimated without accurate exposure and health records, leaving the cause-effect question open and the discourse focused on alternative causal factors. The threat of unfavorable task reassignments kept workers from publicizing procedural violations related to hazardous exposures and consequently barred such information from public discourse.

Reservation and contract physicians drew on their resources of expert knowledge and scientific authority. Science applies "a standards setting logic, with scientifically based risk analyses which do not answer the new questions" (Mol and Spaargaren 1993:441), but which do sustain a kind of scientific mystique. Reservation and contract physicians tactically employed the mantle of expert knowledge to discredit peers who were sympathetic to workers' illness claims. They applied scientific authority in the derogation of ill workers. Reservation physicians held the additional resource of their superior position in the work bureaucracy. From this position, they could make the tactical decision not to inform workers of the results of their medical tests, denying critical information to ill workers.

Reservation authorities used their considerable powers to hide the truth about hazardous exposures, and they invoked the mystique of science to hide the truth in plain sight. The consequences were significant for exposed workers—life-threatening illnesses that might have been avoided—but the consequences for democratic society are even more profound. The exploitation of authority to cloak knowledge of hazardous exposures with the robes of national security directly challenges democratic processes. Indeed, and despite the obvious contributions of our analyses to sociological scholarship on environment, illness, and workplace power dynamics, discursive containment goes far beyond nuclear matters—it is a feature of the risk society in general, not to mention a form of social control that violates democratic principles.

Curtailing public discourse bars citizens from deciding whether a specific risk is acceptable. It excludes citizens from participation in decision-making processes that impact their lives. It prevents the opportunity for an open democratic debate on the costs and benefits of risky technologies. Risk society and democracy, we believe, cannot coexist indefinitely. Cohen (1997) concurs, and envisions two possibilities for the future: democracy's demise or democracy's revitalization. Democracy's demise would occur with increasing reliance on risky production technologies and the global spread of risk societies, causing continued detonation of toxic time-bombs. In this scenario, ever larger segments of the population become ill, and authorities escalate social control tactics to deny illnesses related to risky production materials. Increasingly harsh social control erodes individual rights and alienates citizens until "democratic governance slips away" (Cohen 1997:108). In the revitalization of democracy scenario, in contrast, technical knowledge is shared and interpreted. Public debate on issues of significant social import is encouraged, generating "the possibility for the lay public to gain control over its technology" (Cohen 1997:108). With access to accurate information and open discourse to assess risks, citizens decide which risks they will not accept and can protect themselves from the risks they deem acceptable. . . .

With so much at stake, sociological investigations of contested illness claims, the power dynamics that undergird them, and the complex and changing nature of the risk society are critical.

Note

Cable, Sherry, Thomas E. Chriver, and Tamara L. Mix. Excerpt from "Risk Society and Contested Illness: The Case of Nuclear Weapons Works." *American Sociological Review*. Reprinted by permission of Sage Publications.

References

Beck, Ulrich. 1992. *Risk Society: Towards a New Modernity*. London, UK: Sage.
———. 1995. *Ecological Enlightenment: Essays on the Politics of the Risk Society*. Atlantic Highlands, NJ: Humanities Press.

——. 1996. "Risk Society and the Provident State." Pp. 27–43 in *Risk, Environment and Modernity: Towards a New Ecology*, edited by S. Lash, B. Szerszynski, and B. Wynne. London, UK: Sage.

Brown, Phil, Stephen Zavestoski, Meadow Linder, Sabrina McCormick, and Brian Mayer. 2003. "Chemicals and Casualties: The Search for Causes of Gulf War Illnesses." Pp. 213–36 in *Synthetic Planet: Chemical Politics and the Hazards of Modern Life*, edited by M. Casper. New York: Routledge.

Bullard, Robert D. 2000. *Dumping in Dixie: Race, Class, and Environmental Quality*. Boulder, CO: Westview Press.

Cable, Sherry and Charles Cable. 1995. *Environmental Problems/Grassroots Solutions: The Politics of Environmental Conflict*. New York: St. Martin's Press.

Cable, Sherry, Donald W. Hastings, and Tamara L. Mix. 2002. "Different Voices, Different Venues: Environmental Racism Claims by Activists, Researchers and Lawyers." *Human Ecology Review* 9:26–42.

Cable, Sherry, Thomas E. Shriver, and Donald W. Hastings. 1999. "The Silenced Majority: Quiescence and Government Social Control on the Oak Ridge Nuclear Reservation." *Research in Social Problems and Public Policy* 7:59–81.

Cohen, Maurie J. 1997. "Risk Society and Ecological Modernisation." *Futures* 29(2): 105–19.

Cole, Luke W. and Sheila R. Foster. 2001. *From the Ground Up: Environmental Racism and the Rise of the Environmental Justice Movement*. New York: New York University Press.

Commoner, Barry. 1972. *The Closing Circle*. New York: Bantam Books.

Daniels, Arlene K. 1969. "The Captive Professional: Bureaucratic Limitations in the Practice of Military Psychiatry." *Journal of Health and Social Behavior* 10(4):255–63.

Eder, Klaus. 1996. *The Social Construction of Nature: A Sociology of Ecological Enlightenment*. London, UK: Sage.

Ehrlich, Anne H. and John W. Birks. 1990. *Hidden Dangers: Environmental Consequences of Preparing for War*. San Francisco, CA: Sierra Club Books.

Freudenburg, William R. 1993. "Risk and Recreancy: Weber, the Division of Labor, and the Rationality of Risk Perceptions." *Social Forces* 71:909–32.

Gare, Arran E. 1995. *Postmodernism and the Environmental Crisis*. London, UK: Routledge.

Giddens, Anthony. 1990. *The Consequences of Modernity*. Stanford, CA: Stanford University Press.

——. 1991. *Modernity and Self Identity: Self and Society in the Late Modern Age*. Stanford, CA: Stanford University Press.

——. 1999. "The Transition to a Society in Late Modernity: A Conversation with Anthony Giddens." *Sociologica* 14:201–18.

Habermas, Jurgen. 2001. *The Postnational Constellation: Political Essays*. Cambridge, MA: MIT Press.

Jameson, Frederic. 1991. *Postmodernism; or, The Cultural Logic of Late Capitalism*. London, UK: Verso.

Kinsella, William J. 2001. "Nuclear Boundaries: Material and Discursive Containment at the Hanford Nuclear Reservation." *Science as Culture* 10:163–94.

Kinsella, William J. and Jay Mullen. 2007. "Becoming Hanford Downwinders: Producing Community and Challenging Discursive Containment." Pp. 73–107 in *Nuclear Legacies: Communication, Controversy, and the US Nuclear Weapons Complex*, edited by B. C. Taylor, W. J. Kinsella, S. P. Depoe, and M. S. Metzler. Lanham, MD: Lexington Books.

Mol, Authur P. J. and Gert Spaargaren. 1993. "Environment, Modernity and the Risk-Society: The Apocalyptic Horizon of Environmental Reform." *International Sociology* 8:431–59.

Nelkin, Dorothy and Michael S. Brown. 1984. "Observations on Workers' Perceptions of Risk in Dangerous Trades." *Science, Technology and Human Values* 9:3–10.

Rosenbloom, David H. 2003. *Administrative Law for Public Managers*. Boulder, CO: Westview Press.

Schnaiberg, Allan. 1980. *The Environment: From Surplus to Scarcity*. New York: Oxford University Press.

Smyth, Henry DeWolf. 1945. "Atomic Energy for Military Purposes (The Smyth Report): The Official Report on the Development of the Atomic Bomb Under the Auspices of the United States Government." Washington, DC: National Science Digital Library. Retrieved August 18, 2007 (www.atomicarchive.com/Docs/SniythReport/index .shtml).

Stimson, Henry. 1945. Henry Lewis Stimson Papers. (Diaries and papers from reel 9 of the diary and reels 113 and 128 of the papers.) New Haven, CT: Yale University Library Manuscripts and Archives. Retrieved August 18, 2007 (www.library. yale. edu/un/papers/stimson.htm). Quoted from (www.doug-long.com/stimson.htm).

Thomas, Susan, Laura Frank, and Anne Paine. 1997. "Contamination Even Worse Than Feared." *The Tennessean*, August 17, p. A1.

Udall, Stewart L. 1994. *The Myths of August: A Personal Exploration of Our Tragic Cold War Love Affair with the Atom*. New York: Pantheon.

United States Senate Commission on Protecting and Reducing Government Secrecy. 1997. *Final Report of the Commission on Protecting and Reducing Government Secrecy*. Washington, DC: United States Government Printing Office. Retrieved August 18, 2007 (www.gpo.gov/ congress/commissions/secrecy/index.html).

Vyner, Henry M. 1988. *Invisible Trauma: The Psychological Effects of Invisible Environmental Contaminants*. Lexington, MA: Lexington Books.

Zavestoski, Stephen, Phil Brown, Meadow Linder, Sabrina McCormick, and Brian Mayer. 2002. "Science, Policy, Activism, and War: Defining the Health of Gulf War Veterans." *Science Technology, and Human Values* 27:171–205.

The Knowledge-Shaping Process
Elite Mobilization and Environmental Policy
Eric Bonds

Sociologists emphasize that knowledge, including scientific knowledge, is produced within social structures. Eric Bonds argues that, in order to influence environmental policy, military and corporate elites in the United States worked to shape what the public knew about a chemical used in rockets, ammonium perchlorate. They used four strategies: suppressing information; organizing and funding institutions to produce research helpful to their own goals; attacking or discrediting potentially damaging research; and attempting to influence what information got counted as knowledge and what did not.

Elite Political Mobilization and Environmental Policy

. . . Power structure research is a sociological perspective holding that the corporate wealthy exercise a disproportionate influence in public policy-making; in other words they constitute a power elite (Domhoff, 2006; Dye, 2001; Useem, 1984). Elite dominance, however, does not come automatically; it is not simply "built in" to the state. Rather, elites must continuously mobilize in order to exercise the power needed to enact the policies that best suit their interests (Domhoff, 1990).

Domhoff (2006) argues that elites organize four different power networks in order to influence state policy-making:

1. *The special-interest process*, in which specific corporations and specific business sectors formulate policy proposals and attempt to implement them by lobbying legislative assemblies and by colluding with executive agencies.
2. *The policy-planning process*, in which the general interests of the corporate community are formulated in think tanks. Policy proposals, once formulated, are brought to the attention of the White House and high-ranking congressional committees. They are also broadly disseminated through high-status newspapers and magazines.
3. *The candidate-selection process*, in which the corporate community influences the selection of political candidates most sympathetic to its needs and wants.
4. *The opinion-shaping process*, in which corporations utilize public relations techniques to influence public opinion in ways that promote corporate interests.

By organizing and channeling resources through these networks, elites influence environmental policy. But Domhoff's typology of power networks is not comprehensive. Environmental policy is also likely influenced by a fifth process proposed in this article, *the knowledge-shaping process*, which is similar to and closely interrelated with the power networks identified by Domhoff. In the knowledge-shaping process, elites actively work to influence what is known about a particular subject in an effort to achieve their policy goals. Environmental science, from this perspective, is not a pure reflection of a biophysical world that is separate and distinct from environmental politics. Rather, environmental science and environmental politics are co-produced (Forsyth, 2003). For this reason, environmental knowledge is often a political contest, one into which elites may allocate substantial resources and often prevail.

The knowledge-shaping process involves four distinct exercises of power:

1. *Information suppression*, in which elites purposively act to suppress knowledge damaging to their interests.
2. *Contesting knowledge*, in which elites fund experts to attack and disqualify knowledge that poses a threat to their power base. Elites may also fund diversionary efforts attacking those who have produced or who uphold potentially 'damaging' knowledge (Freudenburg, 2005a; Freudenburg and Alario, 2007).

3. *Knowledge production,* in which elites fund or otherwise promote the production of particular knowledges, either through peer-reviewed scientific research or governmentally administered through tests and analyses.
4. *Knowledge administration,* in which elites influence the selection of what information counts as knowledge and what information does not count.

In this article I present evidence of an elite knowledge-shaping process in a case study regarding the policy debate over rocket fuel contamination.

An Introduction to the Case and its Analysis

The US military and the corporations that manufacture its weapons and provide military services are connected through self-reinforcing relationships of mutual dependence, creating a network of organizations called the military-industrial complex.[1] This network of organizations is capable of exerting major influence on US policy-making. There is a great deal of evidence, for instance, that its constituents play a role determining US foreign policy (Boise, 1994; Cook, 1962; Johnson, 2004; Klein, 2007). So one might then safely make the inference that the military-industrial complex likewise plays a role in determining other national policies, including US environmental policy.

The following case constructed around the policy debate over rocket fuel contamination indicates as much: elites can mobilize substantial resources to determine US environmental policy. The chemical of concern is ammonium perchlorate, both a natural and a manufactured chemical that is the primary constituent of solid rocket fuel. According to the US Environmental Protection Agency (EPA), 'wastes from the manufacture and improper disposal of perchlorate-containing chemicals are increasingly being discovered in soil and water' (EPA, 2007: 1). There have been, according to the EPA (2007), at least 25 *confirmed* releases of the chemical in the USA into ground and surface waters. But the total amount of perchlorate released is likely much more because, according to the EPA (2002b: 37), perchlorate has a 'shelf life' as a rocket fuel, and so 'must be washed out of the USA's missile and rocket inventory to be replaced with a fresh supply. Thus, large volumes have been disposed of in various states since the 1950s.'

Perchlorate is a common contaminant throughout the USA. According to a report by the National Research Council of the National Academies' Committee to Assess the Health Implications of Perchlorate Ingestion, perchlorate exists in the drinking water of at least 11 million people (NRC, 2005). Further, perchlorate has been measured in Lake Mead and the Colorado River system, water from which is drawn to irrigate much of America's supply of winter lettuce (Sharp and Lunder, 2003); this is of potential concern because lettuce concentrates perchlorate taken from irrigation water. A US Food and Drug Administration (FDA) survey found perchlorate in 123 of 137 samples of lettuce taken from different locations in the Southwest (FDA, 2007a). The FDA, however, assures the public that the amount of perchlorate in winter lettuce is, as a whole, below limits established to protect human health (FDA, 2007b). But just how much perchlorate, or rocket fuel, can a person ingest without harm? This question has been a matter of intense scientific *and* political debate in the past decade.

This much is agreed upon: in the human body, perchlorate, in sufficient levels, disrupts the intake of iodine by the thyroid gland and influences the production of thyroid hormones (FDA, 2007a). How much perchlorate is needed to produce this effect within different bodies (for instance in a healthy male compared to a newborn, a pregnant woman, or a person with a thyroid abnormality or iodine deficiency) has been a matter of intense dispute. The US Department of Defense (DoD) and various corporate manufacturers and users of perchlorate have been particularly important players in this conflict.

In order to chart the ways these players exercised power to influence the outcome of the policy debate over perchlorate contamination, I constructed a case study using archival data (including websites, official documents, and news stories),[2] which is a method often employed by power structure researchers (see for instance Domhoff, 1990, 1996; Gendron and Domhoff, 2008). I collected data regarding the perchlorate policy debate in order to 'make sense' of it, utilizing inductive logic while drawing from power structure research and environmental sociology. In doing so, I employed a straightforward methodology in which I determined the goals of elites, in this case officials of the corporations that manufacture weapons and officials working in the Department of Defense. I ascertained what these goals were, following Domhoff (1996), through content analysis of my data. I then sought to determine whether or not these elites were able to achieve their goals (Domhoff, 1996). I further worked to discover the *how* of power (Flyvbjerg, 2001), in other words the ways elites organize themselves and the techniques they employ to achieve their goals. Based on this analysis, I wrote a narrative of the case within which I interwove an analysis of power, as advocated by Flyvbjerg (1999, 2001). The study is intended as a 'paradigmatic case', that is a case particularly useful to the development and illustration of concepts that may be helpful to other social scientists and citizens to understand the world in which we live (Flyvbjerg, 2001). I chose to start the narrative in the 1950s, with the first large-scale disposal of perchlorate, and chose to end it in 2005, when the EPA declared a final 'reference dose' for perchlorate, which is a 'safe' measure of daily ingestion.

Throughout this process, I treat scientific knowledge as a social construction. I do *not* wish to claim that there is no biophysical world 'out there', or that it does not conform to knowable and discoverable laws. My point is simply that our comprehension of this world is imperfect and always incomplete and that, as humans, our ways of knowing are influenced by the organization of the society in which we live.

During the course of this article, I report a number of 'reference doses' for perchlorate, or amounts of perchlorate the EPA has determined are safe for daily ingestion. These reference doses change over time, some being much higher than others. Each reference dose is, in effect, a truth claim: a claim that such and such amount of perchlorate, ingested daily, does not pose a significant risk to the well-being of Americans. As a social scientist I cannot speak to which of these claims is the closest approximation of reality, and for this reason make no attempt to do so. My goal is less ambitious: I attempt to demonstrate that elites associated with the military-industrial complex organized a network and mobilized resources that influenced the course of the EPA's policy-making, or, in other words, influenced the final reference dose the EPA settled on.

Secrecy as a Dimension of Power

This case best begins in the 1950s, when the US military began using tremendous amounts of perchlorate in explosives and as a major constituent of solid rocket fuel. For several decades, waste perchlorate was disposed of when it was dissolved in water and then poured out onto the ground or into waterways. At the time, military officials did not believe that, when ingested in small amounts, it posed a public health risk (Lee, 2004). The American public, given the chance, might have believed differently. While the environmental consciousness of Americans was very different during the 1950s, 1960s, and even 1970s than it is today, some amount of awareness did exist that human-manufactured chemicals may pose health risks and so cannot be released untreated into the nation's ground and surface waters without environmental consequences (Carson, 2002 [1962]; Gottlieb, 2005). The military, however, did not allow the American public to exercise its developing environmental consciousness in relation to perchlorate. It instead exercised secrecy and kept the public ignorant of its rocket fuel disposal practices. In this way, we can see that ignorance about threats to the biophysical world is not something that just happens to organizations or publics in modern industrial societies. It is an achievement and a direct outcome of existing social relations (Bonds, 2007; Flyvbjerg, 1999).

To Boyce (2002), agenda power is an important dimension of environmental inequality. It is the ability to determine which issues enter into public policy debates and which do not, or in other words, it contributes to the 'non-problemicity' of environmental degradation, something of growing concern to environmental sociologists (see Freudenburg, 2005a; McCright and Dunlap,

2003). Secrecy, as here practiced by the military, is an important way elites exercise agenda power to keep knowledge that challenges elite interests out of the public sphere and to avoid the social construction of environmental problems that may pose challenges to the status quo. This is, according to Freudenburg and Alario (2007: 146), part of 'the dark side of legitimation, which depends heavily on evading attention'. Importantly, elite power, exercised here through secrecy, prevented any attempts to rectify past mishandling of perchlorate from emerging for several decades.

The Department of Defense has not abandoned secrecy as an exercise of power since the era of perchlorate dumping. In 2000, the EPA asked the DoD to test all groundwater beneath its bases for perchlorate. In 2002, the DoD prepared standards for testing. In 2003, upon direction from the White House, the Department then made a determination to forgo such tests, claiming that they would be unnecessary and too costly (Waldman, 2003a). When releasing the new policy, the Undersecretary of Defense for the Environment told reporters 'testing is something we should do, and probably will do eventually, but it's a question of priorities' (quoted in Waldman, 2003a). To this day, the Department of Defense has practiced secrecy regarding the extent of perchlorate contamination of groundwater at bases by refusing to conduct a comprehensive survey.

Constructing the Problem of Rocket Fuel Contamination

Despite the Department of Defense's secrecy, the issue of perchlorate was eventually brought to the public's attention and carried into public policy debates by the EPA and civil society groups. In the early 1980s, the Agency identified perchlorate in municipal drinking water sources and classified it as a potential contaminant. In 1992, the EPA declared it a probable danger to human health and set a provisional 'safe dose' at 3.5 parts per billion (Madsen and Jahagirdar, 2006). Native American tribes utilizing Colorado River water to irrigate lettuce fields were among the first civil society groups to express concern, calling on the EPA to study the potential health effects of perchlorate on food crops (Sharp and Lunder, 2003). At an 'eco-summit' organized by the EPA in 1999 in response to Native American concerns—which was attended by five tribes, several major manufacturers and corporate users of perchlorate, and the Air Force—representatives of the DoD pledged $650,000 to evaluate environmental risks posed by the use of perchlorate-contaminated irrigation water (Sharp and Lunder, 2003).

Though the Department of Defense never carried out this research, in this sense again actively choosing not to know potentially damaging information, the EPA continued to pursue the issue. In 1999 the Agency made a decision to list perchlorate under its Unregulated Contaminants Monitoring Rule to gather evidence about the effects of exposure, to gather evidence about the extent to which perchlorate is present in public drinking water systems, and to begin a formal process determining whether or not the contaminant should be regulated (EPA, 2007).

Environmental groups also played a role in the EPA's policy-making process, demonstrating that environmental science and decision-making is a contested arena in which competing actors work to influence what is known about particular topics and what such knowledges should mean. These organizations educated the public about perchlorate contamination and worked to pressure the EPA to impose strict regulations. The Environmental Working Group, an independent non-profit organization, played an especially important role when it paid University of Texas researchers to sample lettuce and spinach from grocery store shelves; the researchers did indeed find perchlorate in 18 percent of the food they tested (Sharp and Lunder, 2003). The study made headlines around the country and put further pressure on the EPA and the Food and Drug Administration to protect public health from the contaminant. Meanwhile, weapons-making corporations and the Department of Defense were organizing on this issue to make the task of regulating perchlorate more difficult, if not politically impossible for the time being.

The Beginnings of a Knowledge-Shaping Network

Soon after the EPA took notice of perchlorate contamination, the Department of Defense, weapons-makers using perchlorate, and perchlorate manufacturers established the Perchlorate Study Group[3] (Madsen and Jahagirdar, 2006). The Perchlorate Study Group is, in its own words, 'a coalition of aerospace, defense, chemical, and allied industries', which includes Lockheed Martin, Aerojet, and the chemical manufacturer Kerr-McGee. The Perchlorate Study Group was not incorporated as an official non-profit organization, but rather, records indicate, more of an informal way to funnel resources toward scientific research, public relations, and policy influence (Madsen and Jahagirdar, 2006).

In the words of its founders, the Perchlorate Study Group was created to work 'cooperatively with the US Environmental Protection Agency to increase scientific and medical understanding of perchlorate's risk to human health' (Council on Water Quality, 2008). The evidence stands, however, to the contrary; all evidence points to a very hostile relationship between the Perchlorate Study Group and the EPA.

What, exactly, these goals are becomes readily apparent by considering the Perchlorate Study Group's earliest efforts. In 1995, the Perchlorate Study Group advocated a 'safe level' of perchlorate at 42,000 parts per billion (Beeman and Danelski, 2004). This proposed level was astronomically higher than the EPA's proposed level of less than 4 parts per billion. The Perchlorate Study

Group, along with scientists and officials at the DoD, later came to advocate a 'safe dose' of perchlorate at 200 parts per billion. Both recommendations would exempt the Department of Defense and perchlorate manufacturers and users from a great deal of liability regarding clean up, as most perchlorate levels that exist in drinking water sources are between the levels of 4 and 100 parts per billion (Lee, 2004).

. . . In an attempt to avoid the environmental regulation of perchlorate, elites associated with the military-industrial complex created the Perchlorate Study Group as something similar to a think tank in the policy-planning process. Sociologists have produced a good deal of work examining the power of think tanks in public policy formation (Altheide and Grimes, 2005; Domhoff, 2006; McCright and Dunlap, 2003). The largest, most well known think tanks are funded by the corporate community to generate policy proposals for consideration by executive branches and legislative committees. They are also funded to attack and discredit policy proposals or existing governmental programs that do not serve the interests of the corporate community (Domhoff, 2006). Think tanks have in the past mobilized the resources of the corporate wealthy in order to achieve particular environmental policy outcomes; McCright and Dunlap (2003) for instance found that think tanks played an integral role in the defeat of the Kyoto Protocol in the USA. The Perchlorate Study Group is something similar to a think tank, but not quite the same. In the knowledge-shaping process such an organization is perhaps best called a 'science tank', in which I intend the militarized sense of the word; that is, a science tank is a vehicle that is built to attack and defend. Unlike think tanks, science tanks do not necessarily work publicly, but channel money surreptitiously behind the scenes. And unlike a think tank, its purpose is not so much to generate policy proposals, but to generate scientific research and fund experts, who attempt to appear unaffiliated, to produce particular knowledges and to contest competing claims. The Perchlorate Study Group is one such organization that fulfilled both roles.

Producing and Contesting Knowledge

. . . Between 1996 and 2005, the Perchlorate Study Group or its individual member companies funded at least 16 studies to assess the human health implications of perchlorate exposure, which were all peer-reviewed and published in scientific journals[4] (Madsen and Jahagirdar, 2006). By 2005, these studies accounted for more than half of all published works on the health impacts of perchlorate. While the Perchlorate Study Group states that it funded these studies to 'help' the EPA understand what the health impacts from perchlorate might be, such statements are misleading, or, at best, incomplete.

Corporations do not exist to help. Their purpose, as defined by their charters and necessitated by the social organization of capitalism, is to maximize profit for shareholders. The Perchlorate Study Group did not fund scientific research to 'help' the EPA, but—for better or worse, depending on one's perspective—to help its member corporations avoid regulation and liability.

... [T]he companies that manufacture and use perchlorate employ the research they have funded to make such public statements as: 'Data from human studies shows that low levels of perchlorate being detected in some drinking water supplies have no adverse health effects on adults, children and newborns' (PIB, 2009a). Similarly companies use this research when making other public statements such as: 'There is no evidence that minute levels of perchlorate pose any health risk to anyone. Credible, peer-reviewed science consistently shows no adverse health effects from perchlorate, which has actually been used as a medicine for more than 50 years' (PIB, 2009b).

Corporations seek out opportunities to fund helpful research that is publishable in peer-reviewed journals, for instance research that may assist corporations in efforts to avoid regulation or limit liability. When corporations do so, they almost always respect the professionalism of scientists; rarely would we expect them to urge researchers to falsify evidence or make unsupported claims. But this does not mean corporate funding does not produce biases within bodies of scientific knowledge. On the contrary, according to Freudenburg (2005b: 3), 'the corporation's most effective techniques of influence may have been provided not by overt pressure, but by encouraging scientists to continue thinking of themselves as independent and impartial'. Freudenburg (2005b) calls this 'seeding science' and 'courting conclusions'. Corporations seed science by providing incentives for researchers to study some particular phenomena out of the infinite milieu of possible research topics, which of course have particular relevance for the corporations involved. And corporations are, of course, not interested in giving this seed money to just any researcher, but to those whom they believe will study the particular topic from a perspective that is useful. Furthermore, to Freudenburg (2005b), corporations court conclusions when they express a willingness to continue funding research as long as the results are helpful. Conclusions are further courted when corporate funders and researchers form professional and congenial relationships with one another, such that researchers may unintentionally anticipate the needs of corporate funders and so feel uncomfortable when results are produced that let friends and colleagues down (Freudenburg, 2005b).

Industry funding of perchlorate research introduced such biases into the body of knowledge regarding the potential human health risks of the contaminant. According to two environmental advocates, the studies funded by the Perchlorate Study Group had designs ill-suited for determining whether or not perchlorate posed a health risk to the American public (Madsen and Jahagirdar, 2006). These advocates note, for example, that some of the studies used very small sample sizes, which makes establishing statistically significant differences more difficult. Officials at the Environmental Protection Agency found industry research lacking for different reasons. In the Agency's 2002 Draft Risk Assessment, its authors stated that no research had been done regarding perchlorate's potential effect on the neurological development of fetuses, infants, or effects on persons with thyroid deficiencies, which are all groups considered more vulnerable to perchlorate contamination (EPA, 2002b). It is for this reason, the Agency stated, that it was proposing a more stringent recommendation based on its review of available scientific information. In its draft review, the Agency proposed a 'reference dose', or a safe daily allowance, of 1 part per billion (EPA, 2002b), a standard lower than its earlier proposal of 3.5 parts per billion.

The experts at the Department of Defense and experts funded by the Perchlorate Study Group, while working simultaneously to produce 'helpful' scientific research, also began work to contest and discredit the EPA's Draft Risk Assessment. Freudenburg et al. (2008) report a long history of corporate efforts to cast doubt upon scientific knowledge in order to reduce liability and/or thwart increased governmental regulation. Corporations often utilize a technique these authors call SCAMS—or scientific certainty argumentation methods—to exploit the uncertainty necessarily part of the scientific method (Freudenburg et al., 2008). The Perchlorate Study Group also used this tactic. It hired the public relations firm APCO Worldwide, which formerly had managed the Philip Morris campaign to avoid health-related tobacco liability, and formed the Council on Water Quality to publicly downplay potential risks associated with perchlorate (Madsen and Jahagirdar, 2006). Other governmental organizations took a more direct approach in efforts to discredit the EPA's work (Waldman, 2003b). For instance, a US Air Force colonel told the press, 'We have reviewed the EPA risk assessment, and we think the document is biased, unrealistic and scientifically imbalanced', while a NASA official, also a major user of perchlorate, told the press, 'We do not believe the EPA has used good science' (Reported in Lee, 2004).

But the DoD and the Perchlorate Study Group went beyond working to downplay potential risks and to discredit the EPA's assessment, they also began working to pressure the White House to intervene and take the decision of a final reference dose away from the EPA. In 2003, the Perchlorate Study Group paid lobbyists to advocate that the White House create a committee from the National Academy of Sciences to conduct a review of the literature and to propose a reference dose—as opposed to letting the EPA continue its own work towards these ends (Beeman and Danelski, 2004). Documents submitted in a response to a Freedom of Information Act request from the Natural Resources Defense Council (NRDC) reveal that representatives from Lockheed Martin and the Department of Defense met with White House officials during this time to discuss perchlorate, though the White House refused to disclose the actual content of the discussions (NRDC, 2005). It seems the weapons manufacturers and the Department of Defense got what they wanted. In 2003 the George W. Bush administration intervened in the EPA's decision-making process and asked the National Academy of Sciences to instead conduct a review of the potential toxicity of perchlorate and to propose a reference dose (Beeman and Danelski, 2004).

This point brings the case to the fourth important dimension of power in the knowledge-shaping process, the administration of knowledge. Elites do not only organize networks and devote resources to fund 'helpful' research and to attack 'damaging' research, they also work to influence the selection of what counts as knowledge and what does not (Flyvbjerg, 1999). Scientific information and environmental data do not, after all, have a pure meaning. Its meaning, like the meaning of all objects in the human universe, is subject to a process of interpretation (Freudenburg and Gramling, 1994). Interpretation is often influenced by position within social structures, which means that *who* gets to interpret what counts and what does not count as scientific knowledge is a political battle fought between individuals and organizations of differing structural locations (Bonds, 2007). Elites organize to win the battle of science administration through lobbying efforts, funding decisions, and via personal and business relationships. The Perchlorate Study Group won this particular battle by convincing the White House to intercede and take decision-making powers away from officials at the EPA. Agency officials had not administered knowledge in ways deemed suitable to the military-industrial complex because they had discounted research funded by industry and relied instead on research that made threatening claims to the military and weapon industry's interests.

Beyond taking decision-making authority away from the EPA, the Bush administration White House took further steps to ensure that the science surrounding perchlorate would be administered in ways amenable to the military-industrial complex. Public documents requested under the Freedom of Information Act by the Natural Resources Defense Council indicate that the White House acted to influence the National Academy of Sciences' review. For instance, the documents indicate that officials from the White House, including the Director and other high ranking officials from the Office of Management and Budget, were involved in writing and editing the 'charge' for the Academy's review, which is a document that frames the issues to be addressed by the Academy's committee (NRDC, 2005). The extent to which the White House was involved in developing and editing the 'charge' cannot be determined because it refused to disclose such information to the public (NRDC, 2005). The public documents released also indicate that the White House influenced or at least sought to influence the selection of the Academy's committee members. The documents indicate that the White House held discussions to develop lists of potential candidates and to discuss 'selection dynamics' (NRDC, 2005). But here again, the extent to which the White House was involved in selecting the review committee's members cannot be clearly determined because the White House withheld this information from the public.[5] However, it may not be coincidence that two individuals appointed to the Committee, including its director, formerly worked as paid consultants to Lockheed Martin, a major perchlorate user and member of the Perchlorate Study Group (NRDC, 2005).

Elite Knowledge-Shaping

The EPA became fairly silent in the public policy debate surrounding perchlorate after the National Academy of Sciences took up its review. The Bush Administration had, in fact, imposed a gag rule prohibiting Agency officials from talking to reporters about perchlorate (Waldman, 2003c). The Perchlorate Study Group, however, was far from silent. Quite the contrary: the Study Group sought to influence the National Academy of Science's review process. The best example is a conference, entitled Perchlorate State-of-the-Science Symposium, held at the University of Nebraska's Medical Center. Though the University's involvement gave the symposium an air of authority and neutrality, it was largely paid for and organized by the Perchlorate Study Group.[6] The Group paid the University $75,000 for its involvement (Waldman, 2005). It also paid the private consulting firm Intertox $128,000 to plan the conference and use the Symposium's outcome for advocacy purposes (Madsen and Jahagirdar, 2006).

The Symposium's planning committee later wrote to the National Academy of Sciences review committee on perchlorate and stated that:

> The Perchlorate State-of-the-Science Symposium was designed to be an *independent and impartial* review of four fundamental science issues related to the potential risk from low-level exposure to perchlorate. Researchers who performed the most important recent studies published since 1999 were asked to present their work (Report of the Planning Committee, 2004, emphasis added).

There is good reason to doubt these claims of independence and impartiality. The framework of the symposium was arranged by the owner and director of Intertox, who billed the Perchlorate Study Group for his work. The owner and director of Intertox was also involved in selecting the presenting scientists, many of whose work was funded by the Perchlorate Study Group or its individual member corporations.[7] The planning committee, however, never disclosed this information to the National Academy's review committee (Waldman, 2005).

The Symposium held two sessions of note. In one session the presenters promoted the value of research conducted on healthy adult subjects that found perchlorate posed little health risk in small amounts. In another session, presenters, including one paid industry consultant, worked to discredit the research used by the EPA when it conducted its 2002 draft review (Waldman, 2005). The organizers of the conference then worked to communicate these proceedings, sending six Symposium participants to share their conclusions with the National Academy's committee, while also sending transcripts and a written report (Waldman, 2005).

It may well be that the National Academy's committee was listening. It gave industry, as well as the Department of Defense, much of what it wanted. In its review, the committee chose to give little weight to the studies utilized by the EPA when it proposed its more stringent 1 part per billion reference dose of perchlorate. It also chose to rely heavily on a study promoted at the industry symposium (Greer et al., 2002) and perhaps not incidentally funded in part by the Perchlorate Study Group (Madsen and Jahagirdar, 2006). In its report, the Committee proposed a reference dose of 24.5 parts per billion, more than 20 times higher than the 'safe' dose proposed by the EPA in 2002. In 2005, the EPA adopted the National Academy's proposal and designated a reference dose of perchlorate at 24.5 parts per billion.

Power Structure Research, Environmental Sociology, and the Knowledge-Shaping Process

In the aftermath of this policy debate, there is much evidence to indicate that military and corporate elites were able to achieve their interests. But their success was not unconditional. For instance, the EPA did end up adopting a reference dose for perchlorate much smaller than the 200 parts per billion standard advocated by industry and the military. And the states of California and Massachusetts have since designated their own standards, both well below that of the EPA's 2005 rule: Massachusetts set a standard at 2 parts per billion, while California implemented a standard at 6 parts per billion.

All the same, weapons manufacturing companies and the DoD did gain much in the sense that state standards often pose less of an imposition than federal standards, and the federal standard is much higher than it would have been without military and corporate involvement. Furthermore, the EPA has since ruled against regulating perchlorate, opting instead to keep it on its list of 'unregulated contaminants' indefinitely (Environmental Working Group, 2008), something surely in the interests of perchlorate-using corporations concerned about profitability, and also something in the interests of a military establishment that has a history of working to avoid regulation and citizen oversight. The military and industry were able to achieve these 'successes', I have argued, through organization and the allocation of resources.

The Knowledge-Shaping Process as a Power Network

Evidence in the case of the perchlorate policy debate supports the contention that elites can achieve major influence in state policies by creating and utilizing what I have termed knowledge-shaping processes. Elites first influence policy through secrecy by suppressing the production of knowledge that may disrupt profitable, even if environmentally harmful, behaviors. Weapons manufacturers and the Department of Defense suppressed information for decades about the widespread perchlorate contamination in America's water systems. Information suppression, however, is never a fail-safe plan to avoid liability or prevent increased regulation in complex industrial societies.

For this reason, elites organize themselves in networks (connecting mutually aligned corporations together along with scientific consulting firms, public relations firms, university researchers, and government decision-makers) to mobilize resources in order to shape what is known about a subject of concern. Elites begin to do so by forming and funding 'science tanks', or private affiliations that channel money to researchers who produce knowledge useful to elites. Elite-funded science tanks also channel money to experts who discredit or raise doubts about 'damaging' scientific research. This was the work of the Perchlorate Study Group.

Finally, elites work to influence policy outcomes through knowledge administration, or by influencing the selection of what counts as knowledge and what does not. This may be accomplished through lobbyists or through the personal and business relationships of elites themselves. It may be that such efforts are further augmented through past or promised campaign contributions or educational endowments. Perchlorate users and manufacturers were able to influence knowledge administration regarding the contaminant by convincing the Bush Administration to take decision-making authority away from the EPA and granting it instead to a National Academy of Sciences committee, the charge for which it sought to influence and the members of which it likely helped select.

The question, however, may justifiably be asked whether or not this is a distinct power network, or if it should be considered something akin to other power networks identified by Domhoff (2006) that are created and utilized by elites, in particular the opinion-shaping process or the special-interest process. Undoubtedly there are important overlaps and similarities; there is likely no absolute defining line between the types. However, there are also important enough differences that warrant speaking about the power network described in this article as something distinct.

There are clear similarities between the opinion-shaping process—as defined by Domhoff (2006)—and the knowledge-shaping process in that both are power networks created to mobilize elite resources toward the production of legitimacy. The kinds of legitimacy they produce, and the means of producing it, however, are very different. In the opinion-shaping process, corporations work through public relations and advertising firms to influence broad publics such as consumers and potential voters. By so doing, they achieve an important type of influence and are often able to maintain the status quo. But legitimation through opinion shaping has its limitations. Publics often prove unwilling to be 'educated' about pollution, typically preferring less than more. One can imagine, for instance, the difficulties the weapons industry would face if it needed to sway American public opinion toward an acceptance of rocket fuel contamination in their water and food.

For these corporations, however, public opinion often has little to do with their everyday operations. The need for legitimation has not gone away, but today it is often achieved via different mechanisms. Facing the losing prospect of trying to convince potentially skeptical publics of accepting the imposition of environmental risks, corporations and state officials sought instead to depersonalize and depoliticize their behaviors, to take such proposals out of normative public debates—and in many ways out of view altogether—by cloaking them in scientific/economic rationality (Thorpe, 2007). While doing so gave corporations and state actors some freedom from the potential constraints of public opinion, it did not make environmental legitimation automatic.

Corporations and state actors faced new constraints and challenges, which explains the need for knowledge-shaping networks. The first constraint is that the utilization of scientific/economic rationality means that environmental decision-making must have at least some accord with evidence—that decisions must not be 'arbitrary and capricious' in the parlance of environmental law— and the evidence itself must have some accord with the biophysical world. A second important constraint is that, when corporations and state actors sought to legitimate environmental actions in scientific/economic rationality, they did not simply eliminate political conflicts; rather, they inadvertently transformed them. Science, environmental science in particular, has since become an important political arena. Environmentalists and other civil society groups also work in this arena, attempting to produce and contest particular knowledges in order to achieve their goals; recall for instance the Environmental Working Group's survey of perchlorate in lettuce and spinach that first attracted widespread attention to the issue of perchlorate contamination. And environmentalists and public health advocates have won important political victories, creating frameworks for environmental decision-making that impose real limitations on corporate and state agencies, even if these decision-making processes favor corporations as a whole (Schnaiberg, 1980).

Taken together, these constraints and conflicts in environmental legitimation explain why corporations and state agency officials need to create power networks, here called knowledge-shaping processes, in order to best secure their desired ends. This also helps explain the particular outcome of the perchlorate policy debate: while the weapons industry and the Pentagon were able to achieve state policies that for the most part protected their interests, they were not able to win everything they sought to achieve.

The importance of scientific/economic rationality for legitimation, along with its associated challenges and constraints, also indicates why knowledge-shaping networks are best thought of as something distinct from the special-interest process identified by Domhoff (2006), in which corporations from particular sectors of the economy secure their interests through lobbying, collusion with executive offices, etc. The knowledge-shaping process is something very similar, in that it was likely through overtly political action that the military and the weapons industry was able to take decision-making authority away from the EPA and, in the end, have a gag rule imposed on the Agency regarding the issue of perchlorate. This was just one side, however, of the power network utilized by the military-industrial complex to achieve a favorable policy regarding rocket fuel contamination. The other side included a network of weapons manufacturers willing to pool funds for research, public and private researchers, a university medical center willing to play host to industry-funded research, an environmental consulting firm, and a public relations firm. Taken together, this network is best called a knowledge-shaping process.

Whether or not the knowledge-shaping process is truly something distinct from the special-interest and opinion-shaping processes, and whether or not it is a useful concept at all, will be borne out by future research, or the lack thereof. Other potential knowledge-shaping networks that might be of interest include such organizations as The Bell Institute of Health and Nutrition, which is funded by General Mills—a maker of high sugar, high fat foods marketed to children—in order to 'contribute to research on whole grains, micronutrients and breakfast, and publish research and scientific articles in leading peer-reviewed journals' (Bell Institute, 2008; see also Simon, 2006). Another potential knowledge-shaping network that may be of interest is that organized and funded by manufacturers of bromine-related flame retardants, represented by the Bromine Science and Environmental Forum, which is 'committed to improving the scientific understanding of bromine products and will commission independent research in this area and share the results with the public' (Bromine Science, 2008). And researchers may want to consider environmental review processes, as required by the National Environmental Policy Act, as state-facilitated knowledge-shaping processes. Further research is also needed to better understand the various constituents of knowledge-shaping networks, for instance to what extent public universities and university researchers are involved in the production of knowledge driven by elites. The more sociologists study and build a public awareness of the ways elites influence environmental policy outcomes, including that achieved through knowledge-shaping, the more able we will be to increase democracy in public policy-making and the more likely we will be to secure increased environmental protection.

Notes

Bonds, Eric. 2010. " The Knowledge-Shaping Process: Elite Mobilization and Environmental Policy." Critical Sociology 37(4): 429–446.

1. The phrase 'military-industrial complex' is widely attributed to President Dwight D. Eisenhower, who in his 1961 farewell speech warned the public of its 'unwarranted influence' in US policy-making. The speech can be read at: http://mcadams.posc .mu.edu/ike.htm (consulted 24 September 2010).

2. The author wishes to acknowledge the important investigative work done by the Environmental Working Group, the Environment California Research and Policy Center, the Natural Resources Defense Council, and the work done by Peter Waldman for the *Wall Street Journal*. Without these efforts, the author and the public as a whole would know much less about perchlorate contamination and the military's and industry's involvement in the policy debate over its regulation.

3. In 2009 the Perchlorate Study Group reorganized itself and now calls itself the 'Perchlorate Information Bureau' (PIB). Its website can be viewed at: www.perch lorateinformationbureau.org.

4. In one notable study, Lockheed Martin paid 100 volunteers $1,000 each to ingest perchlorate—in other words rocket fuel—for 14 days. The study was approved by the Institutional Review Boards of both Loma Linda University and Boston University. . . .

5. In 2003 and 2004, the Natural Resources Defense Council submitted several Freedom of Information Act requests to the White House, requesting any documentation of White House involvement with the Academy's perchlorate review. The White House ignored the requests. The NRDC then sued the White House and a federal court demanded that the White House respond. The Bush Administration did not respond substantively by releasing all such documentation, but instead sent NRDC a description of thousands of documents it was either choosing to withhold or redact—in other words black out (NRDC, 2005). These descriptions of documents provide strong evidence that the White House acted to influence the development of the Academy's charge and to influence the selection of committee members. If the White House was not involved, it might disclose documents concerning discussions over the issue of perchlorate to the public as proof. One can only speculate why, instead, the White House chooses to withhold these documents.

6. The conference website, for instance, displayed the University of Nebraska Medical Center's logo at the top of each page. The website listed the Air Force, Army, Navy, and Department of Defense as co-sponsors, which is fair because these organizations contributed resources. However, the website did not list the Perchlorate Study Group, which footed at least half of the bill for the event, as a co-sponsor (Waldman, 2005).

7. In fact, the owner and director of Intertox selected himself as a presenter.

References

Altheide D. and Grimes J. (2005) War programming: the propaganda project and the Iraq war. *The Sociological Quarterly* 46(4): 617–643.

Beeman D. and Danelski D. (2004) Perchlorate: cost, risks fuel debate over safety; impact on health weighed against billions for clean up. *The Press-Enterprise.* 19 December, p. A1.

Bell Institute (2008) *About Us. General Mills Bell Institute of Health and Nutrition.* Available (consulted 4 April 2008) at: http://www.bellinstitute.com/bihn/about_us/index.aspx?cat_1=28

Boise J. (1994) *Buying for Armageddon: Business, Society, and Military Spending since the Cuban Missile Crisis.* New Brunswick, NJ: Rutgers University Press.

Bonds E. (2007) Environmental review as battleground: corporate power, government collusion, and citizen opposition to a tire-burning power plant in rural Minnesota, U.S.A. *Organization and Environment* 20(2): 157–176.

Boyce J. (2002) *The Political Economy of the Environment.* Northampton, MA: Elgar.

Bromine Science (2008) *BSEF and its Scientific Program.* Bromine Science and Environmental. Available (consulted 30 April 2008) at: http://www.bsef.com/env_health/bsef_science/

Buttel F. (2000) Ecological modernization as social theory. *Geoforum* 31(1): 57–65.

Carson R. (2002 [1962]) *Silent Spring.* New York, NY: Houghton Mifflin.

Cook F.J. (1962) *The Warfare State.* New York, NY: Macmillan.

Council on Water Quality (2008) *The History of Perchlorate: Evolving Science, Technologies and Regulations.* Available (consulted 9 January 2008) at: http://www.councilonwaterquality.org/science/history.html

Domhoff G.W. (1990) *The Power Elite and the State: How Policy Is Made in America.* New York, NY: Aldine de Gruyter.

Domhoff G.W. (1996) *State Autonomy of Class Dominance?* New York, NY: Aldine de Gruyter.

Domhoff G.W. (2006) *Who Rules America? Power and Politics, and Social Change.* Boston, MA: McGraw-Hill.

Downy L. and Strife S. (2010) Inequality, democracy, and the environment. *Organization and Environment* 23(2): 155–188.

Durant R.F. (2007) *The Greening of the U.S. Military: Environmental Policy, National Security, and Organizational Change.* Washington, DC: Georgetown University Press.

Dye T. (2001) *Top Down Policymaking.* New York, NY: Chatham House Publishers.

Environmental Working Group (2008) *Last Minute Mischief: EPA Employed Suspect Chemical Industry Lab to Declare Perchlorate Safe.* Available (consulted 13 May 2009) at: http://www.ewg.org/node/27352

EPA (2002a) *Peer Review Workshop on EPA's Draft External Review Document 'Perchlorate Environmental Contamination: Toxicological Review and Risk Characterization'.* Available (consulted 7 July 2009) at: http://cfpub.epa.gov/si/si_public_record_report.cfm?dirEntryId=51762

EPA (2002b) *Perchlorate Environmental Contamination: Toxicological Review and Risk Characterization.* Washington, DC: US Environmental Protection Agency.

EPA (2007) *Perchlorate.* US Environmental Protection Agency. Available (consulted 9 January 2008) at: http://www.epa.gov/OGWDW/ccl/perchlorate/perchlorate.html

FDA (2007a) *2004–2005 Exploratory Survey Data on Perchlorate In Food*. US Food and Drug Administration. Available (consulted 10 January 2008) at: www.cfsan.fda.gov/~dms/clo4data.html

FDA (2007b) *Perchlorate Questions and Answers*. US Food and Drug Administration. Available (consulted 10 January 2008) at: www.cfsan.fda.gov/~dms/clo4qa.html#effects

Flyvbjerg B. (1999) *Rationality and Power: Democracy in Practice*. Chicago, IL: University of Chicago Press.

Flyvbjerg B. (2001) *Making Social Science Matter: Why Social Inquiry Fails and How It Can Succeed again*. Cambridge: Cambridge University Press.

Forsyth T. (2003) *Critical Political Ecology: The Politics of Environmental Science*. London: Routledge.

Foster J.B. (2002) *Ecology against Capitalism*. New York, NY: Monthly Review Press.

Foucault M. (1995) *Discipline and Punish: The Birth of the Prison*. New York, NY: Vintage Books.

Freudenburg W. (2005a) Privileged access, privileged accounts: toward a socially structured theory of resources and discourses. *Social Forces* 84(1): 89–114.

Freudenburg W. (2005b) Seeding science, courting conclusions: reexamining the intersection of science, corporate cash, and the law. *Sociological Forum* 20(1): 3–33.

Freudenburg W. and Alario M. (2007) Weapons of mass distraction: magicianship, misdirection, and the dark side of legitimation. *Sociological Forum* 22(2): 146–173.

Freudenburg W. and Gramling R. (1994) Bureaucratic slippage and failures of agency vigilance: the case of the environmental studies program. *Social Problems* 41(2): 214–237.

Freudenburg W., Gramling R. and Davidson D. (2008) Scientific certainty argumentation methods (SCAMs): science and the politics of doubt. *Sociological Inquiry* 78(1): 2–38.

Gendron R. and Domhoff G.W. (2008) *The Leftmost City: Power and Progressive Politics in Santa Cruz*. Boulder, CO: Westview Press.

Gottlieb R. (2005) *Forcing the Spring: The Transformation of the American Environmental Movement*. Washington, DC: Island Press.

Gould K., Pellow D. and Schnaiberg A. (2008) *The Treadmill of Production: Injustice and Unsustainability in the Global Economy*. Boulder, CO: Paradigm.

Greer M.A., Goodman G., Pleus R.C. and Greer S.E. (2002) Health effects assessment for environmental perchlorate contamination: the dose response for inhibition of thyroidal radioiodine uptake in humans. *Environmental Health Perspectives* 110(9): 927–937.

Johnson C. (2004) *The Sorrows of Empire: Militarism, Secrecy, and the End of the Republic*. New York, NY: Metropolitan Books.

Klein N. (2007) *The Shock Doctrine: The Rise of Disaster Capitalism*. New York, NY: Metropolitan Books.

Lee J. (2004) Second thoughts on a chemical: in water, how much is too much? *New York Times*. 2 March, p. F1.

McCright A. and Dunlap R. (2003) Defeating Kyoto: the conservative movement's impact on US climate-change policy. *Social Problems* 50(3): 348–373.

Madsen T. and Jahagirdar S. (2006) *The Politics of Rocket Fuel Pollution: The Perchlorate Study Group and its Industry Backers*. Los Angeles: Environment California

Research and Policy Center. Available (consulted 9 January 2008) at: http://www
.environmentcalifornia.org/reports/clean-water/clean-water-program-reports/
the-politics-of-rocket-fuel-pollution

Mol A. (1996) Ecological modernization and institutional reflexivity: environmental
reform in the late modern age. *Environmental Politics* 5(2): 302–323.

Mol A. and Spaargaren G. (2002) Ecological modernization and the environmental
state. In: Mol A. and Buttel F. (eds) *The Environmental State Under Pressure*. Oxford: Elsevier Science, 33–55.

NRC (2005) *Health Implications of Perchlorate Ingestion*. Committee to Assess the
Health Implications of Perchlorate Ingestion, The National Research Council of
the National Academies. Washington, DC: The National Academies Press.

NRDC (2005) *White House and Pentagon Bias National Academy Perchlorate Report*.
National Resources Defense Council Press Backgrounder. Available (consulted 10
January 2008) at: http://www.nrdc.org/media/pressreleases/050110.asp

PIB (2009a) *Summary of Scientific Studies*. Perchlorate Information Bureau. Available
(consulted 7 July 2009) at: http://www.perchlorateinformationbureau.org/science/
studies.html

PIB (2009b) *The Facts about Perchlorate and Milk*. Perchlorate Information Bureau.
Available (consulted 7 July 2009) at: http://www.perchlorateinformationbureau
.org/facts/milk.html

Report of the Planning Committee (2004) *Report Submitted to the Committee to Assess
the Health Implications of Perchlorate Ingestion, The National Research Council of
the National Academies, Based on the Perchlorate State-of-the-Science Symposium*.
Provided by the National Resources Defense Council. Available (consulted 10
January, 2008) at: www.nrdc.org/media/pressreleases/050110.asp

Schnaiberg A. (1980) *The Environment: From Surplus to Scarcity*. New York, NY: Oxford
University Press.

Sharp R. and Lunder S. (2003) *Suspect Salads: Toxic Rocket Fuel Found in Samples of
Winter Lettuce*. Oakland: Environmental Working Group. Available (consulted 9
January 2008) at: http://www.ewg.org/reports/suspectsalads/

Simon M. (2006) *Appetite for Profit: How the Food Industry Undermines Our Health and
How to Fight Back*. New York, NY: Nation Books.

Thorpe C. (2007) Political theory in science and technology studies. In Hacket E et
al. (eds) *The Handbook of Science and Technology Studies*. Cambridge, MA: MIT
Press, 63–82.

Useem M. (1984) *The Inner Circle: Large Corporations and the Rise of Business Political
Activity in the U.S. and U.K.* New York, NY: Oxford University Press.

Waldman P. (2003a) Pentagon backs off water-test plan: fuel-ingredient perchlorate is
center of fight with EPA on evaluations near bases. *Wall Street Journal*. 20 June,
p. A5.

Waldman P. (2003b) Bush seeks liability shield on water pollutant. *Wall Street Journal*.
14 March, p. A2.

Waldman P. (2003c) EPA bans staff from discussing issue of perchlorate pollution. *Wall
Street Journal*. 28 April, p. A3.

Waldman P. (2005) On campus, industry set up a perchlorate confab. *Wall Street Journal*. 29 December, p. A5.

Hurricane Katrina, Contamination, and the Unintended Organization of Ignorance
Scott Frickel and M. Bess Vincent

Sociologists emphasize that science has its own culture and sets of accepted practices. Examining the case of post-Katrina New Orleans, Scott Frickel and Bess Vincent argue that expert systems, including scientific disciplines and regulatory agencies, reinforce knowledge production systems that leave some potential knowledge undone. The result is "organized ignorance", which leaves citizens without accurate or complete information about potential threats to human and environmental health.

> [T]here is no form of knowledge that surpasses the indeterminability of risks.
>
> —Joost Van Loon, Risk and Technological Culture

Introduction

In *Risk Society*, German sociologist Ulrich Beck famously observed that "poverty is hierarchic, smog is democratic."[1] This was another way of saying that the wealthy among us can no longer buy safety from invisible new dangers, be they chemical, nuclear, radiological, genetically modified, or nanotech. Others take issue with Beck's catholic fatalism, countering that persistent inequalities in many parts of the world have concentrated pollution and its attendant health threats disproportionately in poor nations and in poor regions of wealthier nations.[2]

On August 29, 2005 Hurricane Katrina drove home both points of the debate with tragic consequences. Even as the storm's catastrophic destruction exposed in New Orleans the deep racial and economic divisions that characterized the evacuation and rescue efforts, levee breaches across the city wrecked neighborhoods wealthy, middle class, and poor. Down river in St. Bernard Parish, the fences that once physically demarcated political conflicts between industrial polluters and their working-class neighbors were made irrelevant by a million gallon oil spill that oozed crude from the Murphy Oil Refinery, contaminating a square mile of adjacent residential neighborhoods.[3] In the coastal marshes to the south, west, and east, storm surges ravaged coastal wetlands, scouring 30 square miles of newly open water from the marshes just below the tip of Orleans Parish.[4]

As these and other examples illustrate, Hurricane Katrina transformed the nature of risk in southeastern Louisiana in ways that are unlikely to conform to pre-Katrina cultural, political, or socioeconomic realities. Hurricane Katrina's landfall also marks the beginning of an important epistemological moment, an opportunity to engage difficult questions about how and what we know, what we do not know, and why.

This essay considers contamination in Orleans Parish in the wake of Hurricane Katrina. We are interested in how knowledge about contamination and its attendant risks to public health are produced and organized. Our basic argument is that society's understandings of past, present, and future threats are dangerously compromised by expert systems that create and legitimate those understandings. Chief among those expert systems are scientific disciplines and regulatory agencies. In combination, these institutions reinforce a set of expectations and practices for producing knowledge that minimize the ecological and socio-historical contexts in which that knowledge is created and deployed. The result, in effect, is organized ignorance—a system of knowledge production that articulates risk in ways that do not, and perhaps cannot, answer some of our most basic questions concerning safety, health, and sustainability. Answers to such questions will require greater scholarly attention to "the problem of undone science"—explaining why some knowledge never gets made.[5] There is much at stake. What we do not know, or will not know, or cannot know about risks in the new New Orleans matters a great deal (and not just for New Orleanians).

Toxic Gumbo? Hell No!

As the floodwaters in New Orleans rose, so did fears that the city would find itself awash in a "toxic gumbo" of chemical toxins and biological pathogens. Scientists were as quick to arrive at this early conclusion as others, and not without reason. We now know that at a minimum, the floodwaters contained a complex mixture of contaminants. Some areas of the city soaked for weeks in a bath of heavy metals such as arsenic, lead, mercury, and zinc along with Escherichia coli and fecal coliforms, overcoated by a thin layer of petroleum-based volatile organic compounds (VOC).

VOC break down after a week or two, and as they went, so went public discourse on contamination. Measured by "mentions" in newspaper articles, media attention to Hurricane Katrina's contamination peaked during the second week of flooding. By week four, as the last of the floodwaters were pumped into Lake Pontchartrain, newspaper mentions had virtually disappeared.[6] Contrary to widespread expectations, initial test data from floodwater, sediment, and lake water samples indicated that—high levels of biological contaminants notwithstanding—levels of chemical toxicants were generally found to be within regulatory limits set by the Agency for Toxic Substances and Disease Registry, Environmental Protection Agency (EPA), and/or the Louisiana Department of Environmental Quality (LDEQ). Thus, chemical hazards dispersed throughout the city by Hurricane Katrina apparently posed little health risk.[7] Worries of bacterial contagion also dissipated as the expectant period for disease outbreaks came and went. The day after EPA released the first test results showing satisfactory air quality, the mayor announced plans to begin repopulating the city, with further assurance by New Orleans Health Director Kevin Stephens that fecal coliform bacteria was "the only significant health care concern".[8]

By November, the contamination issue had long receded from the national spotlight, and in the local press occasional coverage of contamination emphasized the relative absence of risk from chemical hazards. Illustrating this shift in public discourse, one article featured the owner of a seafood business who blamed the idea of "toxic gumbo" and the resulting public perception of chemical contamination for ongoing revenue losses in that industry.[9] Another article urged readers to "forget about Katrina cough," but without mentioning chemical toxins when describing a Louisiana Office of Public Health study that found "inconsistent" connections between respiratory distress and dust and mold exposure.[10] As the article suggested, mold replaced chemical contaminants as a major focus of local public health campaigns, as fungal geneticists acknowledged that existing science about the vast majority of known molds and fungi is thin.[11][12] Continued testing and follow-up press releases by regulatory agencies through April 2006 reinforced the narrative that, as one January headline at Tulane University put it, "NOLA is Safe for Kids".[13] Rarely, we suspect, has New Orleans—a city culturally divided in so many ways—seen such unanimity around a public-good issue. As the high-stakes mayoral election got under way during the spring of 2006, economic and social interests across the political spectrum lined up behind LDEQ's assertion that returning residents faced "no unacceptable health risks".[14]

Public officials' reactions to environmental groups who continued to press for more testing, better monitoring, and reinterpretation of some of the existing data are one indicator of how important these risk assessments are to the city's recovery. In response to a request from the Natural Resources Defense Council (NRDC) that the state agency make public the details of its environmental assessment, LDEQ Secretary Mike McDaniel issued a public letter deriding the "alarmists" and "scaremongers" whose "inaccurate, misleading, and often outrageous claims y do a grave disservice to New Orleans and the state".[15] Another indicator, less easily measured, is pressure within the local scientific community to join the booster chorus backing the risk assessments. As a few environmental and medical experts have admitted in private conversation, many questions have gone unanswered, and attendant health risks of living in the city remain highly speculative. Nevertheless, state and city public officials and a handful of vocal local experts have hung these questions—and all they imply for the future of the city—on environmental test results.

The Hidden Poverty of Environmental Testing

From September 2005 through April 2006, the EPA in collaboration with several other federal agencies and with the LDEQ, conducted 165,971 tests for chemical and biological contaminants in Orleans Parish.[16] These tests were generated from 1442 samples collected from floodwater, surface (lake) water, sediment, and soil. The timing and scope of sampling efforts was outlined by LDEQ Secretary McDaniel in response to an NRDC request for information. These publicly available results provide the empirical basis of official risk assessments, which in turn have shaped public policies for risk communication and public health and safety education, environmental monitoring, debris removal and disposal, health care, and rebuilding.

Designed to provide technically accurate, objective measures of pollution, testing is also a socially negotiated and organized cultural practice.[17] As such, testing links scientific disciplines that ground test design in a body of established theory and research, and regulatory regimes that set out rules, conventions, and procedures for testing and standards for interpreting test results. We can gain a better understanding of how these paired institutions structure undone science by considering the technical and organizational logics of environmental testing.

Disciplining Nature

Environmental tests are disciplinary activities, in at least two senses. First, tests are the historical products of disciplinary practice. They derive from basic sciences, adapted to fit changing regulatory requirements at particular moments in time. For example, the environmental testing and risk assessment in Orleans Parish owes a considerable debt to analytical chemistry and genetics circa 1970. Many current tests, or their forerunners, were developed by land-grant university chemists and entomologists working in response to heightened public concern about the relationship between pesticide use, the environment, and public health.[18] [19] [20] Similarly, today's risk assessment models incorporate parameters derived from geneticists' earlier efforts to measure the effects of chemicals on the genetic structure of living organisms.[21] While it is common to think about tests in technical terms as precision instruments for extracting specific bits of information from the physical environment or from living tissue, tests embody the disciplinary commitments of the community of scientists that develop them as well as the bureaucratic and political commitments of policy makers and agency managers who legitimate their use in regulatory settings.

We need to recover the history of those commitments and the social, political, and economic contexts of test development decisions if we are to understand how and why testing is organized around certain conventions and not others. For example, fecal coliform bacteria are not a disease pathogen, but tests for the microbe have become standard practice in epidemiology as an indicator species for infectious water-borne disease. High levels of fecal coliform will suggest to public health scientists that disease outbreaks are likely, on the theory that where fecal coliform is present, other, more dangerous bacteria are also present. This is the case even though, as one informant told us, fecal coliform has a "notoriously bad" history of predicting outbreaks. In New Orleans, tests of floodwater showed widespread and extremely high fecal coliform counts. Area hospitals and public health officials were put on alert for patients presenting with symptoms of dengue fever or some other infectious disease and none of the expected outbreaks materialized. That is a good thing, but it raises questions about how a test as relatively unreliable as fecal coliform became the tool of choice for predicting disease outbreaks.[22] [23] [24] It also raises more general questions about the heavy reliance on indicator species as a knowledge production strategy in public health and environmental sciences.

Second, tests are disciplinary activities in the sense that they bring order to natural environments by imposing a particular framework of theoretical assumptions, standards of evidence, and styles of interpretation. As such, tests are not neutral technologies. Instead, cultural expectations—and thus politics—are built in. This notion is captured in cancer biologist Samuel Epstein's trenchant remark that regulatory approaches to science result in "narrow questions, narrowly defined, narrowly posed, and often narrowly answered" [21, p. 93]. Historians and sociologists of science who have studied disciplinary culture in environmental science and biomedicine have similarly noted tendencies in regulatory science to favor ultimate over proximate causes, to describe central tendencies while paying less attention to outliers, to stress the importance of minimizing false-positive over false-negative results, or to view statistical significance as a necessary condition for policy action.[25][26]

Some of these same tendencies, working in complex interaction, seem to be shaping the organization and communication of knowledge about contamination in New Orleans. For example, the EPA's website describes several phases of sediment sampling and testing. In one phase that focused on resampling, the description notes that, "[w]ith the Louisiana Department of Environmental Quality (LDEQ), we revisited approximately 145 previous sediment sample locations where contaminant concentrations exceeded LDEQ and EPA criteria".[27] As this statement suggests, and as our own preliminary analysis of the data from Orleans Parish seems to confirm, resampling has mostly been limited to previously identified contamination hotspots. In other words, sampling has been organized around the agency's interest in minimizing false positives (Type I error). Resampling efforts have not, for the most part, sought to minimize false negatives (Type II error), even though failing to identify actually existing contamination has serious long-term implications for community health.

Precision is another way that tests discipline ecosystems. The simultaneous strength of soil, air, or water testing as explanatory tools, and their weakness as instruments of comprehensive knowledge, lies in the exactness of their measure. Tests will do only what they are designed to do, and nothing more. They will not find chemicals they are not programmed to find; they will not detect parts per billion if they are calibrated to detect parts per million; if sampling occurs near shore, tests will not detect contaminants that have moved into deeper water; if air monitors run during a rain shower, they are not likely to indicate the presence of particulate matter; and so on. In other words, the kinds of results testing produces are programmed into the testing parameters a priori. We find what we seek, not necessarily what is there.

This point has potential significance in the context of post-Katrina New Orleans. Of the approximately 82,000 chemicals in its inventory established under the Toxic Substances Control Act, to date the EPA has issued rules requiring testing on just 185 compounds.[28] In Orleans Parish, the EPA has conducted tests for 199 chemical compounds and heavy metals in 777 sediment samples. As Table 1 shows, frequency distributions of publicly available data show that the number of tests run across the population of sediment samples range from one test (for three samples) to 199 (for 21 samples). Just over a third of the samples received 194 199 tests, but 61% received 124–128. Why the variation? Compounding the concern is the fact that because legal restrictions prevented testing on private property, test results cannot address questions about contaminants that may be in people's yards or inside their houses.

This is an example of how technical precision and accuracy in testing practices can thwart public understanding of risk. Entwined with the requirements of regulatory regimes, disciplinary cultures can produce ignorance by design, even as those same practices and the reams of results they produce lend an aura of legitimacy to the official agencies and offices standing behind the numbers. It is a form of organized ignorance that, among other things, masks ecological complexity.

TABLE 1. **Frequency distribution of tests for chemical compounds run on sediment samples Orleans Parish, La., November 2005–April 2006**

	No. of Samples	No. of Chemical Tests	Percent	Cum. Percent
	3	1	0.39	0.39
	3	2	0.39	0.78
	2	124	0.26	1.04
	5	125	0.64	1.68
	37	126	4.76	6.44
	250	127	32.18	38.62
	179	128	23.04	61.66
	1	144	0.13	61.79
	5	173	0.64	62.43
	4	174	0.51	62.94
	2	176	0.26	63.20
	4	177	0.51	63.71
	1	194	0.13	63.84
	4	195	0.51	64.35
	38	196	4.89	69.24
	124	197	15.96	85.20
	94	198	12.10	97.30
	21	199	2.70	100.00%
Total:	777	118,612	100.00%	

Source: Derived from EPA data [16].

Ecological Complexity

Environmental testing is fundamentally limited in what it can tell us about ecosystem health. Testing proceeds on the assumption that we can understand what is happening in an ecosystem by putting some of it— an air, water, or soil sample—inside a controlled, laboratory-like environment, and then manipulating, and measuring it. Reductionism of this sort allows researchers to make certain-sounding statements such as "benzene is present in the water column at a concentration of 5 parts per billion." The ability to provide technically accurate information is vitally important. Ideally, for example, it allows citizens and regulatory agencies to know whether and when industry violates state or federal emissions standards. But it does not tell us much about the water's condition in an open and dynamic ecosystem. Environmental testing can give us a snapshot image of contamination at one location at one point in time. Lots of testing can give us lots of snapshots. But neither the tests nor their aggregated results come close to mimicking environmental conditions, although scientists and engineers historically have sought to do just that.[29]

These limitations are reproduced in institutions that organize and legitimate test-based knowledge. The tests the EPA and LDEQ have conducted are based on the compartmentalization of ecosystems into discrete media (e.g., air, soil, and water). These testing regimes, in turn, correspond to media-specific disciplines (e.g., aquatic toxicology), regulatory bureaucracies (e.g., LDEQ's Water Quality Assessment Division), and federal regulatory frameworks (e.g., Clean Water Act), each of which develops understandings of environmental contamination in ways that stand at some odds to ecological reality. In short, we have organized knowledge in ways that ensure we will not really know what is happening in the ecosystems we study. This is another form of organized ignorance.

The organization of soil and ground water sampling in Orleans Parish is a case in point. Soil samples are collected 2–3 inches below the surface and are useful for measuring whether chemicals may have leached into the ground during the period when the city was flooded. By taking samples from the same place at different points in time, it is also possible to see whether chemicals or other pollutants are migrating into or out of an area. This is especially pertinent in New Orleans, where this past summer a shattered municipal water system was leaking 85 million gallons of water per day.[30] Treated water from broken pipes saturated the soil and increased subsidence rates to create highly unstable soil conditions. To date, 1552 tests have been conducted from 345 soil samples collected from 264 unique locations. In contrast to sediment testing, for which there has been some limited resampling as noted above, none of the soil samples have been collected to measure change over time. In only two cases were soil samples collected from the same location at significantly different points in time, but in both cases, the new samples were used to test for compounds different than those tested in the original samples. Also, there is no publicly available record of any ground-water tests conducted in Orleans Parish since Hurricane Katrina. It is possible, then, that chemical toxicants in the soil have migrated under the massive infusion of water, and that some of those chemicals may have infiltrated the water table beneath the city. We will not know because the organization of testing has been conducted as if ecological complexity does not matter.

There is a fundamental leap of faith that the logic of testing requires us to make, between what testing tells us happens to contaminants in ecosystems and what does happen. Often it is wise to take that leap, but we should remain conscious of this when agency officials ask that we substitute test results for "what is really going on". This is not merely a philosophical issue but, as our example illustrates, is one with numerous "downstream" implications for what and how we know.

Social History

Environmental testing collapses time and space. Testing happens in geographical space, yet strips away the social history of those locations. Test results replace that history with numerical values that signal the presence or absence of specific contaminants, which then are interpreted in terms of probabilities of a future effect or effects. Thus, past and future are condensed into a one-dimensional present largely devoid of social and historical context.

This is in part why experts can explain away lead found in post-Katrina sediment as being "the same here today as you would expect in any urban area, whether it is Los Angeles or New York or New Orleans". This statement begs the question of acceptable risk associated with lead levels in any major American city, including New Orleans prior to Hurricane Katrina. But regardless, the comparison only works as long as we are prepared to accept the implicit assumption that the social history of urban contamination is largely irrelevant to risk assessment. Unlike Los Angeles and New York—mega-cities with massive populations of people and automobiles—the lead that laces soil in New Orleans comes from vehicles to be sure, but also from pre-1970 paint that has protected and decorated buildings for 300 years. If the sources of lead differ, we should at least be asking whether variation in lead distribution patterns, and population characteristics such as the age and spatial structure of poverty, may differentially affect exposure to vulnerable groups. If we agree to assess risk in New Orleans the same way we assess risk in Los Angeles, it is because we also agree to forget about history.

We know a lot about lead in New Orleans by virtue of the fact that Howard Mielke, a leading expert on urban lead contamination, lives there and has studied the situation for years.[31] We know much less about other forms and sources of local contamination. It is safe to assume, however, that because New Orleans is an old city, manufacturing processes that have been used since the late-eighteenth century have created contaminated waste the disposal of which has not been recorded, much less regulated. We do know that the expansion of the city's manufacturing capacities in the 1940–1980s was tightly linked to the region's rising oil, natural gas, and petrochemical industries. During that period, a number of small firms were established in New Orleans that produced or used petroleum-based products including asphalt, paint, and DDT.[32] Some of these sites have been redeveloped for use as private residences, public housing, parks, and playgrounds. Other old industrial sites are abandoned. These vacant lots are presumably among the 284 locations listed by the Mayor's Office of Environmental Affairs before the hurricane as actual or potential brownfields.[33] While some of these brownfields are known to be contaminated, the vast majority have not been tested, so it is impossible to tell one way or the other. (At present there is no count of the number of new brownfields created by Hurricane Katrina.) This history matters, but most of it remains hidden.

The continued invisibility of contamination owes something to the fact that the logic of testing has largely ignored New Orleans' industrial past. Much of the city's older industrial development concentrated on the higher ground running along the Mississippi River—the area now being referred to locally as the "sliver along the river," which escaped serious flooding. Most of the EPA testing, by contrast, has focused on the other 80% of the city that did flood. Thus, in principle we know more about the parts of the city that were least likely to contain old and hidden contaminants. This has practical relevance because post-Katrina, the city's old industrial corridor has become prime real estate, and the area is likely to soon undergo intense residential and commercial development. Without careful planning and execution, the possibility of inadvertently re-exposing buried contaminants seems very real.

Conclusion: The Politics of Not Knowing

A central feature of contemporary society is uncertainty, and risk management has become an important institutional response to those conditions. Paradoxically, managing risk also creates risk [1]. Joost Van Loon describes the relationship this way: "More uncertainty demands more knowledge, more knowledge increases the complexity, more complexity demands more abstraction, more abstraction increases uncertainty".[34] This process is illustrated on many levels by environmental testing in New Orleans in the wake of Hurricane Katrina.

We suggest that in New Orleans, knowledge about contamination is not well organized to produce comprehensive understanding. Some of this may be intentional. Environmental groups, concerned that the EPA and LDEQ are more invested in controlling public perception and business confidence than in gaining a comprehensive understanding of environmental hazards, have demanded more testing and retesting. Given the reputation of the regional EPA office and the LDEQ as administratively weak organizations, these groups are right to pressure government to do more.[35] But it is important to be clear about what more testing will and will not achieve. In part, at least, the obstacles to usable knowledge are deeply embedded in the machineries of knowledge production itself.

As developed historically through the cultural lens of disciplinary communities and enshrined in our current regulatory regime, environmental testing largely ignores ecological complexity and social history. By missing these dynamics, the power of precision that testing offers is simultaneously enlightening and mystifying. Tests tell us something about some contaminants in certain places at specific points in time. As designed, tests cannot provide comprehensive knowledge. Thus the organization of testing—through which decisions are made about what will be known and what will remain unknown—involves decision making that is as much political as it is technical.

In this context, demands for increased funding for environmental assessments and increased enforcement of existing regulations, while important, are ultimately short sighted. We need more than more testing and more policing. We need to develop and adequately fund new knowledge institutions—for example, a National Institutes of Environment—whose primary mission at both the basic and applied ends of the research stream is to tackle real world environmental and public health problems, doing so in ways that seek to embrace, rather than deny, the complexity of ecological and social systems in interaction.

Notes

Frickel, Scott and M. Bess Vincent. 2007. "Hurricane Katrina, contamination, and the Unintended Organization of Ignorance." *Technology in Society* 29(2): 181–88. Reprinted by permission of Elsevier.

1. Beck U. Risk society: toward a new modernity. London: Sage; 1992. p. 36.

2. Buttel FH. Classical theory and contemporary environmental sociology: some reflections on the antecedents and prospects for reflexive modernization theories in the study of environment and society. In: Spaargaren G, Mol AP, Buttel FH, editors. Environment and global modernity. Thousand Oaks, CA: Sage; 2000. p. 17–39.

3. Environmental Protection Agency press release. These spills affected approximately 1800 homes and several unnamed interceptor canals. Available from: http://epa
.gov/region6/katrina/pdfs/murphy_oil_fctsht_2_2006.pdfS. Accessed 5 January 2005.

4. USGS press release, 14 September 2005. Available at: http://www.usgs.gov/news
room/article.asp?ID=997.

5. Hess D. Alternative pathways in science and industry: activism, innovation, and the environment in an era of globalization. Cambridge, MA: MIT Press; 2007.

6. Frickel S, Vincent MB. Katrina's contamination: media discourses on the risk of return. Paper presented at the annual meeting of the Southern Sociological Society, New Orleans, 24 March 2006.

7. McDaniel to Simms, February 2, 2006. Available from: http://www.deq.loui
siana.gov/portal/portals/0/news/pdf/DEQ-EnvironmentalAssessmentKatrinaRita
-NRDCResponse.pdfs.

8. Russell G. Nagin maps out return to N.O. Some businesses can return Saturday. Times-Picayune 16 September 2005, A-1.

9. Webster R. Toxic soup tales about LA seafood subside. New Orleans City Business 14 November 2005:1.

10. Pope J. LA clears the air on Katrina cough. Respiratory ills not surging, study says. Times-Picayune 19 April 2006:1.

11. Nano S. Accidents, mold pose biggest health problems in hurricane areas. Associated Press state and local wire 11 November 2005.

12. Bennett JW. The molds of Katrina. Update. New York Academy of Sciences; p. 6–9. Available from /http://kerrn.org/pdf/ Katrina_Molds.pdfS.

13. Vann M. Nola is safe for kids. The New Wave; 9 January 2006. Available from: / http://www2.tulane.edu/article_news_details. cfm?ArticleID=6132S.

14. The lone exception is the area near the Murphy Oil spill in St. Bernard Parish. LDEQ Press Release, 9 December 2005.Available from: http://www.deq.louisiana.gov/portal/portals/0/news/pdf/jointenvironmentalassessmentpr.pdfS.

15. The NRDC request and McDaniel's response. Available from: /http://www.deq .louisiana.gov/portal/S. Accessed 3 March 2006.

16. Available from: /http://oaspub.epa.gov/storetkp/DW_resultcriteria_geoS.

17. Pinch T. Testing one, two, three testing: toward a sociology of testing. Sci Technol Human Values 1993;18:25–41.

18. Pinch T. Testing one, two, three testing: toward a sociology of testing. Sci Technol Human Values 1993;18:25–41.

19. Palladino P. Entomology, ecology and agriculture: the making of scientific careers in North America 1885–1985. Amsterdam: Harwood Academic Publishers; 1996.

20. Sawyer RC. To make a spotless orange. Biological control in California. Ames: Iowa State University Press; 1996.

21. Frickel S. Chemical consequences: environmental mutagens, scientist activism, and the rise of genetic toxicology. New Brunswick, NJ: Rutgers University Press; 2004.

22. Schmid, RE. Lack of disease outbreak following Katrina amazing. Associated Press state and local wire, 20 October 2005.

23. Rose JB, Gerba CP, Jakubowski W. Survey of potable water supplies for Cryptosporidium and Giardia. Environ Sci Technol 25(8): 1393.

24. Kramer MH, et al. Surveillance for waterborne-disease outbreaks—United States, 1993–1994. Morbidity and mortality weekly report, 12 April 1996; p. 1–33. Available from: /http://www.cdc.gov/mmwR/preview/mmwrhtml/00040818.htmS.

25. Proctor RN. Cancer wars: how politics shapes what we know and don't know about cancer. New York: Basic Books; 1995.

26. Wynne B, Mayer S. How science fails the environment. New Scientist 1993;5:33–5.

27. Available from: /http://www.epa.gov/katrina/testresults/index.html#sedS; accessed 23 July 2006.

28. United States Government Accounting Office. Chemical regulation: options exist to improve EPA's ability to assess health risks and manage its chemical review program. Report to Congress (GAO-05-458); June 2005.

29. Bocking S. Ecologists and environmental politics: a history of contemporary ecology. New Haven: Yale University Press; 1997.

30 Krupa M. Millions of gallons of water seeping away. Fissures in pipes traced to Katrina. Times-Picayune; 8 June 2006; 1.

31. Mielke HW. Lead in New Orleans soils: new images of an urban environment. Environ Geochem Health 1994;16:123–8.

32. Louisiana Department of Commerce. Louisiana directory of manufacturers. Baton Rouge, LA; various dates.

33. Public Law 107–118 (H.R. 2869) defines brownfields as "real property, the expansion, redevelopment, or reuse of which may be complicated by the presence or potential presence of a hazardous substance, pollutant, or contaminant." Information on the EPA brownfields program is available from: /http://www.epa.gov/brownfields/basic_info.htmS. The list of New Orleans brownfields is available from: /http://www .gcr1.com/epa/pilot-cities/default.cfm?ObjID=4983S.

34. Van Loon J. Risk and technological culture: towards a sociology of virulence. London, New York: Routledge; 2002. p. 41.

35. Roberts TJ, Toffolon-Weiss MM. Chronicles from the environmental justice frontline. New York: Cambridge University Press; 2001.

Media Framing of Body Burdens

Precautionary Consumption and the Individualization of Risk

Norah MacKendrick

Because many of us get our information about health- and environment-related issues from the mainstream media, it is important to think critically about how newspapers cover these issues. Sociologists may look for trends and patterns in reporting—what types of information are routinely discussed? What is left out? What types of people are featured in the news? In this piece, Norah MacKendrick examines how the Canadian press reports on 'body burdens'—chemical contaminants stored up in our bodies—from 1986 to 2006. She finds that news articles focus increasingly on green consuming and self protection (as opposed to protection by the government or business); these have become dominant media frames in reporting on body burdens.

Introduction

Bioaccumulation—the gradual accumulation of environmental contaminants in biological organisms—has long been the concern of natural scientists, but has only recently surfaced in the sociological literature. Attention has now turned to "body burdens," an aspect of bioaccumulation that refers to the internal contaminant load carried by most organisms in the industrialized world. Of special concern are the health effects of body burdens in human populations, particularly children. As individuals, we are not aware of our own internal contaminant load, as detection of body burdens requires specialized technology. But exposure to contaminants is universal and largely involuntary, as chemicals are present in air, water, food, soil, and indoor environments. . . .

As expert systems have considerable control over the definition and subsequent management of chemical hazards (e.g., Cable, Shriver, and Mix 2008), the communication of risk around body burdens to the lay public largely depends on the popular news media. By encouraging certain problem frames, the media shapes public understandings of key causal factors and attributions of responsibility in the management of risk (Brown et al. 2001; Stallings 1990). Consequently, the media plays a vital role in framing body burdens as both a risk and a social problem, and we can assume that public knowledge of body burdens is significantly influenced by the news media. The importance of the news media in interpreting local or regional contamination events is acknowledged in the literature (e.g., Griffin, Dunwoody, and Gehrmann 1995; Robinson 2002; Zavestoski et al. 2004), although to date no study has systematically examined news media coverage of body burdens arising from chronic and universal exposure to environmental contaminants. An understanding of how the news media frames body burdens as a social problem is critical for understanding how this issue is taken up in the public sphere, by policy makers, communities in close proximity to polluting industries, health professionals dealing with environmental illnesses, and individual readers who become aware of their bodies and their environments as "polluted."

Drawing on the sociology of risk literature, this article uses frame analysis to examine the social problem frame around body burdens in the Canadian news media from 1986 to 2006, and links these findings to broader theories of risk and society, particularly the individualization of risk. Most significantly, recent news articles underscore the individual's responsibility to avoid contaminant exposure through what I call "precautionary consumption" behavior. The frame of precautionary consumption communicates a sense of individual empowerment and control through acts of "green" consumption and chemical avoidance. While it transforms body burdens into a manageable risk, it directs attention away from the failure of states and industries to properly manage chemical production and dispersal. . . .

Background: Body Burdens

The internal contaminant load carried by living organisms or "body burden"[1] is associated with intensive industrialization that has released multitudes of persistent chemical compounds into the environment. These chemicals accumulate up the food chain, and predatory organisms, such as polar bears, whales, seals, and fish, contain chemical concentrations far higher than those of their external environments. Chemical bioaccumulation is now a prominent environmental issue for both national and international environmental groups.

Biomonitoring technology—methods for analyzing animal tissue for biological markers of contaminant exposure—has improved significantly in recent years, allowing the detection of compounds not previously known to bioaccumulate (Sexton et al. 2004). Biomonitoring data suggest that the body of nearly every person living in an industrial society contains minute concentrations of contaminants from exposure to a polluted environment, food treated with pesticides, and consumer goods treated with brominated flame retardants, stain repellents, and other compounds (e.g., CDC 2005). Health effects from chronic chemical exposure are uncertain and controversial, although some studies link exposure to certain forms of cancer, fertility problems, behavioral disorders in children, and thyroid disorders (Grandjean and Landrigan 2006). In other words, body burdens represent the contamination of the environment and are a serious health issue.

The industrial production and use of chemicals is regulated in Canada, as in the United States, by state institutions that employ risk assessments to determine the toxicity, persistence and bioaccumulative potential of chemicals, and to remove problematic compounds from production. Human body burdens are frequently cited as evidence of the failure of these risk assessments to prevent universal exposure to bioaccumulative chemicals (CELA 2006; Steinemann 2004).

Such regulatory failures, along with catastrophic localized pollution events, have given rise to a broad-based toxics movement comprised of advocacy groups and community groups fighting for pollution prevention (Szasz 1994) and, more recently, to movements concerned about environmental illness at both the individual and community levels (Brown et al. 2004; Kroll-Smith, Brown, and Gunter 2000; McCormick, Brown, and Zavestoski 2003). Greater accessibility to biomonitoring technology has allowed these groups to track community exposure to environmental contaminants and to raise public awareness of chemical bioaccumulation (Altman et al. 2008; Morello-Frosch et al. 2009).

Technology, Risk and the Environment

Like other forms of contamination and pollution, the bioaccumulation of contaminants in the environment and living organisms represents an environmental and technological risk. This section discusses two separate risk literatures: the institutional and organizational perspective and the risk society and individualization perspective.

Institutional and Organizational Factors

The body burden phenomenon has a clear institutional component in that government agencies regulate chemical production and are responsible for minimizing adverse impacts of chemical exposure on environmental quality and human health. As Perrow (1984) demonstrated in his study of nuclear accidents, risk is not necessarily the product of human error but can be an inherent property of industrial operating systems where sections are so tightly coupled that minor problems quickly develop into systemic failures. Organizational characteristics and configurations are keys to the production of risk, making the institutional perspective on risk a useful analytical tool, as it examines how features of organizations, bureaucracies, and policy-making processes lead to environmental hazards and technological failures (e.g., Clarke 1993) . . .

The "Risk Society" and Individualization

Pointing to widespread ecological degradation (e.g., DDT in breast milk, transboundary pollution, and radioactive fallout), Beck (1992, 1995, 1999) argues that we are moving toward a "risk society" characterized by universal and high-consequence risks that threaten human and ecological existence and transcend geographic and social divisions. He observes that risks have ceased to be managed by traditional institutions associated with the welfare state and are managed instead by institutions with little visibility and public accountability, such as the market, and science and technology. Thus, the production of risks cannot easily be associated with an identifiable actor or institution, a condition he calls "organized irresponsibility" (Beck 1999:6). Elsewhere, Beck has written extensively on individualization and modernity (Beck and Beck-Gernsheim 2002) and the anxiety associated with negotiating universal risks at the individual level (Beck 2006). He suggests that individualization is exacerbated by the inability of state institutions to manage modern risks, such that the market becomes a key institution for individuals to manage their exposure to risk (Beck 2006).

A related, but distinct, body of risk literature has studied the individualization of risk, with a strong focus on risk as a technique of governance related to the dismantling of the welfare state. These authors argue that the individualization of risk is associated with principles of neo-liberalism, emphasizing individual choice, personal responsibility, and the market as an efficient institution for bringing about social and political change (Ericson, Doyle, and Barry 2003; Rose 1999). They note that with the expansion of neo-liberalism, universal risks—such as crime and economic instability—are increasingly managed through the purchase of private insurance and other commodities of self-protection (Doyle 2007; Ericson, Doyle, and Barry 2003; O'Malley 2004). Here, risk is used as a technique of governance, with risk management transferred to "citizen-consumers" (Scott 2007:37) who negotiate their exposure to risk by modifying their consumer choices. While not explicitly embedded in risk theory, Szasz (2007) also observes the growing commodification of risk protection, citing gated communities and the increase in consumption of bottled water and specialty non-toxic products.

Media and Risk

Risks are communicated through the mass media, an important source of information on science, health and environmental issues (Carvalho and Burgess 2005; Nelkin 1987; Seale 2003), and a critical actor in the social construction of risk (Allan 2002; Driedger 2007). The media help to construct phenomena as social problems, identifying which issues are cause for concern, outlining responsibility for these problems, and recommending courses of action (Gamson and Modigliani 1989; Hilgartner and Bosk 1988; Kitsuse and Spector 1973). Public risk perception is shaped by news stories that frame and construct events in ways that amplify or down-play risks. The media can amplify risks through an increase in the volume of news stories about a risk event (Kasperson et al. 2005) or through dramatic language and images (Eldridge et al. 2005). News stories can exacerbate fear and anxiety (Altheide 1997) or offer reassurance to the public by highlighting the actions of "responsible" public institutions purporting to have risks under control (Freudenburg et al. 1996).

Frame Analysis

. . . Frames in news stories do several things: define a problem in a particular way, interpret causal relationships, provide moral evaluation, and recommend courses of action or treatment (Entman 1993). Importantly, frames in news texts represent a choice between what messages to communicate (Tuchman 1978) by drawing attention to certain aspects of reality and ignoring others (Entman 1993; Oliver and Johnston 1999). This article examines the content of frames rather than the conditions behind the construction of frames or the interaction between frames and public opinion formation (see D'Angelo 2002). This approach is useful for identifying general cultural frames and ideological standpoints (Binder 1993; Oliver and Johnston 1999), as news frames deliberately draw on these to increase their resonance or "potency" (Gamson and Modigliani 1989; Scheufele 1999).

It is important to pay attention to the primary sources selected by journalists to define issues and their terms of reference (Coleman, Hartley, and Kennamer 2006). A shift in these "primary definers" (Antilla 2005:344) can coincide with a shift in how risks are framed in the news media. In the case of climate change, for example, what was once almost entirely a scientific issue (with scientists as primary definers) is now also framed as a financial risk because of the involvement of insurance industry representatives as primary definers (Carvalho and Burgess 2005). Journalists seek out "official" sources (often publications or spokespeople from government or industry) from organizations that hold some responsibility for a given event (Stallings 1990), or select sources that lend credibility to the journalist's own viewpoint (Ericson, Baranek, and Chan 1989). Organizations with opposing viewpoints must, therefore, be well organized and persuasive to appear in news articles, and many rarely gain access to reporters (Coleman, Hartley, and Kennamer 2006; Freudenburg et al. 1996). Importantly, frames are not determined by primary definers but are the outcome of an interaction between journalists and their sources (Miller and Reichert 2000).

The Framing of Causal Mechanisms

A key component of the social problem frame in media accounts of risk is the representation of causal mechanisms and attributions of responsibility (Altheide 1997). Media discourse may offer a selective view of causation by failing to identify systemic causes of hazards. In his seminal study of media framing, Stallings (1990) observed that news reports of a bridge failure focused more on the immediate problems associated with environmental conditions and engineering quality than on systemic factors, such as the design of transportation networks or the reliance on cars for transportation. Importantly, Stallings made this observation by noting the absence of systemic causal frames in media representations. In a similar study, Brown et al. (2001) found that references to systemic causes of breast cancer—particularly environmental pollution—decreased over time in the popular print media, while individual-level factors, such as personal lifestyle and genetics were presented as primary causes of the disease.

While the media's influence over public discourse is "neither trivial nor decisive" (Gamson and Modigliani 1989:80), in the case of highly technical risks such as body burdens, we can assume that it exerts a tremendous influence over our knowledge and understanding of risk. Contact with chemicals is part of everyday life, and each of us has a chemical body burden; nevertheless, the ability to detect and observe body burdens is limited to expert systems. Consequently, the news media play a vital role in communicating the risks of chemical bioaccumulation to the lay public—a role that has not yet been examined in the sociological literature . . .

Methods

Over the past 20 years, chemical bioaccumulation has received considerable attention in the Canadian news media, as both an environmental and health topic. Canadian research institutions—including federal government agen cies—actively study the ecological and human health effects of chemical bio-accumulation, and the Canadian government has pushed for the ratification of international treaties to control the production and disposal of persistent organic pollutants as a result of concerns about Arctic pollution.[2] In the last 5 years, several prominent Canadian environmental groups (e.g., Environmental Defense and Pollution Probe) have launched campaigns to raise public aware-ness of chemical pollution and human body burdens.

The first step in the research process was collecting background informa-tion to inform content and frame analysis. This included searching through Canadian newspaper articles from 1986 to 2006, and a careful reading of Centers for Disease Control (CDC) reports on human exposure to chemicals, as well as online publications from several environmental groups. . . . This background research identified the main environmental and health concerns of chemical bioaccumulation, particularly the concern that body burdens are a *universal* and *unavoidable* risk because of frequent exposure to contaminants through normal everyday experiences.

The next step was to find news media articles that reflected these con-cerns, particularly exposure to multiple chemical compounds through normal everyday experiences, such as breathing, eating, drinking, and using common household goods. Articles therefore had to mention *more than one* environ-mental contaminant, so that coverage would not be biased toward issues spe-cific to an individual compound. Because topics around bioaccumulation vary significantly over time (see Figure 1), it was not possible to track one single topic in sufficient depth over a 20-year time period.

Newspaper selection was largely determined by circulation size and geographic representation, but was also influenced by the political economic

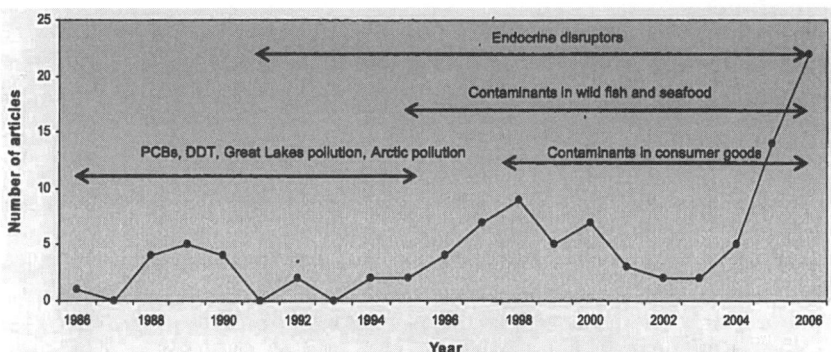

FIGURE 1. Distribution of Articles Over Time by General Topic Area: 1986–2006. (Note: arrows indicate the temporal distribution of the major topic areas related to bioaccumulation.)

realities of newspaper ownership in Canada. *The Globe and Mail*, a national paper, and the *Toronto Star*, a paper serving Canada's largest metropolitan area, were selected as they have the largest circulation in Canada . . .

An electronic database of articles from the four papers was generated through systematic searches in the ProQuest Canadian Newsstand database. All searches were limited from January 1, 1986, to December 31, 2006. . . .

. . . Only news articles and special features were selected for analysis, since these articles are guided by the journalistic norm of objectivity with the purpose of providing information to readers, in comparison with editorials and opinion columns that explicitly state an opinion or take a position in a broader debate (Gamson and Modigliani 1989), and are therefore assumed to be more representative of the media's role in a risk society—as an intermediary between expert and lay systems of knowledge.

Several exclusionary criteria were used to further refine the articles selected for analysis. Articles that focused entirely on bioaccumulation in non-human organisms, for example, were excluded unless there was some mention of human consequences of contamination. Articles were rejected if they covered only accidental or specific point-source pollution (e.g., a chemical spill, contamination from a fire) or exposure to contaminants from certain occupations. Also excluded were those covering "single-instance" food safety scandals (e.g., carcinogens in soft drinks or the contamination of eggs with dioxin) and articles discussing farmed fish.[3] These articles were rejected because single-instance food safety scandals and specific point-source pollution represent a different form of risk from the everyday, normal exposure to contaminants associated with the body burden phenomenon. . . .

Findings

In total, 102 articles were selected for analysis. The greatest proportion came from *The Globe and Mail* (45%), with 25 percent from the *Vancouver Sun*, 22 percent from the *Toronto Star*, and 9 percent from the *Calgary Herald*.

Figure 1 illustrates the distribution of articles and specific topics over the 20-year period. Topics vary according to the period of coverage. PCBs and DDT were two important contaminant issues in the 1980s because of extensive concern over the presence of these chemicals in human breast milk and in large mammals. News reports of chemical bioaccumulation in the Arctic and Great Lakes region were steady throughout the 1980s and early 1990s, but declined after the mid-1990s. Contaminants in wild fish and seafood are consistently covered in the news since the mid-1990s. Coverage of endocrine disruptors began in the early 1990s and became more prevalent in the mid-1990s after the publication of the popular book *Our Stolen Future* (Colborn, Dumanoski, and

Myers 1996). News reports of contaminants in consumer goods began in the late 1990s after the publication of CDC reports and scientific studies identifying these compounds in humans and large mammals such as polar bears. The spike in news coverage around 1998 seems to be explained by a convergence of topics, particularly concerning endocrine disruptors and consumer goods. The considerable increase in articles after 2004 reflects discussions of human body burdens specifically, with an emphasis on health effects in children and consumer goods as contaminant sources.

Content and Frame Analysis

Content analysis is used to identify: (1) the specific pathway of contaminant exposure identified in news articles, and (2) the primary definers used in the article. Frame analysis is used to identify aspects of the dominant social problem frame.

The pathway of chemical exposure reveals the characterization of contaminant origins. Pathways are identified by searching for references to the presence of contaminants in: (1) the external environment, defined as water, soil, and air (including indoor air), as well as reference to bioaccumulation in non-human organisms; (2) food, including wild game and wild-caught fish; and (3) consumer goods, such as electronics and furniture. Primary definers are identified in each article by counting the number of people or organizational representatives quoted, including quotations taken from written statements or organizational publications. . . .

In the first stage of frame analysis, the dominant problem frame is identified, that is, *how* contamination is described as a social problem. Frames in textual materials "are manifested by the presence or absence of certain keywords, stock phrases, stereotyped images, sources of information, and sentences that provide thematically reinforcing clusters of facts or judgments" (Entman 1993). Therefore, frames are identified by examining how the articles used concepts, themes, or metaphors to describe body burdens as a "concern" and assign meaning to this concern. Three different aspects of the problem frame are identified:

1. The overall representation of body burdens as a problem. This includes identifying the specific *characterization* of the problem—whether body burdens are cited as an example of environmental degradation (e.g., references to contaminants as a form of pollution or a threat to nature and wildlife) or a threat to human health (in terms of illness, disease or disorders).
2. The way in which responsibility or blame for contamination is articulated and whether aspects of blame are missing from the article. Here, the particular actors and organizations held responsible for creating contaminant risks are documented (e.g., industry or government).

3. The kinds of solutions to the body burden problem proposed by the article (e.g., changes to regulation, cleaning up the environment, or suggestions for avoiding exposure to contaminants).

In the second stage of frame analysis, the presence of these aspects of the problem frame is documented for each article, making it possible to track variation over time using basic descriptive statistics. Examining annual variation, however, reveals only subtle changes in framing largely because of the small number of articles published each year before 1996. For this reason, coverage is divided into two separate decades to more clearly capture shifts in framing. When divided by decade, 28 percent of the articles (N = 29) appear between 1986 and 1996 and 72 percent (N = 73) appear between 1997 and 2006. T-tests are used to test for significant differences in averages across decades. . . .

Pathway of Exposure and Primary Definers. Most articles note more than one pathway of exposure. . . . [B]etween 1986 and 1996, 86 percent of articles mention an environmental pathway of exposure, and 52 percent mention food as a pathway. In the second decade, there is a drop in articles noting an environmental pathway, and t-tests of statistical difference (p < .05) show that this difference is significant. Moreover, 43 percent of the articles in the first decade connect environmental pollution to the presence of contaminants in food, but this decreases sharply in the second decade (17%). The proportion of articles identifying consumer goods as an exposure pathway, in contrast, increases significantly in the second decade, jumping from 10 percent to 60 percent (p < .001).

Several categories of primary definers are used in the news articles . . . Regardless of time period, academic scientists (those affiliated with universities rather than government) appear most frequently as primary definers. Their presence in the articles contributes to a consistent focus on the "scientific" aspects of body burdens. Although representing a small proportion of primary definers across decades, when individual lay people appear in articles, they typically express fear of contamination or provide information on how others can protect themselves from exposure. With one exception, all of these individuals are women who are presented as mothers (or women wishing to have children) and their advice applies to the social reproductive domain. Some articles, for example, feature women who fear that contaminants in their breast milk are "poisoning" their babies (McInnes 1988), women dealing with infertility problems (Bueckert 1991) or warning against using plastics in the microwave (Ubelacker 2005). These individuals support the frame of precautionary consumption discussed below.

Frame Analysis

Two Major Problem Frames: Health and Environmental. All articles frame body burdens as a "problem" and communicate a sense of fear and anxiety around this issue. They note, for example, the "surprising level of foreign substances" in breast milk (Bergman 1989), express "fears over cancer" (McAndrew 1998), and describe endocrine disruption in aquatic ecosystems as "ominous and frightening" (Simpson 2001).

Across both time periods, all articles identify potential health problems from contaminant exposure, including cancer, birth defects, decreased sperm counts, reproductive disorders, and learning and behavioral disorders. Over time, these health dimensions overshadow the environmental dimensions of body burdens. . . . [F]rom 1986 to 1996, about 83 percent of the articles note environmental problems associated with contaminants (such as compromised ecological integrity or the reduced reproductive success of mammals, fish, and amphibians), but this drops dramatically to 34 percent from 1997 to 2006, and this drop is statistically significant (p < .001). In this later decade, even articles identifying an environmental pathway of exposure often do not explicitly reference environmental concerns associated with chemical bioaccumulation. This shift reflects a broader movement toward seeing environmental degradation through a health lens (Brown and Zavestoski 2004), and attests to the increasing dominance of the health frame in the narrative of environmental problems. The health frame marks a shift in how environmental problems are conceptualized: as a problem separate from humans to an issue directly connected to human well-being.[4]

Responsibility and Blame: Contamination as a Blameless Phenomenon. Given that news articles must reflect journalistic objectivity, it was expected that responsibility for contamination—where actors and organizations are identified as being responsible for creating chemical hazards—would be framed in subtle ways, for example through general references to industrial pollution or regulatory problems and delays. However, even subtle references to responsibility are not articulated in a considerable proportion of the articles from the first decade (48%) and in the majority of articles (66%) from the second decade. More specifically, these articles express concern over contamination and describe how contamination occurs, but do not give the reader any sense of the role of government or industry in creating these problems. In one article, for example, we learn that "the air inside your new home could be 5–20 times more polluted than the outdoor air in the most industrialized cities," owing to chemical off-gassing from paint, furniture, and floor coverings (Gillespie 2005). Despite citing multiple household goods as sources of potentially harmful chemicals, the article does not point to the industrial producers of these household products, nor does it question the efficacy of government safety assessments that allowed these products to go on the market. . . . By failing to identify responsible parties, these articles paint a picture of body burdens as a "blameless" phenomenon.

Of the proportion of articles that *do* identify a responsible party, most of the articles in the earlier period identify industry as responsible, while most of the articles in the later period identify government as responsible. There is a significant decrease in articles identifying industry responsibility between the two decades (p < .01). While industry is blamed for having "saturated" the environment with chemicals (McInnes 1988), government is blamed for being slow "to respond to environmental threats" (Bergman 1989), and is said to have "deliberately ignored and tried to explain away powerful evidence . . . of extremely high toxic doses" (Young 1990).

Solutions: Collective Action Versus Precautionary Consumption. Frames around solutions to body burdens fall into two categories: collective action and what I call "precautionary consumption." Forms of collective action include the implementation of stronger regulations, a reduction in chemical production and improvements in risk assessments. One article, for example, suggests that "clearing the deadly toxins from the animals and fish . . . requires an international ban on the chemicals that contaminate them" (Canadian Press 1989). Another article states that "with an eye on the 1,000 new synthetic chemicals introduced worldwide every year and the 100,000 already on the market, the International Joint Commission is saying that if a chemical belongs to a problem family, manufacturers, importers, and users should have to prove it is not persistent and toxic before it can be introduced or remain on the market" (Smith 1996). Another puts the onus on government, suggesting that we need a "higher level of concern and commitment by the government to find out about the relationship of these chemicals to human disease" (Cone 1998). Articles identifying forms of collective action as a solution decline dramatically (p < .01): from 92 percent in 1986–1996 to 69 percent in 1997–2006.

Corresponding with this drop is a significant increase (p < .001) in the number of articles using a "precautionary consumption" frame (13% in 1986–1996 and 47% in 1997–2006). Many of these articles employ a language related to the precautionary principle—a "better safe than sorry" policy mandate to act despite a lack full scientific certainty to prevent harm to human health or the environment (O'Riordan, Cameron, and Jordan 2001). This principle represents a "public paradigm" (Brown 2007), however, in the case of this frame, precaution is decidedly self-interested and enacted at the individual consumer level. A store owner in one article, for example, is quoted as saying "our store is all about the precautionary principle" (Morphet 2005), while another article quotes a "healthy" shopper who claims to be "very cautious in what I use. I am very good at reading a label" (Wigod 1998). Most importantly, this frame suggests that specific changes to one's behavior as a consumer can reduce exposure to potentially harmful chemicals. Readers are advised to refrain from heating leftovers in plastic, to reduce their use of cosmetics and perfumes, and to buy furniture and electronics that have not been treated with brominated flame retardants. One article entitled "How pure can you get? Worried about how many harmful chemicals are in the food you eat and the air you breathe? There are ways to keep the toxic levels down" notes the universal and involuntary nature of contamination, but concludes with a section advising readers to eat organic food and to avoid many cosmetic products and conventional cleaners (Morphet 2005). Another observes that avoidance is impossible—"don't eat, don't drink and don't breathe"—but includes tips on buying goods without contaminants (Mittelstaedt 2006). The precautionary consumption frame implies that involuntary chemical exposures can be avoided through informed consumer choices or through changes to everyday behaviors.

To summarize, over a period of two decades between 1986 and 2006, we see a significant shift in the framing of body burdens. There is a drop in the proportion of articles whose problem frame discusses forms of collective action as a solution to chemical bioaccumulation, such as the implementation of stronger regulations or placing restrictions on chemical production. The precautionary consumption frame becomes more prominent, while frames articulating institutional or industrial responsibility for contamination fade away. In other words, while news frames in the earlier period reference the broader institutional arrangements involved in the production of chemical hazards, more recently, chemical risks are framed as an individual consumer and health problem, even when the efficacy of individual protective actions are unclear.

Discussion and Conclusions

When we track variations in the framing of body burdens over a 20-year period, we see two important trends. First, the framing of responsibility for contamination becomes increasingly vague. Second, the notion of precautionary consumption, a form of privatized self-protection, emerges as a key frame. Its emergence coincides with the appearance of the "consumption fallacy" (Altman et al. 2008) and "personal commodity bubble" (Szasz 2007) observed in other studies. Self-protection, therefore, is a dominant frame in the discourse of environmental and technological risks, even though it undermines the importance of structural reform.

Precautionary Consumption and the Individualization of Risk

The emergence of the precautionary consumption frame contributes to the individualization of risk and responsibility, and the market for environmentally friendly goods is presented as an alternative whereby individuals can enact their own standards of precaution. When, for example, an article expresses concern about chemicals present in ordinary brands of dish soap (those approved by federal regulators), and readers are advised to avoid these brands in favor of "ecological" alternatives, the article is encouraging the enactment of a precautionary—but individualized—risk assessment. By conceptualizing protection as a consumption problem, a precautionary consumption frame defines responsibility at the individual level, thereby eliminating the discursive space in which one might contemplate the role of the state. The meaning of precaution in this frame contrasts sharply with the precautionary principle, which is inherently supportive of collective mechanisms of universal protection.

The increasing focus on self-protection found in the media articles is at least partly explained by the increasing interest in the human health effects of environmental degradation. As Brown et al. (2001) similarly argue, a focus on the human health dimensions of environmental pollution turns the discussion away from themes of collective responsibility and institutional complicity toward a "personal health" model, prioritizing healthy behaviors and the individual's responsibility in the maintenance of well-being. The individualizing effect is bolstered by the articles' focus on consumer goods as pathways of exposure to chemicals. At the same time, there is a sharp decline in the number of articles linking environmental contamination to the presence of contaminants in food; food is no longer conceptualized as part of the environment, but is seen as a commodity. Unlike universal environmental exposures—such as exposure to polluted air—contact with contaminants in everyday commodities is more personal than collective, as it relates to a specific consumer *choice*. . . .

Precautionary consumption hints at the possibility of controlling a fundamentally uncontrollable phenomenon. It offers self-protection through consumption—a tangible and immediate solution to chemical exposure—thereby suggesting that individuals are empowered to manage this risk. Rather than look to (and wait for) the state to regulate chemical production and prevent pollution at the outset, responsibility is transferred to the individual—in this case, the reader—who gains immediate control over his or her exposure through specific measures of chemical avoidance and "green" consumption. The precautionary consumption frame provides a false sense of empowerment and comfort, given that self-protection through consumption offers a tangible, immediate and artificial solution to the systemic and structural problem of chemical exposure. The tendency of news articles to draw on this frame may furthermore reflect journalistic norms, as articles strive to address the underlying question of "what can I do?" with even the most uncontrollable risk. Ironically, the more inherently unmanageable a universal risk is, the more vulnerable it becomes to this sort of individualization, owing to the struggle to provide the reader with a sense of control.

Theoretical Implications

The growing attention to consumer products highlights how *multiple* sources of risk complicate the framing of responsibility for risk production. Chronic chemical bioaccumulation is an emergent risk. It is created by multiple and integrated sources, making it difficult to identify a single perpetrator and ultimately leading to what Beck calls organized irresponsibility. Although Beck gives brief theoretical consideration to organized irresponsibility, this study of body burdens illustrates how this notion exists empirically as a dominant news frame and is associated with "emergence" as an objective characteristic of risk. In the mid-to late-1980s, for example, when the focus on chemical bioaccumulation centered on industrial activity in the Great Lakes region, articles were more likely to highlight the institutional dimensions of responsibility, especially the failure of government to control pollution. After the mid-1990s, a greater number of articles concentrated on universal exposure through the combination of environment, food, and consumer good path-ways—coinciding with a much weaker framing of blame and responsibility.

Finally, the ideological congruence of precautionary consumption with neo-liberalism cannot be ignored. The precautionary consumption frame draws on the language of choice and individual autonomy, and presents chemical bioaccumulation as a lifestyle and consumer problem. Here, the risk-as-governance perspective is appropriate for understanding shifts in framing. An emphasis on the consumer's role in mitigating environmental and technological risks resonates with a neo-liberal model of governance, where the market, rather than the state, becomes the primary institution for social change. As this literature demonstrates, neo-liberalism is reflected in the discursive transfer of responsibility away from the state to the market, and away from individuals as citizens to individuals as consumers (Ilcan 2009). Owing to their role in producing "safer" consumer alternatives, the green consumer product and organic food industries stand to gain from such a shift, as they are the only organizations that can enable self-protection. The sheer range of green alternatives available to consumers is astounding. Major supermarkets now carry a range of non-toxic water bottles, children's toys, computers, and cosmetics, as well as a full range of organic foodstuffs. As this market expands, the frame of precautionary consumption becomes increasingly accessible to the news media, particularly when such products are marketed as "non-toxic" and "natural."

There are significant social and political implications associated with these shifts in framing. By encouraging individualized responses to a universal risk, news articles divert attention away from the role of state institutions, industry, science and technology in creating and managing the hazards associated with industrialization and chemical production. Individuals may be able to reduce their exposure to some contaminants by changing their shopping habits, but the frame of precautionary consumption overstates this ability, particularly when contaminants are present in air, water, and soil. This frame also leaves unspoken the social and economic constraints on access to "green" products. In fact, universal protection will require collective measures that motivate greater regulatory stringency, better chemical safety assessments, and substantial decreases in chemical production.

Notes

MacKendrick, Norah A. 2010. "Media Framing of Body Burdens: Precautionary Consumption and the Individualization of Risk." Sociological Inquiry 80(1): 126–149.

1. In this article, "body burden" and "chemical bioaccumulation" are used interchangeably. . . .

2. In 1998, Canada hosted the first round of negotiations to draft a global United Nations-sponsored treaty to deal with these pollutants.

3. Farmed fish can contain higher levels of toxins than wild-caught fish, and most retailers use labels to distinguish wild-caught from farmed fish. Farmed fish are a specific commodity with a higher risk of contamination and do not represent a ubiquitous or universal risk.

4. This is especially the case with the discourse of environmental justice. By drawing attention to social and racial stratification in proximity to industrial pollution and toxic waste, this discourse similarly connects environmental degradation to human health (Taylor 2000).

References

Allan, S. 2002. *Media, Risk, and Science*. Philadelphia, PA: Open University Press.

Altheide, D. L. 1997. "The News Media, the Problem Frame, and the Production of Fear." *The Sociological Quarterly* 38:647–68.

Altman, R. G., R. Morello-Frosch, J. G. Brody, R. Rudel, P. Brown and M. Averick. 2008. "Pollution Comes Home and Gets Personal: Women's Experience of Household Chemical Exposure." *Journal of Health and Social Behavior* 49:417–35.

Antilla, L. 2005. "Climate of Scepticism: US Newspaper Coverage of the Science of Climate Change." *Global Environmental Change-Human and Policy Dimensions* 15:338–52.

Beck, U. 1992. *Risk Society: Towards a New Modernity*. London, UK: Sage Publications.

—— 1995. *Ecological Politics in an Age of Risk*. Cambridge: Polity Press.

—— 1999. *World Risk Society*. Malden, Mass: Polity Press.

—— 2006. "Living in the World Risk Society." *Economy and Society* 35:329–45.

Beck, U. and E. Beck-Gernsheim. 2002. *Individualization: Institutionalized Individualism and Its Social and Political Consequences*. Thousand Oaks, CA: SAGE.

Bergman, B. 1989. "Toxins Place Arctic Way of Life in Jeopardy." *Toronto Star* 15:A22.

Binder, A. 1993. "Constructing Racial Rhetoric: Media Depictions of Harm in Heavy Metal and Rap Music." *American Sociological Review* 58:753–67.

Brown, P. 2007. *Toxic Exposures: Contested Illnesses and the Environmental Health Movement*. New York: Columbia University Press.

Brown, P. and S. Zavestoski. 2004. "Social Movements in Health: An Introduction." *Sociology of Health & Illness* 26:679–94.

Brown, P., S. M. Zavestoski, S. McCormick, J. Mandelbaum and T. Luebke. 2001. "Print Media Coverage of Environmental Causation of Breast Cancer." *Sociology of Health & Illness* 23:747–75.

Brown, P., S. Zavestoski, S. McCormick, B. Mayer, R. Morello-Frosch and R. G. Altman. 2004. "Embodied Health Movements: New Approaches to Social Movements in Health." *Sociology of Health & Illness* 26:50–80.

Bueckert, D. 1991. "Pollution, Infertility Studied." *The Globe and Mail* 20:E13.

Cable, S., T. E. Shriver and T. L. Mix. 2008. "Risk Society and Contested Illness: The Case of Nuclear Weapons Workers." *American Sociological Review* 73:380–400.

Carvalho, A. and J. Burgess. 2005. "Cultural Circuits of Climate Change in UK Broadsheet Newspapers, 1985–2003." *Risk Analysis* 25:1457–69.

Centers for Disease Control (CDC). 2005. *Third National Report on Human Exposure to Environmental Chemicals*. Atlanta, GA: Centers for Disease Control and Prevention, National Center for Environmental Health.

Canadian Environmental Law Association (CELA). 2006. *Confidentiality and Burden of Proof under the Canadian Environmental Protection Act (CEPA). Submission to the House of Commons Standing Committee on Environment and Sustainable Development*. Toronto, ON: Canadian Environmental Law Association.

Clarke, L. 1993. "The Disqualification Heuristic." *Research in Social Problems and Public Policy* 5:298–312.

Clarke, L. and J. F. Short. 1993. "Social-Organization and Risk: Some Current Controversies." *Annual Review of Sociology* 19:375–99.

Colborn, T., D. Dumanoski and J. P. Myers. 1996. *Our Stolen Future: Are We Threatening Our Fertility, Intelligence, and Survival? A Scientific Detective Story*. New York: Dutton.

Coleman, C.-L., J. Hartley and D. Kennamer. 2006. "Examining Claimsmakers' Frames in News Coverage of Direct-to-Consumer Advertising." *Journalism and Mass Communication Quarterly* 83:547–63.

Cone, M. 1998. "Pollution Is Feminizing World's Wildlife, Study Indicates." *The Vancouver Sun* September 24:A16.

Corburn, J. 2005. *Street Science: Community Knowledge and Environmental Health Justice*. Cambridge, MA: MIT Press.

D'Angelo, P. 2002. "News Framing as a Multiparadigmatic Research Program: A Response to Entman." *Journal of Communication* 52:870–88.

Doyle, Aaron. 2007. "Introduction: Trust, Citizenship and Exclusion in the Risk Society." Pp. 7–22 in *Risk and Trust: Including or Excluding Citizens?*, edited by Law Society of Canada. Black Point, NS: Fernwood Pub.

Driedger, S. M. 2007. "Risk and the Media: A Comparison of Print and Televised News Stories of a Canadian Drinking Water Risk Event." *Risk Analysis* 27:775–86.

Eldridge, J., J. Reilly, N. Pidgeon, R. E. Kasperson and P. Slovic. 2005. "Risk and Relativity: BSE and the British Media." Pp. 138–54 in *The Social Amplification of Risk*, edited by N. Pidgeon, R. E. Kasperson, P. Slovic. Sterling, VA: Earthscan.

Entman, R. M. 1993. "Framing: Toward Clarification of a Fractured Paradigm." *Journal of Communication* 43:51–8.

Ericson, R. V., P. M. Baranek and J. B. L. Chan. 1989. *Negotiating Control: A Study of News Sources*. Toronto: University of Toronto Press.

Ericson, R. V., A. Doyle and D. Barry. 2003. *Insurance as Governance*. Toronto: University of Toronto Press.

Freudenburg, W. R. 1993. "Risk and Recreancy: Weber, the Division of Labor, and the Rationality of Risk Perceptions." *Social Forces* 71:909–32.

Freudenburg, W. R., C.-L. Coleman, J. Gonzales and C. Helgeland. 1996. "Media Coverage of Hazard Events: Analyzing the Assumptions." *Risk Analysis* 16:31–42.

Gamson, W. A. and A. Modigliani. 1989. "Media Discourse and Public Opinion on Nuclear Power: A Constructionist Approach." *American Journal of Sociology* 95:1–37.

Gillespie, C. 2005. "Guarding Your Home against Pollutants." *Toronto Star*, August 6:N12.

Grandjean, P. and P. J. Landrigan. 2006. "Developmental Neurotoxicity of Industrial Chemicals." *The Lancet* 368:2167–78.

Griffin, R. J., S. Dunwoody and C. Gehrmann, 1995. The Effects of Community Pluralism on Press Coverage of Health Risks from Local Environmental Contamination. *Risk Analysis* 15: 449–58.

Hilgartner, S. and C. L. Bosk. 1988. "The Rise and Fall of Social-Problems—A Public Arenas Model." *American Journal of Sociology* 94:53–78.

Ilcan, S. 2009. "Privatizing Responsibility: Public Sector Reform under Neoliberal Government." *The Canadian Review of Sociology and Anthropology* 46:207–34.

Iles, A. 2007. "Identifying Environmental Health Risks in Consumer Products: Non-Governmental Organizations and Civic Epistemologies." *Public Understanding of Science* 16:371–91.

Kasperson, R. E., O. Renn, P. Slovic, H. S. Brown, J. Emel, R. Goble, J. X. Kasperson, S. Ratick and N. Pidgeon. 2005. "The Social Amplification of Risk: A Conceptual Framework." Pp. 13–46 in *The Social Amplification of Risk*, edited by N. Pidgeon, R. E. Kasperson, P. Slovic. Sterling, VA: Earthscan.

Kitsuse, J. L. and M. Spector. 1973. "Toward a Sociology of Social Problems: Social Conditions, Value Judgments, and Social Problems." *Social Problems* 20:407–19.

Kroll-Smith, J. S., P. Brown and V. J. Gunter. 2000. Illness and the Environment: A Reader in Contested Medicine. New York: New York University Press.

Lupton, D. 1999. *Risk*. New York: Routledge.

MacKendrick, N. A. 2009. *"Protecting Ourselves from Chemicals: A Study of Gender and Precautionary Consumption."* Consuming Chemicals Paper Series. Toronto, ON: National Network on Environments and Women's Health.

McAndrew, B. 1998. "Cleansers Cause Fears over Cancer. Group Thinks It's Possible There's a Link." *Toronto Star* 24:A8.

McCormick, S., P. Brown and S. Zavestoski. 2003. "The Personal Is Scientific, the Scientific Is Political: The Public Paradigm of the Environmental Breast Cancer Movement." Sociological Forum 18:545–76.

McInnes, C 1988. "Chemical Pollution a Motherhood Issue." The Globe and Mail 23:D4.

Miller, M. M. and B. P. Reichert. 2000. "Interest Group Strategies and Journalistic Norms." Pp. 45–54 in *Environmental Risks and the Media*, edited by S. Allan, B. Adam, C. Carter. New York: Routledge.

Mittelstaedt, M. 2006. "Want a Full-Time Job? Live Chemical-Free; Consumers Bombarded by Toxins Are Fighting Back. But There's Really Only One Way to Win -'Don't Eat, Don't Drink and Don't Breathe.'" *The Globe and Mail* 1:A10.

Moneo, M. 2006. "Study Examining Safety of Seafood Eaten by Natives." *The Globe and Mail* 17:S1.

Morello-Frosch, R., J. G. Brody, P. Brown, R. G. Altman, R. A. Rudel and C. Perez. 2009. "Toxic Ignorance and Right-to-Know in Biomonitoring Results Communication: A Survey of Scientists and Study Participants." *Environmental Health* 8:6.

Morphet, S. 2005. "How Pure Can You Get? Worried About How Many Harmful Chemicals Are in the Food You Eat and the Air You Breathe? There Are Ways to Keep the Toxic Levels Down." *The Globe and Mail* 26: F4.

Nelkin, D. 1987. *Selling Science: How the Press Covers Science and Technology*. New York: W.H. Freeman. O'Malley, P. 2004. *Risk, Uncertainty and Government*. London, UK: GlassHouse.

O'Riordan, T., J. Cameron and A. Jordan. 2001. *Reinterpreting the Precautionary Principle*. London, UK: Cameron May.

Oliver, P. and H. Johnston. 1999. "What a Good Ideal Ideology and Frames in Social Movement Research." *Mobilization* 5:37–54.

Perrow, C. 1984. *Normal Accidents: Living with High-Risk Technologies*. New York: Basic Books.

Press, C. 1989. "Inuit Told Food Supply Shows Safe PCB Levels." The Vancouver Sun 8:A.9.

Roberts, J. A. and N. Langston. 2008. "Toxic Bodies/Toxic Environments: An Interdisciplinary Forum." *Environmental History* 13:629–35.

Robinson, E. E. 2002. Community Frame Analysis in Love Canal: Understanding Messages in a Contaminated Community. *Sociological* Spectrum 22:139–69.

Rose, N. 1999. *Powers of Freedom: Reframing Political Thought*. Cambridge: Cambridge University Press.

Scheufele, D. A. 1999. "Framing as a Theory of Media Effects." *Journal of Communication* 49:103–22.

Scheufele, D. A. and D. Tewksbury. 2007. "Framing, Agenda Setting, and Priming: The Evolution of Three Media Effects Models." *Journal of Communication* 57:9–20.

Scott, D. N. 2007. "Risk as a Technique of Governance in an Era of Biotechnological Innovation: Implications for Democratic Citizenship and Strategies of Resistance." Pp. 23–56 in *Risk and Trust: Including or Excluding Citizens?*, edited by Law Society of Canada. Black Point, NS: Fernwood Pub.

Seale, C. 2003. "Health and Media: An Overview." *Sociology of Health & Illness* 25:513–31.

Sexton, K., L. L. Needham, and J. L. Pirkle. 2004. Human Biomonitoring of Environmental Chemicals. *American Scientist* 92: 38–45.

Simpson, S. 2001. "Flushing Is Start of Toxic Journey: No Escaping Daily Load of Chemicals Entering Strait of Georgia, Scientist Discovers." *The Vancouver Sun*, October 25:B7.

Smith, C. 1996. "Of Estrogen Mimics and Breast Cancer." *Toronto Star*, August 3:E6.

Stallings, R. A. 1990. "Media Discourse and the Social Construction of Risk." *Social Problems* 37:80–95.

Steinemann, A. 2004. "Human Exposure, Health Hazards, and Environmental Regulations." *Environmental Impact Assessment Review* 24:695–710.

Szasz, A. 1994. *Ecopopulism: Toxic Waste and the Movement for Environmental Justice*. Minneapolis, MN: University of Minnesota Press.

Szasz, A. 2007. *Shopping Our Way to Safety: How We Changed from Protecting the Environment to Protecting Ourselves*. Minneapolis, MN: University of Minnesota Press.

Taylor, D. E. 2000. "The Rise of the Environmental Justice Paradigm." *American Behavioral Scientist* 43:508–80.

Tuchman, G. 1978. *Making News: A Study in the Construction of Reality*. London, UK: Collier Macmillan.

Ubelacker, S. 2005. "Reheating Leftovers? Make Sure Plastic Containers Are Microwave-Safe." *The Calgary Herald*, December 29:C1.

Wigod, R. 1998. "Cosmetics Crusader Urges Users to Think Critically About Products." *The Vancouver Sun*, October 26:B11.

Young, M. L. 1990. "High Dioxin Found in Mothers' Breast Milk." *The Vancouver Sun* 29:B.2.

Zavestoski, S., K. Agnello, F. Mignano and F. Darroch. 2004. Issue Framing and Citizen Apathy Toward Local Environmental Contamination. *Sociological Forum* 19: 255–83.

PART

Social and Environmental Change—Ideas and Actions

Individualization

Plant a Tree, Buy a Bike, Save the World?

Michael Maniates

This final section of our reader consists of four pieces that present a variety of ways of thinking about and accomplishing social change, from individual-level action to more coordinated efforts at the regional, national, and global levels. In this first selection, Michael Maniates, a political scientist, argues that U.S. environmentalism has become increasingly limited by a model focusing on individual action, where people act mainly as consumers rather than as citizens working to change social and political structures. Maniates points out, as one example, that encouraging consumers to choose more efficient cars deflects attention away from the reality that the structure of the transportation system (based on the needs of the automobile) is inherently polluting, resource inefficient, and destructive. Sustainability requires a much deeper level of change in which citizens are offered a true alternative to automobile travel. This type of progress is only possible with collective action that demands, for instance, that mass transit systems be awarded the same level of government support and subsidy that is presently showered on the automotive industry. Maniates concludes by suggesting that we break out of the individualist approach and search for ways we might foster genuine sustainability by working together to create institutional level, systemic change.

"But now," says the Once-ler, "now that you're here, the word of the Lorax seems perfectly clear. UNLESS someone like you cares a whole awful lot, nothing is going to get better. It's not. SO . . . Catch!" calls the Once-ler. He lets something fall. "It's a Truffula Seed. It's the last one of all! You're in charge of the last of the Truffula Seeds. And Truffula Trees are what everyone needs. Plant a new Truffula. Treat it with care. Give it clean water. And feed it fresh air. Grow a forest. Protect it from axes that hack. Then the Lorax and all of his friends may come back."

—Dr. Seuss

Most people are eagerly groping for some medium, some way in which they can bridge the gap between their morals and their practices.

—Saul Alinsky

One of the most successful modern-day children's stories is *The Lorax*, Dr. Seuss's tale of a shortsighted and voracious industrialist who clear cuts vast tracks of Truffula trees to produce "Thneeds" for unquenchable consumer markets. The Lorax, who "speaks for the trees" and the many animals who make the Truffula forest their home, politely but persistently challenges the industrialist, a Mr. Once-ler, by pointing out again and again the terrible toll his business practices are taking on the natural landscape. The Once-ler remains largely deaf to the Lorax's protestations. "I'm just meeting consumer demand," says the Once-ler, "if I didn't, someone else would." When, finally, the last Truffula tree is cut and the landscape is reduced to rubble, the Once-ler—now out of business and apparently penniless—realizes the error of his ways. Years later, holed up in the ruins of his factory amidst a desolate landscape, he recounts his foolishness to a passing boy and charges him with replanting the forest.

The Lorax is fabulously popular. Most of the college students with whom I work—and not just the ones who consider themselves environmentalists— know it well and speak of it fondly. My children read it in school. The 30-minute animated version of the book often finds its way onto television. The tale has become a beloved organizing touchstone for environmentalists. In years past, for example, the EcoHouse on my campus has aired it as part of its Earth Day observations, as did the local television station. A casual search through the standard library databases reveals over 80 essays or articles in the past decade that bear on or draw from the book. A more determined search of popular newspapers and magazines would undoubtedly reveal additional examples of shared affection for the story.

All this for a tale that is, well, both dismal and depressing. The Once-ler is a stereotypical rapacious businessman. He succeeds in enriching himself by laying ruin to the landscape. The Lorax fails miserably in his efforts to challenge the interlocking processes of industrial capitalism and consumerism that turn his Eden into a wasteland. The animals of the story are forced to flee to uncertain futures. At the end of the day the Lorax's only satisfaction is the privilege of being able to say "I told you so," but this—and the Once-ler's slide into poverty—has to be small consolation. The conclusion sees a small boy with no evident training in forestry or community organizing entrusted with the last seed of a critical species. He's told to "plant a new Truffula. Treat it with care. Give it clean water. And feed it fresh air. Grow a forest. Protect it from axes that hack. Then the Lorax and all of his friends may come back." His chances of success are by no means high.

So why the amazing popularity of *The Lorax*? Why do so many deem it "the environmental book for children"—and, seemingly, for grown-ups too—"by which all others must be judged?" One reason is its overarching message of environmental stewardship and faith in the restorative powers of the young. The book recounts a foolish tragedy that can be reversed only by a new and, one hopes, more enlightened generation. Surely another reason is the comfortable way the book (easily trivialized by adults as children's literature) permits us to look squarely at a set of profoundly uncomfortable dynamics we know to be operating but find difficult to confront—consumerism, the concentration of economic power, the mindless degradation of the environment, the seeming inability of science (represented by the fact-spouting Lorax himself) and objective fact to slow the damage. The systematic undermining of environmental systems fundamental to human well-being is scary stuff, though no more so than one's own sense of personal impotence in the face of such destruction. Seuss's clever rhyming schemes and engaging illustrations, wrapped around the twentieth-century tale of economic expansion and environmental degradation, provide safe passage through a topic we know is out there but would rather avoid.

There is another reason, though, why the book is so loved. By ending with the charge to plant a tree, *The Lorax* echoes and amplifies an increasingly dominant, largely American response to the contemporary environmental crisis. This response half-consciously understands environmental degradation as the product of individual shortcomings (the Once-ler's greed, for example), best countered by action that is staunchly individual and typically consumer based (buy a tree and plant it!). It embraces the notion that knotty issues of consumption, consumerism, power, and responsibility can be resolved neatly and cleanly through enlightened, uncoordinated consumer choice. Education is a critical ingredient in this view—smart consumers will make choices, it is thought, with the larger public good in mind. Accordingly, this dominant response emphasizes (like the Lorax himself) the need to speak politely, and individually, armed only with facts.

For the lack of a better term, call this response the *individualization of responsibility*. When responsibility for environmental problems is individualized, there is little room to ponder institutions, the nature and exercise of political power, or ways of collectively changing the distribution of power and influence in society—to, in other words, "think institutionally," as UC Berkeley sociologist Robert Bellah says. Instead, the serious work of confronting the threatening socioenvironmental processes that *The Lorax* so ably illuminates falls to individuals, acting alone, usually as consumers. We are individualizing responsibility when we agonize over the "paper-or-plastic" choice at the checkout counter, knowing somehow that neither is right given larger institutions and social structures. We think aloud with the neighbor over the back fence about whether we should buy the new Honda or Toyota hybrid-engine automobile now or wait a few years until they work the kinks out. What we really wish for, though, is clean, efficient, and effective public transportation of the sort we read about in science fiction novels when we were young—but we cannot vote for it with our consumer dollars since, for reasons rooted in power and politics, it is not for sale. So we ponder the "energy stickers" on the ultraefficient appliances at Sears, we diligently compost our kitchen waste, we try to ignore the high initial cost and buy a few compact-fluorescent lightbulbs. We read spirited reports in the *New York Times Magazine* on the pros and cons of recycling while sipping our coffee, carefully study the merits of this and that environmental group so as to properly decide on the destination of our small annual donation, and meticulously sort our recyclables. And now an increasing number of us are confronted by opportunistic green-power providers who urge us to "save the planet" by buying their "green electricity"—while doing little to actually increase the quantity of electricity generated from renewable resources.

The Lorax is not why the individualization of responsibility dominates the contours of contemporary American environmentalism. Several forces, described later in this chapter, are to blame. They include the historical baggage of mainstream environmentalism, the core tenets of liberalism, the dynamic ability of capitalism to commodify dissent, and the relatively recent rise of global environmental threats to human prosperity. Seuss's book simply has been swept up and adopted by these forces. Were he alive, Seuss would probably be surprised by the near deification of his little book. And his central character, a Lorax who politely sought to hold a corporate CEO accountable, surely would be appalled that his story is being used to justify individual acts of planting trees as the primary response to the threat of global climate change.

Mark Dowie, a journalist and sometimes historian of the American environmental movement, writes about our "environmental imagination," by which he means our collective ability to imagine and pursue a variety of productive responses (from individual action to community organization to whole-scale institutional change) to the environmental problems before us. My claim in this chapter is that an accelerating individualization of responsibility in the United States is narrowing, in dangerous ways, our "environmental imagination" and undermining our capacity to react effectively to environmental threats to human wellbeing. Those troubled by overconsumption, consumerism, and commodification should not and cannot ignore this narrowing. Confronting the consumption problem demands, after all, the sort of institutional thinking that the individualization of responsibility patently undermines. It calls too for individuals to understand themselves as citizens in a participatory democracy first, working together to change broader polity, and larger social institutions, and as consumers second. By contrast, the individualization of responsibility, because it characterizes environmental problems as the consequence of destructive consumer choice, asks that individuals imagine themselves as consumers first and citizens second. Grappling with the consumption problem, moreover, means engaging in conversation both broad and deep about consumerism and frugality and ways of fostering the capacity for restraint But when responsibility for environmental ills is individualized, space for such conversation becomes constricted. The individually responsible consumer is encouraged to purchase a vast array of "green" or "ecofriendly" products on the premise that the more such products are purchased and consumed, the healthier the planet's ecological processes will become. "Living lightly on the planet" and "reducing your environmental impact" becomes, paradoxically, a consumer-product growth industry.

Skeptics may reasonably question if the individualization of responsibility is so omnipresent as to warrant such concern. As the next section of this chapter shows, it is: the depoliticization of environmental degradation is in full swing across a variety of fronts and shows little sign of abating. The chapter continues with a review of the forces driving this individualization; in particular, it implicates the rise of global environmental problems and the construction of an individualized politics around them. How might these forces be countered? How can the politics of individualization be transcended? How might our environmental imagination be expanded? I wrestle with these questions in the final section of this chapter by focusing on the IPAT formula—a dominant conceptual lens within the field of environmental policy and politics, which argues that environmental impact = population × affluence × technology.

A Dangerous Narrowing?

A few years back Peter Montague, editor of the Internet-distributed *Rachel's Environmental and Health Weekly*, took the Environmental Defense Fund

(EDF) to task for its annual calendar, which this powerful and effective organization widely distributes to its more than 300,000 members and many nonmembers too. What drew Montague's ire was the final page of EDFs 1996 calendar, which details a ten-point program to "save the Earth" (EDF's phrase):

1. Visit and help support our national parks
2. Recycle newspapers, glass, plastic, and aluminum
3. Conserve energy and use energy-efficient lighting
4. Keep tires properly inflated to improve gas mileage and extend tire life
5. Plant trees
6. Organize a Christmas tree recycling program in your community
7. Find an alternative to chemical pesticides for your lawn
8. Purchase only brands of tuna marked "dolphin-safe"
9. Organize a community group to clean up a local stream, highway, park, or beach
10. Become a member of EDF.

Montague's reaction was terse and pointed:

> What I notice here is the complete absence of any ideas commensurate with the size and nature of the problems faced by the world's environment. I'm not against recycling Christmas trees—if you MUST have one—but who can believe that recycling Christmas trees—or supporting EDF as it works overtime to amend and re-amend the Clean Air Act—is part of any serious effort to "save the Earth?" I am forced to conclude once again that the mainstream environmental movement in the U.S. has run out of ideas and has no worthy vision.

Shortly after reading Montague's disturbing and, for me, surprising rejection of ten sensible measures to protect the environment (many of which I myself practice), I walked into an introductory course on environmental problems that I often team-teach with colleagues in the environmental science department. The course, like many taught at the undergraduate level, strives to integrate the natural and social sciences, challenging students to consider not only the physical cause-and-effect relationships that manifest themselves as environmental degradation, but also to think critically about the struggles for power and influence that underlie most environmental problems. That day, near the end of a very productive semester, my colleague divided the class of about 45 students into smaller "issue groups" (energy, water, agriculture, and so on) and asked each group to develop a rank-order list of "responses" or "solutions" to environmental threats specific to that issue. He then brought the class back together, had each group report in, and tabulated their varied "solutions." From this group of 45, the fourth most recommended solution to mounting environmental degradation was to ride a bike rather than drive a car. Number 3 on the list was to recycle. The second most preferred action was "plant a tree," and the top response was, again, "plant a tree" (the mechanics of tabulating student preference across the issue groups permitted a singularly strong preference to occupy two slots).

When we asked our students—who were among the brightest and best prepared of the many we had worked with over the years—why, after 13 weeks of intensive study of environmental problems, they were so reluctant to consider as "solutions" broader changes in policy and institutions, they shrugged. Sure, we remember studying these kinds of approaches in class, they said, but such measures were, well, fuzzy, mysterious, messy, and "idealistic."

The end of the day came soon enough and I began my walk home, a pleasant half-mile stroll. The next day was "garbage day" and my neighbors were dutifully placing their recyclables, carefully washed and sorted, on the curbside. I waved hello and we chatted about the weird weather and all that talk about "global climate change." I made my way through my own front door to find my daughters camped out in front of the television, absorbed in a rare predinner video. The evening's selection, a gift from a doting aunt, was from the popular "Wee Sing" series. Entitled Under the Sea, the production chronicles the adventures of a small boy and his grandmother as they interact with a variety of sea creatures on the ocean floor. Dramatic tension is provided by the mysterious sickness of Ottie, a baby otter meant to tug at the heartstrings of all but the most jaded viewers. The story's climax comes when the entire cast discovers a large pile of garbage on the coral reef, a favorite playground of Ottie, and then engages in a group clean-up of the site while singing a song extolling the virtues of recycling and condemning the lazy, shortsighted tendencies of "those humans." My daughters were enthralled by the video: its message about the need to take personal responsibility for the environment resonated clearly with all that they were then learning about the environment, in preschool and kindergarten respectively.

As I reflect now on these past events, I wonder if they are getting the wrong message, ubiquitous as it has become. Consider the following:

- Despite repeated and often highly public criticism of the "10 simple things to save the planet" focus of its calendars, the EDF pushes forward undaunted. Its 2000–2001 calendar again offers "10 tips to help our planet," which again revolve around individual consumer action: recycle, use energy-efficient lighting, avoid the purchase of products that come from endangered species.
- A colleague recently received a small box in the mail with an attached sticker that read "Environmental Solutions—Not Just Problems." Inside

was a peat pot filled with soil in which was growing a pine-tree seedling, together with a piece of paper about two inches square that said "Rather than sensationalize the problems in our world, Environmental Science provides your students with the tools to develop their own opinions and focus on solutions. Keeping with this theme, you and your students can decide where to best plant the enclosed seedling and watch it grow throughout the year." The package was a promotion for one of the most widely used undergraduate environmental-science textbooks.

- These days, my students argue that the best way to reverse environmental degradation is to educate children now in school. When pressed, they explain that only a sea change in the choices individual consumers are making will staunch the ecological bleeding we are now facing—and it is too late to make much of a dent in the consumer preferences of young adults like themselves.
- The biggest environmental issue to hit our community in the last decade has been the threatened demise, for lack of funding, of "drop-off" centers for recycled products. Primary-school students have distributed their artwork around the theme of "Save the Planet—Recycle" (presumably with their teachers' encouragement). Letters to the editor speak gravely of myriad assaults on the planet and the importance of "buying green" and recycling if we are to stop the destruction. And this is not a phenomenon limited to small-town America, a friend visiting Harvard University recently forwarded a flyer, posted over one of the student copy machines, with a line drawing of planet earth and the slogan "Recycle and Do Your Part to Save the Planet." Recycling is a prime example of the individualization of responsibility.
- Despite the criticism by some academics of the mega-hit *50 Simple Things You Can Do to Save the Earth* (a small book outlining 50 "easy" lifestyle changes in service of sustainability), publications sounding the same theme proliferate.
- My daughters (now in first and fourth grade), like so many children their age, remain alert to environmental issues. A favorite book of the younger one is *The Berenstein Bears Don't Pollute*, which speaks to the need to recycle and consume environmentally friendly products. The older one has been drawn to computer games, books, and movies (e.g., *Free Willy*) that pin the blame for degraded habitat, the loss of bio-diversity, and the spread of environmental toxins on Once-ler-like failings (shortsightedness, greed, materialism) of humans in general.

In our struggle to bridge the gap between our morals and our practices, we stay busy—but busy doing what we are most familiar and comfortable with: consuming our way (we hope) to a better America and a better world. When confronted by environmental ills many confess to caring deeply about—Americans seem capable of understanding themselves almost solely as consumers who must buy "environmentally sound" products (and then recycle them), rather than as citizens who might come together and develop political clout sufficient to alter institutional arrangements that drive a pervasive consumerism. The relentless ability of contemporary capitalism to commodify dissent and sell it back to dissenters is surely one explanation for the elevation of consumer over citizen. But another factor, no doubt, is the growing suspicion of and unfamiliarity with processes of citizen-based political action among masses of North Americans. The interplay of state and market after World War II has whittled the obligations of citizenship down to the singular and highly individualized act of voting in important elections. The increasing fragmentation and mobility of everyday life undermines our sense of neighborhood and community, separating us from the small arenas in which we might practice and refine our abilities as citizens. We build shopping malls but let community playgrounds deteriorate and migrate to sales but ignore school-board meetings. Modern-day advances in entertainment and communication increasingly find us sitting alone in front of a screen, making it all seem fine. We do our political bit in the election booth, then get back to "normal."

Given our deepening alienation from traditional understandings of active citizenship, together with the growing allure of consumption-as-social-action, it is little wonder that at a time when our capacity to imagine an array of ways to build a just and ecologically resilient future must expand, it is in fact narrowing. At a moment when we should be vigorously exploring multiple paths to sustainability, we are obsessing over the cobblestones of but one path. This collective obsessing over an array of "green consumption" choices and opportunities to recycle is noisy and vigorous, and thus comes to resemble the foundations of meaningful social action. But it is not, not in any real and lasting way that might alter institutional arrangements and make possible radically new ways of living that seem required.

Environmentalism and the Flight from Politics

The individualization of responsibility for environmental ills and the piecemeal, counterproductive actions it produces have not gone unnoticed by analysts of contemporary environmental politics. Over a decade ago, for example, social ecologist Murray Bookchin vigorously argued that:

> It is inaccurate and unfair to coerce people into believing that they are personally responsible for present-day ecological disasters because they consume too much or proliferate too readily. This privatization of the environmental crisis, like the New Age cults that focus on personal problems rather

than on social dislocations, has reduced many environmental movements to utter ineffectiveness and threatens to diminish their credibility with the public. If "simple living" and militant recycling are the main solutions to the environmental crisis, the crisis will certainly continue and intensify.

More recently, Paul Hawken, the cofounder of the environmentally conscious Smith and Hawken garden-supply company and widely published analyst of "ecocommerce," confessed that

> it [is] clear to me . . . that there [is] no way to "there" from here, that all companies are essentially proscribed from becoming ecologically sound, and that awards to institutions that had ventured to the environmental margins only underlined the fact that commerce and sustainability were antithetical by design, not by intention. Management is being told that if it wakes up and genuflects, pronouncing its amendes honorable, substituting paper for polystyrene, we will be on the path to an environmentally sound world. *Nothing could be farther from the truth. The problem isn't with half measures, but the illusion they foster that subtle course corrections can guide us to the good life that will include a "conserved nature" and cozy shopping malls.*

Bookchin and Hawken are reacting, in large measure, to a 1980s transformation in how Americans understand and attack environmental problems. The 1980s was a decade in which reenergized, politically conservative forces in the United States promoted the rhetoric of returning power and responsibility to the individual, while simultaneously curtailing the role of government in an economy that was increasingly characterized as innately self-regulating and efficient. Within this context, responsibility for creating and fixing environmental problems was radically reassigned, from government, corporations, and the environmentally shortsighted policies they were thought to have together fostered, to individual consumers and their decisions in the marketplace.

This shift was altogether consistent with then-President Reagan's doctrine of personal responsibility, corporate initiative, and limited government. The new conventional wisdom rejected environmental regulations that would coerce the powerful to behave responsibly toward the environment and slap them hard if they did not. Instead, an alternative environmental politics of "win-win," zero-coercion scenarios flourished, in which a technological innovation here or an innocuous change in policy there would, it was argued, produce real reductions in environmental degradation and higher corporate profits. This "win-win" approach continues to dominate American environmental politics, and a vast range of environmentally friendly, economically attractive technologies, from compact fluorescent lights to ultra fuel-efficient automobiles, are showcased as political-economic means toward a conflict-free transition to a future that works. These kinds of technologies make environmental sense, to be sure, and they typically make economic sense as well, once one accounts for the full range of costs and benefits involved. However, they often fail to make "political sense," insofar as their wide diffusion would drive a redistribution of political or economic power.

As cleaner and leaner (i.e., more efficient) technologies surfaced in the 1980s as the solution to pressing environmental ills, responsibility for the environmental crisis necessarily became increasingly individualized. The new technologies, it was thought, would take root and flourish only if consumers purchased them directly or sought out products produced by them. A theory of social change that embraced the image of consumers voting with their pocketbook soon took root. Almost overnight, the burden for fundamental change in American patterns of consumption and production shifted from government (which was to be trimmed) and corporations (which were cast as victims of government meddling and willing servants to consumer sovereignty . . .), onto the backs of individual consumers.

Scholars of environmentalism, however, caution us against too enthusiastically fixing blame for the individualization of responsibility on the Reagan years. Tendencies toward individualization run deep in American environmentalism; Ronald Reagan merely was adept at tapping into them. Some analysts, for instance, note that mainstream environmentalism has technocratic, managerial roots and thus has always been a polite movement more interested in fine-tuning industrial society than in challenging its core tenets. Environmentalism's essential brand of social change—that which can be had by tinkering at the margins and not hurting anyone's feelings—makes it a movement that tends naturally toward easy, personalized "solutions."

Others pin the blame for the individualization of responsibility on the bureaucratic calcification of mainstream, "inside-the-Beltway" environmental groups. Buffeted by backlash in the 1980s, laboring hard to fend off challenges to existing environmental regulations in the 1990s, and unsure about how to react to widespread voter apathy in the 2000s, mainstream environmental groups in the United States have consolidated and "hunkered down." To survive as nonprofit organizations without government financing (as is common in other countries), these U.S. NGOs have had to avoid any costly confrontation with real power while simultaneously appearing to the public as if they are vigorously attacking environmental ills. The result: 10 easy steps to save the planet of the sort proffered each year by the Environmental Defense Fund.

Other scholars draw attention to the classical liberal underpinnings of environmentalism that bias environmentalism toward timid calls for personal responsibility and green consumerism. As Paul Wapner, a professor at American University, notes:

> Liberal environmentalism is so compatible with contemporary material and cultural currents that it implicitly supports the very things that it should be criticizing. Its technocratic, scientific, and even economistic character gives credence to a society that measures the quality of life fundamentally in terms of economic growth, control over nature, and the maximization of sheer efficiency in everything we do. By working to show that environmental protection need not compromise these maxims, liberal environmentalism fails to raise deeper issues that more fundamentally engage the dynamics of environmental degradation.

And yet mainstream environmentalism has not always advanced an individualized consumerist strategy for redressing environmental ills. Even during the turn of the last century, a time of zealous rediscovery of the wonders of efficiency and scientific management, "the dynamics of conservation," observes famed environmental historian Samuel P. Hays, "with its tension between the centralizing tendencies of system and expertise on the one hand and the decentralization of localism on the other," fueled healthy debate over the causes of and cures for environmental ills. Throughout the twentieth century, in fact, mainstream environmentalism has demonstrated an ability to foster multiple and simultaneous interpretations of where we are and where we should be heading.

But that ability has, today, clearly become impaired. Although public support for things environmental has never been greater, it is so because the public increasingly understands environmentalism as an individual, rational, cleanly apolitical process that can deliver a future that works without raising voices or mobilizing constituencies. As individual consumers and recyclers we are supplied with ample and easy means of "doing our bit"—green consumerism and militant recycling becomes the order of the day. The result, though, is often dissonant and sometimes bizarre: consumers wearing "save the earth" T-shirts, for example, speak passionately against recent rises in gasoline prices when approached by television news crews; shoppers drive all over town in their gasoline-guzzling SUVs in search of organic lettuce or shade-grown coffee; and diligent recyclers expend far more fossil-fuel energy on the hot water spent to meticulously clean a tin can than is saved by its recycling.

Despite these jarring contradictions, the technocratic, sanitary, and individualized framing of environmentalism prevails, largely because it is continually reinforced. Consider, for example, recent millennial issues of *Time* and *Newsweek* that look to life in the future. They paint a picture of smart appliances, computer-guided automobiles, clean neighborhoods, ecofriendly energy systems, and happy citizens. How do we get to this future? Not through bold political leadership or citizen-based debate within enabling democratic institutions—but rather via consumer choice: informed, decentralized, apolitical, individualized. Corporations will build a better mousetrap, consumers will buy it, and society will be transformed for the better. A struggle-free ecorevolution awaits, one made possible by the combination of technological innovation and consumer choice with a conscience.

The "better mousetrap theory of social change" so prevalent in these popular news magazines was coined by Langdon Winner, a political science professor and expert on technological politics, who first introduced the term in an essay on the demise of the appropriate technology movement of the 1970s:

> A person would build a solar house or put up a windmill, not only because he or she found it personally agreeable, but because the thing was to serve as a beacon to the world, a demonstration model to inspire emulation. If enough folks built for renewable energy, so it was assumed, there would be no need for the nation to construct a system of nuclear power plants. People would, in effect, vote on the shape of the future through their consumer/builder choices. This notion of social change provided the underlying rationale for the amazing emphasis on do-it-yourself manuals, catalogues, demonstration sites, information sharing, and "networking," that characterized appropriate technology during its heyday. Once people discovered what was available to them, they would send away for the blueprints and build the better mousetrap themselves. As successful grassroots efforts spread, those involved in similar projects were expected to stay in touch with each other and begin forming little communities, slowly reshaping society through a growing aggregation of small-scale social and technical transformations. Radical social change would catch on like disposable diapers, Cuisinarts, or some other popular consumer item.

Like the militant recyclers and dead-serious green consumers of today, appropriate technologists of the 1970s were the standard-bearers for the individualization of responsibility. The difference between then and now is that appropriate technology lurked at the fringes of a 1970s American environmental politics more worried about corporate accountability than consumer choice. Today, green consumption, recycling, and Cuisinart social change occupy the heart of U.S. ecopolitics. Both then and now, such individualization is alarming, for as Winner notes:

> The inadequacies of such ideas are obvious. Appropriate technologists were unwilling to face squarely the facts of organized social and political

power. Fascinated by dreams of a spontaneous, grass-roots revolution, they avoided any deep-seeking analysis of the institutions that control the direction of technological and economic development. In this happy self-confidence they did not bother to devise strategies that might have helped them overcome obvious sources of resistance. The same judgment that Marx and Engels passed on the utopians of the nineteenth century apply just as well to the appropriate technologists of the 1970s: they were lovely visionaries, naive about the forces that confronted them.

Though the inadequacies of these ideas is clear to Winner, they remain obscure to the millions of American environmentalists who would plant a tree, ride a bike, or recycle a jar in the hope of saving the world. The newfound public awareness of global environmental problems may be largely to blame. Shocking images of a "hole" in the ozone layer in the late 1980s, ubiquitous videos on rainforest destruction, media coverage of global climate change and the warming of the poles: all this and more have brought the public to a new state of awareness and concern about the "health of the planet." What, though, is the public to do with this concern? Academic discussion and debate about global environmental threats focuses on distant international negotiations, complicated science fraught with uncertainty that seems to bedevil even the scientists, and nasty global politics. This is no place for the "normal" citizen. Environmental groups often encourage people to act, but recommended action on global environmental ills is limited to making a donation, writing a letter, or—yes—buying an environmentally friendly product. The message on all fronts seems to be "Act . . . but don't get in the way." Confronted by a set of global problems that clearly matter and seeing no clear way to attack them, it is easy to imagine the lay public gravitating to individualistic, consumer-oriented measures. And it is easy to understand how environmental groups would promote such measures; these measures do, after all, meet the public's need for some way to feel as if it is making a difference, and they sell.

Ironically, those laboring to highlight global environmental ills, in the hope that an aroused public would organize and embark on collective, political action, aided and abetted this process of individualization. They paved the way for the likes of Rainforest Crunch ice cream ("buy it and a portion of the proceeds will go to save the rainforests") because they were insufficiently attentive to a fundamental social arithmetic: heightened concern about any social ill, erupting at a time of erosion of public confidence in political institutions and citizen capacities to effect change, will prompt masses of people to act, but in that one arena of their lives where they command the most power and feel the most competent—the sphere of consumption.

Of course, the public has had some help working through this particular arithmetic. A privatization and individualization of responsibility for environmental problems shifts blame from state elites and powerful producer groups to more amorphous culprits like "human nature" or "all of us." State elites and the core corporations on which they depend to drive economic growth stand to benefit from spreading the blame and cranking the rotary of consumption. And crank they will. One example of this dynamic, though not one rooted per se in global ecology, is found in a reading of the history of efforts in the United States in the 1970s to implement a nationwide system of beverage- and food-container reuse, a policy that would have assigned the responsibility for resolving the "solid waste crisis" to the container industry. The container industry spent tens of millions of dollars to defeat key "bottle bill" referendums in California and Colorado, and then vigorously advanced recycling—not reuse—as a more practical alternative. Recycling, by stressing the individual's act of disposal, not the producer's acts of packaging, processing, and distributing, fixes primary responsibility on individuals and local governments. It gives life to a "Wee Sing" diagnosis of environmental ills that places human laziness and ignorance center stage. The bottling industry was successful in holding out its "solution" as the most practical and realistic, and the state went along.

The same dynamic now permeates mainstream discussions of global environmental ills. Pratap Chatterjee and Matthias Finger, seasoned observers of global environmental politics, highlight the rise of a "New Age Environmentalism" that fixes responsibility on all of us equally and, in the process, cloaks important dimensions of power and culpability. They point, for example, to international meetings like the 1992 Earth Summit that cultivate a power-obscuring language of "all of us needing to work together to solve global problems." In the same vein, academics like Gustavo Esteva and Suri Prakash lament how the slogan "think globally, act locally" has been shaped by global environmentalism to support a consumer-driven, privatized response to transboundary environmental ills. In practice, thinking globally and acting locally means feeling bad and guilty about far-off and megaenvironmental destruction, and then traveling down to the corner store to find a "green" product whose purchase will somehow empower somebody, somewhere, to do good. Mainstream conversations about global sustainability advance the "international conference" as the most meaningful venue for global environmental problem solving. It is here that those interests best able to organize at the international level—states and transnational corporations—hold the advantage in the battle to shape the conversation of sustainability and craft the rules of the game. And it is precisely these actors who benefit by moving mass publics toward private, individual, well-intentioned consumer choice as the vehicle for achieving "sustainability."

It is more than coincidental that as our collective perception of environmental problems has become more global, our prevailing way of framing environmental problem solving has become more individualized. In the end, individualizing responsibility does not work—you cannot plant a tree to save the world—and as citizens and consumers slowly come to discover this fact their cynicism about social change will only grow: "You mean after 15 years of washing out these crummy jars and recycling them, environmental problems are still getting worse—geesh, what's the use?" Individualization, by implying that any action beyond the private and the consumptive is irrelevant, insulates people from the empowering experiences and political lessons of collective struggle for social change and reinforces corrosive myths about the difficulties of public life. By legitimating notions of consumer sovereignty and a self-balancing and autonomous market (with a well-informed "hidden hand"), it also diverts attention from political arenas that matter. In this way, individualization is both a symptom and a source of waning citizen capacities to participate meaningfully in processes of social change. If consumption, in all its complexity, is to be confronted, the forces that systematically individualize responsibility for environmental degradation must be challenged.

IPAT, and Beyond

But how? One approach would focus on undermining the dominant frameworks of thinking and talking that make the individualization of responsibility appear so natural and "commonsense." Among other things, this means taking on "IPAT."

At first glance it would seem that advocates of a consumption angle on environmental degradation should naturally embrace IPAT (impact = population × affluence × technology). The "formula" argues, after all, that one cannot make sense of, much less tackle, environmental problems unless one takes into account all three of the proximate causes of environmental degradation. Population growth, resource-intensive and highly polluting technologies, and affluence (that is, levels of consumption) together conspire to undermine critical ecological processes on which human well-being depends. Focusing on one or two of these three factors, IPAT tells us, will ultimately disappoint.

IPAT is a powerful conceptual framework, and those who would argue the importance of including consumption in the environmental degradation equation have not been reluctant to invoke it. They note, correctly so, that the "A" in IPAT has for too long been neglected in environmental debates and policy action. However, although IPAT provides intellectual justification for positioning consumption center stage, it also comes with an underlying set of assumptions—assumptions that reinforce an ineffectual Loraxian flight from politics.

A closer look at IPAT shows that the formula distributes widely all culpability for the environmental crisis (akin to the earlier-mentioned "New Age Environmentalism"). Population size, consumption levels, and technology choice are all to blame. Responsibility for environmental degradation nicely splits, moreover, between the so-called developed and developing world: if only the developing world could get its population under control and the developed world could tame its overconsumption and each could adopt green technologies, all would be well. Such a formulation is, on its face, eminently reasonable, which explains why IPAT stands as such a tempting platform from which advocates of a consumption perspective might press their case.

In practice, however, IPAT amplifies and privileges an "everything is connected to everything else" biophysical, ecosystem-management understanding of environmental problems, one that obscures the exercise of power while systematically disempowering citizen actors. When everything is connected to everything else, knowing how or when or even why to intervene becomes difficult; such "system complexity" seems to overwhelm any possibility of planned, coordinated, effective intervention. Additionally, there is little room in IPAT's calculus for questions of agency, institutions, political power, or collective action. Donella Meadows, a systems analyst and coauthor of *The Limits to Growth*, the 1972 study that drew the world's attention to the social and environmental threats posed by exponential growth, had long advocated IPAT. But the more her work incorporated the human dimension, including issues of domination and distribution, the more she questioned the formulation. After a 1995 conference on global environmental policy, she had a revelation:

> I didn't realize how politically correct [IPAT] had become, until a few months ago when I watched a panel of five women challenge it and enrage an auditorium full of environmentalists, including me. IPAT is a bloodless, misleading, cop-out explanation for the world's ills, they said. It points the finger of blame at all the wrong places. It leads one to hold poor women responsible for population growth without asking who is putting what pressures on those women to cause them to have so many babies. It lays a guilt trip on Western consumers, while ignoring the forces that whip up their desire for ever more consumption. It implies that the people of the East, who were oppressed by totalitarian leaders for generations, now somehow have to clean up those leaders' messes.

And then, in ways that echo Langdon Winner's assessment of the better-mousetrap theory of social change, Meadows concludes that

> IPAT is just what one would expect from physical scientists, said one of its critics. It counts what's countable. It makes rational sense. But it ignores the manipulation, the oppression, the profits. It ignores a factor that [natural] scientists have a hard time quantifying and therefore don't like to talk about: economic and political power. IPAT may be physically indisputable. But it is politically naive.

. . . [I]nquiry into consumption quickly bumps up against tough issues: consumerism, "manufactured needs," limits, global inequity, the specter of coercion, competing and sometimes conflicting understandings of human happiness. Dealing with these topics . . . demands a practiced capacity to talk about power, privilege, prosperity, and larger possibilities. IPAT, despite it usefulness, at best fails to foster this ability; at worst, it actively undermines it. When accomplished anthropologist Clifford Geertz remarked that we are still "far more comfortable talking about technology than talking about power," he surely had conceptual frameworks like IPAT in mind.

Proponents of a consumption angle on environmental degradation must cultivate alternatives to IPAT and conventional development models that focus on, rather than divert attention from, politically charged elements of commercial relations. Formulas like IPAT are handy in that they focus attention on key elements of a problem. In that spirit, then, I propose a variation: "IWAC," which is environmental Impact = quality of Work × meaningful consumption Alternatives × political Creativity. If ideas have power, and if acronyms package ideas, then alternative formulations like IWAC could prove useful in shaking the environmentally inclined out of their slumber of individualization. And this could only be good for those who worry about consumption.

Take "work," for example. IPAT systematically ignores work while IWAC embraces it. As *Atlantic Monthly* senior editor Jack Beatty notes, "radical talk" about work—questions about job security, worker satisfaction, downsizing, overtime, and corporate responsibility—is coming back into public discourse. People who might otherwise imagine themselves as apolitical care about the state of work, and they do talk about it. IWAC taps into this concern, linking it to larger concerns about environmental degradation by suggesting that consumerist impulses are linked to the routinization of work and, more generally, to the degree of worker powerlessness within the workplace. The more powerless one feels at work, the more one is inclined to assert power as a consumer. The "W" in IWAC provides a conceptual space for asking difficult questions about consumption and affluence. It holds out the possibility of going beyond a critique of the "cultivation of needs" by advertisers to ask about social forces (like the deadening quality of the workplace) that make citizens so susceptible to this "cultivation." Tying together two issues that matter to mass publics—the nature of work and the quality of the environment—via something like IWAC could help revitalize public debate and challenge the political timidity of mainstream environmentalism.

Likewise, the "A" in IWAC, "alternatives," expands IPAT's "T" in new directions by suggesting that the public's failure to embrace sustainable technologies has more to do with institutional structures that restrict the aggressive development and wide dissemination of sustainable technologies than with errant consumer choice. The marketplace, for instance, presents us with red cars and blue ones, and calls this consumer choice, when what sustainability truly demands is a choice between automobiles and mass transit systems that enjoy a level of government support and subsidy that is presently showered on the automotive industry. With "alternatives," spirited conversation can coalesce around questions like: Do consumers confront real or merely cosmetic choice? Is absence of choice the consequence of an autonomous and distant set of market mechanisms? Or is the self-interested exercise of political and economic power at work? And how would one begin to find out? In raising these uncomfortable questions, IWAC focuses attention on claims that the direction and pace of technological development is far from autonomous and is almost always political. Breaking down the widely held belief (which is reinforced by IPAT) that technical choice is "neutral" and "autonomous" could open the floodgates to full and vigorous debate over the nature and design of technological choice. Once the veil of neutrality is lifted, rich local discourse can, and sometimes does, follow.

And then there is the issue of public imagination and collective creativity, represented by the "C" in IWAC. Imagination is not a word one often sees in reflections on environmental politics; it lies among such terms as *love*, *caring*, *kindness*, and *meaning* that raise eyebrows when introduced into political discourse and policy analysis. This despite the work of scholars like political scientist Karen Litfin that readily shows how ideas, images, categories, phrases and examples structure our collective imagination about what is proper and what is possible. Ideas and images, in other words, and those who package and broker them, wield considerable power. Susan Griffin, an environmental philosopher, argues the same point from a different disciplinary vantage point when she writes that:

> Like artistic and literary movements, social movements are driven by imagination. . . . Every important social movement reconfigures the world in the imagination. What was obscure comes forward, lies are revealed, memory shaken, new delineation drawn over the old maps: it is from this new way of seeing the present that hope emerges for the future. . . . Let us begin to imagine the worlds we would like to inhabit, the long lives we will share, and the many futures in our hands.

Griffin is no new age spiritualist. She is closer to rough-and-tumble neighborhood activist Saul Alinsky than ecopsychologists like Roszak, Gomes, and Kanner. Alarmed by the political implications of our collective sense of limited possibility and daunting complexity, she is quick to dispense with claims so prevalent in the environmental movement that a "healed mind" and "individual ecological living" will spawn an ecological revolution. Her argument, like Litfin's, bears restating: ideas and the images that convey them have power;

and though subtle, such power can and is exercised to channel ideas into separate tracks labeled "realistic" and "idealistic." Once labeled, what is taken to be impossible or impractical—"idealistic," in other words—can no longer serve as a staging ground for struggle.

Conclusion

IWAC is more illustrative than prescriptive. It highlights how prevailing conceptualizations of the "environmental crisis" drive us toward an individualization of responsibility that legitimizes existing dynamics of consumption and production. The globalization of environmental problems—dominated by natural- science diagnoses of global environmental threats that ignore critical elements of power and institutions—accelerates this individualization, which has deep roots in American political culture. To the extent that commonplace language and handy conceptual frameworks have power, in that they shape our view of the world and tag some policy measures as proper and others as farfetched, IWAC stands as an example of how one might go about propagating an alternative understanding of why we have environmental ills, and what we ought to be doing about them.

A proverbial fork in the road looms large for those who would seek to cement consumption into the environmental agenda. One path of easy walking leads to a future where "consumption" in its environmentally undesirable forms—"overconsumption," "commodification," and "consumerism"—has found a place in environmental debates. Environmental groups will work hard to "educate" the citizenry about the need to buy green and consume less and, by accident or design, the pronounced asymmetry of responsibility for and power over environmental problems will remain obscure. Consumption, ironically, could continue to expand as the privatization of the environmental crisis encourages upwardly spiraling consumption, so long as this consumption is "green." This is the path of business as usual. The other road, a rocky one, winds toward a future where environmentally concerned citizens come to understand, by virtue of spirited debate and animated conversation, the "consumption problem." They would see that their individual consumption choices are environmentally important, but that their control over these choices is constrained, shaped, and framed by institutions and political forces that can be remade only through collective citizen action, as opposed to individual consumer behavior. This future world will not be easy to reach. Getting there means challenging the dominant view—the production, technological, efficiency-oriented perspective that infuses contemporary definitions of progress—and requires linking explorations of consumption to politically charged issues that challenge the political imagination. Walking this path means becoming attentive to the underlying forces that narrow our understanding of the possible.

To many, an environmentalism of "plant a tree, save the world" appears to be apolitical and nonconfrontational, and thus ripe for success. Such an approach is anything but, insofar as it works to constrain our imagination about what is possible and what is worth working toward. It is time for those who hope for renewed and rich discussion about "the consumption problem" to come to grips with this narrowing of the collective imagination and the growing individualization of responsibility that drives it, and to grapple intently with ways of reversing the tide.

Note

Maniates, Michael. 2002. "Individualization: Plant a Tree, Buy a Bike, Save the World?" Pp. 43–66 in Thomas Princen, Michael Maniates and Ken Conca (eds.), *Confronting Consumption*. Cambridge, MA: The MIT Press.

21

Cleaning the Closet
Toward a New Fashion Ethic
Juliet Schor

The manufacture of cloth and clothing is a major source of social injustice and environmental degradation. Far too often, clothing is made in sweatshops under abominable working conditions. This has been publicized by the antisweatshop movement. What some people do not realize, however, is that clothing production has significant environmental consequences. Schor develops three principles for "a new kind of clothing consumer": (1) emphasizing quality over quantity, (2) a return to small-scale enterprises, and (3) a movement toward socially just and environmentally responsible production practices.

I love clothes—shopping for them, buying them, wearing them. I like good-quality fabrics, such as wool or linen. I cultivate long-term relationships with favorite items, such as sweaters and scarves. I delight in a beautifully tailored suit, everything perfectly in place. And I love to find a bargain.

I confess these sartorial passions with some trepidation. Love of clothes is hardly a well-regarded trait by my friends in the environmental, simplicity, feminist, labor, and social justice movements. And for some good reasons. Much of what we now wear comes from foreign sweatshops. Textile production, with its toxic dyes, often poisons the environment. Fashion is a sexist business, which objectifies and degrades women. Young people adopt a must-have imperative for the latest trendy label. Adults have problems too:

The typical compulsive shopper, deep in credit-card debt, has been supporting a shopping habit focused mainly on clothes, shoes, and accessories. Even
a cursory look at the making, marketing, wearing, and discarding of clothes
reveals that the entire business has become deeply problematic. But my
friends have other objections that I find less compelling. Many believe that
clothes are trivial—not worth spending time or effort on. Some feel they are
irreversibly tainted by the excessive importance society has placed on them,
or the power of the greedy behemoths that dominate the industry.

One school of thought—call it "minimalist"—takes a purely utilitarian
stance. Clothes should be functional and comfortable, but beyond that, attention to them is misplaced. The minimalist credo goes like this: Buy as few
clothes as possible, or better yet, avoid new altogether, because there are so
many used garments around. Make sure your garments don't call too much
attention to themselves. Shun labels and "designers." Purchase only products
whose labor conditions and environmental effects can be verified.

This ethic has gained its share of adherents in recent years. A growing
number of young people critique their generation's slavish devotion to Aber-
crombie, North Face, and Calvin, preferring the thrift-shop aesthetic. Simpli-
fiers advocate secondhand stores, clothes swapping parties, and yard sales.
The market for organic clothing, despite its generally inferior design and high
prices, is expanding. No Logo has developed its own cachet.

Clothing minimalism is certainly a morally satisfying position. But most
people do not and will not find minimalism appealing, and not because they
are shallow or fashion addicted. Rather, minimalism fails because it does not
recognize the centrality of clothing to human culture, relationships, aesthetic
desires, and identity. Ultimately, minimalism lacks a positive vision of the role
of clothing and appearance in human societies.

But what could that positive vision be? First, it will affirm the cultural
importance of clothing, rather than trivialize it. It will embrace the consumer
who buys conscientiously and sustainably, but who also has a prized and beautiful wardrobe hanging in her closet. It will recognize that apparel production,
which after all has historically been the vanguard industry of economic development, should provide secure employment for millions of women and men
in poor countries, a creative outlet for designers and consumers, and a technological staging ground for cutting-edge environmental practices. A "clean-
clothes" movement has begun in Europe. Can we transform it into a "clean
and beautiful clothes" movement here in the United States? If so, it holds the
potential to become a model for a wider revolution in consumer practices. For
if we can work it out with a commodity as socially and economically complex
as clothing, we can do it with anything.

Clothes by the Pound

For an introduction to the insanity of the industry, a good place to start is a used-clothing outlet. I chose the Garment District, a hip, department-style warehouse in East Cambridge, Massachusetts. Inside, it's chockfull of every retro and contempo style one could imagine. Outside, huge eighteen-wheeler trucks deposit giant, tightly wrapped bales of clothing, gleaned from charities, merchandisers, and consumers. These clothes sell for a dollar a pound, and seventy-five cents on Friday. That's a price not too much above beans or rice.

Over the fourteen years that the Garment District has been in business, the wholesale price of used clothing has dropped precipitously, by 80 percent in the last five years alone, according to one source. Renee Weeper, director of retail services at Goodwill International, reports that prices in the salvage market dropped to two to three cents per pound by late 1999 and are now in the seven to eight cent range. In this supply-and-demand oriented "aftermarket," the price decline has been caused by an enormous increase in the quantity of discarded clothing. Throughout the 1990s, donations to Goodwill increased by 10 percent or more each year.

And what of the clothing that is not resold to consumers? The Garment District sells its surpluses to "shoddy mills," which grind up the clothes for car-seat stuffing and other "post-consumer" uses. Or they send it into the global used-clothing market, where it is sold by brokers or given away by charitable foundations. Ironically, the influx of cheap and free clothing in Africa, under the guise of "humanitarian aid," has undermined local producers and created more poverty. And that's not the only irony—the excess clothing that ends up in Africa, the Caribbean, or Asia, probably also started out there.

The Point of Production: Sweated Labor and the Poisoned Landscape

Textiles have become the vanguard industry in the emergence of a new global sweatshop, where women—who comprise 70 percent of the labor force—work for starvation wages, making the T-shirts, jeans, dresses, caps, and athletic shoes eagerly purchased by U.S. consumers. The brutal exploitation of labor and natural resources is at the heart of why clothes have become so cheap.

Consider the case of Bangladesh—which by late 2001 was the fourth largest apparel exporter to the United States. The country, with a per capita income under $1,500 per year, a 71 percent female illiteracy rate, and 56 percent of its children under age five suffering from malnourishment, is one of the world's poorest. While proponents of corporate globalization claim the process is lifting people out of poverty, a recent study by the National Labor Committee reveals otherwise. Wages among Bangladesh's 1.6 million apparel workers range from eight cents per hour for helpers to a high of eighteen cents for sewers. Workers are forced to work long hours and are often cheated of their overtime. When demand is high, they work twenty-hour shifts and are allowed only a few hours of sleep under their sewing machines in the dead of night. The workers, most of whom are between sixteen and twenty-five years old, report constant headaches, vomiting, and other illnesses. Even the "highest" wage rates meet less than half the basic survival requirements, with the result being that malnutrition, sickness, and premature aging are common. Ironically, apparel workers cannot afford to buy clothing for themselves—a group of Bangladeshi women factory workers who recently toured the United States report getting only one new garment every two years. The university caps they sew sell for more than seventeen dollars here; their share is a mere 11.6 cents per cap.

These conditions are not atypical. Disney exploits its Haitian workers who make Mickey Mouse shirts for twenty-eight cents an hour. Wal-Mart, which controls 15 percent of the U.S. market and is the world's largest clothing retailer, has Chinese factories that pay as little as thirteen cents per hour, with the norm below twenty-five cents. High-priced designers also exploit cheap labor—Ralph Lauren and Ellen Tracy pay fourteen to twenty cents, Liz Claiborne twenty-eight cents. Nike, despite years of pressure by activists, continues to exploit its Asian workforce. At the Wellco and Yuen Uren factories where its shoes are made, the company was paying only sixteen to nineteen cents per hour, requiring up to eighty-four hours per week including forced overtime, and employing child labor. A recent estimate for a Nike jacket found that the workers received an astounding one half of a percent of its sale price; a study of European jeans found a mere 1 percent went to workers. By contrast, "brand profit" accounts for about 25 percent of the price.

But low wages are only part of the horror of the global sweatshop. Many factories and worker dormitories lack fire exits and are overcrowded and unhealthy. Workers sewing Tommy, Gap, and Ralph Lauren clothes have been found locked inside the factories. They are routinely harassed—sexually and physically—by their supervisors. The Bangladeshi workers report that beatings are common and that they are forbidden to speak inside the factory. Permission to go to the bathroom is severely curtailed, many are forced to work while ill, and companies typically fire those who become pregnant. Unions are bitterly resisted, with terminations, physical harm, and intimidation by employers. The retailers who contract with local factories have tried to build a wall between themselves and their subcontractors, but this is little more than a callous ruse.

Manufacturers are also exploiting the natural environment. While clothing is not typically thought of as a "dirty" product, like an SUV, plastics, or meat, a closer look reveals that this clean image is undeserved. From raw material production through dyeing and finishing, to transport and disposal, the apparel, footwear, and accessories industries are responsible for significant environmental degradation. Consider cotton, which makes up about half of global textile production. Cotton cultivation is fertilizer-, herbicide-, and pesticide-intensive, endangering both the natural environment and agricultural workers. The crop comprises only 3 percent of global acreage, but accounts for 25 percent of world insecticide use. In some cases, the crop is sprayed up to ten times per season with dangerous chemicals, including, among others, Lorsban, Bladex, Kelthane, Dibrom, Metaphos, and Parathion. The toxicity of these chemicals ranges from moderate to high and has been shown to cause a variety of human health problems, such as brain and fetal damage, cancer, kidney and liver damage, as well as harm to birds, fish, bees, and other animals. Not surprisingly, farm workers suffer from more chemical-related illnesses than any other occupational group. Chemical run-off into the nation's drinking water has also been extensive—Aldicarb, an acutely toxic pesticide, has been found in the drinking water of sixteen states. Conventional cultivation also depletes the soil and requires large quantities of irrigation water.

Additional hazards arise from chemical-based dyeing and finishing of cloth. The most common chemical dye, used in textiles and leathers, is the so-called azo-dye, which is now believed to be carcinogenic and has been banned in Germany. Formaldehyde, pentachloraphenol, and heavy metals remain in use despite their toxicity. A little-known aspect of these toxins is their human health impact on both workers and consumers. One German study found that 30 percent of children in that country suffer from textile-related allergies, most of which are triggered by dyes. An estimated 70 percent of textile effluents and 20 percent of dyestuffs are still dumped into water supplies by factories. In South India, where the (highly toxic) tanning industry grew rapidly in the 1990s, local water supplies have been devastatingly polluted by large quantities of poisonous wastes. The various stages of textile production (from spinning, weaving, and knitting to dyeing and finishing) also require enormous energy and water use. For example, one hundred liters of water are needed to process one kilogram (2.2 pounds) of textiles.

Environmental effects can also be more indirect. The consumer rage for cheap cashmere has led to unsustainable expansion of herds in Mongolia and, subsequently, to overgrazing, desertification, and ecological collapse. The growth of new fabrics, such as the wood-based tencel, is contributing to deforestation in Southeast Asia.

Environmental impact does not end at the point of production. The globalization of the industry has led to increased pollution through long-distance transport. And eventually, the products enter the waste stream. Clothing, footwear, and accessories are a staple of municipal landfills.

Superfluity, Novelty, and Exclusivity:
Hallmarks of the Clothing Industry

At the core of the disposal problem lie two developments: Clothes are cheap and Americans are buying them in record numbers. Since 1991, the price of apparel and footwear has fallen, especially women's clothing, with the drop especially pronounced after 1999. (This was most likely due to declining wages in Asia, caused by the Asian financial crisis.) It is no surprise that as clothes got artificially cheaper, Americans began accumulating more of them. Indeed, when prices are low, the pressure on manufacturers and retailers to sell more becomes intense. In 2000 alone the United States imported 12.65 billion pieces of apparel, narrowly defined (i.e., not including hats, scarves, etc.). It produced another 5.3 billion domestically. That's roughly 47.7 pieces per person per year. (Women and girls rates are higher; men and boys lower.) From Bangladesh alone we imported 1.168 *billion* square meters of cloth. That's a lot of caps.

Paradoxically, the system of low prices and high volume is anchored at the top by outrageously priced merchandise. At the high end, thousand-dollar handbags, dresses running to the many thousands, even undergarments costing a hundred dollars are the rule. A look at the nation's distribution of wealth provides one clue to why high-priced clothing is flying off the shelves: The top 10 percent of the population now own a record 71 percent of the nation's total net worth, and 78 percent of all financial wealth. (The top one percent alone own 38 and 47 percent of net worth and financial wealth.) The existence of such an upscale apparel market is a troubling symptom of a world in which some people have far too much money and far too little moral or social accountability in terms of what they do with it.

But the high-priced venues serve another purpose as well. Designer merchandise becomes available at discount stores at a fraction of its top retail price. This affordable exclusivity is part of what keeps middle-class consumers enmeshed in the system. Clothes cascade through a chain of retail outlets, prices falling at each stage. The system has led many consumers to purchase almost mindlessly when confronted with irresistible "bargain basement" prices of highly regarded designers and to spend much more on clothes than they intend or even realize. Eventually even the desirable designer merchandise ends up being sold for rock-bottom prices—on the web one can find surplus clothing sites selling clothes at a fraction of their retail prices. I found $5,000 designer dresses going for $1,000, women's coats that retail at $129 available for $22 each; men's down jackets for $12. I found Hilfiger, DKNY, Victoria's Secret. Brand-new "high-quality mixed clothing" can be had for twenty-two cents a pound.

The core features of contemporary fashion—fast-moving style, novelty, and exclusivity—also contribute to spending. A seasonal fashion cycle based on climactic needs has been replaced by a shorter timeline, in which the "new" may only last for two months, or even weeks, as in the extreme cases of athletic shoes. The exclusivity that is relentlessly pushed by marketers also contributes to high levels of spending—the product is valued *because* it is expensive. As it becomes more affordable, its value declines. Similarly, when the consumer aspires to be a fashion pioneer, she seeks rarity. The impacts of these core features of the fashion industry are profound. Many middle- and lower-middle class youth are working long hours to buy clothes. For poor youth, with limited access to money and jobs, the designer imperative has been linked to dropping out of school (because of an inadequate wardrobe), stealing, dealing, even violence. Failing to keep up with the dizzying pace of fashion innovation undermines self-esteem and social status.

But it is not only fashion-orientation that accounts for the enormous volume of clothing that is sold in this country. Shopping for clothes, footwear, and apparel have become habits, even addictions, especially for women. Just something to do because we do it. People shop on their lunch hours, on the weekend, through catalogs, or in the mall. They spend vacations at outlet malls. Americans typically have something in mind they want to buy, and, for women that something is often clothing. In my interviews of professional women who subsequently downshifted, a common refrain was the enormous superfluity of their closets. It's clear we need to get our relationship to clothes under control.

Why Clothes Do Matter

To create sustainable, humane, and satisfying apparel, footwear, and accessories industries, we need to understand the functions of these products. Their utilitarian features are obvious. We need garments to cover our bodies, hiking shoes to climb a mountain, a watch to tell time. But this is just the beginning of what clothing really *does*. Throughout history, clothing has been at the center of how human beings interact. Not always with humane purposes, of course. Clothing and footwear have long identified rank and social position. Before the nineteenth century, European governments passed sumptuary laws that regulated dress, particularly to control those of low status. Intense conflict was waged over whether one could wear a wig, choose a certain color, or sport a particular fashion style. Not surprisingly, clothing was equally central to struggles against those very inequities. Working people often asserted their social rights by choosing dress that elites deemed them unworthy of wearing. Clothing has been key to both the repression of social groups and their struggles for human dignity and justice. (Closer to home, consider how incomplete any account of the political challenges of the 1960s would be without attention to blue jeans, tie-dyed shirts, and long hair.)

Clothing has also been at the heart of gender conflicts. As early-twentieth-century American women attempted to break free of patriarchal strictures, they rejected corsets and confining dresses. In the twenties, they defied convention with cigarettes and short skirts. In the 1970s, the women's movement rejected the fashion system and created its own sartorial sensibility. Clothing has historically also been an important site of intergenerational bonding and learning between women, along with hair care and other beauty rituals. I am quite sure that I got my love of clothes from my mother. Being a good shopper, especially in the complex world of women's clothing, requires finely honed skills, which are passed on from generation to generation.

What we wear is important to the way we experience our sexuality. Our age. Our ethnicity. It allows us to show respect for others (by dressing specially for a social occasion) or to signal community (through shared garments or styles). Finally, clothing can be part of the aesthetic of everyday life. There is genuine pleasure to be gained from a well-made, well-fitting garment. Or from a piece of clothing that embodies beautiful design, craftspersonship, or artistry. Throughout history, human beings have exercised their creativity through clothing, footwear, and accessories.

In sum, dressing and adorning are a vital part of the human experience. This is why any attempt to push them into a minimalist, utilitarian box will fail. Clothes embody far more than our physical bodies; they are also a measure of our basic values and culture. So, while we may not all take great pleasure in what we wear, we should all recognize that clothes do matter. They are about as far from trivial as any consumer good can be. Which means that a new fashion ethic will be about affirming social and human values, the commitments of daily life, and our hopes and aspirations for a different kind of world.

Principles for a New Kind of Clothing Consumer

1. Quality Over Quantity. Moving from Cheap and Plentiful to Rarer and More Valuable

In the past, clothing cost more, and its use was far more ecologically responsible. Only the rich bought more clothes than they wore, in contrast to current habits. Expensive clothing was worn sparingly when newly acquired. In some places, as a garment wore out, it cascaded through a social hierarchy of uses, from esteemed social occasions to the everyday public, and eventually to the most mundane private and domestic uses. Clothing was cleaned far less frequently than today, thereby extending its useful life. Women had the skills to make clothes, and even as ready-made garments became more common, to restructure and upgrade them. Style could be attained through "refashioning" garments, rather than discarding them and buying new ones. Such refashioning could also involve new ownership. Historian Nell McKendrick has identified the origins of the eighteenth-century consumer revolution in Britain with the trickle-down from elites to servants, as maids took their mistresses' cast off dresses and turned them into newly stylish outfits. Thus, basic principles of ecology and frugality were maintained—take only what you need, use it until it is no longer useable, repair rather than replace, refashion to provide variety.

The history of clothing practices provides guidance for fashioning a new aesthetic whose central principles are to emphasize quality over quantity, longevity over novelty, and versatility over specialization. For example, if we reject the need to keep up with fashion and can be satisfied with a smaller wardrobe, we can spend more per garment, as consumers do in Western Europe. The impact on the earth is less, and it contributes to longevity, because better clothes last longer by not skimping on tailoring or quality and quantity of yardage. Consumers are better off because high-quality clothing is more comfortable and looks better.

Ultimately we could begin to think of clothing purchases as long-term commitments, in which we take responsibility for seeing each garment through its natural life. That doesn't mean we couldn't ever divest ourselves, but that if we grew tired of a useful garment we'd find it a new home with a loving owner, kind of like with pets. Of course, to facilitate such a change, consumers would need to reject the reigning imperative of variety in clothes, especially as it pertains to the workplace and for social occasions. Just because you wore that dress to last year's holiday party doesn't mean you can't show up in it again.

With such an aesthetic, consumers would demand a shift toward more timeless design, away from fast-moving trends. Clothes could become more versatile in terms of what they can be used for, their ability to fit differently shaped bodies and to be altered. Consider the Indian sari, a simple, rectangular piece of cloth that is fitted around the body. It accommodates weight gain and loss, pregnancy, growth, and shrinkage. Couldn't designers come up with analogous concepts appropriate to Western tastes? Pants with waistbands that are flattering but also can be adjusted through double-button systems or through tailoring. Basic pieces that can be complemented by layering and accessories. Expensive, classic clothes already have some of these qualities— extra fabric for letting out and the capability to remain flattering after they have been altered.

Striving for longevity through versatility facilitates what we might call an ecological or true materialism. The cultural critic Raymond Williams has noted that we are not truly materialist because we fail to invest deep or sacred meanings in material goods. Instead, our materialism connotes an unbounded desire to acquire, followed by a throwaway mentality. True materialism could become part of a new ecological consciousness. Paying more per piece could also support a new structure of labor costs. Workers would work less, produce fewer but higher-quality items, and be paid more per hour. Such a change would help make ecologically clean technologies economically feasible.

Finally, paying more for clothes does not mean adopting the premise of social exclusivity. In luxury retailing, much of the appeal of the product is its prohibitive price or the fact that only elites have the social conditioning necessary to pull off wearing it. An alternative aesthetic would value democracy and egalitarianism through the fashioning of garments that are high-quality but affordable.

2. Small and Beautiful: Creative Clothing for Local Customers

The aesthetic aspect of clothing is and will continue to be important. But the values represented by the fashion industry are unacceptable. Despite decades of feminist criticism, the industry continues to objectify women—and increasingly men—through demeaning, violent, and gratuitously sexualized images and practices. In the late nineties we got "heroin chic," glamorizing drug abuse and poverty. Now it's teen and "tween" styles, with bare midriffs, tightly fitting T-shirts, and sexually explicit sayings emblazoned on the garments. Furthermore, the industry is comprised of megacorporations employing a small number of mostly male designers. They, in turn, produce a monolithic fashion landscape—massive numbers of copycat garments. Suddenly all that's available are square-toed shoes, or short-handled handbags, or hip huggers.

An alternative vision starts from the recognition that many young people, especially young women, yearn to be fashion designers, producing garments that are artistic, interesting, funky, visionary, and useable. And consumers are increasingly desirous of that type of individualized clothing. The industry could return to its roots in small-scale enterprises, run by the designers themselves. The British cultural analyst Angela McRobble has envisioned such a shift, calling for small apparel firms located in neighborhoods, operating almost like corner stores. They would cater to a local clientele whose tastes and needs they come to know. These face-to-face relationships between female designers and the immigrant women who labor in domestic-apparel production also have the potential to reduce the exploitation that currently characterizes the industry. Instead of driving to a mall with its cookie-cutter stores, one might walk to a converted factory housing three or four designers with workshops-cum-show rooms. The consumer could also become active in the creative process, helping to fashion an interesting or unique look for him or herself. If she didn't see what she wanted, it could be made to order, so that fit, color, and style were just right. Such a system would yield substantial savings in the areas of transport, branding, advertising, and marketing as well as a dramatic reduction in overproduction. Those savings could be used to pay decent wages, install environmentally sustainable production technologies, fund better quality materials, and support designers.

Such a vision could be realized through a combination of activist pressure, consumer mobilization, and government policies. The federal government could offer special subsidies for training and education for designers and enterprise loans to small business owners. Local governments could support apparel manufacturers through tax incentives and marketing initiatives.

3. Clean Clothes: Guaranteeing Social Justice and Environmental Responsibility

Relocalization is an important part of a movement toward a just and sustainable apparel industry. But it must go hand in hand with improvements in wages and working conditions in factories and small production units abroad. Such reform is essential to relocalizing on a global scale, because it will be the foundation for creating purchasing power in India, China, Bangladesh, and other southern countries. For now, the north must continue importing in order to provide employment for impoverished foreign workers. But as wages rise abroad, these workers can produce for their own domestic markets.

One of the most important social movements of the past decade has been the coalition of labor, student, and religious activists opposing the exploitation of garment workers around the globe. The Gap, Nike, Kmart, and others have been exposed and embarrassed by their labor practices. Students have demanded that their college's insignia clothing not be produced by sweated labor, and more than ninety institutions have complied. Most American consumers now believe that the workers who make their clothing should be paid decently, and surveys indicate they are willing to pay somewhat more to achieve that goal.

To date, however, the industry response has been inadequate. While some progress has been made, far more energy has gone into winning the PR battle than has been devoted to substantive reform. Companies remain opposed to free association in unions, which is the only true long-term solution to abuse. Nevertheless, the principle of what Europeans call "clean clothes" is making headway. In Europe, major clothing retailers have committed themselves to codes of conduct that ensure reasonable working conditions, free association, and other labor rights. For example, the British chain Marks and Spencer has joined the Ethical Trading Initiative, which is a government-sponsored initiative bringing together nongovernmental organizations (NGOs), unions, and businesses. Next, another British chain, works with Oxfam on ethical trading.

Indeed, the successes of the European clean-clothes movement are worth looking at, particularly for extending beyond labor rights into environmental impacts. In 1996, the Dutch company C&A instituted rigorous controls over its suppliers—monitoring more than one thousand production units annually—to guarantee labor conditions and environmental impacts. It uses the Eco-Tex label for environmental certification, and many of its own brands sport it. Marks and Spencer has begun an organic cotton design project with the Royal College of Art.

The German company Otto Versand, the largest mail-order business in the world, has perhaps gone farthest in terms of environmental sustainability. It has reduced paper use in its catalogs and packaging; its mail-order facility uses wind and solar power; and it is moving to incorporate sustainability throughout its product lines. Otto subsidizes the production of organic cotton in Turkey and India, and last year offered 250,000 organic cotton products. The company has reduced the use of harmful chemicals in textiles and has certified that 65 percent of its clothing passes a strict "skin-test" for dangerous substances. In the late 1990s, Otto worked with Century Textiles (India's largest textile exporter), to phase out azo-dyes. The company has also introduced its Future Collection, which is oriented to production ecology through conservation of energy and water resources. To encourage consumers to adopt a long-term perspective, they offer a three-year replacement guarantee for all their clothes.

To be sure, the shift to just and ecologically sustainable clothing is not simple. The price of organic clothing is currently high, putting it out of reach for many consumers. But activist pressure can help solve this problem, as the European successes are showing. And the U.S. market is already increasing. Nike and The Gap have begun to use some organic cotton. If one or two major U.S. companies commit to a substantial program of organic cotton use, demand will grow and prices will fall. And even a high-priced company such as Patagonia has made some accommodations for affordability—all its clothes carry a no-questions-asked indefinite replacement guarantee and the company operates a number of discount outlets.

The successes of the European campaigns suggest that comparable progress is possible on this side of the Atlantic as well. For example, Eileen Fisher, a high-end women's retailer, has signed on to SA 8000, an international social and environmental standard. U.S. manufacturers and retailers are sensitive to the need to maintain their public image. If we can educate consumers and mobilize activists, we can "clean" the American closet. Doing so would be a substantial step toward a sustainable, but also fashionable, planet.

Note

Schor, Juliet. "Cleaning the Closet: Toward A New Fashion Ethic" from *Sustainable Planet: Solutions for the 21st Century*. Beacon Press. 2002.

Politics by Other Greens
The Importance of Transnational Environmental Justice Movement Networks
David Naguib Pellow

The idea that social inequalities are not separate from—but are instead a fundamental part of—ecological unsustainability is a central theme in environmental sociology. Would wealthy and powerful people really produce hazardous toxins or mountains of garbage if they had to live next door to these? In this reading, David Pellow uses the metaphor of the boomerang to suggest that our actions tend to come back to us. Pellow describes how, with the help of transnational environmental organizations, a small group of activists in Mozambique was able to prevent a Danish development agency from incinerating 900 tons of obsolete toxic fertilizer in southern Mozambique.

The race, class, gender, and national inequalities and ecological violence that are at the core of global capitalism underscore a point that many participants in environmental movements often overlook: social inequalities are the primary driving forces behind ecological crises. That is, we should no longer view race, class, and other inequalities as the most important variables in a general model that might explain environmental injustice. Rather they are also the most important factors for theorizing the overall predicament of ecological unsustainability. Social inequalities are, therefore, not just an afterthought of an environmentally precarious society; they are at its root.

There are times when we must be reminded of the inescapable interdependence among human societies and of those interdependencies we experience with broader ecosystems. Thus a close observation of the myriad forms of institutional violence among human communities always reveals the associated violence visited upon ecosystems. Therefore social movements confronting human rights abuses—particularly in the global South—tend to also confront questions of ecological abuse because the domination over people is reinforced and made possible by the domination of ecosystems. But the interdependencies that human and non-human systems share underscore that no one is exempt from the far-reaching impacts of institutional and ecological violence. Thus radical transformative democratization of societies is a critical component in the global effort to achieve environmental sustainability and social justice.

In this chapter I investigate the phenomenon of transnational environmental justice (EJ) movements, specifically considering the work of activists, organizations, and networks that constitute this new formation. Linking environmental justice studies, environmental sociology, ethnic studies, and social movement theory in new ways, and drawing on interviews and archives, I ask how social movements challenge environmental inequalities across international borders? I argue that transnational EJ movement networks do this (1) by disrupting the social relations that produce environmental inequalities, (2) by producing new accountabilities vis-à-vis nation states and polluters, and (3) by articulating new visions of ecologically sustainable and socially just institutions and societies.

Environmental Sociology and Social Inequalities

In this first section of the chapter I consider theories of environmental conflict and link them to theories of social inequality. I begin with Ulrich Beck's 'Risk Society' thesis, which contends that late modern society is marked by an exponential increase in the production and use of hazardous chemical substances, producing a fundamental transformation in the relationship among capital, the state, civil society, and the environment. What this means is that the project of nation building and the very idea of the modern nation-state are undergirded by the presence of toxins—chemical poisons—that permeate every social institution, human body, and ecosystem. This toxic modern nation-state also depends upon the subjugation of ecosystems and certain human populations designated as "others"—those who are less than deserving of full citizenship. This process attenuates the most negative impacts of such a system on elites. Toxic production systems produce privileges for a global minority and externalize the costs of that process to those spaces occupied by devalued and marginal "others"—people of color, the poor, indigenous communities, and global South nations. The study of such inequalities, of course, is the foundation of the field of environmental justice and inequality studies (Agyeman, Bullard, and Evans 2003).

Thus, according to Beck, advanced capitalism creates wealth for some and imposes risks on others, at least in the short term. In the long run, however, the problem of widespread global ecological harm ends up returning to impact its creators in a "boomerang effect." That is, the risks of late modernity eventually haunt those who originally produced them (Beck 1999). In that sense, Beck acknowledges environmental inequality in the short term, while also maintaining a global, long-range view of what becomes, to some extent, a democratization of risk. Beck confirms the enduring problem of what other scholars have termed the "metabolic rift"—the disruptions in ecosystems that capitalism produces because of its inherent tendency to expend natural resources at a rate that is greater than the ability of ecosystems to replenish those materials (Foster 2000). These rifts are linked to and reinforce social dislocations and inequalities that siphon wealth upward and restrict the economic and political capacities of the working classes and communities of color. Thus environmental harm is necessarily intertwined with the institutional violence that constitutes race, gender, and class hierarchies.

Building on these ideas from within environmental sociology, I now turn to theoretical developments from within the field of ethnic studies. For well over a century, a number of scholars and public intellectuals have used words like *poison* and *toxic* in speech and writings about racism. This is a powerful way to capture the harm racism does to both its victims and perpetrators or beneficiaries. Many authors have described racism as a *poison* that reveals deep contradictions and tensions in this nation, which have periodically erupted in violence, revolts, and wars over the years. Critical race theorists Lani Guinier and Gerald Torres make use of this terminology in their book *The Miner's Canary*. They write:

> "The canary's distress signaled that it was time to get out of the mine because the air was becoming too *poisonous* to breathe. Those who are racially marginalized are like the miner's canary: their distress is the first sign of a danger that *threatens us all*. It is easy enough to think that when we sacrifice this canary, the only harm is to communities of color. Yet others ignore problems that converge around racial minorities at their own peril, for these problems are symptoms warning us that we are all at risk" (Guinier and Torres 2002: 11, emphases added).

Guinier and Torres also introduce a concept they term "political race," which "encompasses the view that race . . . matters because racialized communities provide the early warning signs of *poison* in the social atmosphere"

(Guinier and Torres 2002:12, emphasis added). In other words, political race forces us to think beyond specific instances of culpability and discrimination to produce a broader vision of justice for society as a whole. These concepts push us to rethink and challenge racism because it "threatens us all," not just people of color who may be its primary targets. The concept of political race begins with an emphasis on race and moves to class, gender and other inequalities, so while the principal emphasis is on race, this model is also inclusive of other categories of social difference.

The toxic metaphor for racism—and class and gender domination, for that matter—parallels Beck's "risk society" model in many ways. For example, racism, class domination, and pollution are ubiquitous and deeply embedded in our institutions, our culture, and our bodies. Moreover, while the production of both race, gender, and class hierarchies and toxic chemicals results in widespread harm across human communities and ecosystems, they both can also operate like a boomerang and eventually circle back to impact all members of society through uprisings, social unrest, and other conflicts. Finally, they are also powerful symbols for organizing resistance movements and for bringing people together across social and spatial boundaries. These concepts are helpful for thinking about the power and potential of transnational EJ movements.

Transnational Social Movements for Global Environmental Justice

While the primary focus of this chapter is on anti-toxics struggles, it must be said that the movement for global environmental justice and human rights casts a much broader net. This includes struggles against extractive industries, transboundary pollution and waste flows, free trade agreements, and—more importantly—the ideological and social systems that reinforce such practices, including racism, capitalism, patriarchy, and militarism. For example, hydroelectric dams have catalyzed many communities around the globe where people are fighting water privatization and external control of that most fundamental element on the planet. In response to the massive human rights abuses and environmental impacts associated with large dams, a highly influential and effective international movement emerged to force changes in current dam-building practices. In addition to organizations of dam-affected peoples, this arm of the EJ movement includes numerous allied environmental, human rights, and social activist groups around the world. International meetings in recent years have brought together dam-affected peoples and their allies to network and strategize, and to call for improvements in planning for water- and energy-supply projects. Every year, community and activist groups from around the world show their solidarity with those dispossessed by dams on the International Day of Action, a global event organized to raise awareness about the impacts of dams and the value of dam-free and undammed rivers (McCully 2001).

Groups like the International Campaign for Responsible Technology are primarily focused on the social, economic, and ecological impacts of the global electronics industry, from mineral and water extraction for the production of electronics products, to their manufacture, sale, consumption, and disposal. In other words, this particular global EJ network adopts a lifecycle approach to the problem, following the materials and their effects on people and ecosystems (Smith, Sonnenfeld, and Pellow 2006). Many of these EJ movement networks articulate a critique of broader ideological systems of socio-environmental hierarchy that give life and legitimacy to global environmental injustice. Without such critical guiding frameworks, these movements would be limited in their political power and vision.

Numerous transnational social movement organizations (TSMOs) concerned with EJ and human rights issues focus their efforts on a range of state and industrial sectors. Taken together, these global organizations and networks constitute a formidable presence at international treaty negotiations, within corporate shareholder meetings, and in the halls of congresses and parliaments. Even so, they are only a part of the broader global movement for environmental justice. Arguably the most important components of that movement are the domestic local, regional, and national organizations in the various communities, cities, and nations in which scores of environmental justice battles rage every day. Those groups provide the front line participants in the struggles for local legitimacy within TSMOs and their networks. Together, the numerous local grassroots organizations and their collaborating global networks produce and maintain a critical infrastructure of the transnational public sphere.

Social movements must mobilize resources—funds, technology, people, ideas and imagination—to achieve their goals. Transnational social movements are rarely successful if we narrowly define success as a major change in a specific policy within a nation state (Keck and Sikkink 1998). But they are increasingly relevant in international policy debates, as they seek to make not only policy changes in international law and multilateral conventions, but also to change the terms and nature of the discourse within these important debates. These conventions include, for example: the Montreal Protocol (on the production of ozone-damaging chemicals), the Kyoto Protocol (concerning global warming), the Basel Convention (on the international trade in hazardous wastes), and the Stockholm Convention (on the production and management of persistent organic pollutants). In each of these cases, TSMOs are often a critical source of information for governments seeking information about environmental and social justice concerns, and their presence raises the costs of failing to act on certain issues, thus increasing the possibility of government accountability. In a global society where a nation-state's reputation can be tarnished in international political and media venues, transnational social movements can have surprisingly significant impacts. When movements disseminate information to the point that it becomes a part of common wisdom, such "popular beliefs . . . are themselves material forces" (Gramsci 1971: 165). That is, meaning systems can support or challenge systems of structural and material control. This is a critical point because, as cultural studies scholars and urban political ecologists have argued, social movements are struggling over cultural meaning systems as much as they are fighting for improved material conditions and needs (Moore, Kosek, and Pandian 2003).

In other words, the "natural" environment becomes a symbol of meaning for human communities. It can become a symbol of our attachment to—or contempt for—nature, and as a political or cultural tool for mobilizing against people whom hegemonic actors consider inferior and unimportant. The history of the genocide of Native peoples in the United States and the continued practices of environmental racism are just two examples of associating despised human "others" with landscapes and ecosystems that are also targets of extraction, pollution, or selective valuation. On the other hand, for the same reasons, ecosystems play a cultural role in the mobilization of social movements in favor of protecting ecosystems from risks associated with industrialization. As Moore, Kosek, and Pandian (2003) argue, nature is a terrain of power, through which we discursively and materially advance various meanings, agendas, and politics. Thus transnational EJ movement networks challenge environmental inequality by confronting the social forces that produce these outcomes and by arguing for new relationships of accountability vis-à-vis state and corporate actors.

Boomerang Effects

Recall that Beck's "risk society" and Guinier and Torres's "miner's canary" speak to the relational and interdependent character of industrial chemicals and social inequalities through the phenomena of boomerangs. Research on transnational social movement networks reveals that these formations produce their *own* boomerang effects as well. That is, when local governments refuse to heed calls for change, transnational activist networks create pressure that ". . . curves around local state indifference and repression to put foreign pressure on local policy elites. Thus international contacts amplify voices to which domestic governments are deaf, while the local work of target country activists legitimizes efforts of activists abroad" (Keck and Sikkink 1998). It is the interaction between repressive domestic political structures and more flexible structures in other nations that produces this boomerang.

In their influential book *Activists Beyond Borders*, Keck and Sikkink (1998) explore the significance of the work of transnational social movement networks. These groups of activists in two or more nations, have, for decades, successfully intervened in and changed the terms of important global and national policy debates, pushed for regulation of activities deemed harmful to social groups, and influenced states to embrace practices that might improve the lives of residents in any given nation. Transnational movement networks often do this by gathering critical information and strategically making it available to publics, governments, media organizations, and other movements in order to force change. These movement networks also achieve such goals through mobilizing support for boycotts, letter writing campaigns, and other forms of protest that shine a spotlight on objectionable institutional practices with the goal of halting or transforming them. Transnational movements frequently take advantage of the multiple geographic scales at which these networks operate and sidestep the barriers that nation-states in one locale may create in order to access the leverage available from within other states—the boomerang. Transnational EJ movements use the boomerang to challenge the power that states and corporations enjoy over vulnerable communities, thus confronting the race, gender, and class inequalities that produce environmental injustices.

What Goes around Comes Around

Guinier and Torres underscore the importance of "political race" through the metaphor of the "miner's canary," which symbolizes the role of people of color whose oppression is a sign of a poisonous social atmosphere that ultimately threatens all of society, not just those communities that suffer directly from racism. That is, racism creates its own boomerang effects that reveal systems of interdependence and accountability that impact people from all racial and class strata (albeit unevenly). Wars, revolts, uprisings, and social movements spawned, in part, by demands for racial, gender, and class justice against systems of oppression are among the many examples of such a boomerang effect. While mobilizing the boomerangs of transnational social movements, environmental justice activist networks also draw on analyses of race, class, and inequality to unmask the drivers of environmental injustice and to frame a vision of a more sustainable and socially just world.

There are multiple boomerang effects evident in EJ struggles, and I examine two of them here. The first is the way social movements use transnational activist networks to leverage power across international borders to target states and corporations. The second is the boomerang effect of racial and class inequalities and how such hierarchies often harm both beneficiaries and targets/survivors. After presenting a case study in which both boomerangs are in play,

I then offer a conceptual framework for thinking through the kinds of social and political accountabilities and interdependencies these stories reveal, and their implications for social movements' dreams of freedom and invigorating new political formations.

Something Toxic from Denmark: Mozambique's Battle with Foreign Pesticides

This story begins in 1998, in Mozambique's capitol city of Maputo, where a Danish international development agency (Danida) funded an effort to incinerate nine hundred tons of obsolete toxic fertilizer and pesticide stocks. This case underscores two major examples of global environmental inequality: the massive export of pesticides, which often leads to surplus obsolete pesticide stocks lying unsecured in warehouses, vacant lots, and fields in global South nations, and the massive export of incineration technology to these nations.

Mozambique has a population of nineteen million people, seventy percent of whom live off the land. Located in Southeastern Africa, it is the world's ninth poorest nation. The country is slowly rebuilding itself after five centuries of brutal colonization by Portugal, followed by seventeen years of civil war, which resulted in the deaths of one million persons. Former independence fighters with the group FRELIMO won the country's first democratic elections in 1994, and UN peacekeeping forces finally departed one year later. Since that time, Mozambique has enjoyed relative peace. Even so, the average Mozambican's life expectancy is just forty years and the citizenry experience grinding poverty on a daily basis. The U.S. ecological footprint is 23.7 acres per capita—and a sustainable footprint in that nation would be 4.6 acres. Mozambique represents the other end of the scale, with an ecological footprint of 1.3 acres per capita. Unfortunately, the reason for this lighter footprint is because there is so much poverty and so little industrialization occurring in Mozambique ("Rich Nations Gobbling Resources at an Unsustainable Rate" 2004). Despite this harsh reality, new civil society organizations are emerging and thriving in this once chaotic place. And the first signs of new civil society growth in Mozambique sprang forth from an international struggle for environmental justice.

A Toxic Discovery: Mozambique as a Risk Society

In 1998, in the capitol city of Maputo, community activist Janice Lemos read a story in *Metical*—an independent local newspaper—about Danida's effort to fund the incineration of obsolete toxic fertilizer and pesticide stocks in a cement factory in the southern city of Matola. Danida sought to donate a hazardous waste incineration facility that would be housed in the cement factory, which the aid agency would also pay to have retrofitted for the operation. Ms.

Lemos wrote to the newspaper for more information about the cement kiln incinerator proposal, but none was available. She then contacted Greenpeace International headquarters in the Netherlands, where someone informed her that two U.S.-based toxic waste activists would soon be visiting South Africa, and they might be able to travel to Maputo and Matola if Mozambican community leaders would invite them. With the help of Greenpeace and Oxfam Community Aid Abroad, Lemos and fellow concerned residents met with the U.S. activists Ann Leonard (then with the group Essential Action) and Dr. Paul Connett (a St. Lawrence University chemistry professor and renowned expert on and opponent of incineration), as well as Bobby Peek, a South African toxics expert and activist (with the Environmental Justice Networking Forum).

The visiting activists were quite concerned because they possessed documentation that cement kiln incinerators produce a range of deadly toxins such as dioxins and furans. In fact, scientists estimate that twenty-three percent of the world's newly created dioxin comes from cement kiln incinerators alone (Puckett 1998). Prior to their arrival, the visiting activists were able to access documents about Danida's plans and had additional information about the proposed project. EJNF's Bobby Peek stated, "Whether or not anybody actually became concerned about the issue . . . we strongly felt that we had the moral obligation to pass on what we knew about the plan, and the real risks of cement kiln incineration. They had the right to know. As we feared, almost nobody had heard about the project at all" (Puckett 1998, 25). This lack of public knowledge was particularly disturbing because Danida has a policy of "actively involving individuals, non-governmental organizations and associations and businesses formally and informally in formulating and implementing environmental policies" (Neilsen 1999). Yet few people in Maputo or Matola had heard anything about the project from Danida. In fact, the foreign visitors were the *only* people at the meeting who had seen a copy of the short environmental impact assessment (EIA) Danida had prepared. Moreover, the report was written in English, although the official language of Mozambique is Portuguese. One local activist remembered, "only a few of us could manage to read the report and . . . do a brief analysis" (Lemos 2004). Connett denounced the entire project. He stated: "In the United States or Canada, those proposing a new toxic waste facility would be obliged to fully discuss all of the alternatives, all of the risks, and would have been required to hold several public hearings before decisions could be made about a particular disposal method. The environmental assessment and public involvement in this project is a sham" (Puckett 1998, 25). For its part, Danida conducted an EIA that concluded no serious environmental impacts would result from the incineration of the pesticides (Mangwiro 1999).

The visiting activists also informed the Mozambican citizens of the questionable record of Waste-Tech Ltd, a South African firm that was to be contracted for the Danida effort. At that time, Waste-Tech Ltd. was seeking to import foreign waste into South Africa—a clear violation of law there—and was the subject of an investigation by the South Africa Human Rights Commission concerning possible abuses in the case of two incinerators it had located within close proximity to an economically depressed community. The firm was also confronted with other legal investigations being conducted by the South African Department of Water Affairs and Forestry.

Mauricio Sulila, one of the local community leaders from Maputo present at the meeting, later told a reporter "When we explained [to others attending the gathering] that the government had decided the factory would burn toxic waste, they became terrified" (Lowe 2003). Local people already suspected the presence of toxic materials at the site because, as Sulila recalled, earlier flooding in the area prompted residents to pump the water into a nearby swamp where, soon afterward, "someone ate a fish caught in this swamp and died" (Lowe 2003). The terror that people experienced at the news of a toxic threat underscores risk society theorists' findings that the dangers of modern industrial pollutants often instill fear and dread among exposed communities (Erikson 1995).

At the meeting with U.S. and South African activists, local residents and community leaders founded an organization to address the problem of environmental hazards in the area. Mr. Mazul, one of the attendees who was also an artist, explained that, since the citizens had been kept in the dark by the Danish and Mozambican authorities at the Environment Ministry, the group should be named *Livaningo*, which translates to "all that sheds light" in Shangaan, one of many languages spoken in that region of the country. Mauricio Sulila was appointed the group's general secretary. Janice Lemos and her sister Anabela joined the group's leadership as well. The development of an activist organization in Maputo also reflected the symbolic or cultural dimension of environmental justice politics. This dimension facilitates people's expression of their sense of concern and care for ecosystems in ways that allow them to convert that sentiment into political action. The use of the word *Livaningo* for the new EJ organization was a perfect example. Embodied in this single name lies an acknowledgement of the local culture, the story of how this community came to be under siege, and an intent to make transparent and improve their situation. "All that sheds light" is also an ecological metaphor for the power of the sun and the power of the community.

Action and Networking at Multiple Scales

Soon after its first meeting, Livaningo grew and enjoyed some influence with the local and national governments. They organized public gatherings and meetings, brought their concerns to local residents and businesses, and made strategic use of the independent press. They also held some of the first public demonstrations in post-revolution Mozambique. Sulila explained, "It is important to say that Livaningo was the first organization in Mozambique to really challenge the government" (Pellow 2007, 174). Livaningo was eventually able to secure the services of a firm that conducted an independent environmental assessment of the project. Anabela Lemos proudly recalled that the firm's "conclusion was completely what we thought from the beginning: under no condition should the cement factory should be turned into an incinerator" (Lemos 2004).

However, the organization faced numerous hurdles in its efforts to oppose the incinerator. For example, the Mozambican government refused to consider Livaningo's independent environmental assessment. Activists then tried to secure an audience with the Danish embassy in Maputo, but they were refused. In the fall of 1998, members of the Danida board of directors visited Maputo, but rejected Livaningo's request for a meeting. In response, the activists elevated the struggle and went to the source. Aurelio Gomes of Livaningo and Bobby Peek of the EJNF in South Africa traveled to Denmark to address the Danish Parliament about Danida's pesticide incineration project. As Gomes stated upon arrival in Denmark, with regard to Danida's earlier refusal to meet with them, "This won't prevent us from voicing our concerns, therefore we've come to Copenhagen today to provide the Danish government with information to justify the immediate halt and rethinking [of the incineration effort]" (Basel Action Network 1998). Although the Parliament granted them an audience, its members made no effort to intervene in the conflict. Despite this rebuff, this was a critical moment in the development of a transnational EJ collaboration, because Mozambican, U.S., South African, and Danish activists were working together in close coordination. Allies such as Greenpeace International and the Joint Oxfam Advocacy Program (JOAP, Mozambique) donated the funding support for these activities. Mauricio Sulila remembered:

> "That was great . . . After that, the Mozambique government opened up the door a little. We explained to them that we will not give up, we will not be intimidated. We continued to make pressure, to make noise, to hold international meetings and meetings at the local level. We were working with several organizations, especially Greenpeace Denmark. JOAP's support was fantastic. Say we need to do a demonstration in two days, they were able to provide funds to advertise in the newspaper. When we needed to travel to Denmark, JOAP funded us. It's not a lot of money, but it is at the right time, when we really need it" (Lowe 2003).

When asked later how Livaningo organized so effectively on an international scale, Anabela Lemos stated,

> "It is mostly through the Internet. But whenever we campaign, we make some noise here in Mozambique, and at the same time we have

the international network. When our government told us to stop complaining, we went to Denmark and we spoke to the people *there*, and we realized that, as a result, they started to listen to us *here*. So we realized then that we couldn't just do a campaign here, but instead we had to work both ways, here in Mozambique and in Denmark" (Lemos 2004).

Activists with Greenpeace Denmark were critical to the campaign's success as well. While the Danish government initially refused accountability for the pesticides, Danish activists took responsibility for their nation's involvement in this conflict. Greenpeace Denmark staff member Jacob Hartmann commented on the inconsistency involved in his government's embrace of the Basel Convention on Transboundary Hazardous Wastes (which prohibits wealthy OECD nations trading with or dumping hazardous wastes in poorer non-OECD nations) while also encouraging the incineration of pesticides in Matola: "Considering that Denmark is one of the countries that have taken the lead on this vital treaty, it makes little sense for Denmark to advocate for an elimination of POPs [persistent organic pollutants] globally while promoting new sources of the worst of them in Mozambique" (Puckett 1998, 26). POPs include the most toxic substances known to science such as dioxins, furans, and polychlorinated biphenyls (PCBs), and are common by-products of incineration.

Denmark's Development Minister, Poul Nielsen, denied that his country was seeking to impose incinerators on Mozambique, but activists found this claim suspect, given that Danida had funded a failed incinerator in India in 1986, and because Denmark was considering financial support for garbage incinerators in Zimbabwe and Tanzania in 1998, the year the conflict in Mozambique ignited ("SA Dumping Plan 'Trashed' by NYC" 1998).

Coalition activists consistently called for the pesticide incineration project to be halted, for the pesticides to be exported to a global North nation, for the wastes to be disposed of using non-toxic non-incineration technology, and for all the costs to be borne by the companies that produced the chemicals in the first place ("Mozambique Activists Win Huge Victory" 2000). And although Livaningo activists were only recently beginning civil society organizing on EJ issues, they were familiar with the problem of environmental injustice, since this was something that has been widespread in the region. Anabela Lemos remarked: "In South Africa, always the dumping sites are near the poor people. And we have a waste dump here in the city and there is a concentration of poor people there, so it's the same thing here. The poor, they always get the waste" (Lemos 2004).

Thus, this transnational coalition of environmental justice activists clearly articulated their opposition to Danida's use of local Mozambican ecosystems as waste repositories. Activists channeled these grievances into a vision of environmental justice that communicated an articulation of the symbolic, cultural, and political dimensions of ecosystems—that is, a viewpoint that challenged the dominant perspective of nature as a site of resource extraction and a place for dumping effluence. Thus, they were deeply engaged in disrupting the social relations that produced environmental injustice in their community and sought new relations of accountability locally, nationally, and transnationally.

The Boomerang in Motion

After two years of campaigning, Livaningo had its first major breakthrough. The Mozambican government agreed to a "return to sender" arrangement and allowed the chemicals to be shipped to a global North nation—the Netherlands—for processing and disposal by hazardous waste treatment firms there ("Mozambique Environmentalists Defeat Incinerator Plan" 2000). While the Mozambican government did have to pay some of the costs, Denmark shared the expenses. And, despite EJ activists' hopes that non-incineration technologies would be used, some of the wastes were indeed incinerated in Europe.

Even so, the EJ coalition achieved its primary goal of "return to sender"—exporting the wastes to a global North nation. Livaningo reached out to a broad group of established TSMO's, including the Environmental Justice Networking Forum (South Africa), Essential Action (U.S.), Greenpeace International (Netherlands, Denmark, and Brazil), the Basel Action Network (U.S.), and Oxfam's JOAP (UK), to amplify its voice and augment any leverage it already had in order to achieve one of the most impressive global-local EJ collaborations in the movement's history. The South African-based EJNF lent a critical African presence to the struggle. No less important was the legitimacy that Livaningo provided for its international partner organizations and activists who might otherwise be viewed as "outside agitators" in Mozambique. And Greenpeace Denmark provided much needed credibility for Mozambican activists confronting the Danish government. Drawing on local, regional, and international activist support, as well as international law and aggressive movement tactics, the coalition succeeded. These external resources were critical to the campaign, but the local activists' level of determination and commitment to the struggle was what ultimately sustained the effort. As Livaningo's Aurelio Gomes remarked, "We have nothing against Denmark, and hope they have nothing against us. We just want them to understand that here in Mozambique, while we may not be wealthy, we will never compromise our health—that is all some of us have" (Puckett 1998, 26). Likewise, Livaningo activist Anabela Lemos commented, "We just decided that we would not fail, although there were many times when it looked as if all hope was lost" ("Mozambique Environmentalists Defeat Incinerator Plan" 2000).

Although Mozambique is a democracy, it is still a young one. The government is still slowly becoming accustomed to the idea of being challenged by civil society groups, whether inside or outside its borders. As Anabela Lemos (2004) commented:

> "Mozambique is a country where people are scared to speak out, and still today, but it is getting better. We are going through democracy after so many years. We are the only NGO [non-governmental organization] doing this work. If something is wrong, we speak up, we don't talk just for talking's sake. When we speak, we know we are right and we know we have to say it."

Next Steps for Mozambique: A Broader Vision of Justice and Sustainability

The campaign to halt the incineration project and export the pesticide wastes from Matolo, Mozambique was successful. This was a pleasant surprise for people throughout the international EJ and NGO community as they witnessed activists from one of the world's poorest nations exert uncommon political leverage.

Since this unprecedented success, Livaningo has used the opportunity to broaden its focus beyond toxics to include other environmental justice struggles in the region. As Livaningo expands its work, it is now pursuing projects aimed at introducing ecologically sound waste management systems in health care institutions in Mozambique, in collaboration with international activist groups like Health Care Without Harm. They are also working to oppose harmful "development" projects like the Mpanda Uncua Hydroelectric dam on the Zambezi River in Mozambique, in partnership with TSMOs like International Rivers (based in Berkeley, California). Livaningo is also combating oil extraction efforts by transnational corporations in southern Africa, which would pollute the air, land, and water and return few economic benefits to the people of the region.

Livaningo's victory in the pesticide incinerator case is credited with opening a broader political space for other civil society groups and social movements to work in Mozambique on a host of social concerns. Organizations working on HIV/AIDS, human rights, land rights and global economic justice efforts now enjoy greater support as a result of the political space Livaningo opened. In other words, they forced access into the nation's political process, by challenging and transforming the structure itself. As Anabela Lemos (2004) stated:

> "It is true that we opened things up for people in our nation because we are not scared to speak out and to raise our issues. We think we have the right to do so. And I think that civil society has to get involved, we can't

just sit on our hands and complain. If something is wrong, we should work for it. I think people should start to realize that to have big changes we have to give a lot up and we have to sacrifice. . . . You should not be scared. If you are right, then you have the right to speak, and I think it does make a difference."

Thus, the Danida case allowed activists to build on the success a single environmental justice struggle and expand outward to be inclusive of a greater breadth of environmental and social concerns of civil society. This mobilization also revealed how deeply Mozambique had become apart of the "world risk society" (Beck 1999) through the embrace of ecologically and socially toxic forms of economic development that are rampant throughout southern Africa.

Discussion and Conclusion

The emergence of a transnational movement for environmental justice and the case of Livaningo allows us to think through questions of social hierarchy and the kinds of accountabilities and interdependencies that constrain and enable social and political change from within vulnerable communities. Here I wish to extend Guinier and Torres's "miner's canary" model of a racial metaphor to examine the miner's canary as a *spatial* metaphor. When global South communities are the targets of international environmental injustice (via hazardous waste dumping, illegal waste trading, or resource extraction from the global North), those spaces *and* the people who occupy them constitute the miner's canary. Thus entire communities, nations, and regions are often viewed as disposable or devalued by more privileged actors on the global stage. When social movements mobilize to demand that imported toxics be returned to their points of origin, the receiving nations of the global North serve as a reminder that environmental racism—like racism, class and gender inequality more generally—threatens us all. This analysis allows one to theorize and link the boomerang effects of racism, class inequalities, and social movements across international borders. In this way, the "miner's canary" can signal an impending or potential environmental danger that threatens not only members of vulnerable social groups, but also privileged populations living across vast geographic and social borders. This occurs as a result of the boomerang effects that racial and class inequalities and social movements produce, challenging social hierarchies that create environmental inequality and making hegemonic institutions accountable to vulnerable populations.

The idea of a boomerang effect is productive to theorizing social movements and environmental justice politics because it is a dynamic concept. The boomerang reveals that race and class inequalities and ecological harm associated with global capitalism are not just oppressive of people of color and ecosystems, but may ultimately be unsustainable and hazardous to those who benefit from that system. These race, gender and class inequalities are not just an unfortunate byproduct of an ecologically unsustainable society; they are at its root. Social inequalities are the principal forces driving ecological crises. Thus no one is exempt from racial, class, gender, and ecological violence, and social movements can present important and disruptive challenges to these social forces.

The boomerang is a metaphor. It is also a reminder of the interdependence among human societies and the unavoidable accountabilities we have to each other. The power of the boomerang returns us to the core of the human-environment and human-human interactions and the reason why we should be concerned about the various social dimensions of ecosystems: when we harm ecosystems we also perpetrate harms against other human beings, and vice versa (Harvey 1996; Merchant 1980). When we build relationships of respect and justice within human communities, we tend to reflect those practices in our relationships to ecosystems. Transformative, radical restructuring of societies is required to achieve environmental justice, and creative social movements are an indispensable foundation of that process (Speth 2008).

This chapter links environmental justice studies, environmental sociology, ethnic studies, and social movement theory in new ways, by drawing on key concepts and metaphors from these fields to produce new intellectual space for thinking about environmental politics, transnational movements, and social hierarchies. I began with the question: how do social movements challenge environmental inequalities across international borders? I argued that transnational EJ movement networks do this by disrupting the social relations that produce environmental inequalities, by producing new accountabilities among states and polluters, and by promoting a vision of an ecologically sustainable and socially just society. They achieve these ends by mobilizing bodies, information, and the cultural imaginary.

Note

Pellow, David Naguib. 2011. "Politics by Other Greens: The Importance of Transnational Environmental Justice Movement Networks," pp. 247–265 in *Environmental Inequalities Beyond Borders*, JoAnn Carmin and Julian Agyeman (eds.). Cambridge, MA: The MIT Press.

References

Agyeman, Julian, Robert Bullard, and Bob Evans (eds.). 2003. *Just Sustainabilities: Development in an Unequal World*. Cambridge: MIT Press.

Basel Action Network. 1998. "Danish Development Project Encouraging Toxic Waste Trade into Mozambique?" Press Release. October 5. Copenhagen.

Beck, Ulrich. 1999. *World Risk Society*. United Kingdom: Polity Press.

Erikson, Kai. 1995. *A New Species of Trouble: The Human Experience of Modern Disasters*. New York: W.W. Norton.

Foster, John Bellamy. 2000. *Marx's Ecology: Materialism and Nature*. New York: Monthly Review Press.

Gramsci, Antonio. 1971. *Selections from the Prison Notebooks*. New York: International Publishers.

Guinier, Lani and Gerald Torres. 2002. *The Miner's Canary:" Enlisting Race, Resisting Power, Transforming Democracy*. Cambridge, MA: Harvard University Press.

Harvey, David. 1996. *Justice, Nature, and the Geography of Difference*. Boston: Blackwell.

Keck, Margaret E. and Sikkink, Kathryn. 1998. *Activists Beyond Borders: Advocacy Networks in International Politics*. Ithaca, NY: Cornell University Press.

Lemos, Anabela. 2004. Interview with the author. February 5.

Lowe, Sarah. 2003. "Toxic Waste Victory in Mozambique." *Horizons*. February. Oxfam.

Mangwiro, Charles. 1999. Obsolete pesticides leave Mozambicans with $600,000 problem. *African Eye News Service* (South Africa), July 22.

McCully, Patrick. 2001. *Silenced Rivers: The Ecology and Politics of Large Dams*. London: Zed Books.

Merchant, Carolyn. 1980. *The Death of Nature: Women, Ecology and the Scientific Revolution*. San Francisco: Harper.

Moore, Donald, Jake Kosek, and Anand Pandian (eds.). 2003. *Race, Nature and the Politics of Difference*. Durham, NC: Duke University Press.

"Mozambique Activists Win Huge Victory against Toxic Waste Incineration." 2000. = Coalition Press Release, October 5. http://www.ban.org.

"Mozambique Environmentalists Defeat Incinerator Plan." 2000. Environment News Service (ENS), Maputo, Mozambique, October 13.

Neilsen, Poul. 1999. Letter to Livaningo. January.

Pellow, David N. 2007. *Resisting Global Toxics: Transnational Movements for Environmental Justice*. Cambridge, MA: The MIT Press.

Puckett, Jim. 1998. "Something Rotten from Denmark: The Incinerator 'Solution' to Aid Gone Bad in Mozambique." *Multinational Monitor*, December, Vol. 19, no. 12, pp. 24–26.

"Rich Nations Gobbling Resources at an Unsustainable Rage." 2004. Environment News Service (ENS), March 30.

"SA Dumping Plan 'Trashed' by NYC." 1998. Africa News Service, January 8.

Smith, Andrea, 2005. *Conquest: Sexual Violence and American Indian Genocide*. Cambridge, MA: South End Press.

Smith, Ted, David A. Sonnenfeld, and David Naguib Pellow (eds.). 2006. *Challenging the Chip: Labor Rights and Environmental Justice in the Global Electronics Industry*. Temple University Press.

Speth, James Gustave. 2008. *The Bridge at the Edge of the World: Capitalism, the Environment and Crossing from Crisis to Sustainability*. New Haven: Yale University Press.

23

On the Trail of
Courageous Behavior

Myron Glazer and Penina Glazer

Sociological studies often reveal inequalities and hidden agendas or practices by powerful actors, such as corporations. Myron and Penina Glazer explore how sociological research can also uncover forces that challenge harmful or destructive practices. Examining the courageous behavior of American whistleblowers and environmental activists in the United States, Israel, and the former Czechoslovakia, they ask what enables ordinary people to engage in courageous behavior, such as long-term environmental activism. They identify four factors. First, activists typically have strong social networks, or social capital; second, they believe they can make a difference; third, they are willing to accumulate evidence and expertise; and fourth, they must overcome fear and intimidation.

We ask whether sociology, the study of human behavior in all its forms, can help save all of us from our most destructive proclivities. In an era of mass murder and unleashed genocide, of the production of unsafe and injurious products, of unnecessary waste and pollution caused by individual and corporate greed, can sociology assist us in unraveling the sources of evil, of behavior that intentionally harms others? Can our discipline highlight beliefs and actions that engender moral responsibility for the common good? Can sociology help isolate the social, cultural, and emotional sources of courageous behavior, behavior that embodies taking risks for the well-being of others? Can sociology, through its grounded empirical research, illuminate principles that help sustain opposition to coercive and unaccountable power?

To attempt to answer these questions, and thereby underscore the significance of sociological investigations for maintaining a viable and democratic social order, we draw upon our research on organizational whistleblowers and on community crusaders for a safe environment. Beginning in 1982 we spent six years studying sixty-four American whistleblowers in government and industry. As sociologists we were particularly interested in the values that propelled them to protest unethical and illegal activities. We emphasized the social networks which sustained them and which provided publicity, legitimacy, and legal defense. We scrutinized the organizational retaliation mounted against them as they faced firings, isolation, black lists, and character assassination. Despite their pain and loss, we also highlighted the cultural significance of their victories, their impact on corrupted institutions, and their often successful efforts to rebuild their shattered careers and lives.

After the publication of *The Whistleblowers: Exposing Corruption in Government and Industry*, we decided to continue our study of the social and cultural foundations of courageous behavior. We interviewed scores of grassroots activists in the United States, Israel, and the former Czechoslovakia who would not remain silent when their air was polluted, their wells contaminated, and their children sickened by radiation or other hazardous substances. In continuity with the whistleblowers study, we approached a wide spectrum of environmental crusaders to understand their backgrounds, values, allies, and adversaries (Glazer and Glazer 1998). We wanted to test and advance our theory that environmental crusaders, like the organizational whistleblowers, are on the front lines in exposing and demanding remediation for society's most serious problems; that they often serve as bellwethers heralding crises just over the next horizon; that, in addition, they act as moral exemplars who embody the society's highest ideals of concern for one's neighbors and community. Whistleblowers and crusaders for a safe environment constantly re-assert the boundaries beyond which others, no matter how powerful, shall not pass without encountering serious and sustained resistance. In heralding all these interrelated contributions, sociologists provide a breakwater to the flood of historical and contemporary disasters which threaten a society's moral balance.

The Courage of Ordinary People

Many scholars who study acts of courage focus primarily on military and police situations or on other heroic events that occur in the effort to save the lives of others. Such actions are dramatic, requiring, for instance, the split-second decision to charge a machine gun nest raining lethal fire on one's comrades, or to rush into a burning boiler room to rescue injured sailors before rising waters engulf them (Walton 1986; Rachman 1990). But for grassroots environmental activists and organizational whistleblowers, courage takes another form. The situations they face are usually not immediately life-threatening; rather, their battles demand a longer-term investment of time and energy. They must be ready to withstand withering criticism of their credibility, competence, and integrity. They must face attacks that may sully their reputations, isolate them from one-time friends, neighbors, and coworkers, and even cause rifts within their own families. Under extreme circumstances, grassroots activists and whistleblowers face physical threats, police harassment, and imprisonment.

Knowing these risks, we found that ordinary people in our studies took a courageous stand when they proclaimed the dangers of serious occupational and community situations. We probed into the background and situational factors that led them to commit themselves to building a sustained, collective campaign to demand accountability and remediation. We asked how gender, social class, occupation, religion, and other sociological variables influenced them. Thus, while their decisions did not reflect the single act of heroism associated with military bravery, they had to muster the social and cultural resources to spend years intensively involved in their causes, resulting in stress and the disruption of the rhythm of their lives. Friends and colleagues often experienced burnout, providing a constant reminder of the difficulties of the long-term crusade to remedy organizational irresponsibility or to ensure a safe environment.

This burnout is precisely what occurred to Cheryl Washburn, one of two courageous women who were fighting the effects of a hazardous waste site in Maine. Over time Cathy Hinds continued to demand remediation, but Cheryl Washburn began to withdraw from total involvement. She explained her inability to sustain such intense activity in words that speak for many others:

> It takes a certain person to be able to keep at it all the time. Cathy is one of those people. She's strong, and in some ways strong-willed. For me, it came down to wanting to live a normal life. I didn't want to be faced with this thing every day, or I'd be a basket case. I didn't want to go to all the meetings, to keep butting my head against a wall. As Cathy slowly started doing more, I slowly backed off. Cathy has a way with words—she knows how to put things, and I was glad to let her take over. I'm proud of what we did—and I'm proud of her for keeping it up. (Garland 1988, p. 100)

A similar situation but with a different twist confronted Frank Camps, a senior design engineer for the Ford Motor Company, who protested the construction of the Ford Pinto. Camps believed it was an unsafe car. He helped us record the impact of bureaucracy and its control of financial and career rewards in thwarting collective action. Camps' overriding sense of professional responsibility and his fear of legal liability led him to take bold action despite the risks. After going all the way up the corporation hierarchy and urging redesign without success, he ultimately sued the company to limit his own potential liability. He counted on other engineers to help expose a potentially dangerous situation to consumers, but he soon stood virtually alone. We found comparable reactions in other settings both in industry and government.

> I can recall, right after I filed the suit, other engineers said, "Go get 'em, we wish we could do it, there goes a man with brass balls." While I had tacit support, I was looking for an honest man to stand with me. I found that these guys were suddenly given promotions, nice increases in salary. Next thing I knew, I did not have the support any more. (Glazer and Glazer 1989, p. 19)

The philosopher Douglas N. Walton argues that the courageous behavior of a Cathy Hinds or a Frank Camps is rare in contemporary industrial society:

> Perhaps another reason that courage today seems an absurd or outdated virtue is the growing lack of cohesiveness in social structures and group purposes. In vast modern industrial societies, the individual feels anonymous and often loses identity with the community as a group. This phenomenon in North America has often been remarked upon. Twenty-six bystanders watched as Kitty Genovese was brutally murdered on the street. Not one even calling the police. The current expression is "nobody wants to get involved." A kind of moral anomie is described by Camus in *L'Etranger*—an individual fails to feel even the smallest sympathy or emotion at the death of another. The attitude seems to be a moral aimlessness, a lack of purpose beyond one's own egoistic interests. To one in this frame of mind, *courage—taking personal risks to try and save another or to help the group* or community in time of trouble *seems simply* an irrational risk—no gain at all. (Walton 1986; p. 18, emphasis added)

Invoking our approach that focuses on sustained, long-term confrontations with irresponsible organizational power, we have encountered scores of instances where people have determined to help their communities. In contrast to Walton's assertion, grassroots activists and employee whistleblowers have displayed impressive strength and resilience in caring for others and in their willingness to put themselves at risk. . . .

Why were whistleblowers and grassroots environmental activists able to engage in such behavior when so many of their fellow citizens apparently have not responded with comparable courage? Our research points to several distinctive dimensions. First, a courageous response to a community's problems does not occur in a vacuum. It is not based on a spontaneous decision. Rather, citizens call on a reservoir of social capital, of bonds that they have developed over many years. Those we studied saw their own fate as intertwined intimately with that of others. Whistleblowers expressed an irrevocable allegiance to professional, religious, and community-based values that emphasized responsibility for the well-being of others. They refused, for example, to enact decisions that resulted in the construction of dangerous nuclear power plants or that dumped toxic chemicals into an area's water supply. The whistleblowers assumed individual responsibility rather than acting as agents of hierarchical authority. . . .

Second, both whistleblowers and crusaders had a strong cultural commitment to the efficacy of action. Their past experience led them to believe that they could make a difference. . . . They embodied the democratic tradition that citizens could unite for a redress of grievances; that those in the media or in government would see the justice of their cause, and that their legitimate concerns would be met.

Third, courageous behavior depended on their taking determined action; on their ability and willingness to accumulate the evidence, and expertise. The protesters had to counter with confidence and competence the technological experts and policymakers who belittled their concerns. The whistleblowers usually had direct access to the incriminating data. . . .

To achieve their goals the environmental crusaders had to secure strategically placed allies who could supply firsthand information. At times these allies were whistleblowers within polluting corporations or regulatory agencies. Often, the crusaders also had to become adept at using public records or petitioning through the Freedom of Information Act to secure previously classified material. In this essential effort, public-interest groups often secured mountains of data necessary to prove, for example, that nuclear bomb releases had poisoned the atmosphere or that chemical waste had directly undermined the health of local residents. No campaign for environmental redress could hope to be successful without the crusaders forging a working alliance with others committed to securing governmental and corporate accountability. We designated this essential process as the creation of *alternative networks of power.*

Fourth, purveyors of courage had to overcome fear and intimidation. They knew that the reduction of serious environmental damage or the resolution of other organizational transgressions would not occur without years of struggle. The opposing government bureaucrats and corporate managers would extract a heavy price for challenging the status quo. The protesters' determination to persist in the face of such obstacles attests to their faith in the justice of their cause. Without their willingness to endure on behalf of their beliefs, without their determination to help their communities, serious problems would lie buried beneath the surface with the potential to do great damage to unknowing and unprotected victims.

The Reservoir of Social Capital

Grassroots activists and whistleblowers were deeply involved in the affairs of the community. They were not alienated or passive citizens unwilling and unable to show concern for others. Their sense of self was fully engaged in what happened to their families, neighborhoods, regions, and countries. They may have become protesters later in life, but they had been prepared by a previously developed and strongly held value system. These values included a sense of caring for others, a feeling of responsibility for their safety, and a slowly evolving but nonetheless strong commitment to act when others were in danger. The activists were conveyers of what Robert Putnam and others have labeled social capital (Putnam 1993). For example, women such as Lynn Golumbic in Israel, Jara Johnova in Czechoslovakia, Penny Newman in the United States, and many others may have exercised civic responsibility in more conventional ways until an environmental crisis propelled them into the public arena. But their community-based system of values had been developed and implemented earlier in PTAs, Green Circles, and other organizations, and had been engaged as they prepared to step forward into a leadership role. With their principles intact, they built grassroots organizations and thus joined a militant vanguard in defending communities from victimization by government and corporate bureaucracies. . . .

Each of the women cited above had borne children and had sought to raise them in the safest and healthiest areas. Penny Newman had spent countless hours volunteering to help improve the school system in Glen Avon, California. Jara Johnova had taken the dangerous step of signing the Charter 77 document petitioning the Czechoslovakian government to respect human rights, and for years she was part of a dissident group in Prague. Lynn Golumbic, who had moved to Israel from the United States so that she and her young family could participate in the effort to build a democratic Jewish state, joined the Association of Americans and Canadians in Israel (AACI), which focused on a wide range of social issues. For all of them, assuming a leadership role when they confronted environmental emergencies represented a major commitment and much greater public exposure. Yet this new action was grounded in past experiences and beliefs. Helping the community in a time of crisis was consistent with their strongly held values. While their new roles ruptured old schedules and made many demands, these roles were built on a foundation that could weather the intensive demands of community leadership (Kirp 1989; Hallie 1979; Swidler 1986).

This reservoir of social capital, this principled connection to others, is a core component of courageous behavior, for the risks of speaking out about a problem and assuming leadership could be costly, as Tom Bailie learned. Bailie, a farmer in eastern Washington state whose land abutted the Hanford

Nuclear Reservation, epitomizes the grassroots activist whose past experiences prepared him to announce the existence of a crisis, even if such action was undertaken at his own peril. Bailie had deep roots in the area; he grew up on his parents' farm, raised a family, and ran for local political office. He understood that speaking out against the Hanford nuclear facility entailed substantial risks. He would be a marked man from then on, someone who had punctured the cultural fiction born in the Cold War, the commonly held faith that patriotism demanded the production of nuclear bombs and that everything was safe and under control. But Bailie urged his neighbors and other area residents to face the seriousness of their situation. He told stories of deformed animals and an epidemic of cancer, illness, and death. He drew upon his own personal history of illness and that of neighbors and friends. Bailie urged all who would listen to question the very source of their economic security. He encouraged them to challenge the government and corporations that provided their livelihood. This was not a scenario that was likely to make Bailie a local hero, and for years he and a few allies in the community were objects of ridicule and scorn. His was a dangerous position, but it was one that he was determined to hold, no matter what the personal cost.

> What I have to do goes beyond my marriage and my other family relationships. I'm sorry. I don't know what I have to do to complete this, but I'll be glad when it's done. We still have to find out what the nuclear gang has done to those of us that live here, and how it has affected our lives and affected our health. We've just scratched the surface. (Glazer and Glazer 1998)

Blue-collar and clerical workers in large nuclear organizations who saw practices that entailed serious violations of environmental health and safety standards were also inspired to speak out against such violations. Their protests emanated from a deep sense of community. The nuclear plant construction workers we studied were determined to remain in the communities where they had grown up and thus strongly identified with potential victims who could be relatives, friends, or neighbors. At times, the workers specifically referred to an obligation to the land that had been passed down by parents and ancestors. They often contrasted their sense of responsibility for the community with that of high-placed corporate executives who moved frequently to accommodate their careers and had neither roots nor long-term commitments to the local people with whom they work.

One welder and craftsman at a Texas plant became so deeply concerned about safety at the construction site that he joined a protest to the Nuclear Regulatory Commission despite the likelihood of job loss and blacklisting. His statement captured the spirit espoused by social capital theorists. With his jeans and cowboy boots and Texas drawl, Stan Miles personified the land in which he was raised:

> I was born in this state and this state means a lot more to me than just a place to live. If you will look at my work record, I've never gone out of the state to work. I don't like to leave this land. I like the people here. It's changed a lot, though, since I was a boy. For instance, I was born in west Texas, real west Texas, west of the Pecos. You didn't have car trouble without the next person stopping, and if he had to drive eighty miles out of his way, he did, and you didn't have to pay him anything.
>
> That's gone—all gone, and for the sake of a dollar bill. They took something that was priceless and ruined it for something made of paper. Because if you poison the water, you poison the land. How can the dollar bill replace that? This state means something to me. I was born here, my ancestors came here in 1821, my grandmother was a Comanche Indian, and they've been here for ten thousand years. (Glazer and Glazer 1989, p. 131)

Unlike the environmental crusaders and employees like Stan Miles, many other whistleblowers spoke out to protect potential victims who were unknown to them. As professionals, these whistleblowers invoked a particular brand of social capital. They felt a special responsibility for the safety of others, even if it were a public they might never know. Demetrius Basdekas, an engineer responsible for the safety of control systems essential to avoid nuclear accidents, could not remain uninvolved as he imagined potential victims of a nuclear plant disaster. He protested his supervisors' decision to grant a license to operate a new nuclear facility that he believed did not have proper safety provisions.

> I said to myself, "Look, you are at a crossroads and you have to decide which way to go. You can either roll over and play dead or stand up and say what you think." I hit the wall, the red line. I could not go beyond that line. I was being asked to become a party to an act of fraud on the public where health and safety are concerned.
>
> Management's response was to remove me, to assign a greenhorn to do the job. I was simply told that I was no longer responsible for this part of the work. As a result of this, I and other engineers who were performing in similar situations decided to take our case to the Congress and to the public. (Glazer and Glazer 1989, p. 78)

Basdekas and his colleagues would not rationalize compliance by relegating their decision to the orders of high authority. They would not assume the "agentic role" highlighted by Stanley Milgram in his famous studies of obedience to authority (Milgram 1974). . . . Milgram found that the most telling counterweight to the orders of authorities was the presence of peers or col leagues who would support the decision to protest and resist. For Basdekas that support was essential. For others the stimulus for rebellion also may be professional values and the bond of comradeship. . . .

On the Efficacy of Grassroots Action

Environmental crusaders and employee whistleblowers assumed personal responsibility to confront serious environmental and other problems that affected their communities. Their involvement began when they became convinced that remedial action would not be undertaken voluntarily after they brought the issue to their supervisors or local officials. These grassroots activists and organizational employees believed that gathering information, focusing attention, and organizing to combat social problems could make a difference. These strongly held cultural assumptions about their entitlement to speak out on public affairs and in the efficacy of united action were crucial ingredients in the protesters' willingness to be stigmatized as the bearers of bad news and reinforced their readiness to put themselves at risk. . . . While they sought distant goals, they believed fully that they could achieve them (Russell 1989).

Penny Newman and her peers represent a prime example of a local group who committed themselves to battling the chemical contamination in their community. They began to organize in 1978 when a nearby toxic waste dump, the Stringfellow Acid Pits, overflowed, sending thousands of gallons of poisoned water running through their streets and into their children's school. Their group, Concerned Neighbors, grew increasingly determined to "fight City Hall"—that is, the State of California and some of the largest corporations operating in their region that had dumped tons of dangerous chemicals into a dry pit, without sufficient regard for the safety of the community. Now, twenty years later, Newman summarized how she and her colleagues were transformed from victims to agents of their own victories (letter to authors from Newman 1997).

> I look back at our 20 year battle over the Stringfellow Acid Pits and have a hard time assimilating everything that happened to us and of which we made happen. But as we start listing the accomplishments one can't help but be proud.
>
> We were able to get a new, safe water supply installed throughout the community at no cost to the residents. . . . We made a lot of institutional changes to the Superfund program and how Americans see the issue of toxic dumps. We were the first community to get a technical advisor and become the model used for the Superfund bill in 1986 so that other communities could hire such assistance. We were the first community to

have an office established to answer residents' questions and to be staffed by community volunteers—all paid for by the state. Our community has been the driving force behind each and every improvement at the site.

In more recent years we continued to have an impact both on our site and in public policy. We played a major role in the discussions about the reauthorization of Superfund. In State court, we filed the nation's largest toxic tort, consisting of 5,000 plaintiffs and 200 companies, the County of Riverside, and the State of California. We were able to reach a settlement for over $110 million, one of the first cases in which the plaintiffs were able to prove cause and effect with exposure to chemicals and community health. Another judgment that is certainly precedent setting occurred in Federal court where the court found the State of California 90–98% responsible for the cleanup of the site due to the fact that the state permitted the site, had an obligation to ensure it operated safely, and failed to do so resulting in our community being exposed and damaged.

We were the first community granted Intervenor status by a Federal court which allowed that we had a right to participate in all discussions about the site. Two hundred companies named as Responsible Parties appealed the ruling to the U.S. Supreme Court. We are still intervenors! Since then Superfund has been revised to provide a statutory right of affected communities to participate in such discussions.

In addition to the legal victories, Newman emphasized how their belief in community power transformed many of their members from shy and insecure observers to active participants in the political process. One member of Concerned Neighbors embodied this transformation.

A young Latina woman with 3 young boys at the elementary school was very concerned about the water at the school and attended a meeting where we focused on getting the water tested and filters added to the system. She was extremely shy. But her concern for her boys made her want to participate. She agreed to talk at a school board meeting, but was terrified. We practiced and practiced and that night she stood up and—with voice quivering—gave one of the most touching appeals for peace of mind in protecting the children at the school. Over the 6 month battle, she developed more confidence, was able to stand up and not shake, and helped to win that battle. But more importantly you could see the change in her. She learned that she could stand up and voice her opinion and make a difference. That she was important! This young woman had been in a very abusive marriage where she had been beaten time and time again. Through her participation in this battle, she gained enough strength, confidence and courage to leave that relationship and start a

new life. She works with special education children and is doing great.
(letter from Newman 1997)

Faith in their own efficacy was a crucial weapon on the side of the crusaders. It carried them forth in times of frustration, disappointment, and
temporary defeat. . .

With Facts on Their Side

Because of their central organizational positions, the employee resisters to
illegal or unethical behavior had surer access to incriminating evidence than
did the environmental crusaders. Yet they, too, had to gather evidence that
would convince a skeptical investigative reporter, attract the attention of a
congressional committee, or convince public interest attorneys that a serious
breach had occurred. . . . Hugh Kaufman, working for the EPA, visited scores of
hazardous waste sites to document that chemical contamination was a plague
undermining the health of American communities. His supervisors refused
to acknowledge his evidence until he took his allegations and documentation
to the media (Glazer and Glazer 1989, pp. 135–36). At the same time, Maude
DeVictor, working in the Veterans Administration, gathered voluminous case
material on the effects of Agent Orange (Glazer and Glazer 1989, pp. 231–32).
She became a forerunner in a growing national campaign, to provide compensation for Vietnam veterans who had suffered exposure, incapacitation, and
disease as a result of their wartime service. . . .

For Tom Bailie the unfolding of layer after layer of once-classified information slowly undermined the arguments of his detractors and confirmed his
suspicion that the Hanford Nuclear Reservation had released dangerous emissions onto the local population. The same government and corporations that
were charged with protecting the safety of the region's citizens turned out to be
culpable of knowingly releasing radiation on civilian populations in the area.
Despite their public-relations claims to the contrary, these bureaucratic organizations had shown blatant disregard for the safety of nearby communities. The
testimony of Tom Bailie and other local residents was now supported by government documents and other hard data that had been obtained as a result of a
decision by several organizations to file a Freedom of Information Act inquiry
(FOIA). The Freedom of Information Act, which had been enacted in 1966, was
crucial to furthering the activists' causes. To make full use of the FOIA, Bailie and
the other activists had to rely on the technical assistance of allies in the press and
in the Hanford Education Action League (HEAL), the local public interest group.
Once they had government data confirming their claims of radiation exposure,
their allegations could no longer be dismissed as the statements of paranoid
personalities. Those who had risked their reputations by questioning the secrecy

of the national security state or by challenging the economic viability of the defense-based economy now had the facts on their side. Family members might still be embarrassed and humiliated by the public controversy surrounding the crusaders, but they were also sobered by the evidence, which gave weight to the deadly consequences of the problem.

Not all societies have a Freedom of Information Act, and activists frequently had to use indirect methods to secure the necessary data (Flarn 1996). In our research in Slovakia we found that prior to the fall of the Communists, a group of dedicated environmentalists believed that years of silence on environmental degradation had to end and that the time was ripe to challenge the Communists. . . . They knew they had to secure the documentation that would reveal the desperate state of the environment if they were to raise public awareness and open a serious dialogue with government officials. With retaliation, harassment, and even imprisonment a possible outcome, the environmentalists determined that their effort would be grounded in incontrovertible evidence. The best source of data was the government itself, and the activists spent months surreptitiously gathering information from officials who did not suspect that their contributions would be collated, matched, and eventually integrated into a report. Taken together, the accumulated evidence painted a dismal portrait of government deception, broken promises, and neglected environmental policy.

The publication of *Bratislava Nahlas* [Bratislava Aloud] provided documented assertions about the abysmal failure of the Communists to protect the country from air, water, and land contamination. The writers of the report, drawn from all professional fields, sought to avoid the label of political "dissidents." Rather, they claimed legitimacy as recorders of hard data that pointed to dangerous environmental conditions. The publication of the evidence substantiated their accusations and yet heightened the vulnerability of the activists. Would the government now confiscate the report, harass and arrest them, or subject them to violence? Was assassination a possibility? The *Bratislava Nahlas* group was prepared for the inevitable retaliation, having lived with its threat for years. The report opened with a strong declaration.

> In our city, the basic conditions of life have become problematic. Contamination of the atmosphere is threatening the health of virtually all inhabitants, particularly the aged, the sick, and children. . . . The degradation of values, waste, the damage to human health, and the mass problems which will impact upon future generations are immoral; nevertheless, they occur daily before the eyes of the citizens, no one is ever called to accountability. . . . The moral dimension of the Bratislava situation is, we believe, just as serious as the public health or economic viewpoints.

They ended their courageous introduction with a call to action that had never been heard in Communist Bratislava.

> We expect that the public discussion (which the document would like to introduce) will not only articulate the interests of the citizens of Bratislava, but will mobilize their forces and renew the relationship of the citizens with respect to their city. (*Bratislava-Nahlas* 1987)

Overcoming Fear

Whistleblowers and environmental crusaders undertook the challenge of exposing a major social problem and assuming a leadership role to resolve it. But they knew that they faced risks to their jobs, personal safety, reputations, and more. How did they withstand the fear of retaliation? What are the emotional resources that supported and sustained their decision?

Several factors enabled protesters to move against powerful interests. First, they transformed their anger into a positive determination to take action. Second, they depended on the trust and comradeship that developed in their local groups to sustain their motivation and commitment in the face of frustrations and setbacks. Finally, in their own personal cost–benefit analysis, they overcame the inevitable fear of retaliation by defining the environmental problems they confronted as more severe, more troubling, and more threatening than their anxiety about rejection and isolation. . . .

> . . . According to Anne W. Garland, who studied women activists: Anger is often at the center of [activists'] transformations from private actors in restricted universes to public leaders in universes encompassing all the important issues of the day. The anger comes, of course, from a variety of sources. And it crosses the putative barriers of age and racial differences; differences in education, background, and lifestyle; and differences in religious and political belief. (Garland 1988, pp. xvi–xvii)

Trust also proved essential in sustaining commitment and solidarity among the activists. The accusations, the demeaning comments, even the threats of physical attack or arrest and imprisonment in Czechoslovakia, were all made bearable by the culture of solidarity that existed in the activists' group. . . . Pavel Sˆremer, a longtime dissident and one of the core group in the *Bratislava Nahlas* movement, emphasized how mutual trust in each other sustained them through difficult times. Each Bratislava participant had an assigned set of tasks, and the others had faith that it would be completed. To stop their work, to be paralyzed by the fear of what the government could do to them, would grant their adversaries an unacceptable victory. Faith in their cause and support for each other were strong incentives during their months of intensive, secret activity. . . .

Activists faced fear of failure, fear of criticism and ridicule, fear of attack and assault, and fear of imprisonment and exile, but these fears did not stop them, for they believed that the costs of inaction were even higher. . . .

For organizational whistleblowers fear takes on a particular form. To raise troublesome issues on the job is always risky. Yet as Frank Camps learned at the Ford Motor Company and Maude DeVictor at the Veterans Administration, going outside the organization with your allegations of misbehavior is much more dangerous. It almost always results in threats or actual retaliation. Whistleblowers experienced retaliation that went well beyond their expectations. Some were deliberately isolated from previously congenial colleagues, others faced dismissal from a valued position and the terror of blacklisting from all jobs in that particular industry. There were many witnesses to the career and family dislocation such punishing outcomes entailed.

These kinds of retaliation are not trivial. To withstand them requires the fortitude to stay the course no matter how severe the organizational reaction. The statement of Margaret Henderson (not her real name) best exemplifies the fear, hurt, self-depreciation that results from retaliation. The case also reflects the tenaciousness and moral certainty of her husband. Harry Henderson had joined the federal government after working as a business executive in the South. When he protested the waste of tens of millions of dollars of government funds and the severe impact on the environment, his supervisors ordered him to remain silent and threatened to ruin his career if he spoke outside the agency. When he would not retreat, they initiated a campaign to isolate and later to dismiss him. Here is how his wife described the impact on him:

> Nineteen years ago, I married a man who was outgoing, secure, bold, and optimistic. About his career he was self-confident, enthusiastic, and ambitious. As husband he was interested in and supportive of my activities. Later, as father, he was involved in the lives of his five children and made every effort to spend as much time with them as possible.
>
> From an outgoing person who was involved in the interests and activities of his family, he became withdrawn, spending whatever hours he could in isolation, poring over and over his documents, compulsively reading and rereading every memo dealing with his work situation. When he and I did sit down to talk to each other, he could speak of nothing but what was happening at work and what his supervisors were doing to him, with the pain and suffering he was going through evident in the slump of his shoulders and strained quality of his voice.

All of this, of course, had an effect on the rest of the family. We were afraid to approach Harry with our own needs and concerns, having come to expect his rejection and withdrawal because he no longer had time for or interest in us. One of our children was referred for psychological counseling. I found it necessary to seek work outside the home, having to escape from his oppressive presence and influence. His sleeplessness disturbed our night's rest. We all observed the profound effect of his work situation upon him: the bold man become fearful and intimidated; the aggressive person become reticent and insecure; the optimist become hopeless; the relaxed and outgoing person become tense, withdrawn, and isolated; the well-rounded man become obsessive, paranoid, and neurotic. No longer was he the loving spouse and father. He was the stranger who, although living among us, was not with us. (Glazer and Glazer 1989, p. 154)

Yet, despite all of this, Harry Henderson fought on with the assistance of the Government Accountability Project (GAP) which had taken his case because of its significance and because of their belief that Henderson would not back off. They were right. With GAP representing him, Henderson secured the interest of a congressional committee which held hearings on his allegations. Newspaper articles and television programs featured the seriousness of his testimony of government and industry collusion. Henderson had overcome his fear and disillusionment. His very obsessivenesses ultimately made him an unwavering adversary against government waste. He came to represent the employee who epitomizes devotion to serving the public rather than loyalty to the bureaucracy.

Employees in private industry are susceptible to even harsher retaliation and more paralyzing fear. Chuck Atchison worked as a quality assurance inspector in the nuclear industry, and after reporting several construction problems to the company, he was dismissed for overstepping his area of responsibility. Despite vindication from the Nuclear Regulatory Commission and later from the Department of Labor, he was out of a job. His whistle-blowing action led to his blacklisting in the industry and to deteriorating economic circumstances.

Everything that wasn't nailed down [with] the mortgage was sold. We lost our Visa and MasterCard rights and our gasoline credit cards. Finally we lost the house in July 1983. My wife, Jeanne, has always been employed as a secretary-clerk-bookkeeper. That was the only thing that really kept us going. We let someone take over the payments on the house and found a trailer we could take over the payments on.

The company's reach seemed so pervasive that he even feared physical assault. The ambiguous circumstances of Karen Silkwood's automobile crash ten years earlier in 1974 reinforced his fear of possible organizational revenge:

> Silkwood hit the headlines again. I became paranoid if things happened like a car following me. I'd make several turns and the car would keep up with me. I feared that the company could hire gunmen that would kill someone for big dollars and get back across the border without anyone knowing it. (Glazer and Glazer 1989, pp. 146–47)

Atchison had now lost his job, his home, his credit rating, his sense of personal safety, and his self-esteem as a breadwinner. Forced to leave their familiar surroundings and to live in a mobile home without most of their possessions, the family no longer felt like respected members of the community. Atchison became a living symbol to other workers of the cost of resisting large corporations. The pressure and humiliation penetrated deeply into his sense of self. He dreamed of striking a major blow against his adversaries when in reality he had to settle for the small pleasure of knowing that they had suffered a few defeats in their rush to obtain a license and make good on their investments:

> My emotions went the full gamut from deep depression to hostility. Now most of that part is gone. The main emotion I still get is tickled to death if I see an article in the paper that makes them look a little bit worse as they go along.

Although the costs were very painful, Atchison was not content with these small victories. To fight his case of illegal firing, he contacted the Department of Labor and the press, engaged lawyers, worked with the Government Accountability Project. The reprisals enacted against him for whistleblowing extracted a heavy toll but simultaneously resulted in his developing a new reference group of environmentalists organized to fight against unsafe nuclear plants. He became a principal witness in the campaign of a local grassroots safe-energy group against the plant. He was nationally recognized in 1984 when the Government Accountability Project and the Christic Institute nominated him and several other whistleblowers as the first winners of the Karen Silkwood Award for exposing dangerous working conditions (Glazer and Glazer 1989, pp. 228–29). The citation that accompanied the award was yet another sign that the blacklisting had failed to silence him. Finally in 1988 the company came to an unprecedented agreement with Atchinson and other whistleblowers, and publicly recognized that they had been correct in raising safety concerns. Atchinson had been fully vindicated.

The Allure of Sociology

Sociology can be a significant contributor to the achievement of such vindication. By seeking out these environmental crusaders, employee whistleblowers, and other courageous people, by interviewing them and analyzing their cases from a personal, sociological, and cultural perspective, we provide both publicity and understanding of their accomplishments. By consulting with them as they pursue their cases, we sociologists can contribute useful expertise. By serving on national advisory committees, we assist their battles with the prestige and recognition of our academic positions. By teaching about them, we give our students moral exemplars in a world where irresponsibility and destruction too often hold sway.

By integrating the lives of the crusaders into our theories of resistance to abusive authority, we can emphasize the centrality of moral courage in the building and maintaining of a viable, accountable, and democratic society. . . .

Note

Myron Glazer and Penina Glazer, "On the Trail of Courageous Behavior." *Sociological Inquiry* 69(2): 276–295. Reprinted by permission of Blackwell Publishing Ltd.

References

Bratislava-Nahlas. 1987. Unpublished report. Bratislava: Slovak Union of Landscape and Nature Protectors.

Erikson, Kai. 1966. *Wayward Puritans: A Study in the Sociology of Deviance.* New York: Wiley.

Flarn, Helena. 1996. "Anxiety and the Successful Oppositional Construction of Societal Reality: The Case of Kor." *Mobilization* 1: 103–21.

Freedman, Alix M., and Suein I. Hwang. 11 July 1997. "How Seven Individuals with Diverse Motives Halted Tobacco's Wars." *The Wall Street Journal.*

Garland, Anne Witte. 1988. *Women Activists.* New York: The Feminist Press.

Glazer, Myron Peretz, and Penina Migdal Glazer. 1989. *The Whistleblowers: Exposing Corruption in Government and Industry.* New York: Basic Books.

Glazer, Penina Migdal, and Myron Peretz Glazer. 1998. *The Environmental Crusaders: Confronting Disaster and Mobilizing Community.* University Park: The Pennsylvania State University Press.

Hallie, Philip. 1979. *Lest Innocent Blood Be Shed.* New York: Harper and Row.

Jackall, Robert. 1988. *Moral Mazes.* New York: Oxford University Press.

Kirp, David L. 1989. *Learning by Heart.* New Brunswick: Rutgers University Press.

Milgram, Stanley. 1974. *Obedience to Authority.* New York: Harper and Row.

Putnam, Robert D. 1996. "The Strange Disappearance of Civic America." *The American Prospect* 24:34–48.

————. 1993. "Bowling Alone: America's Declining Social Capital." *Journal of Democracy* 6:65–78.

Rachman, S. J. 1990. *Fear and Courage.* New York: W. H. Freeman.

Russell, Diane E. H. 1989. *Lives of Courage: Women for a New South Africa.* New York: Basic Books.

Schmid, Thomas W. 1985. "The Socratic Conception of Courage." *History of Philosophy Quarterly* 2:113–30.

Stout, David. 21 June 1997. "Ex-Tobacco Official Enjoys the Aftermath of the Deal." *The New York Times.*

Swidler, Ann. 1986. "Culture in Action: Symbols and Strategies." *American Sociological Review* 51:273–386.

Walton, Douglas N. 1986. *Courage.* Berkeley: University of California Press.

Index

Note: *Italic* page numbers indicate illustrations.

AACI. *See* Association of Americans and Canadians in Israel
ABFT. *See* Atlantic bluefin tuna
Abidjan (Ivory Coast), hazardous waste disposal in, 248
aborigines, totemism of, 30
accidents, environmental disasters depicted as, 3
Achebe, Naemeka, 242
Acheson, J. M., 56
acidification, ocean, 39
acid rain, 241, 242
activism: on body burdens, 323, 327; burnout with, 397; against climate change, 48–49; against climate change, lack of, 170–71, 181–83; against coal mining industry, 195–96; against environmental illness, 276; against export of ecological hazards, 242, 248–49, 250–52; against globalization, 252; against lead contamination, 135–36; on perchlorate contamination, 292, 293; in tradition of sociological research, 14; against wild horse removal, 154. *See also* courage of activists; environmental justice

movement; environmental movement; environmental organizations
Activists Beyond Borders (Keck and Sikkink), 383
ACTS. *See* auto-centered transport systems
Administrative Procedures Act of 1946 (APA), U.S., 274
advertising, by West Virginia coal industry, 198–201
AEC. *See* Atomic Energy Commission
Aerojet, 293
Afghanistan, auto ownership in, 255
Africa: export of environmental hazards to, 238–39; used clothing in, 367. *See also specific countries*
African Americans: air pollution affecting, 146, 147; auto ownership among, 145; as farmers, 115, 122nn2–3; without health insurance, 147; public transportation use by, 144; in West Oakland Food Collaborative, 114–17, 122n2. *See also* environmental justice
agenda power, 291–92
Agent Orange, 405
agriculture: in ecological footprint, 96; Green Revolution in, 2; organic, 112–